W9-AZR-941

Jones and Bartlett's Fundraising Series for the 21st Century

Developing Major Gifts

Turning Small Donors into Big Contributors

Jones and Bartlett's Fundraising Series for the 21st Century

Fundraising Basics: A Complete Guide
Barbara Kushner Ciconte, CFRE, and Jeanne G. Jacob, CFRE

Planned Giving Essentials: A Step by Step Guide to Success
Richard D. Barrett and Molly E. Ware

Developing Major Gifts: Turning Small Donors into Big Contributors
Laura Fredricks

Strategic Fund Development: Building Profitable Relationships That Last
Simone P. Joyaux, ACFRE

Capital Campaigns: Strategies That Work
Andrea Kihlstedt and Catherine P. Schwartz

Successful Special Events: Planning, Hosting, and Evaluating
Barbara Levy, ACFRE, and Barbara Marion, CFRE

Corporate and Foundation Fund Raising: A Complete Guide from the Inside
Eugene A. Scanlan, PhD, CFRE

Donor Focused Strategies for Annual Giving
Karla A. Williams, ACFRE

Jones and Bartlett's Fundraising Series for the 21st Century

Developing Major Gifts

Turning Small Donors into Big Contributors

Laura Fredricks, JD
Senior Director of Major Gifts
Temple University
Philadelphia, Pennsylvania

JONES AND BARTLETT PUBLISHERS
Sudbury, Massachusetts
BOSTON   TORONTO   LONDON   SINGAPORE

World Headquarters
Jones and Bartlett Publishers
40 Tall Pine Drive
Sudbury, MA 01776
978-443-5000
info@jbpub.com
www.jbpub.com

Jones and Bartlett Publishers Canada
6339 Ormindale Way
Mississauga, ON L5V 1J2
CANADA

Jones and Bartlett Publishers International
Barb House, Barb Mews
London W6 7PA
UK

Jones and Bartlett's books and products are available through most bookstores and online booksellers. To contact Jones and Bartlett Publishers directly, call 800-832-0034, fax 978-443-8000, or visit our website at www.jbpub.com.

Substantial discounts on bulk quantities of Jones and Bartlett's publications are available to corporations, professional associations, and other qualified organizations. For details and specific discount information, contact the special sales department at Jones and Bartlett via the above contact information or send an email to specialsales@jbpub.com.

Copyright © 2006 by Jones and Bartlett Publishers, Inc.
Originally published by Aspen Publishers, © 2001

All rights reserved. No part of the material protected by this copyright may be reproduced or utilized in any form, electronic or mechanical, including photocopying, recording, or by any information storage and retrieval system, without written permission from the copyright owner.

ISBN 0-7637-4243-0

Production Credits
Chief Executive Officer: Clayton Jones
Production Director: Amy Rose
Production Editor: Renée Sekerak
Director of Marketing: Alisha Weisman
Manufacturing and Inventory Coordinator: Amy Bacus
Printing and Binding: PA Hutchison
Cover Printing: PA Hutchison

Printed in the United States of America
09 08 07 06 05   10 9 8 7 6 5 4 3 2 1

Table of Contents

Foreword

Perhaps I have been reading too many stories to my grandchildren, but the title of this book conjures up the vision of a fairy godmother waving her magic wand over a small donor who miraculously turns into a big contributor. In truth, through my many years of fundraising, I have often earnestly wished that I had some sort of magic wand that would entice those who could be big contributors to become so—contributors to "my" organization, of course. Well, although I never got the wand, I now have Laura Fredricks' book—and so do you!

"A major gift is a well-thought out personal decision," states Laura, and in the following pages she guides us through a process that will enable each of us to assist persons to make such a decision. She moves the cultivation process from one of "selling" an organization's virtues to one of "telling" the organization's story in a systematic, engaging way. Therefore, the journey to the successful "ask" is replete with dialogue evoking the donor's wishes, discovering areas of donor involvement that resonate with the donor's interests, and constantly being mindful of the fact that such decisions take time.

Since we know that the longest journey begins with the first step, the book gives us a first step that we all can do—tap into our existing pool of donors. From there, Laura guides us in an almost paint-by-the-numbers fashion through the process to its successful conclusion. Indeed, we soon become aware that a process that many of us have avoided far too long is, in fact, not rocket science. Almost anyone can do it when they know how. Laura shows us how and is at our side as we proceed.

Having Laura at our side is like having a favorite mentor constantly in touch. Her advice comes from long and varied experience, from successes and failures (both of which she owns), is devoid of jargon, does not necessitate either a cast of thousands or an inordinate investment in databases, and is predicated on her abundant common sense and love of people. She enjoys this work and encourages us to love it as well. Mentors that smile as they work are those who impart the best advice.

Why do you need this book? Because your organization needs some major contributions to continue to do its valuable work. But why *this* book? Because all the evidence confirms that the major source of income for nonprofits is, and will continue to be, from individuals who make major contributions. Since you presently have connected to your organization—in some manner—potential major contributors, it is simply a matter of getting on with it. Given the widely publicized transfer of wealth from generation to generation presently occurring, the timing couldn't be better.

The last chapter of the book relates three success stories. In the first, a donor moved from giving a $2,500 gift to a $50,000 gift. In the second, a donor moved from giving $500 yearly to a $500,000 gift. In the third, the donor moved from giving between $250 and $500 yearly to giving $5 million. The gifts are mighty impressive, but perhaps of even greater note to a neophyte in this process is that all these gifts happened within *one year*! This is persuasive evidence to buy this book, read it, share it, and implement the processes it so eloquently presents.

Don Wells
Director, Certificate Program in
*   Nonprofit Management*
Duke University
Durham, North Carolina

* * *

As the Founder and Executive Director of the Asociacion de Musicos Latinoamericanos (AMLA), a grassroots arts organization located in the heart of Philadelphia's Latino "Barrio," I have personally known the intense struggle necessary for community groups to establish themselves and to grow. We in the trenches of community work are masters of the magic of stretching a dollar to several times its worth. And we must become adept at playing the ongoing chess game that results in our evolving strategy for success.

But as creative as we might be in fundraising from foundations and in generating earned income, the truth is that the *majority of funds in the United States come from private donors*. So our biggest challenge is to connect with those individual major gifts prospects—

people who are interested in our mission and who want to support our group. We need to learn how to approach these new benefactors in a concerted effort to form lasting personal relationships with each one. It is a potentially intimidating task. There are many things that we feel stand in our way—insufficient staff, the seemingly endless needs of our communities, and most important, obtaining the right cultivation skills that will give us the confidence and experience we need to achieve our yearly fundraising goals.

The population of people of color and the number of minority grassroots organizations continue to increase each year. As a frequent panelist on arts grant review committees locally and nationally, I am aware that the mainstream arts organizations are reaching out to minority groups with increasing frequency to build their audiences for the future. The future, for not only the arts, but for business, education, and philanthropic endeavor, is the recognition of our cultures and our needs. This recognition will benefit us all and will lead our partners to market expansion, audience growth, and grant them a place in the future of grassroots community development.

Laura, in *Developing Major Gifts*, guides us through the barriers that stand in our way. She lays out an easy, step-by-step guide to raising from individual donors the large funds that our groups need to stabilize and to grow. She shares with us her personal experiences in working with individuals and offers dozens of ways to keep the entire major gifts process on track.

Developing Major Gifts is a vital tool in that journey toward full empowerment. This book will give our community leaders, our boards, our staff, and our key volunteers, the major gifts fundraising skills necessary for groups like ours to thrive and prosper. Laura, in *Developing Major Gifts*, clearly outlines the steps we need to position ourselves to bridge those gaps leading to recognition of our vital work, for both the current and the future projects we envision for our communities. This is a wonderful resource book we intend to use for many years.

Jesse Bermudez
Founder and Executive Director, AMLA

Acknowledgments

Usually people skip this page and jump right into the book. I encourage you to read along. I think you'll find it entertaining, and you may recognize a name or two or, better yet, pick up a new contact.

The first question many people ask me is, "Why did you want to write this book?" I keep coming back to thoughts about my fundraising students who always wanted something more than the handouts in my classes. Well, now you have it. Teaching and writing this book have made me a better fundraiser, and the optimistic journalist in me hopes that it will help you too. On that note, I am extremely grateful to Emy Halpert, University of Pennsylvania, Special Programs, and Donald Wells, Duke University, Nonprofit Management Program, for giving me the opportunity to teach fundraising courses and for their confidence in me as a teacher and mentor. I owe a great deal to Todd Hunt, my communications professor at Rutgers College, who guided my first career—journalism—and taught me that if you can write while you educate and entertain, you have yourself a best seller and a loyal audience. Here's hoping I accomplished that with this book.

The next question is, "Why did you leave the law?" My answer to that one is, "I never left it!" There is not a day that goes by that I don't use the skills I learned in law school or practicing law. That leads me to one special thank you for Norman Prance, one of my favorite law school professors. As I was writing this book, it dawned on me that I am able to approach each new major gifts fundraising skill with a step-by-step analysis, explaining each step and illustrating each one with real examples, because of my training with him. If you go through each checklist and implement each concept—you've got it covered and you're on your way to getting the major gift. Just goes to show you—you never forget how to ride a bicycle.

The third question I get is, "You really love your job, don't you?" Well, yes I do, and that is because I have worked for and with some wonderful people in some very rewarding places. Thank you to Ronald Costello, Temple University, a model boss who leads by example and is a terrific fundraiser. Ditto for Julius Katz, Deborah Hospital Foundation, and his team where we were able to help so many deserving patients.

You guessed it, the fourth question I am asked is, "What's your secret for finding these great jobs?" as any true fundraiser will surely ask. That's an easy one. My secret weapon is Marianne Anthe, one of my best friends and career consultant supreme. I could not have made a move without her advice, and I would have been a fool if I did.

What follows next is one big "hug" for:

- All of my family, my best cheerleaders, knowing you are behind me gives me all the encouragement in the world.

- Maura Johnston, my good friend, who never let me lose sight that I could write this book and that, yes, people will buy it.

- My friends and colleagues in the National Society of Fundraising Executives, Greater Philadelphia Chapter, who are always ready to help another fundraiser with an answer or a contact or to give professional and personal support.

- All the development professionals and philanthropists who shared with me their thoughts and materials for this book.

- The donors I work with, gracious and wonderful people whom I admire, respect, and thoroughly enjoy knowing.

- My "adopted" family at Aspen Publishers, whose advice and expertise were the driving forces for me to write the best book I could.

Chapter 1
What Is a Major Gift?

CHAPTER OUTLINE

- What Makes a Gift a Major Gift?
- Who Are the Major Donors?
- How Does Major Gift Fundraising Fit within the Overall Fundraising Program?
- Recap and Review

Deciding to make a major gift is an intelligent and strategic decision. It makes you take a hard look at the world and guides you into thinking what it is you want to change and how you can do it. Giving the major gift fills you with joy and passion and connects you to the organization for a lifetime.

Melissa Kohner, 30, Inheritor, Major Donor

WHAT MAKES A GIFT A MAJOR GIFT?

A major gift is not something that donors do on a whim or a lark, or on the spur of the moment. Major gifts generally do not come in the mail, from an unknown or uninvolved person. They do not flow into organizations at a rate of one a week, and in all likelihood, they do not materialize without a great deal of time, talent, or effort attached.

A major gift is a well-thought out *personal decision*. Making the major gift is a very special expression on the part of the donor, which lets the organization know that the donor believes in the organization 100 percent. The donor wants to be an important part of the organization's rich philanthropic tradition and wants that organization to continue its good work well into the future. It is an investment, a bond, a contract that binds the donor to the organization. It is also the highest compliment an organization can receive. Implicit in the gift is the message that the donor truly values the integrity of the organization and holds it in the highest regard.

In most instances, major gifts make it possible for the organization to perpetuate its mission well beyond the donor's lifetime. They are made with the intent of carrying out the donor's values well into the future. The major gift is a way for the donor to leave a meaningful legacy for future generations to be enriched by, and benefit from, the generosity of the major donor.

Major gifts are sometimes called "special gifts," "principal gifts," and "high-end gifts." They represent the most important source of funds for a nonprofit. The rule that 10 percent of the major donors provide 90 percent or more of the organization's funds demonstrates the significance of major gift fundraising. These gifts that represent a significant portion of the organization's entire budget can be used for general operating purposes, special purposes, or capital campaigns.

A prominent feature for any major gift is that it can empower an organization and bring it to new heights. Without major gifts, an organization would not be able to expand its programs or outreach. For example, major gifts can make it possible for a group to open a day care center, to launch a life-saving research project, to conduct public awareness forums, or to provide aid for disaster-stricken families.

Major gifts are very different from annual or direct mail gifts. Annual and direct mail fundraising encompass:

1. Making numerous asks, several times a year, usually in correspondence form.
2. Having limited, if any, personal contact.
3. Emphasizing small-to-moderate increases in gift level.
4. Working with a large donor/membership database.
5. Maintaining and updating a donor/membership database.
6. Expanding the number of donors and members.
7. Updating and disseminating new marketing materials to donors and members.

By contrast, major gift fundraising entails:

1. Selecting top prospects as major gift prospects.
2. Researching prospects' wealth and interests.
3. Sending personal letters, making calls and visits.
4. Personally involving and engaging prospects with every aspect of the organization.
5. Targeting prospects for a specific gift or for a specific project.
6. Selecting the right person to make the right ask at the right time.
7. Overcoming objections and turning "maybe" into "yes."
8. Staying with the prospects when the initial response is "no."
9. Stewarding donors when they agree to make a gift.
10. Tracking the amount and timing of the gift.
11. Personally thanking donors numerous times in numerous ways for their gifts.
12. Replenishing the prospect pool with new major gift prospects.

The comparison of these two areas of fundraising illustrates the importance of the topic of this book. The focus of this book is on the process of taking the top tier of the direct mail/annual donors and turning them into major gift donors. People who have already given to your organization will be the majority of your major gift prospect pool. Those who are consistent givers, and give at an increased level when asked, are more apt to consider a major gift proposal. Those who attend events and give at some level are also your major gift prospects because they have some knowledge and have expressed interest by attending your events.

The key difference between direct mail/annual fundraising and major gift fundraising is that each major gift prospect must be treated specially and individually by you and the leadership in your organization. Each prospect will be cultivated and nurtured in a hand-tailored way that will make the prospect feel special and lucky to receive time and attention from your organization. The more you get to know them, the shorter the time it will take to fashion the right gift opportunity for your prospect.

Remember, the emphasis is on keeping it *personal and sincere*. Major gift donors are very intuitive, and they can detect if you or someone from your organization is not trustworthy, ethical, or sincere. They will often test you, asking numerous questions. They demand accuracy and integrity before they support your cause. Major gift fundraisers must be fully knowledgeable about the organization they represent and how it compares to similar nonprofits. For instance, a major gift prospect who has a family history of heart disease could support the American Heart Association, the leading heart research institute, or a local specialty heart hospital. If the fundraiser represents the research institute, the prospect will want to know why the institute has a greater need for funding over the American Heart Association and the heart hospital.

WHO ARE THE MAJOR DONORS?

Major gift donors are people who have a strong belief in your organization or who have been educated and informed by someone about your organization. As stated above, they have given at some level to your group in the past, have attended an open house or special event, know someone at the organization, or have family or friends who are involved with your group. By and large, they track the progress and publicity of the organization, and they freely give their opinions or comments about the organization when asked. They run the spectrum from a person who wants all the fame and publicity that a gift can buy, to an anonymous donor who strictly forbids that the family name be associated with the gift.

Major donors have accumulated or have inherited assets that can be used for pleasure or for philanthropy. In most instances these assets are in mixed forms such as securities, real estate, retirement accounts, limited family partnerships, insurance policies, and savings.

Major gift donors are protective of their assets and cautious to give them away. In most cases, these assets have taken a long time to accumulate and they want their gift-giving decision to be the best choice possible. They are extremely careful with these assets because they fear that they and their loved ones will outlive their nest egg. They will tell you how hard it was for them during a period of their lives, and how they had to struggle and sacrifice many of their personal goals and ambitions. It is the fundraiser's job to take into consideration all the donor's needs and concerns before fashioning a major gift opportunity.

> **Tip:** *Major gift fundraisers must be sensitive and sympathetic to donor insights, or they will never gain the donor's trust or respect.*

Some major donors view the whole gift process as an investment, and they expect a high return on their investment from your organization. They will often seek the advice of their family, attorneys, financial advisors, accountants, and friends before making any decision. This can take months and even years. The mistake many major gift fundraisers make is that they sense the gift will not occur in a year and stop their cultivation efforts with the donor. You will lose many good prospects and major gifts with this approach.

> **Tip:** *Major gift fundraisers must be prepared to answer all the donor's questions, address their concerns, and above all, be patient, yet persistent.*

Major donors are aware, and sometimes overwhelmed, at the charity choices that exist. Many support a variety of charities, so in their major gift charity selection process they will require detailed information on the questions contained in Exhibit 1–1.

> **Tip:** *The best major gift fundraisers anticipate the donor's questions and are ready to deliver the appropriate answers on behalf of the organization.*

Major donors will give where they have a strong sense that the organization has a solid foundation of support. I use the expression, "people give to forward

Exhibit 1–1 Common Questions Major Gift Donors Ask about the Charity

1. How will their gift be used?
2. How is the project/program being funded currently?
3. Who else is being asked for the gift?
4. Why does the gift have to be made now?
5. Will the project be completed or the program started if the fundraising goal is not met?
6. Have your board members contributed to your organization?
7. How much does the organization spend on fundraising?
8. What percentage of their gift will be spent on the program versus administrative expenses?
9. Have corporations, foundations, and government entities been asked to give?
10. Why do you work for the organization?

moving trains," because it illustrates that major donors will give if others have supported the cause. There is excitement and energy knowing that the gift, coupled with that of others, will make the proposed project a reality. No one likes to think or bear the pressure that if they do not make the gift, the project will fail and never get started. Major gift fundraisers need to seize upon the momentum that past support can build for future support.

> **Tip:** *Prior gifts can and do attract new gifts. Make sure major gift prospects are informed about the benefit prior gifts have brought to your organization.*

Major gift donors insist that they be kept fully apprised of how the gift is being used. Periodic letters, telephone calls, press releases, notes from the gift recipient, letters from the CEO, annual reports, site visits, special receptions, lectures, and seminars are vehicles that fundraisers can use to keep the major donor informed about the gift. Major gift fundraisers know that major donors are by and large not "one-time givers." The best prospects for the organization are the people who just made a gift. Keeping your major donors fully apprised of all the benefits of their gifts will pave the way for their future enhanced gifts.

Major donors also insist that the gift be used for the intended purpose. They have thought long and hard about the type of gift they are going to make and in most instances, they are very specific about how the gift should be used. I have experienced several times a donor's request to include in the contract language of their gift a contingency plan that would protect their gift in case the original purpose cannot be fulfilled. For example, if a donor has endowed a scholarship program in anthropology studies, and the college ceases to offer an anthropology program, the donor could select another academic program to support with the endowed scholarship money.

HOW DOES MAJOR GIFT FUNDRAISING FIT WITHIN THE OVERALL FUNDRAISING PROGRAM?

It is essential that major gift fundraising be an integral part of your entire fundraising program. It must be closely linked with your direct mail/annual, prospect research, membership, corporation and foundation, planned giving, stewardship/recognition, and volunteer fundraising components. This is not always an easy task to accomplish. In many organizations, each development department has its own budget and its own list of prospects. Fundraisers feel the yearly pressure of making their fundraising goals, often to the exclusion of other development departments. People responsible for increasing the numbers and dollars brought in by membership programs and direct mail/annual giving programs may be less than enthusiastic about sharing or giving names of their top givers to the major gifts department. Planned giving specialists may not want the major gifts department to see their prospects because the prospects may make an outright gift, instead of a planned gift. Volunteer and auxiliary groups may want to see the major gift prospect alone and may not share donor information with the major gifts department. These damaging approaches, coupled with high turnover of development staff, can produce disastrous results. They can sabotage the organization's overall fundraising goals and can prevent preservation of important institutional history. It can give your organization a bad internal atmosphere, which will most assuredly reflect on the quality of contact your organization has with its constituency.

So how can major gift fundraising successfully integrate with the entire development operation? Exhibit 1–2 contains some suggested ways to produce a highly successful fundraising program.

Exhibit 1–2 Suggested Ways To Produce a Highly Successful Fundraising Program

1. Create and implement a three-to-five-year fundraising strategic plan that includes prospect lists, tasks, timelines, and goals for each fundraising division.
2. Have everyone responsible for fundraising from staff to board members be aware of the strategic plan.
3. Revisit the plan and evaluate all components on a yearly basis.
4. Have a top official of the development office (CEO, president, vice president, executive director, director of development, etc.) make decisions regarding prospect assignments.
5. Meet twice a month with all fundraising staff to review the progress of each department and to exchange information and ideas about assigned prospects.
6. Encourage fundraisers to learn the roles and responsibilities of their coworkers.
7. Emphasize teamwork and overall goals, not individual fundraiser's goals.
8. Reward fundraising staff for creative fundraising ideas.
9. Be flexible to new developments and new projects that take place within your organization.
10. Praise everyone when a gift is received.

Tip: Major gift fundraising must work in conjunction with every aspect of the development office to ensure the present and future success of the organization's overall fundraising goals.

RECAP AND REVIEW

1. Major gifts are personal decisions based on a personal relationship the donor has formed with the organization.
2. Major gifts make it possible for the organization to perpetuate its mission well into the future.
3. Major gifts can empower an organization and expand its outreach and breadth of programs and service.

4. Unlike direct mail/annual fundraising, major gift fundraising emphasizes one-on-one personal contact, over time, with emphasis placed on specific gift ideas for each prospect.

5. Major donors demand your trust, sincerity, and honesty.

6. Major donors have strong beliefs in the cause and direction of your organization.

7. Major donors are protective of the assets they have worked hard to accumulate.

8. Major gift fundraisers must anticipate the donor's questions and listen to their concerns before crafting a major gift proposal.

9. Major gift fundraisers must keep donors fully apprised of the people and programs that have benefited by the generosity of the donor's gift.

10. Major gift fundraising must be an integral part of the organization's entire fundraising program.

SUGGESTED READINGS

Gary, T., and M. Kohner. 1998. *Inspired philanthropy: Creating a giving plan.* Oakland, CA: Chardon Press.

Kelly, K. 1998. *Effective fund-raising management.* Mahwah, NJ: Lawrence Erlbaum Associates.

Muir, R., and J. May. 1993. *Developing an effective major gift program: From managing staff to soliciting gifts.* Washington, DC: Council for Advancement and Support of Education.

Williams, J. 1997. Overview of major giving. In *The Nonprofit Handbook: Fund Raising*, ed. J.M. Greenfield, 360–361. New York: John Wiley & Sons, Inc.

Chapter 2
The Essentials To Starting a Major Gifts Program

CHAPTER OUTLINE

- Identifying Your Best Prospects
- Sorting It All Out
- Assessing the Number of Major Gifts Prospects
- Creating Donor Profiles
- Gathering Donor Information
- Developing a Personal Calendar System
- Recap and Review

Our giving is an extension of our commitment to building relationships with our customers. For that reason, we form partnerships with organizations that serve the needs of our customers and their communities. By focusing our giving, integrating it into our business goals and making it a core value of our company, we can have a long-term positive impact in the areas we support.

Arthur M. Blank, President and CEO, The Home Depot, and Philanthropist

---

IDENTIFYING YOUR BEST PROSPECTS

Every four months, Mr. D faithfully sent a $100 check to the local hospital where he had heart surgery. The checks were gratefully acknowledged by the hospital and properly recorded. Mr. D's gift record showed a series of $100 gifts that made him a direct mail donor. After reviewing the cumulative gifts for all the direct mail donors, the hospital's direct mail manager and major gifts manager decided that Mr. D might be a major gift prospect. The major gifts manager met with Mr. D and discovered that Mr. D gave $100 each quarter because that was when he made pledge payments to his church. To him, the church's pledge envelope served as a convenient reminder for him to send his gift to the hospital. During their conversation it was revealed that Mr. D supported the hospital because he received individual attention by all the nurses, and it was his "insurance" just in case he needed follow-up care. The major gifts manager proposed that Mr. D increase his quarterly gifts to $250, and the hospital

would send him their pledge envelopes. Mr. D agreed. Now that Mr. D was making yearly gifts of $1,000 he became a major donor to the hospital.

This is just one example of how many major gift prospects may go undetected. Choosing the best prospects for your major gifts program may seem like a piece of cake. For a college it may be the highest alumni givers, for a museum it may be long-standing members, for an environmental group it may be their top membership level. Any organization could simply take the 20 largest, most recent gifts, and—voila—those donors would become major gift prospects.

That might seem like a good start, but organizations that use this limited approach will miss some of the real jewels. It is those diamond donors who can be long-time major gifts donors to the organization.

Take the example of Mr. D. He would have given the hospital $400 per year, instead of $1,000 per year, for as long as his pledge payments continued to the church. Worse yet, Mr. D's gifts to the hospital may have ended when he fulfilled his payments to the church.

SORTING IT ALL OUT

Before organizing a major gifts program, you should examine your office computer capabilities. At a minimum your system should record donor names, addresses, telephone numbers, date and amount of gift, gift pledges, gift purpose, and acknowledgment. Most computer software companies have programs that go well beyond these basics to include the type of gift (cash, stock, in-kind), gift restrictions, pledge history, and the solicitor or solicitation team. In addition, the program can include prospect research, donor contacts, association with the organization, cultivation and solicitation strategies, events attended, contact reports, links to their business addresses, matching gifts program, and corporate or foundation support.

It is possible, but highly labor intensive, to do this manually. A variety of moderately priced fundraising computer software companies are available that can save hours of valuable time. Some include JSI Fundraising Systems, Inc., Blackbaud Inc., Campagne Associates, Target Software Inc., and Donor II. It is highly recommended that you use a computer system that can sort your donors by geographic regions, gift amount, date of gift, gift history, pledges, and pledge payments.

Each major gift fundraiser will have to make the determination of what constitutes a major gift for their organization. There is no magic number or gift level that all organizations use for their major gifts program. For a large university, it may be $250,000 or more. For an elementary school, it may be $75 or more. For a national environmental group, it may be $100,000 or more. For a local clean air council, it may be $50 or more. The range is set by the size and scope of the organization. Use the number of donors, number of highest gifts, and number of cumulative gifts that reach the highest gifts as guides to determining your major gift range. Keep in mind that the smart fundraiser should not set a range that is too high or too low. Your goal is to set the major gift range that will produce a workable number of major gifts prospects who will receive personal attention from your organization. A high range will narrow the pool and frustrate the development professional with a limited number of prospects. A low range will overwhelm the development professional and jeopardize the individual treatment effort needed in major gift fundraising.

For example, let's define a major gift as a gift of $10,000 or more.

Step 1: Sort by gifts of $10,000 or more that the organization received within the last year.

Step 2: Sort by gifts of $10,000 or more *ever* received.

Step 3: Sort by gifts in the last five years or less that total $10,000 or more.

Step 4: Sort by gifts that come close to $10,000 *and* the donor has attended an event.

Analysis Step 1

Individuals who gave $10,000 or more within the last year are your top prospects. The more recent the gift was given, the higher the position the prospect will have on your priority list. These folks are already giving at the major gift level and have the potential to make repeat enhanced gifts. They are on the top of your priority list because you will want to move very quickly to get to see them and thank them in person for their outstanding gifts to your organization. They have demonstrated that they have the capacity to make these types of gifts, and in all likelihood, have the capacity to make even larger gifts. This is the group to which you will devote most of your time and attention.

Analysis Step 2

Gifts of $10,000 *ever* received will capture those prospects who at one time felt very strongly about your organization. Some event in their lives or something your organization did certainly tugged on their heartstrings and motivated and inspired them to support your group. You will want to work with the most recent $10,000 gifts first and then move on to the prospects who made this type of gift in later years. Capturing these lapsed prospects on the list is important because in time you will want to convince them to give frequently and at higher levels. Keep in mind that if the donor has not made the gift within the last five years or more, it is going to take more work and time to persuade the donor to give again at that level. They will require more information and cultivation from your organization. If the donor gave once, you will need to find out why they did not give in later years. It could be they chose to support other groups; they were less than thrilled with some project, program, or leader in your organization; they felt your group did not properly acknowledge their significant gift; or they had a change in their personal finances. In time you will want to win them back to support your organization.

Analysis Step 3

One of the most overlooked areas in targeting major donors is what has been termed the cumulative givers. Some organizations are surprised to learn that they have a significant pool of donors who have given a large gift, say $1,000 a year, for the past 10 years. Why are their gifts that total $10,000 any less significant than the recent one-time $10,000 gift? They are not, and that is why an organization must capture this group by following Step 3.

Remember our story of Mr. D earlier? He is a classic example of the cumulative giver. If the development office at the hospital just looked at his yearly giving, he would have been classified as a $400 donor, and not a major gift prospect. Yet sorting by 10 years or more, Mr. D's combined gifts over this time placed him well into the hospital's major gift range.

Analysis Step 4

Finally we have the prospects whose gifts come close to the $10,000 and they have attended, volunteered, or participated in some event, project, or program for your organization. Just when you are ready to discount these prospects as low-end givers, they attend an opening, volunteer for an open house, or in some way show their interest. It would be easy to draw the conclusion that if they are this interested in your organization, they will *naturally* send in a gift. It would also be easy to sit back and wait for it to arrive. In all likelihood, time will go by, there will be no gift. These folks need to be part of your list because they have the potential to make gifts *and* be involved. The more involved they are, the better chance you have of bringing them along your path that will lead to consistent major gifts.

Take, for example, Mrs. C. Every gift she ever gave to the local food bank was $100 or less. The food bank would invite her to volunteer organizing holiday meal baskets to needy individuals in the area, but she always declined. One year, she showed up on Thanksgiving and helped the food bank serve meals to the homeless and less fortunate families in the area. The food bank thought that since Mrs. C attended the meal drive, she would naturally respond to their December mailing and give more than her usual $100 gift. To their disappointment, she sent her usual $100. The food bank learned that Mrs. C needed more individual cultivation before she felt comfortable giving at a higher level.

ASSESSING THE NUMBER OF MAJOR GIFTS PROSPECTS

At this point a fundraiser should add up the number of direct/annual donors that emerge from the four steps. This number is very important because you must decide how many major gifts prospects you can work with comfortably and competently. Now is the time to take a realistic view of the following items:

1. Are you devoting 100 percent of your time to major gift fundraising, or do you have other fundraising/administrative responsibilities?
2. Do you have administrative help?
3. If so, can the support person/staff mail letters, set appointments, and make follow-up telephone calls?
4. Are they experienced at setting appointments and making follow-up telephone calls?
5. Do they *like* performing these tasks or does it seem like drudgery?
6. Do you have the time to tackle the whole process yourself?

Use these questions as a guide in determining the number of prospects you select. Pay particular attention to numbers 3 through 5 above. One should not assume that since you have a secretary/administrative assistant, that this person is skilled at setting telephone appointments or that he or she would enjoy this task. One organization learned the hard way. The CEO gave the list of her top 25 prospects to her administrative assistant with current business and home telephone numbers and asked the assistant to set up the visits. One week went by, two weeks went by, and the assistant did not make any calls. It turned out that the assistant was petrified that the prospects would say no to the visits and feared that the CEO would blame the assistant for not getting the appointments.

Another organization thought they were doing well because their secretary was making 12–15 calls a week. The director thought that eventually his secretary would land him at least a few visits a week. It turned out that the secretary hated making the calls. She could not get off the telephone fast enough with the prospect or the prospect's secretary, and the director never got in the door with one prospect.

If you do have support, you may need to spend upfront time training your support person/staff. I suggest that you give him or her telephone scripts of what you want to say, and tailor the script to each prospect or small pool of prospects that have something in common. For example, if a group of prospects just made a gift, you could have one script thanking them. If you read in a recent newsletter, newspaper, or journal article that a few prospects just started a new company, the script could include a congratulatory opening line. You will also have to work out the issue of what dates and time you are available to make calls. Don't make the mistake that some fundraisers do by letting someone else set the appointments without specifying the dates and times you are unavailable.

Take for example, political fundraiser, Ms. S. She was delighted that she had a list of over 100 top political supporters for the upcoming governor's race in November. She gave the list of names to her assistant six months before the election and asked her to make appointments. What she failed to do was detail where she would be over those six months. Half of her time was spent on the road with the candidate, so she was unavailable even if the assistant set up the prospect meetings.

A one-person development shop or small nonprofit should keep the number of prospects to about 25–50 people. For instance, The Balch Institute for Ethnic Studies in Philadelphia has a director of development who handles about 25 prospects. The Boys & Girls Club of Bentonville/Bella Vista in Arizona has a one-person development shop and handles approximately 47 major gifts prospects. The additional help from a senior manager, an assistant, or reliable part/full-time volunteer would prop the number of major gifts prospects to 50–75.

A development office with two to four development professionals and administrative help could handle 100–150 prospects. For example, at the World Affairs Council in Philadelphia, the president, with help from her development and administrative staff, handles about 125–150 prospects. Lehigh Valley Hospital and Health Network's director of major gifts and capital campaigns, together with a senior development professional, two directors, and one part-time assistant, handles about 125 major gifts prospects. Similarly, at the Philadelphia Zoo, the vice president for development, with two directors and support staff, handles about 150 major gifts prospects.

At large organizations, such as a major university, or a nationally based organization with more than seven development professionals, senior staff, and administrative assistants, the ratio of prospects to development help depends on how the organization is structured. For instance, at Cornell University, at the $1 million special gifts level, seven gift officers plus one part-time officer work with 250 prospects each. At their major gifts level, $1 million to $10 million, five individual gift officers plus one part-time officer work with 100–150 major gifts prospects each. At Lehigh University, three people from top level management handle a group of 750 major gift prospects rated $100,000 and above, while five major gift officers handle a group of 1,000 major gift prospects rated $25,000 and above.

CREATING DONOR PROFILES

Now that you have your pool of prospects, you will need to assess what you know about each person and what you need to know. The more you know about them, the easier it will be for you to get in the door to see them, establish common links and connections to your organization, and effectively cultivate them. For each prospect, you will create a donor profile (see Exhibit 2–1).

Start with the facts you know about every donor, such as their gift history. Examine carefully the years they made their gifts, if their gifts increased, decreased, or stayed the same. The "same gifts each year" donors may be your best prospects because it is unlikely that anyone *personally* spent the time needed to convince this group to increase their gifts or pledge at a higher gift level. Did the donor skip a year or two? This could signal a myriad of possibilities, such as shift in financial priorities, illness or death in the family, lack of contact by your organization, or they simply forgot to send in their end-of-year gift. These are all important issues you will want to find out once you meet your prospects.

Next, examine where they live and vacation. If most of your constituency lives in one area, then break the area down by neighborhood or block. Most nonprofits have certain neighborhoods that are viewed as "affluent centers." Beyond the obvious areas of Boca Raton, Florida; Greenwich, Connecticut; Scottsdale, Arizona; or the Silicon Valley in California there are pockets of wealth in every state. Your organization must be aware of where your supporters live in proximity to these wealthy areas. It is *one* of many facts you will want to explore as you get more acquainted with your prospects. Be aware, however, that just because a prospect lives in a wealthy area, it does not automatically mean that they have the disposable wealth to make gifts.

Exhibit 2–1 Elements for a Donor Profile

1. History that details the gift amount, dates of the gifts, and pledge payments.
2. Gift restrictions—gifts that are targeted for a program, project, or campaign.
3. Current home, vacation home, and business addresses, e-mail addresses, telephone/cell numbers.
4. Net worth, including salary, securities, real estate holdings.
5. Business title and business connections.
6. Length of time they owned their home or vacation home.
7. Educational background for the prospect and the prospect's family.
8. Attendance to any special event, athletic event, concert, groundbreaking, meeting, seminar, lecture, open house.
9. Prior contact reports or any communication by other development professionals.
10. Details of their family history, such as the names, ages, and residencies of spouse/significant other, children, grandchildren, stepchildren, parents, and grandparents.
11. Religious affiliation.
12. Support to other charitable organizations and, if possible, level of support.
13. Volunteer activities, board affiliations, and memberships.
14. Hobbies, interests, and recreation activities.

Tip: An address in a wealthy neighborhood may mean that the donor has the capacity to make a large gift or that the money is needed to maintain their affluent lifestyle.

If your prospects are scattered regionally or nationwide, it may be a good idea to "cluster" them by areas in preparation for visits and cultivation events. If your organization has a budget that allows for some travel, clustering offers a great way to organize prospect visits to this area. It also serves as an important factor for a nonprofit to know where its top prospects are located, which could provide a pattern to follow to capture additional prospects.

For example, when I first started working at Temple University in Philadelphia, Pennsylvania, I had a concentration of alumni living not only in the Philadelphia region, but also in New York City, Washington, DC, and Florida. I separated my pool of 165+ major gift prospects by these geographic locations. Each geographic area had a separate folder and each folder contained donor profiles. If I needed to see a donor in one of those regions, say New York City, I would schedule my time so that I could see other prospects living in the New York area. Throughout your major gifts development work, you will get leads of other major gifts prospects. Maybe you will read about them in the newspaper. Maybe someone you just visited will give you a name or two of other people who would be interested in learning more about your organization. While you may be tempted to put those names in a folder for a later time, I encourage you to take the time to place them in your folder by geographic area. This way when you are in one area, you can see this new prospect or lead without making a special trip. This may increase your prospect pool slightly; however, you do not want to miss the opportunity of exploring a possible important lead.

Tip: Create geographic area files for prospects in preparation for future area meetings and visits.

This exercise is also helpful if you are separating your donor pool by town or county. It will streamline your cultivation efforts because you will be able to drive to one area and make several visits. It will also help you organize small special events for your top prospects. For example, you can gather a small group of donors living in the same county for a breakfast meeting or to meet your CEO, a volunteer, or someone who has benefited by the good work of your organization, such as a girl scout, a big brother/little brother, or a camp director.

GATHERING DONOR INFORMATION

Outside of knowing the donor's name, address, and giving history, you may, at first, know very little about your prospect. Unless someone from your organization or a volunteer has had prior contact with, or knowledge of, the prospect, it would be highly unlikely that you could know their family life, their hobbies and interests, or if they support other charities. Luckily, fundraisers have many avenues available to them to uncover this vital information.

Research—From a Distance

Your local library may be the most underused resource tool. Most local libraries have copies of local newspapers, business and trade journals, corporate and foundation guides, chamber of commerce publications, *Who's Who in America*, *Who's Wealthy in America*, or Internet access to these publications. You can research your prospects, your prospects' companies, community activities, and board memberships in these publications. For example, almost every local newspaper has a "society column" that will let you know if your prospect has served on any social committees or has attended any social events. This will tip you off that your prospect supports or is active with other charities.

Other sources of written material you can use for research are annual reports, alumni lists, and membership lists. An annual report will give you the big picture of your prospects' companies or side investments. Alumni lists, especially yearly honor rolls, will let you know if your prospects support their alma mater and the level of their support. This will be an important guide when you are ready to ask this prospect for a gift to your organization. Membership lists will give you a clue about your prospects' recreational activities, such as hiking, fishing, golf, or tennis, or cultural activities, such as art, theater, dance, or music.

There is a wealth of material written about prospect research and Appendix 2–A lists suggested readings, Web sites, and prospect research information providers on this topic. One research tool, however, should be specifically mentioned. Some fundraisers may be unaware of the prospect information contained in the U.S. Department of Treasury, Internal Revenue Service Form 990 (see Appendix 2–B). Tax-exempt organizations that have annual gross receipts over $25,000 must file this form with the government each year. This would include most charities and non-profit organizations. Organizations that are not required to file this form include church affiliated groups, schools below college level affiliated with a church, an exclusively religious activity, a mission society sponsored by a church that conducts more than half its activities in foreign countries, and a governmental unit.

Of key interest to fundraisers is Part V of Form 990. The filing organization must list for each officer, director, trustee, and key employee all cash and non-cash compensation, contributions to employee benefit plans and deferred compensation, and taxable and non-taxable fringe benefits. Key employees include chief financial officers, chief management, and administrative officials. If your prospects are officers or directors for nonprofit boards, this would be an excellent resource to find out if they are paid for their positions, and if so, at what salary and benefit level.

In Part III of Form 990, the filing organization must report the amounts of awards and grants given to individuals and organizations in the past year. This includes scholarships, fellowships, and research grants. If your prospect list contains a grant-making organization, or an individual who plays a key role in a grant-making organization, you will want to research the past few years of the organization's Form 990.

Tax-exempt private foundations, such as family foundations, must file Form 990-PF (Appendix 2–C). Part VIII of this form details compensation and expense account information about officers, directors, trustees, foundation managers, highly paid employees, and independent contractors, such as consultants. The filing foundation must list information on the foundation's assets and capital gains and losses. Of particular interest to many fundraisers is Part IX–A, which lists the foundation's four largest direct charitable activities, and Part XV, which lists the grants and contributions paid by the foundation during the year, or approved for future distribution, such as multi-year grants.

Here is an example of how researching a prospect's Form 990 and Form 990-PF can reap big benefits. Senior Services fundraiser had Mr. E on her prospect list. Mr. E was well known in the local business community as a frequent gift giver, for many different causes, but none that to her knowledge included Senior Services. She wanted to find out the amount of these gifts to these organizations. She went to her local library that kept on file all tax-exempt organizations that filed a Form 990. There she found Mr. E's Form 990-PF. It turns out Mr. E had a family foundation and all his gifts came from the assets of the foundation. In Part XV where it lists grants distributed for the prior year, she discovered that the foundation made a grant to a religious nursing home. She also learned that the foundation's average gift to any one organization was in the $20,000 range.

Armed with this knowledge, Senior Services fundraiser made an appointment with Mr. E and brought him to the organization for a tour. After several meetings between Mr. E and the executive leadership of Senior Services, it was proposed that Mr. E's foundation make a $25,000 gift to support the Senior

Services new senior mentoring program. Funding for this program would make it possible for 15 seniors to help kindergarten and first-grade students in a local elementary school improve their reading skills. Mr. E agreed to make the gift in the following fiscal quarter.

In addition to researching Form 990 and Form 990-PF in local libraries, fundraisers with Internet access can check the Web site *nccs.urban.org* to see if the organization has filed their forms online. Under the Taxpayer Relief Act of 1997, if you request Form 990-PF from a private foundation, the foundation is required to send you a copy by mail.

Internet research can give you information about the prospects' publicly held stocks, their company's publicly traded stocks, real estate holdings, and commercial property holdings. Almost every brokerage has their own Web site and there are numerous sites you can access for this information (see Appendix 2–A).

Time and Deadlines

Depending on the size of your organization, you may have a prospect researcher or have a full prospect research department. Small or one-shop nonprofits may not have the resources to hire a full-time researcher; however, it is highly recommended that this component be factored into their long-range fundraising plans. Possibilities include hiring a part-time researcher, hiring a consultant, or simply devoting part of your time on doing the research yourself. In the end you will find this is well worth the extra expense and time, *if* the research is focused and timelines are established.

For example, if you have a prospect researcher, you should give your list of major gifts prospects with the information you need on each prospect to the researcher with a *deadline* for getting back to you with this information. Here is an illustration of what can happen if deadlines are not set and met.

Fundraiser P for a children's welfare advocacy group read in a weekly business journal that one of her prospects just became managing partner for a large tool and die company. She sent the prospect a congratulatory card, with a note that she would like to meet the prospect and congratulate him personally at the company. At the same time, she sent her prospect researcher a request for information about this company *without a deadline*. Several weeks went by, and fundraiser P never called the prospect to set up the meeting because she had not received the information from the researcher. Without the information, she would feel unprepared for the meeting. This prospect fell to the bottom of fundraiser P's prospect list. About two months later, fundraiser P received the information from the prospect researcher. By now it was too late to call the prospect and reference her congratulatory note. Fundraiser P missed an excellent opportunity to get an initial visit with her prospect.

Two important points must be made. First, prospect research is helpful information; however, too many fundraisers postpone their important initial contacts with their major gifts prospects because they are waiting for prospect information. Do not become overly reliant on prospect research and Internet searches.

Second, tying prospect research to a deadline is important. The information-gathering process can break down and drag on for weeks if deadlines are not set and met. Give the prospect researcher or department three weeks at most for collecting information, and then move on.

Another avenue your organization may want to consider is hiring a prospect research firm. Even if you have a prospect research department, this may be a worthy investment. These firms can work with your research department to select the areas of research you need on your major gifts prospects. They have access to a variety of research tools and can hand tailor prospect information profiles and ratings systems for your organization. In addition, some companies will interface their newly created research data with your existing donor files, to create one computer software system that you can use as your major gifts donor tracking system (see Appendix 2–A).

Research—Up Close and Personal

Once you have gathered all the information you can on paper or have hired a research firm to do the task, you will need to find out everything you can about your prospect as an *individual*. Whereas the facts and figures on your prospects in the previous section could be gathered by book or computer, the information you need here requires an investment of time getting to know each prospect on a personal level. Start with your coworkers, development professionals, boards, upper management, contacts, volunteers, and staff. Does anyone know anything about your prospect? Arming yourself with as much information about the person as possible prepares the fundraiser to write the initial letter and to make the first telephone call. It also sets the stage for future meetings and visits. While you may know about the prospect's wealth and property hold-

Preface

The only way you can raise major gifts is to have confidence in yourself and enjoy the process.

This is easy to say and very difficult to deliver. I wanted to write a book that would give executive directors, development directors, board members, volunteers, staff, political fundraisers, and entrepreneurs a step-by-step process of how to raise major gifts from their existing pool of direct mail or annual donors. In the course of teaching major gifts fundraising classes, I have learned that many people think that there is this "magic layer" of top prospects who will, in time, make large gifts. While that may be true, the better source for your major gifts is your existing direct mail/annual donors. This book will show you how to:

- Identify and segment your top donors from your existing pool of direct mail/annual donors.
- Create donor profiles and gather prospect research.
- Manage your time and organize your calendar for donor cultivation.
- Write prospect letters and make telephone calls that will get you "in."
- Use all the information during cultivation to craft individual gift proposals.
- Work effectively with leadership and volunteers before, during, and after solicitations.
- Ask for major gifts and be prepared to respond to any concern or question.
- Select the most meaningful and personalized donor recognitions that prepare the donors for the next gift.
- Creatively involve and educate your donors with stewardship programs that will lead to the next gift.
- Track the frequency of gifts and activity with your top prospects as a guide for weaving in new prospects from which to cultivate and solicit new major gifts.

Each chapter contains real examples and tips to help you incorporate these skills into your major gifts program. The book is designed for you to share it with your development coworkers, other development units in your organization, supervisors, board members, and volunteers. Major gifts affect every aspect of your organization so it is essential that you include all staff and all departments in this process. This book will provide your organization with a clear road map and a timeline of moving your prospects from small gifts to significant gifts.

I left the best for last and that is in the last chapter. It illustrates a few heart-warming success stories of donors whose gifts of $250–$2,500 became gifts of $50,000–$5 million in less than one year. It is my intention that the book, and particularly this last chapter, will motivate, encourage, and energize you. The more energy and enthusiasm you bring to this process, the easier it will be for you to get the gift. Why? Prospects and donors expect you to be upbeat and to be the cheerleader for your organization. They can tell if you are feel awkward and unsure or if your proposal and your ask are less than convincing. Now you have a book that gives you and others all the skills, the real life stories to draw upon, plus all the encouragement and motivation to raise many, many major gifts.

I have purposely written this book in a conversational tone and with some humor, so that you will relax and learn. The best part about major gifts fundraising is getting to know your donors and developing friendships with them so that they feel good about making a meaningful gift to your organization. You have to find your voice and share some of your own experiences with your donors to make this work. I hope this book helps you to find your voice and your own personal, successful style of raising major gifts.

> Please feel free to e-mail me your comments and suggestions to "majorgifts@yahoo.com."

ings, experienced fundraisers have learned that other bits of information, such as family involvement, religious activities, hobbies, club memberships, community activities, athletic interests, and support of other charities, can be extremely important.

Peer Screening

If someone has information about your prospect, make the time to sit down with that person and learn all you can about the donor. These "peer screenings" will provide invaluable information throughout the entire process of working with your prospects. Many organizations conduct peer screenings in a group setting, inviting board members, contacts, and volunteers to meet with the development officers. At these meetings, a list of major gifts prospects, with all the known information, is circulated and discussed. If the peer screeners have additional information about the prospects, it is the responsibility of the development officers to research this information and follow through. Any size organization can conduct peer screenings. If meetings are too time consuming and/or costly, they can send their peer screeners a list of prospects and discuss each prospect on the telephone or by conference call.

Peer screening works better in a group atmosphere. For instance, one board member may see the name of a prospect and say, "I believe she just became president of the Chamber of Commerce." This may trigger another board member to add "yes, and I think she just ended her board membership with Land Trust Foundation so that she could take on this new role with the Chamber." Now you have two new facts about the prospect that you did not have prior to the peer screening. You can use this new information to get you in the door to see your prospect or to continue your cultivation. Just think, if this prospect is high on your list, all you need to do is go to the next Chamber of Commerce meeting and introduce yourself to your prospect.

Peer screening is not an isolated process, restricted to the major gifts department or person responsible for raising major gifts. If you or anyone from your organization, including coworkers in other departments and staff, have met the prospect, in the past or present, or have had any contact with the prospect whatsoever, it is important that this information be shared in the peer-screening process. Your organization will be better served, and you will be preserving institutional history if many people in your organization participate in these peer screenings.

Keep in mind that the *prospect-initiated contact or communication*, such as a letter, attendance at any

event, or meeting with an auxiliary group, is important information that must be shared with the group. This information, combined with information from the peer-screening process, will paint the most accurate and complete donor profile.

Confidentiality

It is important that you and your peer screeners, whether they are staff, volunteers, board members, or community leaders, be extremely sensitive with the information you receive. Always ask your peer screeners if this is common knowledge or if they think the prospect would not want this information revealed. In the example above, the election of a new president to the Chamber of Commerce would be public knowledge. What if, however, that same prospect just became divorced or was seriously ill? Obviously this is useful information for you to know, especially in planning your contact and the timing of your gift proposal. You would not want others outside your organization to know because it would be looked upon with disfavor and would cast your organization in a very bad light. The National Society of Fund Raising Executives Code of Ethical Principles and Standards of Professional Practice specifically states that its members "shall not disclose privileged information to unauthorized parties," and that "all donor and prospect information created by, or on behalf of, an organization is the property of that organization" (see Appendix 2–D). This illustrates the need to be very discrete and aware of the confidential nature of the information you uncover in peer screenings.

> ***Tip:*** *Make sure that you ask your peer screener if you can use his or her name or information when working with the prospect. If they say "no," make certain that you keep confidential any information that you've gathered from the peer screener.*

Recordkeeping

A very important part of peer screenings is maintaining accurate records. Good recordkeeping will ensure that your organization preserves institutional history on your major gifts prospects. Records should be kept in computer files, and to the extent possible, in hard copy. Many nonprofits experience turnover in staff, and without good records, the new development officers have to start from the beginning of the information-gathering stage. This can be a set back to any nonprofit organization and can forestall the organization's campaigns and fundraising goals. It is equally important that this information is shared with coworkers who have responsibilities other than major gifts fundraising (Dean 1998, 12). If you have other departments such as direct mail, annual giving, corporate and foundation giving, planned giving, or prospect research, make sure you circulate your information to these departments. You may discover that your major gift prospect just made a high-end gift to the annual fund, or that they just started a new business from your corporate development coworker.

The best way to ensure that all your prospect information is properly recorded and can be accessed by your development team is to create a contact report (see Exhibit 2–2). Any time a fundraiser, someone from your organization, or a volunteer contacts or communicates with your prospects, or if the prospect initiates the contact, attends an event, or accepts an invitation, a contact report should be made. It should include the prospect's name; address; time, date, and place of the contact; type of contact (telephone call/visit/meeting/tour/concert/site visit/gift proposal); people in attendance; comments; and, most important, next step with proposed date of completion.

> **Tip:** *Make sure you fill out a contact report as soon as possible after the contact with the prospect. This will ensure the accuracy and thoroughness of the report.*

DEVELOPING A PERSONAL CALENDAR SYSTEM

It is absolutely essential for any major gifts fundraiser to have a personal calendar system. The rule is to get one system that works well for you and that can be made available to administrative help for setting and confirming your prospect appointments. Too often fundraisers have a personal calendar, a calendar on their desk, and a calendar with their assistant. The downfall of that system is that when you do get an

---

Exhibit 2–2 Contact Report

Contact Report
By: Laura Fredricks

Date: _____

Prospect's Name: _____

Prospect's Home Address: _____

Prospect's Business Address: _____

Date/Place/Time of Contact: _____

Type of Contact:

____ Telephone	____ Cultivation Visit	____ Meeting	____ Special Event
____ Tour	____ Site Visit	____ Letter	____ Solicitation
____ Follow-Up Solicitation	____ Gift Closing	____ Stewardship	____ Recognition
____ Other			

People in Attendance: _____

Comments: _____

Next Steps with Dates: _____

appointment, or one is set for you, you have to record it in three or more places. The worst scenario, which has happened to many fundraisers, is that they finally get in the door to see a prospect they have been trying to see for several weeks, only to find out they were looking at only one calendar. Another calendar had them scheduled to see someone else.

Many fundraisers use a daily planner to pencil in appointments and engagements. Others use computer calendars, digital calendars, or pocket and hand-held electronic calendars. The system that works best for me is a combined monthly and daily planner. It contains the names, addresses, telephone numbers, and birthdays of my top 50 prospects; the current month and next two months in a two-page format; daily pages in a one-page format for three months; and a section for appointments and events for one full year. I bring my planner everywhere I go, and it serves as my only calendar. My assistant has her own calendar she keeps for my appointments. Each day I give her my planner so that she can transfer my dates into her calendar. If I get an appointment when I am traveling or away from the office, I call her right after the appointment is set so she can record it on her calendar. This ensures that she does not schedule me for an appointment or meeting when I am unavailable.

It is also critical to major gifts fundraising that if tasks and calls are not completed during the day, that they are transferred to later days. This is where your planner can be most helpful. If I was scheduled to call four prospects, and I only called two, I take the uncalled two names and place them on the next day's to-do list. This will ensure that you are maintaining consistent contact with all your prospects. Appendix 2–E illustrates a sample of my monthly and two-day daily planner. In Chapter 3, Getting in the Door, you will really see how useful it is to have an organized personal calendar system.

RECAP AND REVIEW

1. Assess your computer capabilities for recording and sorting donor records.
2. Sort your donors by gifts of $10,000 or more, years of giving, cumulative giving, and involvement with your organization.
3. Select the number of major gifts prospects you can work with, taking into consideration the size of your organization and your administrative/volunteer help.
4. Create a donor profile for each prospect.
5. Cluster your prospects by geographic area, including region, state, county, or town.
6. Use a local library, government tax forms, the Internet, and peer screenings to gather as much information as you can about each of your prospects.
7. Prospect researchers must be given deadlines for each research request.
8. Be aware that some prospect information may be confidential.
9. Maintain timely and accurate contact reports.
10. Select and use a personal calendar system.

REFERENCES

Dean, J. March 1998. Development Dynamics. *Fund Raising Management*: 12.

National Society of Fund Raising Executives Code of Ethical Principles and Standards of Professional Practice. Adopted 1991, amended 1999: Standards 12–13.

Taxpayer Relief Act of 1997, 26 U.S.C. 1.

U.S. Department of Treasury Internal Revenue Service Form 990 Return of Organization Exempt From Income Tax, IRC 501 c.

U.S. Department of Treasury Internal Revenue Service Form 990-PF Return of Private Foundation, IRC 501 c.

Who's Wealthy in America, 1999. 9th ed. Farmington Hills, MI: The Taft Group.

Who's Who in America 1999, 53rd ed. New Providence, RI: Reed Elsevier, Inc.

Appendix 2–A

Suggested Readings, Web Sites, and Prospect Information Providers

SUGGESTED READINGS

Bergan, H. 1996. *Where the information is.* Alexandria, VA: Bio Guide Press.

Blanchard, L. 1998. *Fundraising and friend-raising on the Web.* Chicago: American Library Association.

Jenkins, J., and M. Lucas. 1986. *How to find philanthropic prospects.* Ambler, PA: Fund-Raising Institute.

Hudson, M., ed. 1997. *Prospect research fundamentals.* Sioux City, IA: Stevenson Consultants, Inc.

Norsworthy, A., ed. 1991. *FRI prospect research resource directory.* 2d ed. Rockville, MD: The Taft Group.

Stanley, T. 2000. *The millionaire mind.* Kansas City, MO: Andrews McMeel Publishing.

Stanley, T., and W. Danko. 1996. *The millionaire next door.* New York: Pocket Books.

Bibliography: Resources for prospect development. 1997–1998. Minneapolis, MN: Bentz Whaley Flessner.

WEB SITES FOR PROSPECT RESEARCH

www.stockmaster.com

www.etrade.com

www.suretrade.com

www.finance.yahoo.com

www.tenkwizard.com

www.investorhome.com

www.realestate.yahoo.com

www.lexis-nexis.com

www.dnb.com

www.dataquick.com

www.hoovers.com

www.knowx.com

www.martindale.com

www.ama-assn.org

www.salesleadsusa.com

www.wealthengine.com

www.wealthknowledge.com

PROSPECT RESEARCH INFORMATION PROVIDERS

Amergent, 9 Centennial Drive, Peabody, MA 01960, (978) 531–1800.

Bentz Whaley Flessner, 2150 Norwest Financial Center, 7900 Xerxes Avenue South, Minneapolis, MN 55431, (612) 921–0111.

Claritas, 1525 Wilson Blvd., Suite 1000, Arlington, VA 22209, (800) 234–5973.

Database America, 100 Paragon Drive, Montvale, NJ 07645, (201) 476–2300.

Equifax, P.O. Box 740241, Atlanta, GA 30374–0241, (888) 997–2493.

Marts and Lundy Inc., 1200 Wall Street West, Lyndhurst, NJ 07071, (800) 526–9005.

Prospect Information Network, 295 Madison Avenue, 43d Floor, New York, NY 10017, (888) 557–1326.

Prospect Research Online, 53 Grafton St., Charlottetown, Prince Edward Island C1A1K8, (800) 655–7729.

REDI Real Estate Information Service—Experian, Inc., 5601 East Lapalma Ave., Anaheim, CA 92807, (800) 345–7334.

Thomas Financial Wealth Identification, 1455 Research Boulevard, Rockville, MD 20850, (800) 933–4446.

Appendix 2–B

U.S. Department of the Treasury Internal Revenue Service

Form 990 Return of Organization Exempt from Income Tax

Form **990**

Return of Organization Exempt From Income Tax

Under section 501(c) of the Internal Revenue Code (except black lung benefit trust or private foundation) or section 4947(a)(1) nonexempt charitable trust

Department of the Treasury
Internal Revenue Service

Note: *The organization may have to use a copy of this return to satisfy state reporting requirements.*

OMB No. 1545-0047

19 99

This Form is
Open to Public
Inspection

A For the 1999 calendar year, OR tax year period beginning _____ , 1999, and ending _____ ,

B Check if:
- ☐ Change of address
- ☐ Initial return
- ☐ Final return
- ☐ Amended return (required also for state reporting)

Please use IRS label or print or type. See Specific Instructions.

C Name of organization

Number and street (or P.O. box if mail is not delivered to street address) | Room/suite

City or town, state or country, and ZIP+4

D Employer identification number

E Telephone number

F Check ▶ ☐ if exemption application is pending

G Type of organization—▶ ☐ Exempt under section 501(c)( ) ◀ (insert number) OR ▶ ☐ section 4947(a)(1) nonexempt charitable trust

Note: *Section 501(c)(3) exempt organizations and 4947(a)(1) nonexempt charitable trusts MUST attach a completed Schedule A (Form 990).*

H(a) Is this a group return filed for affiliates? . . . . ☐ Yes ☐ No

(b) If "Yes," enter the number of affiliates for which this return is filed: . ▶ _____

(c) Is this a separate return filed by an organization covered by a group ruling? ☐ Yes ☐ No

I If either box in H is checked "Yes," enter four-digit group exemption number (GEN) ▶ _____

J Accounting method: ☐ Cash ☐ Accrual
☐ Other (specify) ▶

K Check here ▶ ☐ if the organization's gross receipts are normally not more than $25,000. The organization need not file a return with the IRS; but if it received a Form 990 Package in the mail, it should file a return without financial data. **Some states require a complete return.**

Note: *Form 990-EZ may be used by organizations with gross receipts less than $100,000 and total assets less than $250,000 at end of year.*

Part I — Revenue, Expenses, and Changes in Net Assets or Fund Balances (See Specific Instructions on page 15.)

Revenue

1	Contributions, gifts, grants, and similar amounts received:		
a	Direct public support	1a	
b	Indirect public support	1b	
c	Government contributions (grants)	1c	
d	**Total** (add lines 1a through 1c) (attach schedule of contributors) (cash $ _____ noncash $ _____)	1d	
2	Program service revenue including government fees and contracts (from Part VII, line 93)	2	
3	Membership dues and assessments	3	
4	Interest on savings and temporary cash investments	4	
5	Dividends and interest from securities	5	
6a	Gross rents	6a	
b	Less: rental expenses	6b	
c	Net rental income or (loss) (subtract line 6b from line 6a)	6c	
7	Other investment income (describe ▶)	7	

8a	Gross amount from sales of assets other than inventory	(A) Securities	(B) Other	
		8a		
b	Less: cost or other basis and sales expenses	8b		
c	Gain or (loss) (attach schedule)	8c		
d	Net gain or (loss) (combine line 8c, columns (A) and (B))			8d

9	Special events and activities (attach schedule)		
a	Gross revenue (not including $ _____ of contributions reported on line 1a)	9a	
b	Less: direct expenses other than fundraising expenses .	9b	
c	Net income or (loss) from special events (subtract line 9b from line 9a)	9c	
10a	Gross sales of inventory, less returns and allowances . .	10a	
b	Less: cost of goods sold	10b	
c	Gross profit or (loss) from sales of inventory (attach schedule) (subtract line 10b from line 10a) .	10c	
11	Other revenue (from Part VII, line 103)	11	
12	**Total revenue** (add lines 1d, 2, 3, 4, 5, 6c, 7, 8d, 9c, 10c, and 11)	12	

Expenses

13	Program services (from line 44, column (B))	13	
14	Management and general (from line 44, column (C))	14	
15	Fundraising (from line 44, column (D))	15	
16	Payments to affiliates (attach schedule)	16	
17	**Total expenses** (add lines 16 and 44, column (A))	17	

Net Assets

18	Excess or (deficit) for the year (subtract line 17 from line 12)	18	
19	Net assets or fund balances at beginning of year (from line 73, column (A))	19	
20	Other changes in net assets or fund balances (attach explanation)	20	
21	Net assets or fund balances at end of year (combine lines 18, 19, and 20)	21	

For Paperwork Reduction Act Notice, see page 1 of the separate instructions.   Cat. No. 11282Y   Form **990** (1999)

Part II　Statement of Functional Expenses　All organizations must complete column (A). Columns (B), (C), and (D) are required for section 501(c)(3) and (4) organizations and section 4947(a)(1) nonexempt charitable trusts but optional for others. (See Specific Instructions on page 19.)

Do not include amounts reported on line 6b, 8b, 9b, 10b, or 16 of Part I.		(A) Total	(B) Program services	(C) Management and general	(D) Fundraising
22	Grants and allocations (attach schedule) . . (cash $ _____ noncash $ _____) **22**				
23	Specific assistance to individuals (attach schedule) **23**				
24	Benefits paid to or for members (attach schedule). **24**				
25	Compensation of officers, directors, etc. . . **25**				
26	Other salaries and wages **26**				
27	Pension plan contributions **27**				
28	Other employee benefits **28**				
29	Payroll taxes **29**				
30	Professional fundraising fees **30**				
31	Accounting fees **31**				
32	Legal fees **32**				
33	Supplies **33**				
34	Telephone **34**				
35	Postage and shipping **35**				
36	Occupancy **36**				
37	Equipment rental and maintenance **37**				
38	Printing and publications **38**				
39	Travel **39**				
40	Conferences, conventions, and meetings . . **40**				
41	Interest **41**				
42	Depreciation, depletion, etc. (attach schedule) **42**				
43	Other expenses (itemize): **a** **43a**				
b	.... **43b**				
c	.... **43c**				
d	.... **43d**				
e	.... **43e**				
44	**Total functional expenses** (add lines 22 through 43). *Organizations completing columns (B)-(D), carry these totals to lines 13—15* . **44**				

Reporting of Joint Costs. Did you report in column (B) (Program services) any joint costs from a combined educational campaign and fundraising solicitation? . . . . ▶ ☐ Yes ☐ No

If "Yes," enter **(i)** the aggregate amount of these joint costs $_____; **(ii)** the amount allocated to Program services $_____; **(iii)** the amount allocated to Management and general $_____; and **(iv)** the amount allocated to Fundraising $_____

Part III　Statement of Program Service Accomplishments (See Specific Instructions on page 22.)

What is the organization's primary exempt purpose? ▶--

All organizations must describe their exempt purpose achievements in a clear and concise manner. State the number of clients served, publications issued, etc. Discuss achievements that are not measurable. (Section 501(c)(3) and (4) organizations and 4947(a)(1) nonexempt charitable trusts must also enter the amount of grants and allocations to others.)

Program Service Expenses
(Required for 501(c)(3) and (4) orgs., and 4947(a)(1) trusts; but optional for others.)

a --

(Grants and allocations　$　　　　　　　　　)

b --

(Grants and allocations　$　　　　　　　　　)

c --

(Grants and allocations　$　　　　　　　　　)

d --

(Grants and allocations　$　　　　　　　　　)

e Other program services (attach schedule)　(Grants and allocations　$　　　　　　　)

f **Total of Program Service Expenses** (should equal line 44, column (B), Program services) . . . . . ▶

Form **990** (1999)

Part IV Balance Sheets (See Specific Instructions on page 22.)

	Note: *Where required, attached schedules and amounts within the description column should be for end-of-year amounts only.*		**(A)** Beginning of year		**(B)** End of year
Assets	**45** Cash—non-interest-bearing			**45**	
	46 Savings and temporary cash investments			**46**	
	47a Accounts receivable	**47a**		**47c**	
	b Less: allowance for doubtful accounts . .	**47b**			
	48a Pledges receivable	**48a**		**48c**	
	b Less: allowance for doubtful accounts . .	**48b**			
	49 Grants receivable			**49**	
	50 Receivables from officers, directors, trustees, and key employees (attach schedule)			**50**	
	51a Other notes and loans receivable (attach schedule).	**51a**		**51c**	
	b Less: allowance for doubtful accounts . .	**51b**			
	52 Inventories for sale or use			**52**	
	53 Prepaid expenses and deferred charges .			**53**	
	54 Investments—securities (attach schedule)			**54**	
	55a Investments—land, buildings, and equipment: basis	**55a**		**55c**	
	b Less: accumulated depreciation (attach schedule).	**55b**			
	56 Investments—other (attach schedule) . .			**56**	
	57a Land, buildings, and equipment: basis . .	**57a**		**57c**	
	b Less: accumulated depreciation (attach schedule).	**57b**			
	58 Other assets (describe ▶ _____)			**58**	
	59 **Total assets** (add lines 45 through 58) (must equal line 74)			**59**	
Liabilities	**60** Accounts payable and accrued expenses			**60**	
	61 Grants payable			**61**	
	62 Deferred revenue			**62**	
	63 Loans from officers, directors, trustees, and key employees (attach schedule).			**63**	
	64a Tax-exempt bond liabilities (attach schedule)			**64a**	
	b Mortgages and other notes payable (attach schedule)			**64b**	
	65 Other liabilities (describe ▶ _____)			**65**	
	66 **Total liabilities** (add lines 60 through 65)			**66**	
Net Assets or Fund Balances	**Organizations that follow SFAS 117, check here ▶** ☐ **and complete lines 67 through 69 and lines 73 and 74.**				
	67 Unrestricted			**67**	
	68 Temporarily restricted			**68**	
	69 Permanently restricted			**69**	
	Organizations that do not follow SFAS 117, check here ▶ ☐ **and complete lines 70 through 74.**				
	70 Capital stock, trust principal, or current funds			**70**	
	71 Paid-in or capital surplus, or land, building, and equipment fund . .			**71**	
	72 Retained earnings, endowment, accumulated income, or other funds			**72**	
	73 **Total net assets or fund balances** (add lines 67 through 69 OR lines 70 through 72; column (A) must equal line 19 and column (B) must equal line 21)			**73**	
	74 **Total liabilities and net assets / fund balances** (add lines 66 and 73)			**74**	

Form 990 is available for public inspection and, for some people, serves as the primary or sole source of information about a particular organization. How the public perceives an organization in such cases may be determined by the information presented on its return. Therefore, please make sure the return is complete and accurate and fully describes, in Part III, the organization's programs and accomplishments.

| **Part IV-A** | **Reconciliation of Revenue per Audited Financial Statements with Revenue per Return** (See Specific Instructions, page 24.) | **Part IV-B** | **Reconciliation of Expenses per Audited Financial Statements with Expenses per Return** |

a Total revenue, gains, and other support per audited financial statements . . ▶ **a**

b Amounts included on line **a** but not on line 12, Form 990:

(1) Net unrealized gains on investments . . $

(2) Donated services and use of facilities $

(3) Recoveries of prior year grants . . . $

(4) Other (specify):

------------------ $

Add amounts on lines (1) through (4) ▶ **b**

c Line **a** minus line **b**. . . . . ▶ **c**

d Amounts included on line 12, Form 990 but not on line **a**:

(1) Investment expenses not included on line 6b, Form 990 . . . $

(2) Other (specify):

------------------ $

Add amounts on lines (1) and (2) ▶ **d**

e Total revenue per line 12, Form 990 (line **c** plus line **d**) . . . . . ▶ **e**

a Total expenses and losses per audited financial statements . . ▶ **a**

b Amounts included on line **a** but not on line 17, Form 990:

(1) Donated services and use of facilities $

(2) Prior year adjustments reported on line 20, Form 990 . . . . $

(3) Losses reported on line 20, Form 990 . $

(4) Other (specify):

------------------ $

Add amounts on lines (1) through (4)▶ **b**

c Line **a** minus line **b** . . . . . ▶ **c**

d Amounts included on line 17, Form 990 but not on line **a**:

(1) Investment expenses not included on line 6b, Form 990. . . $

(2) Other (specify):

------------------ $

Add amounts on lines (1) and (2) ▶ **d**

e Total expenses per line 17, Form 990 (line **c** plus line **d**) . . . . . ▶ **e**

Part V **List of Officers, Directors, Trustees, and Key Employees** (List each one even if not compensated; see Specific Instructions on page 24.)

(A) Name and address	**(B)** Title and average hours per week devoted to position	**(C)** Compensation (**If not paid, enter -0-.**)	**(D)** Contributions to employee benefit plans & deferred compensation	**(E)** Expense account and other allowances

75 Did any officer, director, trustee, or key employee receive aggregate compensation of more than $100,000 from your organization and all related organizations, of which more than $10,000 was provided by the related organizations? ▶ ☐ **Yes** ☐ **No**
If "Yes," attach schedule—see Specific Instructions on page 25.

Form **990** (1999)

Part VI	**Other Information** (See Specific Instructions on page 25.)		Yes	No
76	Did the organization engage in any activity not previously reported to the IRS? If "Yes," attach a detailed description of each activity .	**76**		
77	Were any changes made in the organizing or governing documents but not reported to the IRS? . . . If "Yes," attach a conformed copy of the changes.	**77**		
78a	Did the organization have unrelated business gross income of $1,000 or more during the year covered by this return?.	**78a**		
b	If "Yes," has it filed a tax return on **Form 990-T** for this year?	**78b**		
79	Was there a liquidation, dissolution, termination, or substantial contraction during the year? If "Yes," attach a statement	**79**		
80a	Is the organization related (other than by association with a statewide or nationwide organization) through common membership, governing bodies, trustees, officers, etc., to any other exempt or nonexempt organization? . . .	**80a**		
b	If "Yes," enter the name of the organization ▶ --- -- and check whether it is ☐ exempt **OR** ☐ nonexempt.			
81a	Enter the amount of political expenditures, direct or indirect, as described in the instructions for line 81.	**81a**			
b	Did the organization file **Form 1120-POL** for this year?.	**81b**		
82a	Did the organization receive donated services or the use of materials, equipment, or facilities at no charge or at substantially less than fair rental value?	**82a**		
b	If "Yes," you may indicate the value of these items here. Do not include this amount as revenue in Part I or as an expense in Part II. (See instructions for reporting in Part III.).	**82b**			
83a	Did the organization comply with the public inspection requirements for returns and exemption applications?	**83a**		
b	Did the organization comply with the disclosure requirements relating to quid pro quo contributions? . .	**83b**		
84a	Did the organization solicit any contributions or gifts that were not tax deductible?	**84a**		
b	If "Yes," did the organization include with every solicitation an express statement that such contributions or gifts were not tax deductible?	**84b**		
85	*501(c)(4), (5), or (6) organizations.* **a** Were substantially all dues nondeductible by members?	**85a**		
b	Did the organization make only in-house lobbying expenditures of $2,000 or less?	**85b**		
	If "Yes" was answered to either 85a or 85b, **do not** complete 85c through 85h below unless the organization received a waiver for proxy tax owed for the prior year.			
c	Dues, assessments, and similar amounts from members	**85c**		
d	Section 162(e) lobbying and political expenditures	**85d**		
e	Aggregate nondeductible amount of section 6033(e)(1)(A) dues notices . . .	**85e**		
f	Taxable amount of lobbying and political expenditures (line 85d less 85e) . .	**85f**		
g	Does the organization elect to pay the section 6033(e) tax on the amount in 85f?.	**85g**		
h	If section 6033(e)(1)(A) dues notices were sent, does the organization agree to add the amount in 85f to its reasonable estimate of dues allocable to nondeductible lobbying and political expenditures for the following tax year?. . .	**85h**		
86	*501(c)(7) orgs.* Enter: **a** Initiation fees and capital contributions included on line 12 .	**86a**		
b	Gross receipts, included on line 12, for public use of club facilities.	**86b**		
87	*501(c)(12) orgs.* Enter: **a** Gross income from members or shareholders.	**87a**		
b	Gross income from other sources. (Do not net amounts due or paid to other sources against amounts due or received from them.)	**87b**		
88	At any time during the year, did the organization own a 50% or greater interest in a taxable corporation or partnership, or an entity disregarded as separate from the organization under Regulations sections 301.7701-2 and 301.7701-3? If "Yes," complete Part IX	**88**		
89a	*501(c)(3) organizations.* Enter: Amount of tax imposed on the organization during the year under: section 4911 ▶_____ ; section 4912 ▶_____ ; section 4955 ▶_____			
b	*501(c)(3) and 501(c)(4) orgs.* Did the organization engage in any section 4958 excess benefit transaction during the year or did it become aware of an excess benefit transaction from a prior year? If "Yes," attach a statement explaining each transaction.	**89b**		
c	Enter: Amount of tax imposed on the organization managers or disqualified persons during the year under sections 4912, 4955, and 4958. . . . . ▶ _____			
d	Enter: Amount of tax on line 89c, above, reimbursed by the organization. . . . . ▶ _____			
90a	List the states with which a copy of this return is filed ▶ ---------------------------------------			
b	Number of employees employed in the pay period that includes March 12, 1999 (See inst.) .	**90b**		
91	The books are in care of ▶ ------------------------------ Telephone no. ▶ (_____) ---------------- Located at ▶ --- ZIP + 4 ▶ --------------------------			
92	*Section 4947(a)(1) nonexempt charitable trusts filing Form 990 in lieu of **Form 1041**—*Check here . . . . ▶ ☐ and enter the amount of tax-exempt interest received or accrued during the tax year . . ▶	**92**		

Form **990** (1999)

| Part VII | Analysis of Income-Producing Activities (See Specific Instructions on page 29.) |

Enter gross amounts unless otherwise indicated.	Unrelated business income		Excluded by section 512, 513, or 514		(E) Related or exempt function income
	(A) Business code	**(B)** Amount	**(C)** Exclusion code	**(D)** Amount	
93 Program service revenue:					
a _____					
b _____					
c _____					
d _____					
e _____					
f Medicare/Medicaid payments					
g Fees and contracts from government agencies					
94 Membership dues and assessments . . .					
95 Interest on savings and temporary cash investments					
96 Dividends and interest from securities . . .					
97 Net rental income or (loss) from real estate:					
a debt-financed property					
b not debt-financed property					
98 Net rental income or (loss) from personal property					
99 Other investment income					
100 Gain or (loss) from sales of assets other than inventory					
101 Net income or (loss) from special events . .					
102 Gross profit or (loss) from sales of inventory .					
103 Other revenue: **a** _____					
b _____					
c _____					
d _____					
e _____					
104 Subtotal (add columns (B), (D), and (E)) . . .					

105 Total (add line 104, columns (B), (D), and (E)) . . . . ▶ _____

Note: _Line 105 plus line 1d, Part I, should equal the amount on line 12, Part I._

| Part VIII | Relationship of Activities to the Accomplishment of Exempt Purposes (See Specific Instructions on page 30.) |

Line No. ▼	Explain how each activity for which income is reported in column (E) of Part VII contributed importantly to the accomplishment of the organization's exempt purposes (other than by providing funds for such purposes).

| Part IX | Information Regarding Taxable Subsidiaries and Disregarded Entities (See Specific Instructions on page 30.) |

(A) Name, address, and EIN of corporation, partnership, or disregarded entity	(B) Percentage of ownership interest	(C) Nature of activities	(D) Total income	(E) End-of-year assets
	%			
	%			
	%			
	%			

Please Sign Here

Under penalties of perjury, I declare that I have examined this return, including accompanying schedules and statements, and to the best of my knowledge and belief, it is true, correct, and complete. Declaration of preparer (other than officer) is based on all information of which preparer has any knowledge. (**Important:** See General Instruction U, on page 14.)

▶ _____   _____   ▶ _____
  Signature of officer   Date   Type or print name and title.

Paid Preparer's Use Only

Preparer's signature ▶		Date	Check if self-employed ▶ ☐	Preparer's SSN or PTIN
Firm's name (or yours if self-employed) and address ▶			EIN ▶	
			ZIP + 4 ▶	

✿   Form **990** (1999)

Appendix 2–C

U.S. Department of the Treasury Internal Revenue Service

Form 990-PF Return of Private Foundation

Form **990-PF**

Department of the Treasury
Internal Revenue Service

Return of Private Foundation
or Section 4947(a)(1) Nonexempt Charitable Trust
Treated as a Private Foundation

Note: *The organization may be able to use a copy of this return to satisfy state reporting requirements.*

OMB No. 1545-0052

1999

For calendar year 1999, or tax year beginning _____ **, 1999, and ending** _____

Use the IRS label. Otherwise, please print or type. See Specific Instructions.	Name of organization	**A Employer identification number**
	Number and street (or P.O. box number if mail is not delivered to street address)　　Room/suite	**B Telephone number** (see page 9 of the instructions) ( )
	City or town, state, and ZIP + 4	**C** If exemption application is pending, check here ▶ ☐

H Check type of organization: ☐ Section 501(c)(3) exempt private foundation
☐ Section 4947(a)(1) nonexempt charitable trust ☐ Other taxable private foundation

I Fair market value of all assets at end of year *(from Part II, col. (c),* line 16) ▶ $ _____

J Accounting method: ☐ Cash ☐ Accrual
☐ Other (specify) _____
(Part I, column (d) must be on cash basis.)

D 1. Foreign organizations, check here . ▶ ☐
2. Organizations meeting the 85% test, check here and attach computation . ▶ ☐
E If private foundation status was terminated under section 507(b)(1)(A), check here . ▶ ☐
F If the foundation is in a 60-month termination under section 507(b)(1)(B), check here . ▶ ☐
G If address changed, check here . . ▶ ☐

Part I Analysis of Revenue and Expenses *(The total of amounts in columns (b), (c), and (d) may not necessarily equal the amounts in column (a) (see page 9 of the instructions).)*

		(a) Revenue and expenses per books	(b) Net investment income	(c) Adjusted net income	(d) Disbursements for charitable purposes (cash basis only)
Revenue	**1** Contributions, gifts, grants, etc., received (attach schedule)				
	2 Contributions from split-interest trusts				
	3 Interest on savings and temporary cash investments				
	4 Dividends and interest from securities				
	5a Gross rents				
	b (Net rental income or (loss) _____)				
	6 Net gain or (loss) from sale of assets not on line 10				
	7 Capital gain net income (from Part IV, line 2) . .				
	8 Net short-term capital gain				
	9 Income modifications				
	10a Gross sales less returns and allowances				
	b Less: Cost of goods sold . .				
	c Gross profit or (loss) (attach schedule)				
	11 Other income (attach schedule)				
	12 **Total.** Add lines 1 through 11				
Operating and Administrative Expenses	**13** Compensation of officers, directors, trustees, etc.				
	14 Other employee salaries and wages				
	15 Pension plans, employee benefits				
	16a Legal fees (attach schedule)				
	b Accounting fees (attach schedule)				
	c Other professional fees (attach schedule) . . .				
	17 Interest				
	18 Taxes (attach schedule) (see page 12 of the instructions)				
	19 Depreciation (attach schedule) and depletion .				
	20 Occupancy				
	21 Travel, conferences, and meetings				
	22 Printing and publications				
	23 Other expenses (attach schedule)				
	24 **Total operating and administrative expenses.** Add lines 13 through 23				
	25 Contributions, gifts, grants paid				
	26 **Total expenses and disbursements.** Add lines 24 and 25				
	27 Subtract line 26 from line 12:				
	a Excess of revenue over expenses and disbursements				
	b Net investment income (if negative, enter -0-) .				
	c Adjusted net income (if negative, enter -0-) . .				

For Paperwork Reduction Act Notice, see the instructions.　　　Cat. No. 11289X　　　Form **990-PF** (1999)

Part II	**Balance Sheets** Attached schedules and amounts in the description column should be for end-of-year amounts only. (See instructions.)	Beginning of year	End of year	
		(a) Book Value	**(b)** Book Value	**(c)** Fair Market Value

Assets

1	Cash—non-interest-bearing			
2	Savings and temporary cash investments			
3	Accounts receivable ▶................................			
	Less: allowance for doubtful accounts ▶................			
4	Pledges receivable ▶................................			
	Less: allowance for doubtful accounts ▶................			
5	Grants receivable			
6	Receivables due from officers, directors, trustees, and other disqualified persons (attach schedule) (see page 14 of the instructions)			
7	Other notes and loans receivable (attach schedule) ▶..............			
	Less: allowance for doubtful accounts ▶..............			
8	Inventories for sale or use.			
9	Prepaid expenses and deferred charges			
10a	Investments—U.S. and state government obligations (attach schedule)			
b	Investments—corporate stock (attach schedule)			
c	Investments—corporate bonds (attach schedule)			
11	Investments—land, buildings, and equipment: basis ▶..............			
	Less: accumulated depreciation (attach schedule) ▶..............			
12	Investments—mortgage loans			
13	Investments—other (attach schedule)			
14	Land, buildings, and equipment: basis ▶..............			
	Less: accumulated depreciation (attach schedule) ▶..............			
15	Other assets (describe ▶..................................)			
16	**Total assets** (to be completed by all filers—see page 15 of the instructions. Also, see page 1, item I)			

Liabilities

17	Accounts payable and accrued expenses			
18	Grants payable			
19	Deferred revenue.			
20	Loans from officers, directors, trustees, and other disqualified persons			
21	Mortgages and other notes payable (attach schedule) . .			
22	Other liabilities (describe ▶..............................)			
23	**Total liabilities** (add lines 17 through 22).			

Net Assets or Fund Balances

	Organizations that follow SFAS 117, check here ▶ ☐ and complete lines 24 through 26 and lines 30 and 31.			
24	Unrestricted			
25	Temporarily restricted			
26	Permanently restricted			
	Organizations that do not follow SFAS 117, check here ▶ ☐ and complete lines 27 through 31.			
27	Capital stock, trust principal, or current funds			
28	Paid-in or capital surplus, or land, bldg., and equipment fund			
29	Retained earnings, accumulated income, endowment, or other funds			
30	**Total net assets or fund balances** (see page 16 of the instructions)			
31	**Total liabilities and net assets/fund balances** (see page 16 of the instructions)			

Part III	Analysis of Changes in Net Assets or Fund Balances

1	Total net assets or fund balances at beginning of year—Part II, column (a), line 30 (must agree with end-of-year figure reported on prior year's return).	**1**	
2	Enter amount from Part I, line 27a	**2**	
3	Other increases not included in line 2 (itemize) ▶.................................	**3**	
4	Add lines 1, 2, and 3	**4**	
5	Decreases not included in line 2 (itemize) ▶....................................	**5**	
6	Total net assets or fund balances at end of year (line 4 minus line 5)—Part II, column (b), line 30 . .	**6**	

Form **990-PF** (1999)

| Part IV | Capital Gains and Losses for Tax on Investment Income |

(a) List and describe the kind(s) of property sold (e.g., real estate, 2-story brick warehouse; or common stock, 200 shs. MLC Co.)	**(b)** How acquired P—Purchase D—Donation	**(c)** Date acquired (mo., day, yr.)	**(d)** Date sold (mo., day, yr.)
1a			
b			
c			
d			
e			

(e) Gross sales price	**(f)** Depreciation allowed (or allowable)	**(g)** Cost or other basis plus expense of sale	**(h)** Gain or (loss) (e) plus (f) minus (g)
a			
b			
c			
d			
e			

Complete only for assets showing gain in column (h) and owned by the foundation on 12/31/69

(i) F.M.V. as of 12/31/69	**(j)** Adjusted basis as of 12/31/69	**(k)** Excess of col. (i) over col. (j), if any	**(l)** Gains (Col. (h) gain minus col. (k), but not less than -0-) **or** Losses (from col.(h))
a			
b			
c			
d			
e			

2 Capital gain net income or (net capital loss). { If gain, also enter in Part I, line 7   If (loss), enter -0- in Part I, line 7 }   **2**

3 Net short-term capital gain or (loss) as defined in sections 1222(5) and (6):
If gain, also enter in Part I, line 8, column (c) (see pages 11 and 16 of the instructions). }
If (loss), enter -0- in Part I, line 8 . . . . }   **3**

| Part V | Qualification Under Section 4940(e) for Reduced Tax on Net Investment Income |

(For optional use by domestic private foundations subject to the section 4940(a) tax on net investment income.)

If section 4940(d)(2) applies, leave this part blank.

Was the organization liable for the section 4942 tax on the distributable amount of any year in the base period? ☐ Yes ☐ No
If "Yes," the organization does not qualify under section 4940(e). Do not complete this part.

1 Enter the appropriate amount in each column for each year; see page 16 of the instructions before making any entries.

(a) Base period years Calendar year (or tax year beginning in)	**(b)** Adjusted qualifying distributions	**(c)** Net value of noncharitable-use assets	**(d)** Distribution ratio (col. (b) divided by col. (c))
1998			
1997			
1996			
1995			
1994			

2 Total of line 1, column (d) **2**

3 Average distribution ratio for the 5-year base period—divide the total on line 2 by 5, or by the number of years the foundation has been in existence if less than 5 years **3**

4 Enter the net value of noncharitable-use assets for 1999 from Part X, line 5 . . . .   **4**

5 Multiply line 4 by line 3 . . . .   **5**

6 Enter 1% of net investment income (1% of Part I, line 27b) **6**

7 Add lines 5 and 6 . . . .   **7**

8 Enter qualifying distributions from Part XII, line 4 . . . .   **8**

If line 8 is equal to or greater than line 7, check the box in Part VI, line 1b, and complete that part using a 1% tax rate. See the Part VI instructions on page 16.

Form **990-PF** (1999)

Part VI	Excise Tax Based on Investment Income (Section 4940(a), 4940(b), 4940(e), or 4948—see page 16 of the instructions)		

1a Exempt operating foundations described in section 4940(d)(2), check here ▶ ☐ and enter "N/A" on line 1.
Date of ruling letter: .... **(attach copy of ruling letter if necessary–see instructions)**

b Domestic organizations that meet the section 4940(e) requirements in Part V, check here ▶ ☐ and enter 1% of Part I, line 27b . . . .

c All other domestic organizations enter 2% of line 27b. Exempt foreign organizations enter 4% of Part I, line 12, col. (b)

1	

2 Tax under section 511 (domestic section 4947(a)(1) trusts and taxable foundations only. Others enter -0-) **2**

3 Add lines 1 and 2 **3**

4 Subtitle A (income) tax (domestic section 4947(a)(1) trusts and taxable foundations only. Others enter -0-) **4**

5 **Tax based on investment income.** Subtract line 4 from line 3. If zero or less, enter -0- . . . **5**

6 Credits/Payments:

a 1999 estimated tax payments and 1998 overpayment credited to 1999 **6a**

b Exempt foreign organizations—tax withheld at source **6b**

c Tax paid with application for extension of time to file (Form 2758) . **6c**

d Backup withholding erroneously withheld **6d**

7 Total credits and payments. Add lines 6a through 6d **7**

8 Enter any **PENALTY** for underpayment of estimated tax. Check here ☐ if Form 2220 is attached **8**

9 **TAX DUE.** If the total of lines 5 and 8 is more than line 7, enter **AMOUNT OWED** . . . . ▶ **9**

10 **OVERPAYMENT.** If line 7 is more than the total of lines 5 and 8, enter the **AMOUNT OVERPAID** . ▶ **10**

11 Enter the amount of line 10 to be: **Credited to 2000 estimated tax** ▶ | **Refunded** ▶ **11**

Part VII-A	Statements Regarding Activities		

		Yes	No
1a During the tax year, did the organization attempt to influence any national, state, or local legislation or did it participate or intervene in any political campaign?.	**1a**		
b Did it spend more than $100 during the year (either directly or indirectly) for political purposes (see page 17 of the instructions for definition)?	**1b**		

*If the answer is "Yes" to **1a** or **1b,** attach a detailed description of the activities and copies of any materials published or distributed by the organization in connection with the activities.*

c Did the organization file **Form 1120-POL** for this year?. **1c**

d Enter the amount (if any) of tax on political expenditures (section 4955) imposed during the year:
(1) On the organization. ▶ $ _____ **(2)** On organization managers. ▶ $ _____

e Enter the reimbursement (if any) paid by the organization during the year for political expenditure tax imposed on organization managers. ▶ $ _____

2 Has the organization engaged in any activities that have not previously been reported to the IRS? . . . **2**
If "Yes," attach a detailed description of the activities.

3 Has the organization made any changes, not previously reported to the IRS, in its governing instrument, articles of incorporation, or bylaws, or other similar instruments? *If "Yes," attach a conformed copy of the changes* . **3**

4a Did the organization have unrelated business gross income of $1,000 or more during the year? **4a**

b If "Yes," has it filed a tax return on **Form 990-T** for this year? **4b**

5 Was there a liquidation, termination, dissolution, or substantial contraction during the year? **5**
If "Yes," attach the statement required by General Instruction T.

6 Are the requirements of section 508(e) (relating to sections 4941 through 4945) satisfied either:
● By language in the governing instrument; or
● By state legislation that effectively amends the governing instrument so that no mandatory directions that conflict with the state law remain in the governing instrument?. **6**

7 Did the organization have at least $5,000 in assets at any time during the year? *If "Yes," complete Part II, col. (c), and Part XV.* **7**

8a Enter the states to which the foundation reports or with which it is registered (see page 18 of the instructions) ▶ ....

b If the answer is "Yes" to line 7, has the organization furnished a copy of Form 990-PF to the Attorney General (or designate) of each state as required by General Instruction G? *If "No," attach explanation* . **8b**

9 Is the organization claiming status as a private operating foundation within the meaning of section 4942(j)(3) or 4942(j)(5) for calendar year 1999 or the taxable year beginning in 1999 (see instructions for Part XIV on page 23)? *If "Yes," complete Part XIV* **9**

10 Did any persons become substantial contributors during the tax year? *If "Yes," attach a schedule listing their names and addresses.* **10**

11a Did anyone request to see either the organization's annual return or its exemption application (or both)? . **11a**

b If "Yes," did the organization comply pursuant to the instructions? (See General Instruction Q.) **11b**

12 The books are in care of ▶ .... Telephone no. ▶ ....
Located at ▶ .... ZIP+4 ▶ ....

13 Section 4947(a)(1) nonexempt charitable trusts filing Form 990-PF in lieu of **Form 1041**—Check here . . . . . ▶ ☐ and enter the amount of tax-exempt interest received or accrued during the year. . . . . . ▶ | **13**

Form **990-PF** (1999)

Part VII-B **Statements Regarding Activities for Which Form 4720 May Be Required**

		Yes	No

File Form 4720 if any item is checked in the "Yes" column, unless an exception applies.

1 Self-dealing (section 4941):

a During the year did the organization (either directly or indirectly):

    (1) Engage in the sale or exchange, or leasing of property with a disqualified person? . ☐ **Yes** ☐ **No**

    (2) Borrow money from, lend money to, or otherwise extend credit to (or accept it from) a disqualified person? . . . . ☐ **Yes** ☐ **No**

    (3) Furnish goods, services, or facilities to (or accept them from) a disqualified person? ☐ **Yes** ☐ **No**

    (4) Pay compensation to, or pay or reimburse the expenses of, a disqualified person? . ☐ **Yes** ☐ **No**

    (5) Transfer any income or assets to a disqualified person (or make any of either available for the benefit or use of a disqualified person)? . . . . ☐ **Yes** ☐ **No**

    (6) Agree to pay money or property to a government official? (**Exception.** Check "No" if the organization agreed to make a grant to or to employ the official for a period after termination of government service, if terminating within 90 days.) . . . . ☐ **Yes** ☐ **No**

b If any answer is "Yes" to 1a(1)–(6), did ANY of the acts fail to qualify under the exceptions described in Regulations section 53.4941(d)-3 or in a current notice regarding disaster assistance (see page 18 of the instructions)? **1b**

Organizations relying on a current notice regarding disaster assistance check here . . . . ▶ ☐

c Did the organization engage in a prior year in any of the acts described in 1a, other than excepted acts, that were not corrected before the first day of the tax year beginning in 1999? **1c**

2 Taxes on failure to distribute income (section 4942) (does not apply for years the organization was a private operating foundation defined in section 4942(j)(3) or 4942(j)(5)):

a At the end of tax year 1999, did the organization have any undistributed income (lines 6d and 6e, Part XIII) for tax year(s) beginning before 1999? . . . . ☐ **Yes** ☐ **No**

If "Yes," list the years ▶ 19 .... , 19 .... , 19 .... , 19 .....

b Are there any years listed in 2a for which the organization is **NOT** applying the provisions of section 4942(a)(2) (relating to incorrect valuation of assets) to the year's undistributed income? (If applying section 4942(a)(2) to ALL years listed, answer "No" and attach statement—see page 18 of the instructions.) **2b**

c If the provisions of section 4942(a)(2) are being applied to ANY of the years listed in 2a, list the years here. ▶ 19 .... , 19 .... , 19 .... , 19 .....

3 Taxes on excess business holdings (section 4943):

a Did the organization hold more than a 2% direct or indirect interest in any business enterprise at any time during the year? . . . . ☐ **Yes** ☐ **No**

b If "Yes," did it have excess business holdings in 1999 as a result of **(1)** any purchase by the organization or disqualified persons after May 26, 1969; **(2)** the lapse of the 5-year period (or longer period approved by the Commissioner under section 4943(c)(7)) to dispose of holdings acquired by gift or bequest; or **(3)** the lapse of the 10-, 15-, or 20-year first phase holding period? *(Use Schedule C, Form 4720, to determine if the organization had excess business holdings in 1999.)* **3b**

4 Taxes on investments that jeopardize charitable purposes (section 4944):

a Did the organization invest during the year any amount in a manner that would jeopardize its charitable purposes? **4a**

b Did the organization make any investment in a prior year (but after December 31, 1969) that could jeopardize its charitable purpose that had not been removed from jeopardy before the first day of the tax year beginning in 1999? **4b**

5 Taxes on taxable expenditures (section 4945) and political expenditures (section 4955):

a During the year did the organization pay or incur any amount to:

    (1) Carry on propaganda, or otherwise attempt to influence legislation (section 4945(e))? ☐ **Yes** ☐ **No**

    (2) Influence the outcome of any specific public election (see section 4955); or to carry on, directly or indirectly, any voter registration drive? . . . . ☐ **Yes** ☐ **No**

    (3) Provide a grant to an individual for travel, study, or other similar purposes? . . . ☐ **Yes** ☐ **No**

    (4) Provide a grant to an organization other than a charitable, etc., organization described in section 509(a)(1), (2), or (3), or section 4940(d)(2)? . . . . ☐ **Yes** ☐ **No**

    (5) Provide for any purpose other than religious, charitable, scientific, literary, or educational purposes, or for the prevention of cruelty to children or animals? . . . ☐ **Yes** ☐ **No**

b If any answer is "Yes" to 5a(1)–(5), did ANY of the transactions fail to qualify under the exceptions described in Regulations section 53.4945 or in a current notice regarding disaster assistance (see page 19 of the instructions)? **5b**

Organizations relying on a current notice regarding disaster assistance check here . . . . ▶ ☐

c If the answer is "Yes" to question 5a(4), does the organization claim exemption from the tax because it maintained expenditure responsibility for the grant? . . . . ☐ **Yes** ☐ **No**

If "Yes," attach the statement required by Regulations section 53.4945–5(d).

Form **990-PF** (1999)

Part VIII Information About Officers, Directors, Trustees, Foundation Managers, Highly Paid Employees, and Contractors

1 List all officers, directors, trustees, foundation managers and their compensation (see page 19 of the instructions):

(a) Name and address	(b) Title, and average hours per week devoted to position	(c) Compensation (If not paid, enter -0-)	(d) Contributions to employee benefit plans and deferred compensation	(e) Expense account, other allowances
----------------------------				

----------------------------				

2 Compensation of five highest-paid employees (other than those included on line 1—see page 19 of the instructions). If none, enter "NONE."

(a) Name and address of each employee paid more than $50,000	(b) Title and average hours per week devoted to position	(c) Compensation	(d) Contributions to employee benefit plans and deferred compensation	(e) Expense account, other allowances
----------------------------				

Total number of other employees paid over $50,000 . . . . ▶

3 Five highest-paid independent contractors for professional services—(see page 19 of the instructions). If none, enter "NONE."

(a) Name and address of each person paid more than $50,000	(b) Type of service	(c) Compensation
----------------------------		

Total number of others receiving over $50,000 for professional services . . . . ▶

Part IX-A Summary of Direct Charitable Activities

List the foundation's four largest direct charitable activities during the tax year. Include relevant statistical information such as the number of organizations and other beneficiaries served, conferences convened, research papers produced, etc.	Expenses
1 --	
--	
2 --	
--	
3 --	
--	
4 --	
--	

Form **990-PF** (1999)

Part IX-B **Summary of Program-Related Investments** (see page 20 of the instructions)

Describe any program-related investments made by the foundation during the tax year.	Amount
1	
2	
3	

Part X **Minimum Investment Return** (All domestic foundations must complete this part. Foreign foundations, see page 20 of the instructions.)

1	Fair market value of assets not used (or held for use) directly in carrying out charitable, etc., purposes:	
a	Average monthly fair market value of securities	**1a**
b	Average of monthly cash balances	**1b**
c	Fair market value of all other assets (see page 21 of the instructions)	**1c**
d	**Total** (add lines 1a, b, and c)	**1d**
e	Reduction claimed for blockage or other factors reported on lines 1a and 1c (attach detailed explanation) **1e**	
2	Acquisition indebtedness applicable to line 1 assets	**2**
3	Subtract line 2 from line 1d	**3**
4	Cash deemed held for charitable activities. Enter 1½% of line 3 (for greater amount, see page 21 of the instructions)	**4**
5	**Net value of noncharitable-use assets.** Subtract line 4 from line 3. Enter here and on Part V, line 4	**5**
6	**Minimum investment return.** Enter 5% of line 5	**6**

Part XI **Distributable Amount** (see page 21 of the instructions) (Section 4942(j)(3) and (j)(5) private operating foundations and certain foreign organizations check here ▶ ☐ and do not complete this part.)

1	Minimum investment return from Part X, line 6		**1**
2a	Tax on investment income for 1999 from Part VI, line 5	**2a**	
b	Income tax for 1999. (This does not include the tax from Part VI.)	**2b**	
c	Add lines 2a and 2b		**2c**
3	Distributable amount before adjustments. Subtract line 2c from line 1		**3**
4a	Recoveries of amounts treated as qualifying distributions	**4a**	
b	Income distributions from section 4947(a)(2) trusts	**4b**	
c	Add lines 4a and 4b		**4c**
5	Add lines 3 and 4c		**5**
6	Deduction from distributable amount (see page 22 of the instructions)		**6**
7	**Distributable amount** as adjusted. Subtract line 6 from line 5. Enter here and on Part XIII, line 1		**7**

Part XII **Qualifying Distributions** (see page 22 of the instructions)

1	Amounts paid (including administrative expenses) to accomplish charitable, etc., purposes:	
a	Expenses, contributions, gifts, etc.—total from Part I, column (d), line 26	**1a**
b	Program-related investments—total of lines 1-3 of Part IX-B	**1b**
2	Amounts paid to acquire assets used (or held for use) directly in carrying out charitable, etc., purposes	**2**
3	Amounts set aside for specific charitable projects that satisfy the:	
a	Suitability test (prior IRS approval required)	**3a**
b	Cash distribution test (attach the required schedule)	**3b**
4	**Qualifying distributions.** Add lines 1a through 3b. Enter here and on Part V, line 8, and Part XIII, line 4	**4**
5	Organizations that qualify under section 4940(e) for the reduced rate of tax on net investment income. Enter 1% of Part I, line 27b (see page 22 of the instructions)	**5**
6	**Adjusted qualifying distributions.** Subtract line 5 from line 4	**6**

Note: *The amount on line 6 will be used in Part V, column (b), in subsequent years when calculating whether the foundation qualifies for the section 4940(e) reduction of tax in those years.*

Form **990-PF** (1999)

Part XIII **Undistributed Income** (see page 22 of the instructions)

	(a) Corpus	(b) Years prior to 1998	(c) 1998	(d) 1999
1 Distributable amount for 1999 from Part XI, line 7				
2 Undistributed income, if any, as of the end of 1998:				
a Enter amount for 1998 only				
b Total for prior years: 19____ ,19____ ,19____				
3 Excess distributions carryover, if any, to 1999:				
a From 1994				
b From 1995				
c From 1996				
d From 1997				
e From 1998				
f **Total** of lines 3a through e				
4 Qualifying distributions for 1999 from Part XII, line 4: ▶ $ _____				
a Applied to 1998, but not more than line 2a.				
b Applied to undistributed income of prior years (Election required—see page 23 of the instructions)				
c Treated as distributions out of corpus (Election required—see page 23 of the instructions)				
d Applied to 1999 distributable amount . .				
e Remaining amount distributed out of corpus				
5 Excess distributions carryover applied to 1999 *(If an amount appears in column (d), the same amount must be shown in column (a).)*				
6 **Enter the net total of each column as indicated below:**				
a Corpus. Add lines 3f, 4c, and 4e. Subtract line 5				
b Prior years' undistributed income. Subtract line 4b from line 2b				
c Enter the amount of prior years' undistributed income for which a notice of deficiency has been issued, or on which the section 4942(a) tax has been previously assessed				
d Subtract line 6c from line 6b. Taxable amount—see page 23 of the instructions .				
e Undistributed income for 1998. Subtract line 4a from line 2a. Taxable amount—see page 23 of the instructions				
f Undistributed income for 1999. Subtract lines 4d and 5 from line 1. This amount must be distributed in 2000.				
7 Amounts treated as distributions out of corpus to satisfy requirements imposed by section 170(b)(1)(E) or 4942(g)(3) (see page 23 of the instructions).				
8 Excess distributions carryover from 1994 not applied on line 5 or line 7 (see page 23 of the instructions)				
9 **Excess distributions carryover to 2000.** Subtract lines 7 and 8 from line 6a . . .				
10 Analysis of line 9:				
a Excess from 1995 . . .				
b Excess from 1996 . . .				
c Excess from 1997 . . .				
d Excess from 1998 . . .				
e Excess from 1999 . . .				

Form **990-PF** (1999)

| Part XIV | **Private Operating Foundations** (see page 24 of the instructions and Part VII-A, question 9) |

1a If the foundation has received a ruling or determination letter that it is a private operating foundation, and the ruling is effective for 1999, enter the date of the ruling . . . . ▶

b Check box to indicate whether the organization is a private operating foundation described in section ☐ 4942(j)(3) or ☐ 4942(j)(5)

	Tax year		Prior 3 years		
	(a) 1999	**(b)** 1998	**(c)** 1997	**(d)** 1996	**(e)** Total
2a Enter the lesser of the adjusted net income from Part I or the minimum investment return from Part X for each year listed					
b 85% of line 2a					
c Qualifying distributions from Part XII, line 4 for each year listed					
d Amounts included in line 2c not used directly for active conduct of exempt activities .					
e Qualifying distributions made directly for active conduct of exempt activities. Subtract line 2d from line 2c . . .					
3 Complete 3a, b, or c for the alternative test relied upon:					
a "Assets" alternative test—enter:					
(1) Value of all assets					
(2) Value of assets qualifying under section 4942(j)(3)(B)(i) .					
b "Endowment" alternative test— Enter ⅔ of minimum investment return shown in Part X, line 6 for each year listed . .					
c "Support" alternative test—enter:					
(1) Total support other than gross investment income (interest, dividends, rents, payments on securities loans (section 512(a)(5)), or royalties) . .					
(2) Support from general public and 5 or more exempt organizations as provided in section 4942(j)(3)(B)(iii) . .					
(3) Largest amount of support from an exempt organization					
(4) Gross investment income .					

| Part XV | **Supplementary Information (Complete this part only if the organization had $5,000 or more in assets at any time during the year—see page 24 of the instructions.)** |

1 **Information Regarding Foundation Managers:**

a List any managers of the foundation who have contributed more than 2% of the total contributions received by the foundation before the close of any tax year (but only if they have contributed more than $5,000). (See section 507(d)(2).)

b List any managers of the foundation who own 10% or more of the stock of a corporation (or an equally large portion of the ownership of a partnership or other entity) of which the foundation has a 10% or greater interest.

2 **Information Regarding Contribution, Grant, Gift, Loan, Scholarship, etc., Programs:**

Check here ▶ ☐ if the organization only makes contributions to preselected charitable organizations and does not accept unsolicited requests for funds. If the organization makes gifts, grants, etc. (see page 24 of the instructions) to individuals or organizations under other conditions, complete items 2a, b, c, and d.

a The name, address, and telephone number of the person to whom applications should be addressed:

b The form in which applications should be submitted and information and materials they should include:

c Any submission deadlines:

d Any restrictions or limitations on awards, such as by geographical areas, charitable fields, kinds of institutions, or other factors:

Form **990-PF** (1999)

Part XV Supplementary Information (continued)

3   Grants and Contributions Paid During the Year or Approved for Future Payment

Recipient Name and address (home or business)	If recipient is an individual, show any relationship to any foundation manager or substantial contributor	Foundation status of recipient	Purpose of grant or contribution	Amount
a *Paid during the year*				
Total . . . . ▶ **3a**				
b *Approved for future payment*				
Total . . . . ▶ **3b**				

Form **990-PF** (1999)

Part XVI-A Analysis of Income-Producing Activities

Enter gross amounts unless otherwise indicated.

	Unrelated business income		Excluded by section 512, 513, or 514		(e)
	(a) Business code	**(b)** Amount	**(c)** Exclusion code	**(d)** Amount	Related or exempt function income (See page 24 of the instructions.)
1 Program service revenue:					
a _____					
b _____					
c _____					
d _____					
e _____					
f _____					
g Fees and contracts from government agencies					
2 Membership dues and assessments					
3 Interest on savings and temporary cash investments					
4 Dividends and interest from securities . . .					
5 Net rental income or (loss) from real estate:					
a Debt-financed property					
b Not debt-financed property					
6 Net rental income or (loss) from personal property					
7 Other investment income					
8 Gain or (loss) from sales of assets other than inventory					
9 Net income or (loss) from special events . . .					
10 Gross profit or (loss) from sales of inventory .					
11 Other revenue: **a** _____					
b _____					
c _____					
d _____					
e _____					
12 Subtotal. Add columns (b), (d), and (e) . . .					

13 Total. Add line 12, columns (b), (d), and (e) . . . . ▶ **13** _____

(See worksheet in line 13 instructions on page 25 to verify calculations.)

Part XVI-B Relationship of Activities to the Accomplishment of Exempt Purposes

Line No. ▼	Explain below how each activity for which income is reported in column (e) of Part XVI-A contributed importantly to the accomplishment of the organization's exempt purposes (other than by providing funds for such purposes). (See page 25 of the instructions.)

Part XVII	Information Regarding Transfers To and Transactions and Relationships With Noncharitable Exempt Organizations

		Yes	No
1	Did the organization directly or indirectly engage in any of the following with any other organization described in section 501(c) of the Code (other than section 501(c)(3) organizations) or in section 527, relating to political organizations?		
a	Transfers from the reporting organization to a noncharitable exempt organization of:		
	(1) Cash . . . . **1a(1)**		
	(2) Other assets. . . . . **1a(2)**		
b	Other Transactions:		
	(1) Sales of assets to a noncharitable exempt organization . . . . **1b(1)**		
	(2) Purchases of assets from a noncharitable exempt organization . . . . . **1b(2)**		
	(3) Rental of facilities, equipment, or other assets . . . . **1b(3)**		
	(4) Reimbursement arrangements. . . . . **1b(4)**		
	(5) Loans or loan guarantees . . . . **1b(5)**		
	(6) Performance of services or membership or fundraising solicitations . . . . . **1b(6)**		
c	Sharing of facilities, equipment, mailing lists, other assets, or paid employees **1c**		

d If the answer to any of the above is "Yes," complete the following schedule. Column **(b)** should always show the fair market value of the goods, other assets, or services given by the reporting organization. If the organization received less than fair market value in any transaction or sharing arrangement, show in column **(d)** the value of the goods, other assets, or services received.

(a) Line no.	(b) Amount involved	(c) Name of noncharitable exempt organization	(d) Description of transfers, transactions, and sharing arrangements

2a Is the organization directly or indirectly affiliated with, or related to, one or more tax-exempt organizations described in section 501(c) of the Code (other than section 501(c)(3)) or in section 527? . . . . . . ☐ Yes ☐ No

b If "Yes," complete the following schedule.

(a) Name of organization	(b) Type of organization	(c) Description of relationship

Part XVIII	Public Inspection (see page 26 of the instructions and General Instruction Q)

1 Enter the date the notice of availability of the annual return appeared in a newspaper ▶ --------------------

2 Enter the name of the newspaper ▶ --------------------

3 Check here ▶ ☐ to indicate that you have attached a copy of the newspaper notice required by the instructions on page 26. (If the notice is not attached, the return will be considered incomplete.)

Under penalties of perjury, I declare that I have examined this return, including accompanying schedules and statements, and to the best of my knowledge and belief, it is true, correct, and complete. Declaration of preparer (other than taxpayer or fiduciary) is based on all information of which preparer has any knowledge.

Please Sign Here

▶ _____   _____   ▶ _____
Signature of officer or trustee   Date   Title

Paid Preparer's Use Only

Preparer's signature ▶	Date	Check if self-employed ▶ ☐	Preparer's SSN or PTIN
Firm's name (or yours if self-employed) and address ▶		EIN ▶	
		ZIP+4 ▶	

✶   Form **990-PF** (1999)

Appendix 2–D

National Society of Fund Raising Executives Code of Ethical Principles and Standards of Professional Practice

STATEMENT OF ETHICAL PRINCIPLES
Adopted November 1991

The National Society of Fund Raising Executives (NSFRE) exists to foster the development and growth of fund-raising professionals and the profession, to promote high ethical standards in the fund-raising profession and to preserve and enhance philanthropy and volunteerism. Members of NSFRE are motivated by an inner drive to improve the quality of life through the causes they serve. They serve the ideal of philanthropy; are committed to the preservation and enhancement of volunteerism; and hold stewardship of these concepts as the overriding principle of their professional life. They recognize their responsibility to ensure that needed resources are vigorously and ethically sought and that the intent of the donor is honestly fulfilled. To these ends, NSFRE members embrace certain values that they strive to uphold in performing their responsibilities for generating philanthropic support.

NSFRE members aspire to:

- practice their profession with integrity, honesty, truthfulness and adherence to the absolute obligation to safeguard the public trust;
- act according to the highest standards and visions of their organization, profession and conscience;
- put philanthropic mission above personal gain;
- inspire others through their own sense of dedication and high purpose;
- improve their professional knowledge and skills in order that their performance will better serve others;
- demonstrate concern for the interests and well being of individuals affected by their actions;
- value the privacy, freedom of choice and interests of all those affected by their actions;
- foster cultural diversity and pluralistic values, and treat all people with dignity and respect;

- affirm, through personal giving, a commitment to philanthropy and its role in society;
- adhere to the spirit as well as the letter of all applicable laws and regulations;
- advocate within their organizations, adherence to all applicable laws and regulations;
- avoid even the appearance of any criminal offense or professional misconduct;
- bring credit to the fund-raising profession by their public demeanor;
- encourage colleagues to embrace and practice these ethical principles and standards of professional practice; and
- be aware of the codes of ethics promulgated by other professional organizations that serve philanthropy.

STANDARDS OF PROFESSIONAL PRACTICE
Adopted and Incorporated into the NSFRE Code of Ethical Principles November 1992

Furthermore, while striving to act according to the above values, NSFRE members agree to abide by the NSFRE Standards of Professional Practice, which are adopted and incorporated into the NSFRE Code of Ethical Principles. Violation of the Standards may subject the member to disciplinary sanctions, including expulsion, as provided in the NSFRE Ethics Enforcement Procedures.

Professional Obligations
1. Members shall not engage in activities that harm the member's organization, clients, or profession.
2. Members shall not engage in activities that conflict with their fiduciary, ethical, and legal obligations to their organizations and their clients.
3. Members shall effectively disclose all potential and actual conflicts of interest; such disclosure does not preclude or imply ethical impropriety.

Source: Copyright NSFRE. Used with permission. All rights reserved.

4. Members shall not exploit any relationship with a donor, prospect, volunteer or employee to the benefit of the member or the member's organization.
5. Members shall comply with all applicable local, state, provincial, federal, civil and criminal laws.
6. Members recognize their individual boundaries of competence and are forthcoming and truthful about their professional experience and qualifications.

Solicitation and Use of Charitable Funds

7. Members shall take care to ensure that all solicitation materials are accurate and correctly reflect the organization's mission and use of solicited funds.
8. Members shall take care to ensure that donors receive informed, accurate and ethical advice about the value and tax implications of potential gifts.
9. Members shall take care to ensure that contributions are used in accordance with donors' intentions.
10. Members shall take care to ensure proper stewardship of charitable contributions, including timely reports on the use and management of funds.
11. Members shall obtain explicit consent by the donor before altering the conditions of a gift.

Presentation of Information

12. Members shall not disclose privileged or confidential information to unauthorized parties.

13. Members shall adhere to the principle that all donor and prospect information created by, or on behalf of, an organization is the property of that organization and shall not be transferred or utilized except on behalf of that organization.
14. Members shall give donors the opportunity to have their names removed from lists that are sold to, rented to, or exchanged with other organizations.
15. Members shall, when stating fund-raising results, use accurate and consistent accounting methods that conform to the appropriate guidelines adopted by the American Institute of Certified Public Accountants (AICPA)* for the type of organization involved. (* In countries outside of the United States, comparable authority should be utilized.)

Compensation

16. Members shall not accept compensation that is based on a percentage of charitable contributions; nor shall they accept finder's fees.
17. Members may accept performance-based compensation, such as bonuses, provided such bonuses are in accord with prevailing practices within the members' own organizations, and are not based on a percentage of charitable contributions.
18. Members shall not pay finder's fees, commissions or percentage compensation based on charitable contributions and shall take care to discourage their organizations from making such payments.

Appendix 2–E
Sample Personal Calendar

Thursday, November 9

8:00	
9:00	Full Staff Meeting—Bring Agenda
10:00	
11:00	Meet Dean School of Music—Bring Mr. B file
12:00	Lunch with Mr. B—Bring new university catalogues and School of Music Fall Concert Series
1:00	
2:00	
3:00	
4:00	Update Dean on meeting with Mr. B
5:00	
6:00	
7:00	
8:00	

To Do	Done
Contact Report—Mr. B	x
Call Mr. W—Change time to meet 2:30	
Call Mr. J—Next month's open house	x
Schedule lunch with Ms. S	
Get more NY calls for 11/29	

Friday, November 10

8:00	Breakfast Meeting Mr. D
9:00	
10:00	
11:00	
12:00	
1:00	Meet with Assistant VP Development—Plan Nov. Florida visits
2:00	
3:00	Meet with Annual Fund Director—Coordinate next mailing to Major Gifts Prospects
4:00	
5:00	
6:00	
7:00	
8:00	

To Do	Done
Call Mr. W	x
Schedule lunch Ms. S	x
Call NY prospects for 11/29 visits	
Prepare Top 5 Prospect Reports for 11/13 meeting	x

November

Sunday	Monday	Tuesday	Wednesday	Thursday	Friday	Saturday
			1 9:00 Coffee with Ms. T 1:30 Conf. Call	**2** 12:00 Dedication 4:00 Meet Mr. G at football game	**3** 12:00 Lunch Mr. Z—Princeton	**4**
5	**6** 11:15 Staff Meeting	**7** 10:00 Call top 5 prospects 3:00 Meet Ms. D at art gallery	**8** 8:30 Meet with Assist VP 3:00 Meet with Dean School of Art	**9** 9:00 Staff Meeting 11:00 Meet with Dean 12:00 Lunch Mr. B 4:00 Update Dean	**10** 8:00 Breakfast Mr. D 1:00 Meet with Assist VP—FL visits 3:00 Annual Fund Dir. mtg.	**11**
12	**13** 10:00 Top Prospect Meeting 11:15 Staff Meeting	**14** 12:00 Lunch with Mr. G	**15** 5:00 Art opening—meet Ms. D	**16** 8:00 Mr. W 12:00 NSFRE Meeting 6:00 Meet Business Prospects Downtown	**17** 2:00 Corp. Sponsor Program Art Gallery Meeting	**18**
19	**20** 11:15 Staff Meeting	**21** 3:30 Meet Mr. J Dedication Ceremony 6:00 Reception	**22** 10:00 Meet with Dean Business School 3:00 Follow-Up visit Ms. D	**23** Off	**24** 9:00 Meet with Dev. Staff—Strategize on top 10 prospects	**25**
26	**27** 11:15 Staff Meeting 2:30 Meet with Mr. M—proposal?	**28** 9:00 Meet with Dir. of Dev.—coordinate prospect list	**29** 10:00–4:00—NYC prospect calls	**30** 12:00 Lunch and tour with Mr. and Mrs. Z		

Chapter 3
Getting in the Door

CHAPTER OUTLINE

- Selecting a Contact To Open the Door for You
- Writing to Prospects Initially
- Writing to Prospects with Unlisted Telephone Numbers
- Contacting Prospects by E-Mail
- Calling the Prospects Instead of Sending a Letter
- Calling Your Prospects after the Initial Letter
- Fundraiser Versus Administrative Assistant Calls
- Leaving Messages on the Answering Machine
- Leaving the Message with the Prospect's Assistant
- Calling the Prospects at Home or at Work
- Overcoming the Telephone Brushoff
- Staying in Touch with the Prospect When the Prospect Says "No" to a Visit
- Recap and Review

We look for and support organizations that are making a difference in the community. These agencies are not only reaching diverse populations with critical needs, but they are doing so in fresh and innovative ways. We feel fortunate to be in a position that allows us to contribute to the future.

Dr. Henry Samueli, Co-Founder of Broadcom Corporation,
and Susan Samueli, Philanthropists

SELECTING A CONTACT TO OPEN THE DOOR FOR YOU

Now that you have your pool of prospects, you must plan and form a strategy of how you will contact them. It is important to review each prospect's file to see if someone connected with your organization knows the prospect or has had some significant contact with the prospect. If a board member, major donor, staff person, or volunteer knows the prospect *and has a good relationship with the prospect*, ask the contact to write an introductory letter or place an introductory call to your prospect for you. Note here that the mention of your contact's name should bring a smile to your prospect's face. It should not be someone the prospect has a vague recollection of meeting. For instance, if a major donor tells you that she belongs to the same choir as your prospect and they car pool together, this would be a good opportunity to ask the major donor to place an introductory call to your prospect. If your executive director attended the same honorary dinner as your prospect, but they did not meet, using the executive director's name might not open the door for you. In fact, it could cause confusion during your first contact. If you reference the honorary dinner, and the prospect says "I don't remember meeting any executive director that night," you will be getting off to a poor start with your prospect.

Tip: *Only use the contact's name or ask the contact to place an introductory call for you if there is a recognizable positive relationship or strong acquaintance between your contact and your prospect.*

After you have determined that your contact would be an appropriate person to make the initial move with your prospect, the contact should be asked to either send a letter and follow up with a telephone call, or simply call the prospect. If the contact wishes to send a letter first, the letter should contain the following elements:

1. A brief description of the overall good work of the organization.
2. The reason why the contact supports the organization.
3. The need for the organization's leaders and fundraisers to meet personally with all supporters as well as with people who may be interested in giving their support.
4. A closing line that either the contact or you (name and title) will be calling the prospect to set a date and time to meet.

(See Appendix 3–A.)

It is important for the contact to give your name and title to the prospect for several reasons. First, your contact most likely will have many other responsibilities, both at work and at home, and contacting prospects for you may be on the bottom of the "to do" list. If the contact does not call the prospect within two or three weeks after the prospect receives the letter, it will be up to the fundraiser to place the call. Since the contact's letter references that the contact *or* the fundraiser will be calling, the prospect will not be caught off guard when the fundraiser calls. Second, if the fundraiser has to place the call, it will not be considered a "cold call." The introduction has been made by the contact, and the door is open for the fundraiser to follow up with the prospect.

Your contacts must be aware that they need to make the call to the prospect within two to three weeks after the letter is sent. If the contact needs *a little more time*, give the contact one more week. Excluding vacation season, illness, and extended business travel, if the call has not been placed after this time, then the fundraiser must thank the contact and call the prospect.

The ideal situation would be for your contact simply to place a call to the prospect soon after you have given the contact the prospect's name, address, and telephone number. At that time, the contact can arrange to see the prospect either alone or with the fundraiser. If during the conversation the prospect has questions or concerns about the organization, the contact can say, "these are great questions, and I would like to answer these and any other questions you have in person with our director of development."

Tip: *Make sure your contacts are thanked for their efforts, even if they never call their assigned prospects. Contacts may be beneficial volunteers and spokespeople for your organization at a later time.*

WRITING TO PROSPECTS INITIALLY

If you do not have a contact who can do the initial letter or call, then you need to decide whether you will write or call the prospect as your initial move. If the donor has had *very little contact* with your organization, it is wise to send a letter before making a call. The letter will:

- Introduce the fundraiser to the prospect.
- Thank the prospect for his or her past support.
- Reference a common bond between the prospect and the organization, or the prospect's interest in the organization.
- Tie the prospect's interest with the organization's recent accomplishments or new programs.
- Tell the prospect that the fundraiser will call in *one week* to set a *brief* meeting.

A letter eliminates the awkwardness that may occur on the first-time "cold call." If the prospect has had very little contact with the organization, and one day receives a call from a development officer, the prospect is more than likely going to think the officer is a telemarketer asking for money. Remember, donors and prospects receive many calls, at all times during the day, from charities asking for money or to volunteer and from companies looking for new business. Your initial contact with the prospect sets the tone for their future involvement with your organization.

The letter also gives the prospect some time to think about your organization before your call. The letter puts your organization on the forefront of the prospect's mind. This is why it is crucial for the fundraiser to call the prospect no later than one week after the prospect receives the letter. The more time that goes by, the more likely the prospect will not remember your letter or the purpose of your call. This illustrates the need to have a calendar system as discussed in Chapter 2. Once the introductory letters are sent to your prospects, you must use your calendar to mark the day in the week that you will be making your calls. Try not to let other projects and meetings deter you from making the calls. If they do, use your calendar to set the *next closest free time* period to make your calls and mark it in your calendar.

The letters to your prospects should reference any connection that the prospect has with your organization, or if the prospect has demonstrated an interest in the organization. For instance, if the prospect volunteered for a clothing drive, sent a personal note back to the organization on a direct mail piece, sent a holiday card to the staff, or called and asked for an annual report, place it in the letter. If the prospect lives near you or someone in your organization, let them know in the letter. This may be the first common bond you establish with the prospect. It will separate your major gift work from a mass mailing and will bring you one step closer to your prospect.

If you are traveling out of your area to see prospects, make them feel special by saying that it is your privilege to visit people on behalf of your organization. Express that you would like to see them personally so that you can tell them about the new developments at your organization. State that you would like to hear their views so that you can bring their thoughts and suggestions back to the organization. It will make the prospects feel that their input is valued, and they will be more willing to say yes to a visit when you call. If the prospect insists that it is not necessary for you to go out of your way to see them, respond that you intend to see several supporters in their area. There is comfort knowing that many people, especially in their area, support and care about the same philanthropic organizations. People like to give to a "winning" and successful charity so be sure to stress that there is local support for your group.

Additionally, if you have clustered your prospects by geographic location as "Creating Donor Profiles" in Chapter 2 recommends, then it will be easy for you to call upon several prospects in one area. Again, the more personal you make this process the more successful you will be.

Sometimes there is no bond, the prospect has not initiated an interest, and there is nothing special to link the prospect to your organization. Many good prospects have made gifts but, for one reason or another, the prospect has yet to be personally contacted by the organization. In those instances, tell the prospect in one sentence what your organization has been able to accomplish with the prospect's gifts. This should be something more than a fundraising goal that was reached. For instance, if twenty more children attended summer camp this year than last year, or if enough funds were raised over the year to keep a congregation open nights and weekends for adult education classes, put it in the letter. It is a much better approach than stating that the charity surpassed its fundraising goal by x percent.

Sometimes your prospects have no giving history, yet they are good prospects. For instance, you may read about someone in a journal or newspaper who has the means to make a gift and has a public broadcasting background. If you are a publicly supported radio station, you will want to explore this prospect's gift potential further. Since you cannot use the prospect's prior gifts as leverage to get you in the door, connect the prospect's interest to your group and let the prospect know what the support from others has done for your constituency. If there is no connection, just elaborate on how the support of others has made it possible for your organization to achieve great things and tell the prospect that there is a need to expand this base of support (see Appendix 3–A).

Perhaps the most important part of any initial letter to prospects is the sentence that you only want to meet with them *briefly*, at their home or office (see Appendix 3–A). Brief means approximately 20 minutes. This will let the prospects know right away that you do not intend to spend the whole morning or afternoon with them. The prospects will be more willing to see you if they know that they can "squeeze" you in their schedule and not have to devote a large block of time for this meeting. Once you call the prospects and they suggest that you meet for a meal or see you for more time, then be available to meet their timetable. The prospects will respect you and your professionalism for making the initial offer to have a short meeting.

Major gifts fundraisers often hesitate giving their title at the end of the letter fearing that prospects will never say "yes" to a meeting if they know they are going to meet someone with a title of "major gifts director" or "major gifts officer." The fear is that the prospects will think they will be pressured at the first meeting to make a gift that will be way above their means. I always include my title for several reasons.

First, prospects should know right from the start that it is my job to raise large gifts for the organization. This does not mean that I am going to ask them for a large gift on the first visit. You will never establish a trusting relationship with your prospects if you are not honest about what you do right from the start. Second, if you send a letter with just your name, the prospects have no idea the level of leadership that is trying to contact them from the organization. They may think you are the president or CEO and when you call, they may be disappointed to find out that it was not the top leader calling them. Third, it lets the prospects know that your organization is really working hard to raise significant money. Prospects are usually flattered that your group "thinks" they have "that much money" to make major gifts. Giving your title will weed out those prospects who on the initial call will let you know that they have no desire to see you, to give, or to increase their gift. It is best to find this out early in the process so that you can focus on prospects who are interested in making major gifts.

WRITING TO PROSPECTS WITH UNLISTED TELEPHONE NUMBERS

Fundraiser Pete, Major Gifts Officer for Good Person Charities, sent 10 letters to his top prospects. The letter informed the prospects that he was going to be in their area and it was important for him to see them to hear their views on Good Person Charities. Their input would help shape the future fundraising efforts by the organization. Fundraiser Pete said he would call them in one week to set a brief meeting.

One week goes by and fundraiser Peter picks up the file to call his first prospect. He opens the prospect's file and searches for a telephone number. He goes to his computer database, but no telephone number is listed. He calls telephone information, and the number is unlisted.

> **Tip:** *Make sure you have the prospect's home, work, or cell telephone number before you write the initial letter telling the prospect you will call.*

Fundraiser Pete, like many development professionals, learned that each letter should be tailored to each prospect. Had he reviewed the prospect's donor profile first, he would have discovered that his prospect had an unlisted telephone number. Fundraiser Pete would have sent a very different letter to the prospect.

Now fundraiser Pete must write another letter and tell the prospect to call him since he just learned that the prospect has an unlisted telephone number.

The best way to contact your unlisted telephone number prospects is to send them a letter introducing yourself, referencing their involvement, thanking them for their gift, and asking them to call you. If your organization has a toll-free number, put it in bold in the letter. It is important to mention that you know they have an unlisted number, you respect their privacy, and you would rather have the task of making the call, but under the circumstances that is not possible (see Appendix 3–A).

Another way to contact this group is to send a self-addressed prepaid postage envelope with your letter. This way the prospects can write to you and let you know when they are available to meet. It is important that you send three letters to these prospects with unlisted telephone numbers because they are among your top prospects. Three tailored letters will let them know you are very serious about meeting them.

Keep in mind, however, that if prospects have an unlisted telephone number, they may not want to be contacted at all. The very nature of the fact that they have unlisted telephone numbers suggests they want to control the people that contact them. Since they are your top prospects, you have to try to contact them and be persistent with them until they let you know they do not want to be contacted by your organization.

CONTACTING PROSPECTS BY E-MAIL

The donor profile or your donor database may contain the prospect's e-mail address. Communicating with your prospects via e-mail has its pluses and minuses. On the plus side, it is an excellent way to reach your prospects if they have unlisted telephone numbers. You can put everything you would have said in a letter in an e-mail and send it to the prospect's home or office. Since this is your first communication with the prospect, however, it is important to include a note or a postscript asking the prospect how he or she would like to be contacted. Some prospects may not like being contacted by charities via their computers. Others may find it the best and fastest way to communicate.

Another positive feature of using e-mail to contact your prospects is that it can really speed the process of getting an appointment. This works particularly well with business prospects. E-mail can eliminate the several telephone calls it may take to speak with your prospect in person and can eliminate leaving numerous messages with the prospect's voice mail, receptionist, or administrative assistant. Again, be sure to ask the prospect's permission to contact him or her using e-mail in the future.

The downside of using e-mail is that it keeps the process detached and impersonal. Remember this is the first contact you will be having with the prospects, and your goal is to get in to see them and build a solid relationship that will lead to a major gift. Some prospects may not let you in to see them because they feel they can accomplish "whatever it is you had in mind for them" via e-mail. If you do not have the opportunity to see them or visit their office or home, it will be extremely difficult to conduct any meaningful cultivation that will lead to a gift if all your contact is confined to e-mail.

Similar to the prospects with unlisted telephone numbers, some prospects may feel that you have invaded their privacy if you contact them initially by e-mail. One should not assume that just because a person has an e-mail address, he or she wants to be contacted by a charity via e-mail. Some business prospects do not use their business e-mail to conduct any personal business. Whether you reach a prospect at home or at work via e-mail, some prospects may only want their personal friends or family to contact them this way. With these uncertainties in mind, the preferred way to initially contact your prospects is by letter, followed by a call. You can always use e-mail to stay in communication with your prospects once you have met them and you have their permission.

CALLING THE PROSPECTS INSTEAD OF SENDING A LETTER

Many fundraisers have had great success calling their top prospects first instead of sending an initial letter. I suggest that if you take this approach, make sure the prospect's donor profile reveals that the prospect has had *recent, frequent, and meaningful contact* with someone in your organization. For instance, if the prospect has spoken several times with your direct mail or membership director, or the prospect has written letters to your president, CEO, or executive director, the prospect may not mind a call from you and may not need an introductory letter. This approach is similar to the "Selecting a Contact To Open the Door for You" section, earlier in this chapter, but here you are the one from the start to place the call. If your call would be a *natural and logical next step* to cultivating the prospect, then certainly call the prospect. This type of

call would be considered an extension of an already existing relationship between the prospect and your organization. The key is to make sure the contact was recent and something more significant than one or two calls or letters to someone connected to your group.

When you make the call, you should introduce yourself to the prospect and quickly reference the contact they have had with the individual from your organization. Let the prospect know right away that this connection has led you to call them. Then state that you would like the opportunity to meet with them personally and ask them when it would be convenient for them to meet with you. If the prospect asks about the person they have been dealing with prior to your call, ask the prospect if you can bring that person with you on your visit. This will serve as a natural progression of the prospect's involvement with your organization and will lead toward well-planned cultivation by the major gift fundraiser.

> *Tip: Before calling your prospect, speak with the person who has connected with your prospect. Ask that person if they would be willing to accompany you on the visit.*

CALLING YOUR PROSPECTS AFTER THE INITIAL LETTER

At this point you are ready to call the prospects that received your initial letters. The idea of "cold calling" prospects can be overwhelming and intimidating to some fundraisers. There is the fear that the prospects will automatically say "no" to the visit or that the calling process will take so much time that the task is pushed to the bottom of a large work pile. With the right approach, calling prospects can be a positive task. Think of it as getting one step closer to getting your next gift. It will not take an enormous amount of time if you have a system to this process. Exhibit 3–1 shows you the steps you need to streamline the calling process.

It is important to refresh your recollection of the prospect's donor profile, particularly the giving history and involvement with your organization before calling the prospect. This will help you make "small talk" with the prospect in the opening moments of the call. For instance, if the prospect just made a gift, you should thank him or her for the gift and say that the organiza-

Exhibit 3–1 Guide for Calling Prospects

1. Have the initial letter and donor profile at your fingertips.
2. Review the donor profile before you make the call.
3. Call at a time you are feeling upbeat and can project energy and enthusiasm in your voice.
4. Good times to reach prospects are 10 AM–11 AM or 2 PM–3 PM.
5. Review your personal calendar and select whole days in the current week and following weeks that you are available for visits *before* you make the calls.
6. Be ready to quickly identify yourself and reference the initial letter.
7. Be prepared for the prospect to have no recollection of the letter.
8. State that your purpose is to *personally meet* key supporters or new friends of the organization to share information about your group's new programs or projects.
9. Tell them it is critical to the growth of your organization that you spend some time in person with them, listening to their views about the organization so that you can bring these insights to the leadership of the organization.
10. Emphasize that the meeting will be *brief.*
11. Quickly suggest a few dates you have set aside in the current week and the following week to meet.
12. Once the date is picked, ask the prospect the time he or she would like to meet.
13. Ask the prospect if you can meet him or her at home, at work, or at your organization.
14. If the prospect wants to meet at a more neutral location, suggest meeting for coffee, breakfast, or lunch, depending on your travel budget.
15. If you are meeting the prospect at his or her home or work, ask for directions.
16. Make sure the prospect has your name and telephone number in case he or she has to reschedule the meeting.
17. Reconfirm the date, time, and meeting place.
18. Thank the prospect for his or her time and state that you look forward to seeing him or her very soon.

"warm them up" and start the conversation on a positive note. If the prospect just attended an event, reference that activity.

You should make your calls on days when things are going well, and you can project some energy. Prospects will be more willing and open to the suggestion of a visit if they think they will be meeting a "likeable" person, one who is upbeat, personable, and enjoyable. Not every day can be a "good" day. Meetings, special events, and travel can be wearing on fundraisers so you do not want to call on the days you will sound drained and tired.

I have found that the best times to reach prospects are either 10 AM or after 2 PM. Calling the prospects around 10 AM at home is good because you do not know their morning routine and you do not want to wake them up or call during breakfast. Calling after 2 PM will catch your prospects after lunch or after they have run errands. Calling prospects at work during these times gives them time to sort through their morning routine and will likewise catch them right after lunch.

Here is yet another illustration of the importance of having a personal calendar as discussed in Chapter 2. Using your calendar, you must clear a block of dates in the current month and the next month when you will be free to see these prospects. This must be done *before* you make your calls. Then if the prospects say they cannot meet for several weeks, you have future dates when you are available to meet. It is suggested that you block whole days for your appointments. This will give the prospects several time periods in the selected days to meet with you. Remember, the easier you make it for your prospects, the more willing they will be to see you.

When the prospect answers the call, you should quickly identify yourself and reference your letter. This will let the prospect know that you are not a telemarketer, and you are not soliciting money for an annual fund or campaign. The prospect may or may not remember your letter. It is possible he or she never received the letter. The mailing address could have changed, the prospect may have two addresses and your letter could have been sent to the other residence or vacation home. Ask if your letter was received. If it was, reiterate that you want to meet *briefly* to personally share some new projects or past successes and to get feedback. Quickly suggest some dates to meet. If the letter was not received, tell the prospect what the letter said and again quickly suggest some dates to meet.

Once the date is set, ask for the most convenient time and place to meet. Whenever possible, try to meet

tion feels that it is important to *personally thank* donors as well as to send them a written thank you. This will prospects at their homes or businesses. You will learn so much more about them by seeing how they live or work, than you will if you meet them at your organization or a restaurant. This point will be covered in depth in "Meeting Your New Best Friends" in Chapter 4.

If the meeting place selected is the prospect's home or place of business, do not forget to ask for directions. Even if you have the street address in your donor profile, it is important to confirm this detail. Many fundraisers have arrived at an old address, or have been detoured through some major road construction, and have arrived well beyond the set time. Prospects usually like to share "the best way" to their homes or offices so ask, write down the directions, and be sure to take them with you the day of your meeting. If the address or location given to you is unfamiliar, ask the prospect how long it should take you to get there. Then you can gauge your time appropriately and avoid the embarrassment of being late.

It is also a good idea to give your prospects your telephone number in case something comes up and they have to cancel and reschedule. It would be very inconvenient for them to have to look up your number in the telephone book, call telephone directory assistance, or find a direct mail piece to get your organization's telephone number. I also like to give my prospects my direct number so that when they call they get me immediately and do not have to go through a receptionist. This begins the donor relationship on a much more personal basis and sends the strong message that *you* are personally interested in them.

As a close to your conversation, reconfirm your meeting date, place, and time and tell the prospect you are looking forward to meeting him or her. If the prospects are donors, ALWAYS thank them for their interest and support of your organization.

FUNDRAISER VERSUS ADMINISTRATIVE ASSISTANT CALLS

If the fundraiser's primary role is to raise major gifts, then it is the fundraiser's responsibility to make the prospect calls. This is recommended for several reasons:

1. You will gain valuable information about the prospect over the telephone.
    -   The prospect's voice will clue you into his or her approximate age.
    -   The prospect's tone will let you know if the prospect is willing to meet you or is hesitant and will need much convincing and persuasion on your part.

2. Telephone information about the prospect may or may not be conveyed to you if an assistant makes the calls.
3. The fundraiser is much more prepared to answer the prospect's questions by the very nature of the fundraising position.
4. The fundraiser will probe the prospect to find out why the prospect is unwilling to meet and may be able to change the prospect's mind.
5. It sets a personal tone between you and the prospect right from the start.
6. Top prospects deserve time and attention from the major gifts fundraising leaders of the organization.

Larger organizations or organizations that are well staffed have used assistants, secretaries, and interns to make prospect calls. The advantage, of course, is that it gives the fundraiser time to devote to other tasks and someone sets your schedule for you. The preferred approach, however, is to have the fundraiser call and have the staff person confirm the meeting the day before the appointment.

LEAVING MESSAGES ON THE ANSWERING MACHINE

In all likelihood, you will get a message machine during your prospect calling period. I always leave a message that lets the prospect know who I am and the purpose of my call. If there is some connection between the prospect and someone in your organization, be sure to state this right away. It is critical that you ask the prospect to call you and let you know the best time you can reach them. This works very well if your office has voice mail and the prospect can call you back and leave the message on your machine. Be sure to repeat your name and telephone number.

You should call the prospect once a week. If after three weeks you keep getting the answering machine, send a letter stating that you have tried to reach him or her on the telephone, give the telephone number you are calling, and ask the prospect again to call you and let you know when you can meet. The prospect may be away on business or extended vacation. If you sense this is the case, let a month go by, then call again. Be sure to state that it is not your intention to "barrage" your prospect with calls, however, it is important that you speak with the prospect. This may seem time consuming, but these are your top prospects and they are worthy of this time.

LEAVING THE MESSAGE WITH THE PROSPECT'S ASSISTANT

Business prospects will, by and large, always have an assistant who in many instances will "screen" the calls. Sometimes it is very difficult to get past the assistant or to get your message to your prospect. In these situations, you have no choice but to work with the assistant. If the prospect is unavailable or the assistant will not put the call through, it is important that you give the complete details of the purpose of your call (see Exhibit 3–1). Treat the assistant as if the assistant were the prospect. Ask the assistant to give you times and dates when you can reach the prospect. Likewise, you should let the assistant know the best time the prospect can reach you and the dates you wanted to see the prospect. This will avoid playing "telephone tag."

CALLING THE PROSPECTS AT HOME OR AT WORK

If the donor profile contains the prospect's work telephone number, most fundraisers call the prospect at work. The fundraiser must be sensitive to the prospect's time on the telephone because some people may not like using their office time to discuss their charitable interests. When calling a prospect at work, after your initial introduction be sure to ask the prospect if you have reached them at a good time. The prospect may be just going into a meeting, may need that time to finish a report, or may be expecting an important call. Ask the prospect if you can call back in an hour or so. That way you will have a firm telephone appointment with the prospect, and he or she will be more prepared for your call.

Calling a prospect at home is a bit more difficult. If this is the only number you have, it is suggested that you call at 10 AM and 2 PM, then various times during the day. The prospect may work a night shift, volunteer, or work hours other than nine to five. The best thing you can do when trying to reach prospects is to let them know that you do not know when to reach them and to ask them to call you. Again, prospects can leave good dates and times on your office voice mail.

To reach these prospects, you may have to take donor profiles home and make night calls from your home. Under these circumstances, be sure you tell the prospect *immediately* that you are not a telemarketer and apologize for having to call in the evening. I always find that if you tell prospects you do not want to deter them from their evening time with friends or

family, this helps to "soften" them. They will be more apt to give you a minute or two at this time to set an appointment.

> **Tip:** *If you have reached the prospect at a bad time, ask if you can call the next day. Be sure to confirm a time and the telephone number where you can reach the prospect.*

OVERCOMING THE TELEPHONE BRUSHOFF

Perhaps the hardest part of contacting prospects on the telephone is to convince them to see you. Many will want you to simply place something in the mail. Others will say they are too busy, or they will be away for an extended period of time. Here are some suggested persuasive pitches you can use to counter the telephone brushoff.

Just Put the Information in the Mail

- "As part of our personal outreach, it is important that we meet with our special supporters like you. We cannot maintain our level of quality service to our constituency and supporters if we do not have input from you."
- "You've been a great supporter, and it would be a disservice to you to just drop a brochure in the mail."
- "I really would like the opportunity to spend just a few minutes with you, introduce myself, and give you a brief outline of our new initiatives. I promise it will not take long, but it will be worth your time."

I'm Really Busy Right Now

- "I am sorry to catch you at a bad time. Can I call you tomorrow at this number around 2 PM?"
- "I know it is a very busy time. We never seem to have enough hours in our day to get it all done. When is a good time for me to reach you?"
- "I apologize for the timing of my call. I will call you at whatever time you suggest. It is important to us at (the charity name) that we maintain excellent relations with our supporters like you. When do you suggest I call back?"

Is This about Money?

- "The purpose of my call is to introduce myself and to be a personal contact for you on behalf of (the charity name)."
- "I want to meet with you so that I can personally share with you the new developments and directions at (the charity name)."
- "I promise during our meeting that I will not mention money."
- "I will not bring up the topic of money unless you do."

I Don't Want Anyone in My House

- "Perfectly understandable, can we meet somewhere close to your home?"
- "I understand completely. Perhaps we could meet for coffee, at a park, or at our organization?"
- "If you're like me, I like to go out to lunch now and then. Would you like to join me for lunch next Tuesday, say around 12:30?"

Tip: The key to overcoming the prospect's telephone objection is to acknowledge the objection, reiterate the importance of a personal meeting, and then quickly suggest alternative ways, dates, or places to meet. Fundraisers must be flexible and project a sincere, not a pushy, voice during this process.

STAYING IN TOUCH WITH THE PROSPECT WHEN THE PROSPECT SAYS "NO" TO A VISIT

Sometimes, no matter how persuasive or prepared the fundraiser is, the prospect will not agree to a visit. In those instances, it is still possible to keep the prospect personally involved with your organization. Exhibit 3–2 illustrates the various ways you can bring the prospect closer to your organization. These methods also serve to let prospects know that they are being treated specially by you on behalf of the organization. In time, they may be willing to meet with you.

Sending handwritten notes on prospects' mailings will make the prospects feel that they have been elevated from the direct mail list and placed on your orga-

Exhibit 3–2 Ways To Keep Prospects Involved When They Refuse a Visit

1. Ask prospects if they like receiving your organization's mailings. If so, ask prospects which materials they like the best.
2. Send personal handwritten notes on each of these materials.
3. Call to personally invite them to any special event.
4. Tell prospects that you wanted them to know about this event before any mailings were sent.
5. Call the prospects just to say hello.
6. Call the prospects during holiday seasons.

nization's VIP list. It lets prospects know that you listen to what they say and follow through on their interests. For example, if the prospects like the charity's newsletter or the holiday card the charity sends each year, make sure those materials are signed with a personal note from you. If your group hosts an open house, dedication, cultural event, special dinner, or area meeting, be sure to call and personally invite the prospects *before* invitations are sent. This will make the prospects feel very special. It connects you to the prospects and gives them someone from your organization that they can rely on.

Perhaps the most important way you can show your prospects that you are genuinely interested in bringing them closer to your organization is to call them *just to say hello*. How often do we hear from our donors that the only time we contact them is when we are looking for money? Too many to count, which is why you need to call them and let them know your organization is thinking about *them*. You can call these prospects every six to eight weeks. This is just enough time and contact without being overbearing. Some fundraisers may feel very uncomfortable with the idea of calling prospects with nothing to say. Quite the contrary, you will have much to say with the right approach. If you have reached prospects at a good time, ask them how their family and friends are doing and tell them that you were "just checking in" to make sure everything was all right. You will be amazed at how grateful your prospects will be when they know you are just calling to say hello.

The holiday seasons are also a great time to call your prospects and extend warm wishes on behalf of your organization. If you called your prospects during the appropriate holidays of New Years, Easter/Passover, Rosh Hashanah, Thanksgiving, Christmas, and Hanukkah, you will really solidify your relationship with them. Tack on a call or two during the summer months to ask them about their travels. This would give you plenty of meaningful contact with your prospects throughout the year.

During these telephone calls, you will learn a great deal of valuable prospect information. Prospects generally start to talk about themselves and their family, business life, and health with each call. Now is the time you can weave in the conversation a word or two about how well your organization is doing. Give the prospect any update on a campaign and share any news about recent major gifts. After a few months of these calls, renew your request to see them. You can say, "We have spoken so much over the past few months, I feel like we know each other. Why don't we get together sometime soon?" With the proper and consistent contact by you, the prospects will be receptive to a meeting. A trust has been established, and it will open the door for you.

RECAP AND REVIEW

1. Whenever possible, ask a contact who knows your prospect to write the initial letter or to make the initial call for you.
2. If you do not have a contact, write a letter to your prospects requesting a *brief* meeting.
3. Make sure the prospect has a listed telephone number before you state in your letter that you will call to set a date and time to meet.
4. Use e-mail to communicate with your prospects after you have their permission to contact them this way.
5. Call the prospect first instead of writing a letter, *only* if the prospect has had recent, frequent, and meaningful contact with someone in the organization.
6. Before calling the prospect one week after they receive your initial letter, make sure you have cleared dates and times over the next two months when you are available to meet.
7. Call the prospects around 10 AM and 2 PM and be ready to suggest various dates, times, and places to meet.
8. Leave detailed messages on the prospect's answering machines and ask the prospect to call you with good times for you to call.
9. Befriend the prospect's administrative assistant and deliver the same message, in the same tone as if you were speaking to the prospect.
10. Whenever possible, call the prospect at work. Make sure you have reached the prospect at a good point in the workday to discuss your prospective visit.
11. Overcome the prospect's telephone objections by acknowledging the objection and reiterating the importance of the meeting. Project a sincere and convincing voice, not a pushy and overbearing voice.
12. If the prospect refuses initially to see you, call the prospect just to say hello, during holiday seasons and summer travel months. After a few months, renew your request to meet.

SUGGESTED READINGS

Gillespie, J. 1999. What Am I Gonna Say? Negotiating the Planned Gift. 1999 National Society of Fundraising Executives International Conference. Miami, FL.

Kelly, K. 1998. *Effective Fund-Raising Management.* Mahwah, NJ: Lawrence Erlbaum Associates, Inc.

Warwick, M. 1994. *How to Write Successful Fund Raising Letters.* Berkeley, CA: Strathmore Press.

Weinstein, S. 1999. *The Complete Guide to Fund Raising Management.* New York: John Wiley & Sons, Inc.

Appendix 3–A
Sample Letters

Dear Tom:

It was great to see you at our art opening last week. Tom, as you know, I have been on the Advisory Board for Great Art Gallery for the past four years. I think you'll agree, it's a vibrant, avant-garde gallery. What you may not know is that in addition to putting on great exhibits, we also give *free* art classes to underprivileged children in the surrounding areas. I can't tell you how rewarding it is to see these young talented children use art as a creative outlet.

You said to me a while ago that you were thinking about doing something for the gallery. Ms. M, our major gifts director, has been with the gallery for over five years. She knows the gallery inside and out and can fill you in with all the details about our art classes and the other educational programs we offer. She would be the best person to answer any questions you may have. Besides, Ms. M is very personable, and I think you will enjoy meeting her. She's a real gallery enthusiast!

Tom, I can't thank you enough for your time. I will have Ms. M give you a call. See you at the next show.

Sincerely,

(Contact's name)

P.S. The next gallery exhibit promises to be "a trick of the eye." Be sure to have Ms. M explain!

Dear Mr. Prospect:

I read with interest the story about you and your farm in the last issue of *The Business Times*. Family-owned businesses are treasures here in the United States, and we often take them for granted. You and your family should be very proud of your rich history and the accomplishments you have achieved over these past decades.

Your business follows the same philosophy as our community hospital. While your challenge is maintaining your independence with pressure from wholesalers and retailers, our challenge is to maintain our excellent patient care with pressure from health maintenance organizations and for-profit hospitals.

You see, Mr. Prospect, we both have a "personalized style" that has kept us in business for years. We both serve the needs of our friends and neighbors. Our supporters have made it possible for us to provide life-saving medical treatment for our community. Our goal is to expand this base of support so that *your community hospital* will always be there when you need us.

I would very much like the opportunity to meet with you *briefly* to talk more about your business and community hospital. I would like to hear your views about our hospital, and how we can better serve *our* community and neighbors.

I will call you next week to set a date and time that is best for you.

Most cordially,

Director of Development
P.S. Our family loves your new produce stand next to your farm!

Dear Mrs. Donor:

We may not say this enough, but we at the Beach Preservation Society really do appreciate your loyal and most generous yearly gifts. It takes a special person to think so highly of our precious beach land, and you, Mrs. Donor, are a very special person to us.

As a major gifts officer, I have the enjoyable opportunity to meet as many of our Beach Preservation Society members as possible. I would like to meet with you, *briefly*, at home or at work, just to learn more about your views of our Society. I can share with you at that time some new projects we have underway.

I will call you at the end of the week so that we can set a mutually convenient time to meet. Mrs. Donor, I am very much looking forward to speaking with you.

Most cordially,

Major Gifts Officer

Dear Dr. and Mrs. Donor:

Greetings from your alma mater! We hope all is well with you, your family, and friends.

As a director here at the college, part of my enjoyable job is to meet with our top alumni, like the two of you. The purpose of my visit is to hear about your experiences at the college and to share with you some of the latest news about your college. I will be in your area next month and would very much like the opportunity to meet with you *briefly*. You should know we have quite a few alumni who live near you. If you like, when we get together, I can let you know if anyone from your class is living or working nearby.

I will call you next week to set a date and time that is convenient for you. In the meantime, stay well and know that we at the college are thinking of you.

Sincerely,

Major Gifts Director

Dear Mrs. Supporter:

This year we are celebrating our 25th Anniversary as the first regional arts center in the area. From a small recital hall to a state-of-the-art multipurpose center, we certainly have come a long way. All this would not be possible, but for the generosity of our loyal supporters like *you*!

As a songwriter and performer, you know how important it is to reach out to your audience and touch their lives with your talent. We too, Mrs. Supporter, need to reach out to our loyal donors and share with them our future plans. Very few people know that in a few months we will be providing scholarships for elementary school children to learn music and dance. Additionally, next year we will launch our first gifted young musicians concert series. If all goes as planned, we will raise enough funds to send these young musicians on a national tour.

It would be my pleasure to meet with you *briefly* to talk more about these and other exciting music programs at our arts center. Since you travel a great deal, I will accommodate your schedule. Next week, I will call your office to arrange a date and time to meet.

From all of us at *your regional arts center*, thank you for your genuine interest and support. I look forward to meeting with you soon.

Sincerely,

Executive Director

Dear Honorable and Mr. Donor:

We at the horticultural society just wanted to let you know that we think of you all the time and hope that you and your family are doing well.

Our annual spring show is just around the corner, and we wanted to make sure our loyal supporters like the two of you have the dates MARCH 21–23 marked on your calendars. You will be receiving a special pre-event reception invitation, which will be held on MARCH 20 starting at 6 PM. We know that last year you could not attend our pre-event reception, so we're hoping that this "early invitation" will make its way to the front of your calendar!

An important part of our mission at the horticultural society is to personally meet our loyal friends like you, Honorable and Mr. Donor. Few people know just how many programs and classes we offer throughout the year, as well as the numerous volunteers we coordinate for neighboring arboretums and gardens.

I would love to have the chance to speak with you *briefly* in person about these and many more exciting programs we do at the society. Since you do not have a listed telephone number, could you please be so kind to call me at **(800) 000–0000** so that we could set a date and time that is best for us to meet. If you prefer, send a note in the enclosed self-addressed envelope and let me know when we can meet.

Honorable and Mr. Donor, we cannot thank you enough for all you have done for the horticultural society. But we'll keep trying!

Most cordially,

Associate Director

Chapter 4
Meeting Your New Best Friends

CHAPTER OUTLINE

Mrs. Haas and I support organizations that we have felt a deep commitment towards and personal involvement with. We also give to the educational institutions we attended, religious institutions we attend, organizations led by persons we respect, and organizations that are important to our city. Worthwhile human service and environmental organizations receive our support because of their important role in making our region a better one in which to live and work.

John C. Haas, Chairman Emeritus of Rohm and
Haas Co., and Philanthropist

MAKING THE MOST OF YOUR FIRST VISIT

The Friends School Director of Development, John, was really looking forward to meeting prospect Q at prospect Q's office. He had tried for weeks to get this appointment, and finally prospect Q agreed to see him. John knew that prospect Q owned several prosperous Quaker continuing care retirement villages and planned to build more. Prospect Q, not an alumnus of The Friends School, made one gift of $5,000. Director John was hoping that the meeting would give him the chance to find out why he made the gift and to set the stage for a future gift to the school's capital campaign.

At the meeting, prospect Q described in detail every feature of his "highly successful" retirement villages. He showed Director John the 15 development models for the upcoming new villages. Director John barely had the opportunity to talk about The Friends School or to find out anything more about prospect Q

other than the success of his business. After 20 minutes or so passed, prospect Q received an important telephone call and had to end the meeting. Director John left prospect Q's office unsure what to do next with the prospect.

What went wrong? While Director John had high hopes of planting the seed for prospect Q to support the school's capital campaign, he learned very little about prospect Q and his connection with The Friends School. He did not learn some essential information, such as why prospect Q made the one-time $5,000 gift; if prospect Q had a family member or friend who ever attended the school; or prospect Q's views about the school. Furthermore, Director John was so preoccupied with trying to look attentive during prospect Q's presentation of the next phase of the retirement villages that he failed to observe anything else in prospect Q's office. He never saw the pictures on his desk, the diplomas and awards on his walls, or the bronze sculpture pieces inside the curio. If he asked some open-ended questions about prospect Q's first gift, or commented on the awards or sculpture pieces, Director John would have gained invaluable knowledge about prospect Q. He would have gotten closer to his prospect, and it would have been easier for Director John to map out his next moves.

GETTING THE COMPLETE INFORMATION ABOUT YOUR PROSPECT ON THE FIRST VISIT

Whether you meet your prospects at their offices, in their homes, at your organization, or at a restaurant, there is a checklist of questions every fundraiser should carry with them on the first visit (see Exhibit 4–1). These are *open-ended questions* that will give the fundraiser essential information about the:

- Prospect
- Prospect's views on giving
- Prospect's views on your organization
- Prospect's family life
- Prospect's interests
- Prospect's volunteer activities

The answer to these questions will add valuable research to the donor profile and will give the fundraiser many topics to discuss during future meetings. The questions in the checklist are listed in order of importance. It is suggested that you review them before each visit.

The first question, why the prospect gives to your organization, is most important because it will let you know the prospect's connection with your organization. It is critical for you to know the prospect's reason or reasons for giving to your group because from that moment on, you will be designing your next steps and tailoring your ask to the prospect's interests. Sometimes fundraisers are quick to make assumptions about why the prospect supports the organization, and they never ask the question. For instance, while working for a hospital foundation, fundraiser Amy assumed that the prospect gave because he or a loved one had been a patient. When she asked the question, the prospect said, "A long time ago, you ran a television advertisement with a Polish girl who came to your hospital and received life-saving treatment. My wife is Polish, and the ad got to us!" Never in a million years would fundraiser Amy have guessed this as a reason for his support. This illustrates the importance of why you must ask prospects their reasons for giving to your

Exhibit 4–1 Checklist of Questions for the First Visit

1. Why did you give your first gift and/or later gifts to our organization?
2. Was this your decision or did you and other family members or friends decide together?
3. What do you like the most about our organization?
4. Is there a particular program, project, award, or scholarship fund that interests you most?
5. Do you know any of the organization's staff, board/committee members, volunteers, or other supporters?
6. Are there other organizations that you support?
7. Have you been to the organization, and if not, would you like to take a tour and meet some of our volunteers and staff?
8. Have you attended any of the organization's special receptions or special events?
9. Do you like receiving our mailings, and if so, do you like any one in particular?
10. Have you lived/worked in this geographic area a long time?
11. Have you always been in this line of work or did other jobs lead you to this point?
12. Do you have family in this area?

group. Once you have your answer, you can steer all your future cultivation and solicitation efforts in that direction. In the case of fundraiser Amy, the prospect was interested in the hospital's international pediatric program. From that time forward, fundraiser Amy could send the prospect every piece of information on the program. She could have some of the pediatric patients from abroad, as well as the nurses who cared for them, write letters to the prospect and his wife. Remember, if you only have time to ask your prospect one question, make sure it's "why do you support us?"

Once you have your answer, follow up with the question, "Is this something you decided, or is this a family decision?" This will let you know if you will be cultivating the prospect, the prospect and the spouse/significant other, the prospect and another family member, or the prospect and a friend. If you have just met with the prospect alone, and the prospect tells you that she and her husband decide on all their charitable gifts, then the next visit you set up must include both parties. To ignore one of the decision makers could jeopardize future gifts to your organization. Both parties should be present for future visits, and all invitations and mailings should be addressed to both of them. This will let your prospects know that you recognize how their charitable gifts are made and that the prospects will be treated with equal attention from you.

The next piece of information you need to find out is what the prospect likes most about your organization. It may be, "Its overall good work," "It's close to where I live, and I can see where my money goes," or "I like to help those who cannot provide for themselves." This question hones in on the prospect's emotional ties with your group and gives the fundraiser the opportunity to talk more about the success of the organization. Sometimes the prospect cannot answer that question on the spot, or they never really thought about it. It is up to the fundraiser to ask the next question, "Is there a particular program, project, or area of outreach that interests you?" This puts the prospect more at ease and gives the prospect some time to reflect on a few of your organization's accomplishments. These questions are also useful even if the prospect cannot respond. The fundraiser now has the chance to discuss the organization's past and present activities, which serves to update the prospect on new developments.

Sometimes the prospect's primary connection and continued connection with your organization is with a board member, committee member, executive director, staff member, volunteer, or another supporter. For instance, board members recruit friends to support the charity in which the member holds a board position. Likewise, volunteers are some of the best marketers for the charity, and they are able to "sell" the charity to many of their family members and friends. More often than not, these connections are strong and long lasting. They are the foundation for your prospect relationship. These relationships pave the way to solicit a gift from these prospects because they already favor your group and know and like someone connected with it. The way to find out if such a connection exists is to ask the open-ended question, "Do you know any of our leaders, board/committee members, staff, volunteers, or other supporters?"

If everything is going well at this point, and the prospect has more time to spend with you, ask the prospect if he or she has ever visited your organization. Try to get the prospect to give an approximate timeframe of when he or she visited the site. From there you can update the prospect on any new growth, internal and external, that has taken place since that time. For example, if the prospect has not been back to the local YMCA for several years, talk about the new equipment and any evening programs that the YMCA offers the surrounding neighborhood. If the prospect supports the local zoo, update the prospect on all the special exhibits, rare animals, and children's programs the zoo has had since the time of the prospect's last visit.

The natural next question is, "Have you attended any of our special events?" This will give you the opportunity to let the prospect know about past events and any upcoming events. It will also let you know if your prospect likes to attend certain events or prefers to skip them altogether. If your prospect seems interested in what your charity does to gather your supporters socially, now is your chance to find out which events he or she likes. You will also learn from this question which events do not interest your prospect. Here, again, you do not want to be making any assumption about your prospect's interests. For instance, if the prospect is an art historian/lecturer and you represent a museum, do not assume that the prospect would be naturally interested in supporting your guest lecturer series. The prospect may be interested in your senior arts program or a specific exhibit. Likewise, many college and university fundraisers have made the mistake of assuming most physical education majors would gladly go to a football game or basketball game with them. The reality is that while some do, others prefer a music event, a play, or alumni networking reception on campus. The key is to let prospects tell you their interests, then invite them to some of your organization's activities that match or come close to their interests.

One of the questions I find most helpful in gaining prospect insight is, "Do you like receiving our mailings, and if so, which ones?" You will be amazed at the variety of responses you will receive. You will find out if:

- They like receiving your mail.
- They think your organization is spending "their donations" on unnecessary mail.
- You mail too much or not enough.

> **Tip:** *Be conscious of the time spent with the prospect. When you set the appointment, you said you would make it BRIEF. If more than 20 minutes have passed, ask the prospect if you can spend additional time with him or her. If not, ask the prospect when and where you can meet again to continue discussing his or her interests with your group.*

- They do not get any information about your organization from the mailings.
- You send them mail that lists a deceased family member in the address.
- They like your response envelope or find it too confusing.
- They think the pieces are "too busy" or the print is not "large enough."
- They like, hate, or are neutral about your annual report, magazine, and newsletters.
- They do not want to receive any mail at all.
- They only want to receive certain mailings.
- Your organization is one of a "hundred requests" they get for donations.
- They only occasionally read what you send.
- They never read what you send.

At first this may seem like a question that would only be important to the direct mail development officer, but I assure you it is not. There is a wealth of information in these answers. For starters, now you know the image they have about your organization through direct mail. If prospects tell you that they do not read any of it or they really would prefer that you not send the literature, then the fundraiser must go back to the office and delete them from the mail list. This is not to suggest that they be taken off of the direct mail pieces that *ask for an annual gift.* They should only be deleted from lists that send your organization's other marketing materials. You can always bring these with you on future visits and give them to your prospects after your visit. Most prospects will read it if you "hand-deliver" them as opposed to sending them in "bulk mail." Again, it keeps the prospect–fundraiser relationship on a personal basis.

If the prospect tells you they like certain mailings, then the fundraiser has an excellent new cultivation tool. The fundraiser can write handwritten notes on those mailings that will bring the prospect one-step closer to your organization. If the prospect tells you the mailings should only come to him or her, under a different spelling of his or her name, or that your group keeps including a deceased person in the address, then the fundraiser must immediately correct that in the database at the office. Nothing turns off prospects more than if the organization spells their name incorrectly, or if the organization fails to correct the mistake after the prospect has brought it to their attention.

It tells them the organization "is too busy" to handle this simple matter and that the organization really does not care about *them.* This will most assuredly be a roadblock to your major gift fundraising efforts.

Asking the prospect about your direct mail pieces will also let you know the prospect's views on how your organization spends its money. One time a donor asked me, "Since you send several mailings throughout the year, how much of my donation actually was used by the charity for nonadministration costs?" Fundraisers must be prepared to answer this question and know the organization's administrative costs versus the amount spent by the charity for its intended purpose. Fundraisers can use this question to their advantage by telling the donor that the mailings keep your supporters well informed about the charity. Mailings can be an important educational service that the donors deserve and that your organization feels an obligation to provide. If during the conversation the fundraiser senses that the donor thinks the mailings are a "waste of the organization's money," then offer to take the donor off the extraneous mailing list. You will gain the respect of your prospects if you listen to their requests on which mailings they like to receive and follow through accordingly.

Prospects expect that you will listen to them and that you will take their concerns very seriously (Pearce and Kushner 1997, 165). If the fundraiser has been a good listener, prospects will be more relaxed and more comfortable. This translates into their willingness to answer the few questions you may have. Now is the time to casually talk about their family, where they live, and what jobs they have had over the years. The more at ease you are with asking the questions, the more likely they will be to treat this as a friendly conversation. A few suggested questions to ask at this time are:

- "Many of our donors come from this area. Have you lived here a long time?"
- "Do you still have family in this area, or are they living, working, or going to school in other areas or states?"
- "You seem to really like what you do. Have you had this job/company for many years?"

The purpose of asking these questions is that you need to know as much as you can about the prospect's family and employment history before you can ask for a major gift. You need to know about a prospect's children, stepchildren, grandchildren, and parents, including where they are and what they are doing. You need to know about the prospect's employment history, and if possible, any investments the prospect may have. These important facts will clue you in to the prospect's ability and propensity to make a major gift. If the prospect tells you that she is caring for her mother in a retirement home, her middle child is in her freshman year at a private college, and her oldest child and his family just moved in with her because he just lost his job, this will let you know that the prospect may not be in the best position at the current time to make a large gift. On the other hand, if the prospect tells you she owns a minor league baseball team, she has one child who is doing very well as artistic director for a regional opera company, and she has lived in her house for over 23 years, this will let you know that things are going well for the prospect and she may be ready to discuss major gift opportunities very soon.

Many fundraisers may feel uncomfortable asking these open-ended questions because it may appear as if they are "prying" into the prospect's personal life. If the questions are asked in the right manner as suggested above and delivered with sincerity, prospects will think that the fundraiser is just trying to get to know them better. This is an important conversation that you need to have with all your prospects. Without it you will not have the background facts necessary to formulate the right major gift ask.

If the fundraiser really has a hard time asking these questions, it is suggested that the fundraiser talk a little bit about why they work for the organization and share with the prospect a few personal background facts. For instance, the fundraiser could say, "I really like working for this charity because I grew up in this area. Over the years, I've seen what a tremendous difference it has made for financially needy families." This would give the fundraiser a smooth entry to ask the prospect, "Have you been in this area a long time?" If you are really committed to the organization you work for, this type of dialogue will come naturally. The key is to present yourself as a highly committed and dedicated fundraiser (Walton 1999, 3). Your commitment to your organization will instill confidence in your prospects that your group is strong, solid, and staffed with top-notch development professionals. This in turn will make it easier for you to discuss major gifts with them. There is an expression that I use, "Everyone likes to give to forward moving trains." Prospects and donors want to give to "the best charities," the ones that provide the best programs, are managed well, have strong leadership, and will be around forever (Smith 1997, 36). The more confidence and commitment you project on behalf of your organization, the more major gifts you will raise.

Tip: It is important on your first visit to tell the prospect a little bit about you, why you work for the organization, where you grew up, and experiences that have led you to your position. Remember, this is a conversation, not an interview. You will make the prospect uneasy if all you do is ask questions without sharing some information about yourself.

Always end the meeting by setting up your next meeting. You must keep your prospect involved. Suggesting a date, time, and place to meet next will keep the prospect cultivation process on track. If the prospects said they would like to see the organization, set up a date and time when they can come. If an event is coming up, and they expressed interest in attending, make sure you say that you will meet them there. You want the prospect to know that you are the main contact with the organization and that this was not a "one-time meeting–never see you again" event. If you have no event coming up, and it is clear that the prospect will see you only if you come to the prospect, say "I have really enjoyed getting to know you a little better, and I would like us to stay in touch. How about if we get together again very soon?" This will keep the prospect relationship going, and it will be very easy for you to call in a month or so to see the prospect again. When you get back to the office, mark in your personal calendar to call the prospect in one month to set up the next meeting.

OBSERVING EVERYTHING YOU CAN ON THE FIRST VISIT

In addition to asking the right questions on your first visit, it is equally important that the fundraiser *observe the prospects' surroundings.* Whether you see them at their homes or in their offices, it is important that you take the time to see and absorb as much as you can. Details about how they live and work, and how they chose to decorate and display cherished items, will give you further insight into your prospects. In the example of fundraiser John at the opening of this chapter, he never saw prospect Q's pictures, diplomas, or rare sculpture pieces in the curio. The meeting would have gone entirely different if fundraiser John said to prospect Q, "I see that you enjoy sculpture. They are great works of art. Where did you find these?" Fundraiser John may have found out that prospect Q travels quite a bit, and it is his hobby to collect rare art, or that his son made them for him. Fundraiser John could have also inquired about the pictures on prospect Q's desk, which may have revealed prospect Q's entire family tree. He would have known so much more about the prospect than he did before he walked through the door.

> *Tip: When inquiring about the prospect's pictures, do not assume that they are family members. Let the prospect tell you who the people are in the picture. Some prospects may be estranged from their families, and it may make them uncomfortable if you assume it is a family photo.*

If possible, it is always preferable to meet prospects at their home. You can learn so much about prospects from the location and contents of their homes. You can observe their decoration style, the types of books they like to read, the size of their home, their property, the kind of car they drive, their pets, and many more details (see Exhibit 4–2). At first it may appear that this is "background" information and that the fundraiser's real job is to focus on the conversation of promoting the charity. Nothing could be further from the truth. This information is as important as any discussion you will have with the prospects because you will learn as much, if not more, about them by observing their surroundings. This will clue you into how they live, what they value, and how they spend their leisure time. These facts will help you during the cultivation process, as well as when you are ready to prepare the major gift ask.

Here is an example of how meeting a prospect at home and observing the surroundings can lead to meaningful next steps with your prospects. Over the past few months, my boss and I visited a donor who was considering making another gift. During our prior visits, we always picked him up in the lobby of his retirement home and took him to lunch. He was a shy man who had few visitors. We thought that we would get closer to him if we took him out of his retirement community and spent some time with him over lunch. We heard about his activities of ordering videos for the library at the home and doing bookkeeping for some of the residents. This became routine after several visits, so my boss and I decided that the next time we saw the donor, we should meet with him at his apartment and not take him to lunch. We wanted to focus our meeting entirely on the donor's next gift and not get sidetracked

Exhibit 4–2 Prospect's Home or Office—Important Observations

1. Location, neighborhood, and size of the property
2. Type of cars or recreational vehicles
3. Hired help—nurse, housekeeper, landscaper, nanny, or au pair
4. Style of furnishings—contemporary, art deco, or rustic
5. Ramps or childproof devices
6. Objects on table tops and desks—paperweights, clocks, maps, brochures, picture albums, or cards
7. Objects on the floor—toys or tools
8. Pictures, art work, awards, or diplomas
9. Reading materials—books, magazines, newspapers, digests, newsletters, or brochures
10. Videos
11. Entertainment units and equipment
12. Computers
13. Pets
14. Hobbies—crafts, astronomy, performing arts, writing, reading, or choir
15. Recreational activities—tennis, swimming, golf, running, boating, fishing, hiking, skiing, bird watching, hunting, coaching, or volunteering

over lunch. We also wanted to learn more about him and how he lived. It was getting difficult to find new ways to keep the donor interested in the university, since he didn't drive, he didn't want to come back to campus, and he declined our prior invitations to university events.

We made an appointment to see him at his apartment. When I walked in, I saw his computer on a card table, with an unusual mouse pad. It was a picture of a small mouse singing away, with the words "Metropolitan Opera." I commented that I thought the mouse pad was clever, and asked if someone gave it to him. The donor told me he ordered it from the Metropolitan Opera and that he was a big fan of the opera. My boss and I immediately launched into a conversation about the university's upcoming black tie opera gala and invited the donor to attend. He accepted on the spot. We would have never known about the donor's interest in opera music if we had not visited with him in his apartment. This donor bonding made it very easy for us to find our next step with the donor. It also gave us an opportunity to make a smooth transition into the topic of the donor's next gift. The donor was more relaxed because we tapped into one of his major interests, the opera. During this same visit, the donor brought up the topic of his next gift and said that he would give it his top priority and get back to us soon. We would have never gotten this close to the donor had we not spent some time with him in his home.

Visiting a prospect at home can also give the fundraiser more complete information about the prospect's wealth. Observations of everything inside and outside the prospect's home can produce vital information for the donor profile. For instance, prior to her prospect appointment, Major Gifts Officer Megan reviewed Mr. Y's donor file. He lived in a semi-wealthy area, on a lake. Major Gifts Officer Megan knew that Mr. Y was a widower and that he retired about three years ago. Based on these facts, she estimated initially that Mr. Y may be a major gifts candidate for an outright gift of $25,000 or perhaps a charitable remainder trust in the nature of $100,000.

When Mr. Y greeted Major Gifts Officer Megan at the door, she noticed that the foyer contained many tools. She saw a crowbar, buckets of spackle, several hammers, screwdrivers, a leveler, and stacks of wood. She could have ignored what she saw and moved into the living room for her visit. If she did, she would have made some initial small talk, followed by an update on her charity and concluded with a request to visit again. The meeting would have gone very well, but Major Gifts Officer Megan would have missed some crucial prospect information.

Instead of moving right to the living room for the visit, Major Gifts Officer Megan said to Mr. Y, "Gee, it looks like you're having some construction done?" Mr. Y replied that his two sons and one brother were "giving him a hand *with the other houses.*" Major Gifts Officer Megan, now curious about that statement said, "Oh, you have other houses that you maintain?" Mr. Y then brought Major Gifts Officer Megan to the back of the house, away from the living room and showed her the lake in his backyard and several properties situated on the far side of the lake. "See those two houses on the end? I rent those and own the vacant lots on the opposite end," said Mr. Y. It turned out that Mr. Y and his family were fixing some windows in the two rental properties. Had Major Gifts Officer Megan not commented about the tools in the foyer, she would never have known about the additional properties and land that Mr. Y owned. Armed with this new information, she could begin to formulate a much higher major gifts ask when the time was right.

The fundraiser's observations during the initial visits are so important to building close ties with prospects. Assessing the prospect's wealth is just one part of the process. Learning about the prospect's life, family, business, health, hobbies, and interests is the other. These are the facts that you will want to remember for the duration of your prospect relationship. The goal is to treat each prospect *individually*, and these facts will let you make sure each prospect receives individual treatment. They will key you into the prospect's needs and interest in your organization, which in turn will guide you when you are ready to ask for the gift.

For example, while driving up to a prospect's home for a visit, Jake, Development Associate for a telephone crisis hotline, noticed a long concrete ramp leading up to the prospect's home. Once inside, he saw that all the furniture, cabinets, table, chairs, and countertops were all waist high. Development Associate Jake knew the prospect was not disabled, but upon introduction of her husband, he quickly learned that the husband had a disability. Had the meeting taken place at the prospect's office or at a restaurant, Development Associate Jake would have never known about the husband's disability. Development Associate Jake knew from these facts that the couple may be interested in hearing how the crisis hotline was instrumental in sending rescue crews to disabled people who needed aid. As it turns out, the couple was deeply empathetic to this cause and wanted to know how they could help. After explaining the various outreach programs and the benefits of each, the couple said they would give serious thought to supporting one of these services. Development Associate Jake set a date with the couple to meet two weeks later to further discuss "the prospective gift."

Not every observation or comment by the fundraiser will lead to a discussion of gifts, but it does make prospects feel "special." The mere fact that the fundraiser is devoting the time and attention on the prospects is flattering to them. It makes prospects feel that the fundraiser really cares about them as individuals, and not just as fundraising dollars. The key is to weave those observations into your conversation. Here is an example of how easy it is to get to know your prospect very quickly and to set up your next meeting.

While I was visiting a prospect at his home, he wanted to give me a grand tour. As we entered the kitchen, I saw that it was filled with spectacular culinary tools and state-of-the-art kitchen appliances. I asked the prospect, "Who is the gourmet chef?" He said it was his "hobby" to cook and that he loved to entertain relatives, friends, and neighbors. I told him that was a great hobby and that I would "love to take a lesson from him someday." On the spot, he invited me to come the following Saturday because he and his wife were entertaining friends from abroad. I told him I would come on one condition—that I could help him or at least watch him prepare any part of the meal. He agreed. Not only did I set up the next visit, I also had the chance to meet his wife and some of his close friends. One observation and one comment led to this great next step with the prospect. If you relax and enjoy the process of meeting, observing, and listening to prospects, they will want to see you again and again. It is this kind of "bonding with your prospects" that will lead to future major gifts.

ASKING FOR MONEY ON THE FIRST VISIT

One of the most frequently asked questions from fundraisers is, "Do you ask for money on the first visit, and if not, how many visits do you make before you ask?" Some fundraisers feel they need to do three in-person visits within one year before they ask for a major gift (Dickey 1997, 28). Others feel that if the donor made steady and increased gifts previously, the donor should be ready on the first visit for a major gift ask. There are several factors to consider before one can be sure that it is beneficial to the donor relationship to ask for a major gift on the first visit.

A past giving record may or may not be a good indication that the donor would be in a position to talk about a prospective major gift on the first visit. What if the organization never properly acknowledged the donor's gifts, or if the donor had to make several calls before the organization would send the right tax deduction letter? If the fundraiser prior to the visit just looked at the giving history without finding out if the gifts were properly acknowledged, the donor may be far from ready to discuss giving more money on the first visit.

> **Tip:** Past giving records should not be used as the only factor in determining whether to ask for a major gift on the first visit. Fundraisers need more information about the prospect before this determination can be made.

I visited a dentist who had made several gifts of $10,000 or more to the dental school. On his giving record alone, I thought he was a prime candidate to consider a $25,000–$50,000 endowed scholarship to the dental school. As soon as I was seated in his office, he told me the only reason he agreed to see me was so that I could let the dental school know that he would never give again. He told me he made gifts previously to support his school "in hopes that they would continue to accept the most qualified applicants that would enhance the school's reputation." Recently, his daughter had applied to the dental school. He called the dean and reminded him of his loyal gifts. Two months prior to my visit, the daughter was notified that she was not accepted at the dental school. The donor used our meeting to sound off his anger with the dental school. This example illustrates how a fundraiser should not use a donor's previous giving record as the sole reason for asking for a major gift on the first visit. Giving records can be misleading, and you need much more information and time to determine whether or not a prospect is ready to make a major gift.

Another factor to consider is whether the prospect contacted the organization or whether the fundraiser initiated the contact. If the prospect contacted the fundraiser for more information about major gifts or in response to the organization's major gift mailing, the fundraiser MUST be prepared to discuss in person the charity's giving opportunities on the first visit. In all likelihood, the prospect thought about making some kind of large gift well before your first meeting. Since the prospect contacted the organization, it is expected that the fundraiser will come prepared to answer questions and leave major gift options for the prospect to consider.

There are several strong arguments to be made in favor of *not asking for a major gift* on the first visit. This applies even if the prospect initiated the contact with the organization. At the first meeting, the fundraiser does not know the prospect well enough to match his or her interests with the right gift opportunity. The best and most successful major gift solicitations require that the fundraiser:

- Visit with the prospect a few times to learn the key link between the prospect and the organization.
- Educate the prospect about the organization and involve the prospect with the organization.
- Cultivate the prospect.
- Assess the prospect's giving level.
- Formulate the right gift proposal that matches the prospect's interests.

- Decide who would be the right person to do the ask.
- Decide when the prospect is ready to be solicited.

Furthermore, one meeting may not be enough time to build a rapport between the fundraiser and the prospect. Most major gifts are made *after* the prospect forms a solid and trustworthy relationship with the fundraiser and the charity's leaders. Large gifts require time, education, involvement, and preparation. They are usually done in person and followed up with a written proposal, marketing materials, and letters by the leadership of the organization (Edwards and Benefield 1997, 107). It is far better to ask for the gift when all of these elements are in place. Prospects deserve well thought-out and hand-tailored asks that will meet their specific needs and will fulfill their philanthropic aspirations. The fundraiser never wants to "shoot from the hip" when asking for a major gift. It certainly will appear that way if the fundraiser "jumps the gun," becomes overly zealous, and asks for a major gift on the first visit.

Most fundraisers on the first visit have the mind-set that they are there to learn as much as they can about the prospect, then plot and plan their next steps, which will lead to getting the major gift (Williams 1991, 38). Even though the prospect knows or has a hunch that you are there to get them to give to your charity, your primary goals are to:

1. Get closer to the prospect.
2. Listen to the prospect's opinions and concerns.
3. Learn as much as you can about the prospect's interests.
4. Set up the next meeting.
5. Plan your next moves.

On the first visit I *rarely* bring up the donor's prior gift record or ask the donor to increase his or her gift. I learned this the hard way. Upon my first visit with a donor in his nursing home, I referenced his prior gifts and asked him to double his gift. He quickly replied, "I thought you said when you called this wouldn't be about money?" The donor was right. When I called to make the appointment, he was extremely hesitant. I repeated on the telephone that I wanted to come to learn more about him and his views about the charity. In hindsight, I should have gotten to know him better, gained his trust, and then broached the topic of his increased gift. Also, I did not have enough background information about his family, his work, or his interests to know that doubling his gift would be the right ask. He could have owned and sold a major cable television station and had the assets to make a much higher gift. This illustrates why fundraisers should rarely ask for the major gift on the first visit.

On the flip side, it is always recommended that the fundraiser *be prepared* to discuss major gift opportunities with the prospect. Note, this is not the same as *asking* for a major gift. Instead, you are discussing your group's major giving programs and planting the seeds for the prospect to consider and reflect. Sometimes during a fundraiser's initial visit, the prospect will bring up the topic of gifts or the fact that they would "like to do more for the charity." That is an open door for the fundraiser to detail the benefits of each of the charity's gift vehicles. The fundraiser can follow up with probing questions like, "Did you have something specific in mind?" and "As I just described them, do any of these gift opportunities interest you more?"

In preparing for the possibility that the prospect will raise the issue of major gifts on the first visit, fundraisers should always take with them any written materials or videos on major gift opportunities. This way if the prospect brings it up, the fundraiser can quickly *describe and show* how each gift opportunity works. Pictures of people benefiting from your organization and brochures or videos that detail how your organization makes a real difference in the community are great marketing tools to further educate your prospects on your organization and to lay the foundation for a major gift.

CULTIVATION—WHAT IS IT? HOW DOES IT WORK?

Once a fundraiser has met the prospective donors and has learned about their interests, family life, and work experiences, it is time to plan individual cultivation strategies for each prospect. For development professionals, cultivation simply means planning steps to take to educate and involve your prospects with your organization so that they will make an investment in a particular program, project, or service that they care about deeply. Donor cultivation programs are essential for any nonprofit organization because they lead to big gifts (Warwick 2000, 244–245). Now you realize the importance of knowing the prospect's interest in your organization, as well as the importance of getting to know each prospect on an individual basis. Cultivation requires that you:

- Match the prospect's interests with your organization's ongoing activities, meetings, and events.
- Consistently call and visit your prospects.
- Send appropriate cards, letters, and informational materials to prospects.

The more creative and consistent you are with your cultivation moves, the more involved the prospects will be with your group. The goal is to get your prospects to the point where their education and involvement with your organization will naturally lead to a major gift (Schaff and Schaff 1999, 104).

Fundraisers must take the time to carefully plan a timeline for the series of steps to cultivate each of their prospects. Since the fundraiser is the primary contact for the prospect, it is the fundraiser's responsibility to coordinate and oversee all cultivation activities. Prospects who are on the top of your list should be given first priority. If a fundraiser is working with 100 prospects, the top 10 prospects must receive one cultivation move a month. The next group of prospects, 11–30, should be cultivated every six to eight weeks. Prospects 31–60 should be cultivated four or five times a year. The last 40 prospects should receive at least three contacts a year (Smith 1997, 35).

In order for all these cultivation moves to take place, the fundraiser must map out each move with each prospect over a one-year calendar. Start with your top 10 prospects and end with your last 40. Use your personal calendar system, discussed and illustrated in Chapter 2, to help you plan and schedule each cultivation move. (Chapter 9 will address how to track your prospect's involvement, solicitations, and gifts.) This may seem like an overwhelming task at first, but once you key into what each prospect likes about your organization, it will be easy to elevate his or her level of interest and involvement with the right cultivation moves. Exhibit 4–3 lists suggested ways to cultivate your prospects.

Bringing prospects to your site is an excellent cultivation tool. The prospects can meet your top leadership and see first hand your organization. To the extent possible, arrange ahead of time to have your prospect spend some time with your staff and volunteers.

Special events, such as award dinners, openings, lectures, walk-a-thons, concerts, athletic events, and film series, are great ways to keep your prospects active. Make sure that you attach a handwritten note to each invitation to let the prospects know that you thought enough not to "mass mail" the invitation.

Exhibit 4–3 Suggested Ways To Cultivate Your Prospects

1. Arrange a personal meeting with the executive director, president, or vice president, followed by a tour.
2. Send handwritten notes on all special event invitations.
3. Invite prospects to be a speaker or lecturer or to do a workshop.
4. Ask prospects to volunteer and to bring a friend to your fundraising events.
5. Visit with prospects in a variety of places, such as their homes or offices, a park, or a restaurant.
6. Ask their advice on a special project or program.
7. Send handwritten notes on all annual reports, brochures, or newsletters.
8. Have people who have benefited from your organization call your prospect.
9. Send newspaper clippings of special interest.
10. Feature your prospect in one of your publications.
11. Send birthday, anniversary, holiday, and congratulatory cards.
12. Take prospects out on their birthday or send a special gift.
13. Ask the prospect to host a small reception of special supporters at his or her home or office.
14. Ask prospects to serve on an advisory board or committee.
15. Ask prospects to introduce you to people they know who may be interested in your group.
16. Invite prospects to a game, concert, play, movie, or art opening unrelated to your organization.

Follow this up with a telephone call to make sure they received the invitation and to let them know how important it is to have them at the event. Let them know you will be there, and, if possible, sit near the prospects or have the prospects seated with your senior management.

Volunteer opportunities with your group, such as being a speaker or lecturer, participating in food and clothing drives, or serving on an advisory or auxiliary board or a committee, will increase the prospect's involvement and participation with your group. Be sure to send your prospects a thank you once they have committed to a volunteer activity.

Whenever your group has a fundraising event, ask your prospect to participate and to bring a friend. For instance, many prospects like to participate in walk-a-thons, bike-a-thons, honorary dinners, and galas. Bringing a friend will foster a strong relationship with your organization. It will also give you access to a new prospect.

Invitations to these special events and volunteer opportunities should be mixed with ongoing personal meetings between the fundraiser and the prospects. These meetings will serve to keep the relationship on a *personal basis* and will remind the prospects that they are important to the future of your organization. You must personally visit them from time to time so that you, as the primary contact, can keep them up to date on your organization, and they can let you know what is going on in their lives (Williams 1991, 33). It is best to visit them in a variety of places, such as their homes or offices, a park, or a restaurant, so that the meetings do not become mechanical and predictable. You will also learn more about your prospects if you see them in different environments.

Sometimes fundraisers forget to ask their prospects their views and advice on a new project or program. It is very easy to get caught up with invitations and events, which are excellent cultivation tools, but that will overlook your prospects' input into your organization. Do not run the risk of keeping the cultivation process one-sided, that is, the organization is on the inviting, active side, and the prospect is on the receiving, passive side. For example, if your organization is considering moving to a new location because you have outgrown your facility, ask your prospects how they feel about the prospective move. If you are launching a capital campaign to add a new day care center, ask your prospects how they feel about this decision.

Handwritten notes on marketing materials, such as annual reports, brochures, and newsletters, and telephone calls to your prospects from people who benefit from your organization will let your prospects know that you are focused on their needs and interests. It makes the prospects feel very special because you took the time to coordinate these thoughtful and heart-warming gestures. Newspaper clippings of articles that feature one or more of your prospects' interests will really show that you are thinking about your prospects all the time. For example, if your prospect loves to spend her free time in her boat with family and friends and you see an article about an upcoming boat show, clip the article and send it to her with a note saying, "Read this and thought of you. Are you going?"

If your newsletters or appeal letters spotlight interesting donors, such as a donor with an unusual hobby or a donor who has reached a milestone in his or her life or career, ask your prospects if you can feature them in one of your publications. For instance, a fundraiser for a college could use the alumni magazine to feature an alumni couple who got married while skydiving. A preservation group fundraiser could use a newsletter to feature a prospect who spent four weeks whitewater rafting. A social service fundraiser could use a brochure to feature a supporter who reached his or her 100th birthday or 35th year conducting the local choir.

Cards are also a terrific way to draw your prospects closer to your organization. Try to send your top prospects every holiday card and a birthday card. If you know that they received a promotion, or that they just became a grandfather, send them a congratulations card. If you know your prospects' anniversary date, send them a card. To the extent you have a miscellaneous budget to cover the expense, take your top donors out to lunch or dinner around their birthday, or send them a special gift that shows you know and appreciate their interests. For example, one of my top prospects was a doctor who loved to paint. For his birthday, I sent him a book on the relationship between art and medicine. The book showed that our organization knew he was a multi-talented person. Not only was he a well-respected physician, he was also an accomplished painter. He sent me not one, but two thank you notes. This small present brought him much closer to my organization. It said that he was special and important and that we thought about him as a friend, not just as a potential donor.

If your prospect has a terrific home or an office with a conference room, ask the prospect if they would host a small reception of special supporters. This will make the prospect feel that he or she is on the "top tier" of your organization's list of supporters. Be sure that the leadership of your organization is present and spends time with your prospect at this important event. It will give the prospect and the small group of other supporters a chance to get to know each other in a relaxed and informal setting.

Many prospects would like to be more active and to help out on a committee or board. It gives them the opportunity to participate with the success of current programs as well as to help guide the organization's direction for the future. Invite these prospects to serve on an advisory board or a committee in which your organization needs strength and new members. Many supporters like to do something more than just send a check. Your prospects may really enjoy having a "hands-on" approach to helping your group. Additionally, they will have the opportunity to meet new friends who have the common bond of liking your group well enough to offer their time and talent. For business prospects, it also gives them the opportunity to meet potential clients. This can be a real selling feature when you want to cultivate your top business prospects.

If the fundraiser has done several of the suggested cultivation steps listed previously, it may be the right time to ask your prospects if they know any friends or business colleagues who may be interested in supporting your organization. This is a cultivation move because now your prospects will have to reflect on the importance of your group, which draws the prospects closer. It also motivates your prospects to think of their inner circles of friends, business colleagues, and family who may be interested in supporting your group. Some prospects will always have a name or two to suggest. Sometimes they even invite these new friends on their own to one of your events. Others may not know anyone or do not wish others to know about their philanthropic activities.

> **Tip:** *Some prospects may feel uncomfortable giving names of some of their family, friends, or business colleagues to the charity, even if they think these people may be potential supporters. Fundraisers must always be sensitive to how the prospect feels about suggesting names of potential supporters and respect the prospect's wish to have their charitable activities remain private.*

Fundraisers can always invite their prospects to events that are unrelated to the charity's events. Fundraisers can scan the daily newspaper to find an event that is of particular interest to the prospect. This can be extremely helpful to organizations that do not conduct many events during the year. Fundraisers can use these outside events as cultivation tools to keep in good contact with their prospects. Suggested events include:

- Football, basketball, baseball, soccer, hockey, or lacrosse games
- Music concerts, recitals, plays, or movies
- Art exhibits, art lectures, or art classes
- Book signings or book readings
- Flower shows or arboretum tours
- Antique shows, flea markets, or estate sales

Here is an example of how a fundraiser for a city library who has a prospect that loves the library's rare book collection could cultivate the prospect using the library's events as well as outside events. Natural and logical cultivation steps would be to:

1. Invite the prospect to see the rare book collection.
2. Send every piece of literature on the rare book collection to the prospect with a handwritten note from the fundraiser or the library's senior management.
3. Ask the librarian who oversees this department to write the prospect a thank you letter for his or her support and interest in this important area of the library.
4. Ask the prospect if he or she collects rare books and which ones are of particular interest. Send the prospect an autographed rare book on that topic.
5. Invite the prospect to book readings and book signings held at your library as well as in local bookstores.
6. Set up a meeting between the executive director of the library and the prospect.
7. Ask the prospect what books he or she thinks should be added to the rare book collection.
8. Ask the prospect if he or she has family, friends, or colleagues who are also rare book enthusiasts who may be interested in supporting this "treasured area" in the library.
9. Send the prospect newspaper clippings about rare books and newly discovered first editions.
10. Invite the prospect to an estate sale where the seller has an extensive library or is a known author.

Fundraisers must keep in mind during their cultivation activities that cultivation *takes time and that it lasts throughout the lifetime of the donor relationship.* It does not end when the prospect is contemplating making the major gift. It does not end when the prospect makes the gift. It does not end when the prospect has made the first gift. Numerous organizations make the mistake of letting their cultivation efforts fall to the back burner or end once the gift proposal is delivered. It is equivalent to "dropping your prospects," and no one knows it more than your prospects. Put yourself in their shoes. If you have come to enjoy some thoughtful personal calls, letters, special invitations, and visits from an organization, then suddenly it all stops, how would you feel? Like the organization is not as sincere as it made itself out to be? That all they were interested in was your money? Your cultivation moves should continue on the same steady basis as you originally planned, until the prospect tells you he or she will not make a gift EVER, and they do not want to see you or anyone from your organization. Chances are you will not hear this often. In fact, since these are your organization's top prospects, and if you have properly educated and involved them with your cultivation moves, it is more likely that the prospect in time will make a gift. This emphasizes the importance of maintaining a consistency with your cultivation steps.

JUDGING THE PROSPECT'S READINESS TO MAKE A MAJOR GIFT

If the prospect has been sufficiently educated and involved, has the assets, and has demonstrated a willingness to make a gift, then the time is right to make the ask. With some prospects, this will be an easy task to decipher; with others, it will be more difficult. There is no magic formula that spells out the time period or number of cultivation moves that need to be made before it is time to make the ask. Rather, the fundraiser must make this determination by considering each prospect individually. In most instances, the fundraiser is the primary contact between the prospect and the organization and has conducted most of the cultivation moves. In those instances, it is the fundraiser's call on when the prospect is ready to be solicited (Williams 1997, 358).

There are a number of factors a fundraiser can use as a guide to judge prospects' readiness to make a gift (see Exhibit 4–4). The most obvious is to look at the prospects' giving record. If prospects have made steady increases to their gifts each year, there have been sudden and dramatic gift increases in the current year from the past year, and all the past gifts were in the major gift range, then the prospects may be ready to entertain a hand-tailored gift proposal. Make sure that the donors' prior gifts were properly acknowledged and that the donors received the appropriate recognition for their level of giving.

Another factor to consider is whether the prospect contacted the organization about major gift opportunities or whether the prospect was identified and cultivated by the fundraiser. Many times charities send out mailings advertising their gift opportunities that contain either a toll-free telephone number to call or a mail-in tear-off form to send for more information. If this is the case, then the prospect may be further along

Exhibit 4–4 Factors To Consider in Judging a Prospect's Readiness To Make a Gift

- Has the prospect made gifts previously?
- Do the gifts fall within the major gift range?
- Has the donor received proper stewardship for the prior gifts?
- Did the prospect contact the organization or did the fundraiser contact the prospect?
- Has the prospect been sufficiently educated and involved with the organization?
- Does prospect research or prior personal meetings indicate the prospect has the means to make the gift?
- Does prospect research or personal meetings indicate the prospect wants to make the gift?
- Does the organization have enough prospect information to determine the amount and purpose of the solicitation?
- Is there a well thought-out gift proposal for the prospect that connects his or her interest to the gift opportunity?
- Has the prospect been successfully and consistently cultivated by the organization?

on the readiness scale to make a gift.

A prospect must be educated to the point in which he or she could be a fundraiser or volunteer for your group. If the prospect asks about the progress and success of certain programs, services, or campaigns or wants to be updated on a regular basis about your group's new direction or initiatives, then in a short period of time, the prospect will be educated enough to be a spokesperson for your group. This in turn may signal that the prospect is ready to entertain a major gift ask (Goettler 1996, 42).

A prospect's involvement level can be another good factor to use when judging major gift readiness. If the prospect knows your cycle of special events, meetings, and activities; actively participates; and on some occasions volunteers or brings new prospects; the prospect's level of involvement would be considered high. Even with this involvement, some prospects require months and years of this type of cultivation before being ready to make a gift. Others will require less time. Each prospect is different, which is why you need to be aware of individual involvement activities.

The prospect must have the *assets and be willing* to invest these assets in your organization. Both of these elements must exist before the prospect can make the major gift. The prospect could have more than enough assets to make the gift, but if the prospect has no desire to part with them at this time, then the prospect is not ready. The prospect could have the desire to invest in your organization but is not in a financial position to do so at this time, then the prospect is not ready.

It is critically important that the fundraiser know through prospect research, personal meetings, or peer screenings the amount of the prospect's assets that could be used to make a gift. You need this information in order to pitch the right gift level during the solicitation process. This is much different from knowing the prospect's total financial portfolio. The prospect may have the capacity to make a million-dollar investment but has numerous financial commitments that would make a million dollar ask out of the question.

If after examining all of these readiness factors, the fundraiser determines that the time is right to make the ask, the fundraiser must be sure to have the right gift proposal that includes the prospect's main interest in the organization. A prospect may be ready to make an endowed gift to ensure the organization's future but would never be ready to make an outright gift that supports one specific program. If you have done your cultivation work, you will know exactly what the prospect would want to support once the time is right.

Keep in mind that these are only *factors for you to consider* when you think a prospect may be ready to make that significant investment with your group. The bottom line is that the prospect will give *when the prospect is good and ready*, and when they feel it is the right time (Bates 1988, 55). Sometimes this will be easy for you to know, while other times you may be quite unsure. Fundraisers in either circumstance are encouraged to consult with senior management and development coworkers, and board members and volunteers where appropriate, to determine the prospect's readiness. The more development expertise that is involved in judging the prospect's readiness, the more likely your organization will ask the prospect for a major gift when the time is right for the prospect.

RECAP AND REVIEW

1. Try to meet prospects at their homes or offices, as opposed to a restaurant or your office.
2. Review the first visit checklist of questions before meeting the prospect.
3. Use open-ended questions that suggest that the fundraiser is genuinely interested in the prospect. Avoid using a tone that suggests you are prying or conducting an interview.
4. Make sure the prospect tells you why he or she supports your group and his or her main interest in your group.
5. Find out the prospect's views on your organization's mailings and follow up with any request by the prospect to correct a name/address or to be deleted from extraneous mailings.
6. Share your fundraising background and reasons why you work for your organization with the prospect.
7. Always set up the next meeting with the prospect before you leave the first meeting.
8. Observe every detail in the prospect's home or office and weave those observations into the conversation.
9. Be prepared on the first visit to discuss all of the organization's giving programs and gift vehicles.
10. In most instances, asking for a major gift will not occur on the first visit, but be prepared if it does happen.
11. Avoid being overly zealous to get the major gift by asking for it prematurely.
12. Ask for the major gift when the prospect is educated, interested, involved, and ready and when the fundraiser has the right gift opportunity that will match the donor's interest.

REFERENCES

Bates, M. 1988. Advanced fund raising endeavors. In *Getting started: A guide to fund raising fundamentals.* Chicago: National Society of Fund Raising Executives.

Dickey, M. 1997. Taking time to secure large gifts. *Chronicle of Philanthropy*, 24 July.

Edwards, R., and E. Benefield. 1997. *Building a strong foundation: Fundraising for nonprofits.* Washington, DC: NASW Press.

Goettler, R. 1996. Announcing the "Four Ws" of major gift solicitation. *Fund Raising Management*, April.

Pearce, E., and R. Kushner. 1997. Making the face-to-face visit. In *Planned giving: Making IT happen.* Vol. II. Toronto, ON: Strategic INK Communications Ltd.

Schaff, T., and D. Schaff. 1999. *The fundraising planner.* San Francisco: Jossey-Bass Publishers.

Smith, P. 1997. Managing a successful major gifts program. *New Directions for Philanthropic Fundraising,* no. 16.

Walton, C. 1999. The psychology of major gift. *Fund Raising Management*, February.

Warwick, M. 2000. *The five strategies for fundraising success.* San Francisco: Jossey-Bass Publishers.

Williams, J. 1991. *Big gifts.* Rockville, MD: Taft Group.

Williams, J. 1997. Overview of major giving. In *The nonprofit handbook: Fund raising*, ed. James M. Greenfield, 368–369. New York: John Wiley and Sons.

SUGGESTED READINGS

Brehmer, D., ed. 1996. *Communicating effectively with major donors.* San Francisco: Jossey-Bass Publishers.

Burlingame, D., and J. Hodge, eds. 1997. *Developing major gifts.* San Francisco: Jossey-Bass Publishers.

Making sure your personal visit program works. 1998. *National Fund Raiser*, October.

Stevenson, S., ed. 1996. Setting the appointment. In: *Solicitation skills builder.* Sioux City, IA: Stevenson Consultants, Inc.

Chapter 5
Preparing the Right Gift Proposal

CHAPTER OUTLINE

- Creating Hand-Tailored Gift Opportunities
- Components of an Effective Gift Proposal
- Gift Proposals by Letter
- Gift Proposals Formal, Yet Personal
- Gift Proposals That Include a Planned Gift
- Recap and Review

What motivates me the most in my giving is knowing that it will help someone get the tools they need to become an equal participant in our society. Whether it be understanding their rights, and testifying in a city council meeting; asking for improved schools for their children from their school board; or protesting against lack of emission standards at a local factory, I want my money to help those people to speak up and be heard.

Diane Feeney, 32, President, French American Charitable Trust,
daughter of billionaire, Charles F. Feeney

CREATING HAND-TAILORED GIFT OPPORTUNITIES

Any major gifts proposal, whether it be verbal or in writing, must be tailored specifically for each prospect. This important part of the major gifts process requires a great deal of time and attention. Fundraisers must reflect on the entire prospect relationship, including all conversations, meetings, site visits, and personal visits the fundraiser and others from the organization have had with the prospect. Now is the time to pull in all the facts you and others know about the prospect so that you can suggest a major gift that will hone in on the prospect's connection with your organization and the prospect's key interests and motivations to give.

In order to shape the right major gifts proposal for each prospect, there are several questions fundraisers must answer:

1. What is the prospect interested in supporting?
2. Can the organization match the prospect's interest with an existing gift opportunity?
3. What is the prospect's gift range?
4. What gift vehicle would be best for the prospect?
5. Has the prospect been targeted/solicited by another department/person in your organization?

The Prospect's Interests

At this point in the prospect relationship, the fundraiser and/or others, such as senior management, a board/committee member, or a volunteer, have met and spent time with the prospect. There should be a clear idea of the prospect's top interests and priorities. If the organization has listened to the prospect's reasons for giving as well as his or her preferences on how to utilize the gift, then the organization will be ready to suggest an appropriate gift plan (Mammone 1996, 10). In many instances, during the cultivation steps, fundraisers have taken the time to discuss informally the type of gift and the amount of the gift the prospect would like to make in the future. These are sometimes called pre-solicitation conversations. During these conversations, the prospect shares ideas on what he or she would like the gift to support, such as:

- The overall good work of the charity
- A specific program
- A specific service
- A department
- New equipment
- Technical supplies
- A special campaign

For instance, during a site visit of a senior services organization that cares for the infirm, a prospect tells fundraiser Jim that she feels it is really important that the elderly have access to the latest physical therapy programs. Later in their conversation, fundraiser Jim learns of the prospect's struggle with a nursing home over the proper care of her late aunt. The prospect felt that the home did not give her aunt the right physical therapy that would have made a tremendous difference in her aunt's quality of life. Fundraiser Jim now knows how to shape his future gift proposal to this prospect. It must include a gift to the organization's physical therapy center.

For the most part, during your cultivation visits prospects will reveal if they want to give their gift to a specific area or program. Their deep sense of commitment and "need to give something back" comes through as you get closer and more involved with your prospects. All prospects like to see tangible benefits of their gift, and there is no better way to do this then to invest it in a specific project or program. This is why it is so important for the fundraiser to know their prospects' motivation to make the gift and their ideas on what they would like to support.

Some prospects, however, may not have a preconceived idea of how they would like their gift spent, and this will require more effort on the fundraiser's part. This is a golden opportunity for the fundraiser to consider the organization's needs and funding priorities. For example, if a prospect wants to make a major gift to the hearing-impaired society but has no clear idea how the gift should be targeted, the fundraiser has an open door to suggest the organization's funding priorities. If the organization needs money for volunteers to learn sign language, the fundraiser can discuss the details of the program. If the fundraiser spoke about the program previously and perhaps even brought the prospect to the organization, the fundraiser could introduce the prospect to the people who would train the sign language volunteers as well as the volunteers. It gives the prospect the chance to interact with the future recipients of the gift and to witness how beneficial the gift will be for these deserving people. It makes the gift process an engaging and energizing event, rather than a cold and clinical process. It makes the prospect realize that if the gift is made, the prospect will become a very significant owner and investor in the organization. Once you have the prospect thinking in this direction, you will be very close to securing the gift.

Tip: If the prospects are open to suggestions from the fundraiser on the best use of their gifts, make sure that the prospects are given a few choices along with the organization's top funding needs. This way the prospects have a few options to consider, and the prospects will not feel that the organization is "strong-arming" them to make a certain gift.

The Match between the Prospect's Interest and a Gift Opportunity

Sometimes the prospects' interests are obvious and a natural extension of their fondness for the organization. An alumna from a university who received a scholarship when she was a student may want to make her gift to a scholarship fund. A prospect who was raised by a single parent may want to give to a children's family services after-school program. A minority farmer who received financial aid from a land assistance fund may want to target his gift to the fund's minority farmer loan assistance program. These are a few examples of how it can be a very simple, but important, task to match the prospect's interest with an organizational need.

It is always tempting for a fundraiser to try to fit the prospect's interest into an existing gift opportunity, even if it seems like a "stretch" at first. I highly recommend that you take some time and really think about this crucial step in the major gifts process. You can wind up spending a great deal of time convincing and selling your gift idea to your prospect, when the time might be better spent focusing on the prospect's interest and using your creativity to find a better match. For instance, while working for a university, I had a prospect who was an education graduate. He wanted to make a major gift, but not necessarily to the school of education. Right from the start it would have been very easy for me to spend some time with the prospect convincing him that the school of education had several worthwhile programs that he could support. Instead, I spent the time listening and learning that what he cared about most was educating and helping children. His family foundation often supported unique learning programs for youths in third-world countries. As a university, we had several comprehensive student internship programs in which our students taught children, but he felt that was not unique. He said if I could come up with something different, some other service of educating children besides our student intern programs, he would consider a gift proposal.

I met with the dean and several department heads to brainstorm on what we could offer the prospect. This process took months and much investigative work until we felt that we had the right gift opportunity. The university had a center for intergenerational learning that participated in a pilot program to mobilize teams of senior citizen volunteers to teach reading to inner city elementary schools. During the pilot program 72 trained senior citizen volunteers provided one-on-one tutoring several times a week to more than 360 children in kindergarten through second grade. These were students who came from very impoverished areas of the city and who tested to be "at-risk" to fail at reading.

The reading skills of the students markedly improved, and the parents of the students began book club meetings so that they could be more involved with their children's education. The senior citizen volunteers had a tremendous impact, not only on the lives of the elementary school children, but also on the quality of life for their families. The program was a great success and received national attention.

The pilot program was targeted to expand to more schools, provided that it could receive private support. To date the project was funded by the government and foundation support. I knew that there was an area of the city from which the prospect was most interested in helping children because it was where he was raised. I asked the program directors if the project could be expanded to include this area with private support. They agreed. I now had the right gift proposal for the prospect. It matched his desire to educate children in a unique way, in an area of the city that he wanted to improve. It also fulfilled his desire to do something for the university where he received his education. It gave him a way to give something back to children who needed it the most. The gift idea did not come easily, but it was well worth the time and effort. This is just one example that it may require "going the extra mile" before you can find just the right gift opportunity for your prospect.

> **Tip:** *Avoid the temptation to "pigeonhole" the prospect's interests into an existing gift opportunity. Spend time exploring different ideas and collaborative projects before you select a gift opportunity for your prospect.*

If the prospect's interests do not match an existing gift opportunity at the organization, it gives the fundraiser a chance to work with the leadership of the organization in an effort to expand and enhance existing programs. For example, let's say you are the fundraiser for an Asian arts center that offers art classes, programs, and exhibits, as well as theater productions. Your prospect loves everything about the center, except the fact that it does not encompass enough of dance, which is her primary interest. Your prospect studied dance in college and was the choreographer for a regional dance company. You know that the only way you can secure this gift is if you can show the prospect that the center has a continuing commitment to include dance.

Now is your chance to work with the leadership of your organization and volunteers to come up with some original ways to meet the prospect's interests. You might inquire:

1. If the center would let the prospect teach a special dance class or two on a weeknight when there were no rehearsals or productions.
2. If the center had any plans to do a joint production that would include dance.
3. If any upcoming theater productions would be predominantly dance.

This would show the prospect that the center has an important and evolving dance program, and that her major gift is needed to ensure the future growth of the program. It also shows the leadership of your organization, volunteers, and coworkers that with a little creativity and some thinking outside the existing categories of gift opportunities, the organization can reap the big benefits.

The Prospect's Gift Range

In addition to knowing your prospects' ideas on where they would like their gifts to be used, it is equally important that the fundraiser, or fundraising team, know the *gift range for each prospect*. If the prospect has been properly cultivated, this information should be apparent. For instance, during the presolicitation discussions with a prospect who wants to support an animal shelter, fundraiser H mentioned that the organization needs $150,000 to open a new animal shelter site. Fundraiser H took the prospect to see the proposed site and introduced the prospect to the executive director and the staff at the shelter. Fundraiser H and the prospect discussed in detail over several meetings how the new site was chosen and why it was needed. The prospect said that he always wanted to do something for animals. He had some "old stock" and wanted to avoid capital gains on it. During these discussions, fundraiser H learned that the prospect's stock was valued in the $150,000–$175,000 range. This was a clear indication to fundraiser H that the prospect had the capacity and motivation to make a gift in the $150,000–$175,000 range, and that he could comfortably suggest a major gift of this size.

Keep in mind that when you are deciding on the suggested gift amount for the prospect, err on the high end (Stevenson 1996, 27). This is not to say that one should go way beyond the gift range. Rather, it will be more beneficial to your organization if you start on the higher end of the range. In the example above with fundraiser H and the new animal shelter, fundraiser H should ask for a $175,000 gift because that is the top end of the anticipated gift amount. If she asked for $150,000, that's all she may get. It is a rare instance that the prospect would come back and say to fundraiser H, "Oh, you asked for $150,000 but you should have asked me for $175,000!"

> **Tip:** *If you know the prospect's gift range, always ask for the gift at the top level of that range. It is much harder to work your way up to a higher gift once you have suggested a lower gift level.*

Even if you know all you can about the prospect's wealth and disposable assets through your cultivation efforts and prospect research, you may still have to probe the prospect to find out the approximate size of the gift the prospect would make (Lawson 1996, 46). If you think the prospect can make a $250,000 gift, talk about gifts other donors have made in this gift range. Watch the prospect's body language and listen to the prospect's remarks about the size of the gift (Williams 1991, 40). If the prospect seems really uncomfortable or is so thrilled that *others* support your group at this outstanding level, the prospect may not consider himself or herself a quarter of a million dollar donor. On the other hand, the prospect may not react at all and be at ease discussing gifts in this range. You need to find the size of the gift that will make the prospect comfortable about the gift, otherwise the gift idea may be rejected immediately, or worse, you may not get a major gift at all. When in doubt, simply ask the prospect, "We thought you would be interested in making a gift in the $250,000 range?" This will give the prospect the opportunity to let you know the approximate size gift he or she would consider giving. It opens the door to further presolicitation discussions about the size of the prospective gift.

The Right Gift Vehicle

Once you know the prospect's interests, and you've matched those interests with a gift opportunity at an appropriate gift level for the prospect, it is time to consider the right gift vehicle. Gift vehicles include an outright gift, in which the prospect funds the gift with cash, securities, insurance proceeds, retirement benefits, or family foundation grants; personal and real property; a planned gift such as a gift annuity, charitable trust, pooled income fund, or life insurance; or the blend gift that consists of an outright gift and a planned gift (Barrett and Ware 1997, 35). If you know that your prospect has assets such as stock that can be used for charitable gifts, then suggesting an outright gift may be just right for the prospect. However, what if the prospect would like to use these assets to make the gift, but needs the gift to produce some extra income? An outright gift could not fulfill the prospect's financial need for an income-producing gift.

Each prospect has different assets to give, as well as to use as a means of support. Fundraisers must analyze the prospect's financial situation very carefully before suggesting how the prospect should make the gift. Exhibit 5–1 lists several financial factors to consider before suggesting a gift vehicle.

All four questions in Exhibit 5–1 must be considered at the same time. Let's use the example of a prospect who wants to make a $50,000 stock gift to a foster care agency. The first question the fundraiser

Exhibit 5–1 Selecting the Right Gift Vehicle

1. What assets will the prospect use to make the gift?
2. Are the assets available now or at a later time?
3. Is the prospect seeking to avoid or reduce income, capital gains, and/or estate taxes?
4. Does the prospect need the gift to produce income?

must ask is if the prospect wishes to transfer the stock now or wait until a certain period when the prospect will be ready to make the transfer. Many major gifts prospects keep a careful watch of their stock portfolios, and they know exactly when they are willing to buy, sell, trade, liquidate, or transfer the stock. If the stock market is very good, and the stock has appreciated significantly, the prospect may want to transfer the stock to the foster care agency at this peak period to maximize on the size of the gift and to avoid capital gains tax. Conversely, if the market takes a down turn, and the stock depreciates, the prospect may want to hold onto the stock until the market rebounds. This illustrates the importance of knowing the type of asset that will be used to fund the gift as well as the timing of when the asset can be used to make the gift.

It is important that you communicate to your organization how and when your prospects' major gifts will be made so that your organization has a good idea on the gifts it can count on for special projects or campaigns, as well as those that are projected to come in at a later time. This will ensure that funding goals for any project, program, or campaign stay on track. For instance, if the prospect cannot make the $50,000 stock gift to the foster care agency until the stock appreciates in value, then the foster care agency should not count on this gift to fund any immediate project or program. In fact, it may take so much time that the stock gift might not be included in the yearly fundraising goal. In this example, the fundraiser should continue to work with the prospect, and the gift would be targeted to fund an institutional need at a later time. Major gifts fundraisers must be particularly aware of this important communication task because it directly impacts on the progress of the institution's overall fundraising goals.

The final piece to the gift vehicle puzzle is finding out if the prospect needs the gift to produce income for the prospect or another beneficiary. In the example of the stock gift to the foster care agency, if the prospect

is making the gift with appreciated securities and is just looking for an income tax deduction and a way to avoid the capital appreciation on the stock, then giving the stock outright would accomplish those financial goals. If, however, the prospect needs the stock gift to supplement his or her income, then the fundraiser should suggest that the stock be used to fund a charitable gift annuity, charitable trust, or pooled income fund. These planned gifts would give the prospect an income tax deduction, avoidance of capital gains on the stock, and a stream of income. In some instances, it may even reduce the size of an estate, and thereby reduce the estate tax (Barrett and Ware 1997, 48). (See *Suggested Readings* at the end of this chapter for more information on planned gifts.) The bottom line is that the major gifts fundraiser must listen to the prospect's financial needs then assist the prospect with selecting the right gift vehicle that will benefit the prospect and the organization.

For example, a prospect in his mid 70s wanted to give the Boy Scouts a gift in the nature of $125,000. In his youth, the prospect was a boy scout and felt that this experience was one of the best things he ever did in his life. The prospect's sister died recently, and he received the $125,000 from her estate. He told fundraiser Steve from the Boy Scouts that while he wanted to give them $125,000, he really wouldn't mind having just a little extra cash each year.

Fundraiser Steve suggested a variety of ways to meet the prospect's philanthropic interest as well as his financial goals. He suggested that since the prospect was in his mid 70s, he could establish a charitable gift annuity with the $125,000. With a charitable gift annuity, the prospect would irrevocably gift the $125,000 to the Boy Scouts. At his age the charitable gift annuity would pay him approximately 8.2 percent a year, the rate suggested by the American Council on Gift Annuities (Andersen 1999, 160). The prospect would receive this fixed dollar amount for his lifetime, and at his death, the Boy Scouts would receive the remainder of the trust. For tax purposes, the prospect's income stream in this example would be divided into two parts: (1) a tax-free part, since part of this income is considered a return on principal; and (2) an income-taxed part, since the gift would be made with cash (Barrett and Ware 1997, 41).

Fundraiser Steve told the prospect to consult with a tax attorney. Depending on his income and the size of his estate, he may be entitled to take an income tax deduction of $125,000 and possibly reduce his estate by $125,000 to avoid estate taxes.

While the prospect liked this idea, he was concerned that he would have to pay income taxes on part of the 8.2 percent income that he would receive from the charitable gift annuity. At his age, he had very little income and worried that it would not be enough to cover the tax he would owe on part of the 8.2 percent supplemental income. He asked if there were some other way that he could make the gift and receive an income at a slightly lower level. Fundraiser Steve suggested a charitable remainder annuity trust. This trust pays a fixed income stated in percentage set by the donor at the time the trust is created. It must be at least 5 percent of the initial trust assets. This type of trust is very attractive to older prospects who want a fixed payment over a number of years. The fixed payment can be set for the lifetime of one or more beneficiaries, or it can be set for a period of years. When the last beneficiary dies, or at the end of the set period of years, the charity receives the remainder (Clifford and Jordon 1996, 7, 20).

Knowing that the prospect wanted only a small stream of income, fundraiser Steve suggested a 5 percent charitable remainder annuity trust. The trust would generate a fixed income at 5 percent of the trust assets that would give the prospect a slightly lower rate of income than the gift annuity. Again, depending on the prospect's income and size of the estate, the annuity trust could reduce the prospect's income tax and estate taxes. After the prospect met with his attorney and financial advisor, the prospect decided to establish a $125,000 charitable remainder annuity trust with the Boy Scouts. The charitable remainder annuity trust was the best gift vehicle to meet the prospect's financial needs while accomplishing his desire to make a major gift to the Boy Scouts.

Many organizations place a heavy hand on fundraisers to ask for the outright gift first and then ask for a planned gift as a fallback position. It is no secret that groups need the money now, not at some time in the distant future, to carry out the organization's mission and to fund special projects and programs. Fundraisers should, whenever possible, ask for the gift outright first, *if an outright gift would be appropriate for the prospect*. You will know if a prospect is a candidate for an outright gift if you and/or others from your organization have discussed this with the prospect and the prospect is willing and able to make all or part of the gift outright.

For example, fundraiser C was working with a prospect who wanted to donate his vacation home in Colorado. The property, in a ski resort community, was valued at over $300,000. Fundraiser C knew that the prospect did not have $300,000 cash or securities to give to the organization and that the property was the prospect's only means to make a major gift to the group. In this instance, asking the prospect to make an outright gift in the range of $300,000 would be totally inappropriate.

A change in the facts would yield different results. If fundraiser C knew that the prospect could donate the property and that the prospect had made several wise investments that yielded large returns, fundraiser C could ask the prospect to consider making an outright gift of stock, together with the gift of property. This would enable the organization to use the outright gift for immediate purposes and the donated property for a charitable purpose in the future. This is an attractive gift package to prospects who want to see immediate benefits of their gifts, while at the same time, want to ensure the continued good work of the organization.

> *Tip:* *When considering the right gift vehicle for a prospect, the prospect's financial needs come before organizational funding needs. While an outright gift always makes the best major gift for the organization, it may or may not be the best gift vehicle for the prospect.*

Competing Proposals and Conflicting Ideas for Prospects

The final point to consider when preparing a gift proposal for a prospect is whether there may be a competing proposal within your organization for this prospect or whether the prospect has been targeted to make a gift to a special project or campaign (Dunlop 1993, 114). This is true no matter what size organization you represent. A development director for a university's business school may be ready to ask a prospect for a gift for an endowed scholarship, while at the same time, the university's central major gifts officer may be targeting the same prospect for an outright gift to the university. A director of a local hospice agency may think it is time to ask a prospect for an outright gift of $75,000, while the president of the hospice board may be targeting that same prospect to make a leadership gift during the silent phase of an upcoming campaign. The key here is to have open communication about prospects among all departments *and* the organization's top leaders and volunteers.

Many organizations have staff meetings and top prospect meetings with the development directors and department heads, but fail to include or inform on a regular basis the executive director, key board members, or the president of the organization. This is chemistry for disaster. I know of several fundraisers who have had to withdraw their gift proposals to their prospects because the organization wanted to "save" those prospects for a larger campaign. While this can happen in any size organization, it especially holds true for larger organizations and nationally based organizations. It is very difficult to keep all front line fundraisers, staff, organizational leaders, board/committee members, and volunteers fully informed about the progress and readiness of major gifts prospects. However, if everyone from the organization participates in monthly meetings or conference calls or receives monthly reports on major gifts prospects, an organization of any size will protect itself from competing with itself to secure major gifts. Additionally, if fundraisers who are working with major gifts prospects routinely input their prospect information in their computer software programs, all prospect information will be accessible to key fundraisers in the organization (Dunlop 1993, 115–116). This will keep everyone in the organization fully apprised of who is working with each prospect as well as the progress on anticipated gifts. It should avoid, or at a minimum alleviate, the dilemma of having two fundraisers working on the same prospect for different major gifts.

COMPONENTS OF AN EFFECTIVE GIFT PROPOSAL

Unlike a gift proposal to a corporation or a foundation for a grant, a major gifts proposal to an individual is *extremely personal*. No two proposals are ever alike. It entails tying together all the facts you and others have gathered during your cultivation efforts and fashioning the best gift plan for each prospect. Gift proposals usually occur in two stages. The first stage takes place throughout the course of your cultivation moves, when you are informally discussing the amount, purpose, and timing of the gift. During this stage, the fundraiser sketches in his or her mind the type of proposal the prospect should receive when the time is right. In some instances, a draft of the proposal is given

to the prospect for comments and questions, then is later refined and presented at the formal ask. The second stage of the gift proposal is this final presentation of a written document or letter of understanding that codifies the terms of the gift opportunity.

During the first stage of the gift proposal process, there are certain elements that must be thoroughly discussed by the prospect and the fundraiser well in advance of any written gift proposal (see Exhibit 5–2). This is an exploratory phase where the fundraiser must get the prospect to express any feelings, motivations, opinions, or expectations about the gift. It is also the time to get the prospect to think about certain issues, such as gift recognition, that the prospect may not have given prior consideration. This takes the open-ended question phase discussed in Chapter 4 "Meeting Your New Best Friends," one step further. Now is the time to really get close to your prospect by asking very heartfelt questions. The key is to be an excellent listener and to follow through on any issue that is left open.

Exhibit 5–2 Elements of a Gift Proposal

- The amount of the gift.
- The purpose of the gift.
- When the gift will be made.
- How the gift will be made.
- How the gift will be recognized.

This process should be a relaxed and natural extension of your prospect meetings and discussions. You will know when the moment is right to turn to the prospect and say, "Julie, I know that you told me you want to support our historical preservation society because it meant a great deal to your father and uncle. Is there anything about our society that you personally like, or do you want to make this gift in time because you have a rich family history with our group?" Notice how you are now getting to the very core of the purpose of the prospective gift. Fundraisers must get close to their prospect at this stage and explore each gift proposal element.

This may seem painfully obvious, however, it is crucial to this phase of the major gifts process that the prospect and the fundraiser have a clear understanding about the prospective gift. One misconception on either the prospect's or the organization's part, and the gift could be jeopardized. It is very easy to make assumptions at this point of the major gifts process. Take for instance the purpose of the gift. The prospect may state that she wants the gift to benefit a center for literacy. She really believes that the center is a marvelous way to empower people who cannot read and write. A fundraiser who knows this information may feel secure knowing that the prospect wants to make a gift because it will benefit the mission of the organization and enhance the quality of life for her community. What the fundraiser may not know is that the prospect has in her mind certain restrictions for the gift. She may want to make the gift only if the center never moves from its present location. She has come to love its presence in her neighborhood. She did not feel the need to reveal this fact to the fundraiser, because she did not think it was important and felt that her gift would ensure the center's permanent home in her neighborhood. This is why it is so important to constantly probe the prospect's interests until the fundraiser is sure he or she knows the prospect's purpose and motivations for making the major gift.

Likewise it is equally important that the details of the amount of the gift, how the gift will be funded, and when the gift will be made be thoroughly discussed during the prospect-fundraiser relationship. A fundraiser may know the prospect's gift range, but may not know if the prospect intends to fund the gift with cash, securities, retirement benefits, insurance proceeds, property, or trust fund payments. How the gift is funded will directly impact on when the gift can be made. For instance, if the prospect wants to donate her second home to the charity, the charity will not realize the income from that gift until the property is sold. This could take months, or it may take years. A prospect who intends to fund the gift with cash may seem at first glance to be able to make the gift in a relatively short period of time. What if that prospect intends to use cash to make the gift, but only at such a point when there is enough in the prospect's savings account? Similar to the gift of property, this cash gift may take just as long. Now you see why these gift proposal elements must be explored in great detail with the prospect.

It may seem premature at this point in the first stage of the proposal process to address the issue of gift recognition. Many prospects may be reluctant and quite hesitant to talk about publicity for the gift, while others will let you know right away what they expect the organization will do for them once the gift is made. Fundraisers should always try to broach this topic with their prospects. It will accomplish several goals. First,

it will give the prospect some time before the formal proposal is drawn to think about the type of honor he or she may or may not want. Now is the time to explore with the prospect the types of honors the organization had in mind for the prospect and to let the prospect decide. Second, it will let the fundraiser know the prospect's expectations for the gift. Some prospects may expect a recognition dinner, a special dedication ceremony, a plaque, or feature article in the organization's newsletter. Others may want total anonymity. Third, it will make it much easier for the fundraiser at the final presentation of the gift proposal to "seal the deal" with the agreed upon details of the gift recognition. It will give the fundraiser the chance to complete the gift proposal by incorporating the previously discussed details on gift recognition.

Keep in mind that discussing the prospect's views on gift recognition occurs at a point in the prospect relationship when the prospective gift is being discussed. It should be a natural and progressive next step in the conversation. If it isn't, you run the risk of sounding presumptuous. For instance, if the prospect says he is considering a gift to an Alzheimer's group, but when he makes the gift he doesn't want "a lot of fanfare," this is the golden opportunity for the fundraiser to ask the prospect what he does and does not want in terms of publicity for the prospective gift. If on the other hand, the prospect says he would like to make a gift to the Alzheimer's group, but not until next year, then it would be premature at this point to discuss gift recognition for the prospect. It would not be a natural and logical next step to the discussion.

Tip: Gift recognition should be discussed with the prospect when the prospect is ready to make the gift and the parameters of the gift are being discussed.

Fundraisers often ask the next set of questions about major gifts proposals:
- Must the proposal always be in writing?
- How specific and detailed should it be?
- Does it have to include gold seals, drawings, renderings, or testimonials or be in a special folder?
- Should someone other than the fundraiser review it before it is presented?
- At what point should the fundraiser present the proposal?

Most major gifts proposals are in writing. Even if the writing consists of a one-page letter, it is necessary for the prospect to have something in writing that states the amount, timing, purpose of the gift, and how the gift will be funded. The proposal must "speak" to the prospect with convincing and persuasive language. When the prospect reads the proposal he or she should feel honored, valued, and treasured by the organization. The prospect should feel that by making this gift, he or she will be an important benefactor, a life-long friend of the organization, and a generous and caring individual to all those who benefit from the organization's good work. Saying these words to your prospect is one thing—having the prospect see it in print creates a bigger impact and lasting impression.

Since each proposal is tailored to meet the interests of each prospect, the details of the proposal vary from the very simple letter, to the very detailed and illustrated proposal. A rule of thumb is that the larger and more complex the gift, the more detailed the gift proposal. For instance, if you have been meeting several times with a prospect who wants to make a $100,000 gift to endow a study abroad program, and the prospect knows all about the program and is ready to make the gift, a simple letter outlining the details of the gift may suffice. If however, the same prospect wants to set up a $100,000 charitable trust for the same purpose, your gift proposal would look quite different. You would need to send the prospect a planned giving illustration along with a personal cover letter explaining the benefits of the gift.

The nature of the gift, together with the personality of the prospect, will dictate whether or not your proposal should contains gold seals, drawings, renderings, or testimonials or be in a specific folder. If you are asking the prospect to name a unit, wing, or building, and you have the resources to hire a good photographer or artist to depict the area you want the prospect to name, then it would be ideal to include the illustration in your proposal. It gives the prospect the chance to see and experience the magnitude of the prospective gift. Likewise, you may be working with certain prospects that have "healthy egos" and would love to see how their names would look on the unit, wing, or building. If you are working with these types of prospects, then it would be a good idea to include the illustration and give them all the "bells and whistles" your budget will allow. The bottom line is that the "look" of the proposal will depend upon the type of gift you are asking for as well as the type of prospect you are asking to make this gift.

Gift proposals should ALWAYS be reviewed by someone, preferably your boss. This will serve many purposes. First, it keeps your development operation apprised of your moves with your prospects. Second, you need a proofreader just in case you have typographical errors in your proposal. Third, it will give you reassurance that you are making the right ask, for the right amount, for the right gift, at the right time. If possible, have the people who went with you on visits review the proposal. The more input you have into this process, the better the proposal will be. They may have some great suggestions that will make a good proposal even better.

Taking into consideration the material previously covered in Chapter 4, "Judging the Prospect's Readiness To Make a Major Gift," the gift proposal cannot be presented until the prospect is ready to make the gift. You are at the point now when gift details and timing of the gift are being discussed. At such time, the proposal can be either hand delivered and discussed during a visit or mailed followed by a later telephone call. It is always preferable to meet with prospects to present the proposal in person. It gives you the chance to answer questions and address their concerns right away. This alleviates the need to try to "catch them at a good time" on the telephone. It keeps the process on a more personal level, and it can speed up the process of acquiring the gift.

Sometimes, however, prospects will prefer that you send it to them. They may not have the time or desire to meet with you because your prior meetings have covered the gift details. In those instances, thank your lucky stars that you are this far along with your prospects. Honor their wishes by sending them the proposal and be sure to follow-up with all the telephone calls it takes to get them to discuss the proposal with you.

The best way to see how this whole gift proposal process comes together is through illustrations. Appendixes 5–A through 5–H contain several examples of gift proposals. By discussing each one in detail, you will get a firm grasp on:

- What the proposal should contain.
- How the proposal should look.
- How each proposal is personally tailored to meet the needs and interests of each major gifts prospect.
- What is the best way to present the proposal.

GIFT PROPOSALS BY LETTER

The first gift proposal in Appendix 5–A is the gift idea previously discussed in this chapter under "The

Match between the Prospect's Interest and a Gift Opportunity." This is the example of the prospect who wanted to make a gift to Temple University's School of Education only if we could suggest some unique way of improving the reading skills of children in Philadelphia who needed it the most. We suggested that he make a $50,000 gift to our Center for Intergenerational Learning so that we could expand our Experience Corps program to improve the reading skills of elementary children in an area where the prospect was raised.

The proposal is presented in a letter. The first two paragraphs reference the last meeting I had with the prospect, Mr. R, and the specifics of his ties with Temple University. It is important that you add right upfront in your proposal the reasons why the prospect wants to make the gift. In this instance, I used the line, "It was particularly moving to hear you say that one of the best experiences you had in your distinguished career was teaching seventh and eighth grade students in disadvantaged areas of Philadelphia." This makes the gift proposal personal. It shows the prospect that you have listened to him and have given much time and attention to his life experiences that have brought him to this point of making a gift. It sets the right tone because it puts the prospect at ease. Now the prospect is ready to hear the details of the gift you have in mind for him.

The second paragraph continues to bring in more details of the conversation we had about Mr. R's prospective gift and introduces the gift idea. This is where fundraisers need to spell out the match between the prospect's interests with an institutional need. In this example, I matched his desire for a new way of educating inner city children with a very different university program that fulfilled his wishes.

Notice in the last sentence of the second paragraph, there is a reference that the proposal is being submitted to Mr. R at his request. While discussing the prospective gift, if the prospect says something like, "Sure, I'll give that idea some thought," then make sure you put this reference in your proposal. It serves to remind the prospect that it was his idea to have you send or hand deliver the gift proposal to him. It keeps the ball in his court, which is where you want it to be. You want the prospect to think it was his idea all along, and you were merely crystallizing his ideas in the proposal *that he requested*.

The next several paragraphs explain the details of how the program works and the success the program has made to date. It emphasizes the positive impact the gift will have on the lives of the children and their families. Remember, whenever possible, it is important to place the emphasis on people, not intangible programs, buildings, or equipment. Even if your prospect is making a gift toward new equipment or to name a building, emphasize how wonderful it will be for the doctors, technicians, and researchers to have this new equipment or for the students, professors, and patients to have a new building.

Your gift proposal must contain the reason for the suggested gift amount. In Mr. R's gift proposal, it states, "Your $50,000 investment is needed to cover the costs of screening, training, placing, monitoring, and evaluating volunteers, as well as the costs for the small group literacy activities and parental outreach programs for two new sites for the program." Prospects expect that you will tell them how you came to select the gift level. Most want to know and see a breakdown of how the gift will be utilized by the organization. The last page of this gift proposal gives a simple chart of how the $50,000 is needed to cover the costs of starting the program in two new schools. Charts are a great way to show your prospect how every dollar will be wisely invested with your group. The key word is "investment." Whenever possible, use this word in your gift proposals. Prospects have worked hard, saving and *investing* their assets. If they use part of their investments to make the gift, then they want to be sure the assets will continue to be invested prudently.

I always try to close my gift proposals on a personal note. In this instance, I reminded Mr. R that teaching inner city children who came from difficult backgrounds was one of the most rewarding things he ever did in his life. Thanks to his dedication and love for children, he earned the trust and respect of his students, and they in turn learned from him. I let him know that his gift would be used to help many children, just like the ones he taught several years ago. Your gift proposals should end on a similar note. Be sure to close with a sentence or two that will make the prospect feel lucky to be at a point where he can now give something back. With his gift, he can make a difference in the lives of future generations.

Mr. R was extremely busy with his business, which often included extended trips abroad. Getting appointments with him took several weeks, and on several occasions he had to cancel our appointment to go abroad. I knew all along that when it came time to deliver a proposal to him, it would probably have to be by mail. When Mr. R was ready to hear my gift suggestions, I incorporated into the conversation the fact that while I would love to deliver the proposal in person, I respected his limited time and suggested that I send it to him in writing. I let him know the week he would receive it and asked him how much time it would take before he would make his decision. He told me that he could not get to it for a few months because he wanted to make the gift from the family foundation. He said he needed time to consult with his brothers. I asked him if I could set up an appointment now to meet after a few months. He agreed.

This example shows how you must take the lead from the prospect with respect to the delivery and follow through of the gift proposal. It would have damaged the prospect-fundraiser relationship if I had pressed to hand deliver the proposal. In fact, knowing how difficult it was to get an appointment with Mr. R, it may have really delayed the delivery of the proposal to him. Similarly, there was no point in my pressing Mr. R to consult with his brothers sooner. This was Mr. R's time frame, and I had to go on his schedule, not the university's or mine.

> *Tip: When presenting the prospect with the gift proposal, be sure to listen to how and when he or she would like you to follow-up, and then follow the prospect's wishes. If the prospect is neutral on this subject, quickly suggest that you will call in a few days to follow through.*

The gift proposal example in Appendix 5–B is a simple letter that speaks to the prospect as if I were still in the room with her. I like to use this approach after I have had a really good visit with a prospect. In this case, I visited with Mrs. G at her home. Mrs. G had been visited by a development director for the school of art several times before my visit, had been involved for a number of years with the school, and was prime for a major gift ask when I met her. She spent much of the visit reminiscing of how she was in the third graduating class, which at that time had only a handful of women. She viewed herself as extremely lucky to have been given a scholarship to attend the school "back in the old days." It was extremely difficult for some students to concentrate on their work because they were worried that they did not have enough money to buy art supplies, to rent studio space, or to pay for tuition bills. Mrs. G felt it was time for her to give something back to help future art students.

Over lunch, she asked me what were the art school's greatest needs. I told her that we needed endowed scholarships. While Mrs. G may have gone to the school many years ago, students still have the same concerns about paying for art supplies, studio space, and tuition. I told her that endowed scholarships also help to attract the best art students, which furthers the outstanding reputation of the school.

Mrs. G wanted to know the details of how an endowed scholarship works. I explained that with an endowed gift, the interest from the principal gift amount would be used each year to award scholarships. She asked very good questions such as, "Who selects the students for these scholarships?" and "How much of a gift do I have to make for this to be a 'meaningful' scholarship each year?" I told her that the dean and a committee of faculty would select the scholarship recipient each year. She, of course, could refine the criteria for the scholarship by stipulating that the students have a concentration in painting, ceramics, printmaking, or photography. Mrs. G thought that the dean and the faculty would be the best people to select the scholarship recipient and that there was no need to further define the parameters of the scholarship.

Mrs. G's donor profile revealed that she had made steady gifts of $5,000 each year and that someday she would like to make a "larger gift." I knew that she had appreciated stock, so I suggested that she make a $100,000 gift, using her stock, for an endowed scholarship. This size gift would produce a "meaningful scholarship" each year, especially considering the rising costs for our art students. I knew that I was giving her a lot of information at this lunch meeting, so I told her to think about our conversation and that I would include the information in a letter to her.

Appendix 5–B contains the letter I sent Mrs. G two days after our meeting. Mrs. G only needed the essence of our conversation in writing. I just stated a few facts that we had gone over about her prospective endowed scholarship. Any more information would have been too much. Furthermore, she did not need to be convinced or persuaded. I sensed she liked the gift idea and just needed some time to think it over.

The tone of the letter is warm and sincere because Mrs. G is a warm and gracious lady. She values sincerity, honesty, and directness. If you say that the school needs scholarship dollars, she will trust that you are guiding her in the right gift direction. I ended the letter by bringing her back in time to when she was a student at the art school and reminding her of how important it is for students not to worry about money and instead to concentrate on their art work. In this instance, a simple, warm letter followed-up with a telephone call was the right approach for Mrs. G.

Tip: Let the personality of your prospect be reflected in the gift proposal. If the prospect is a warm, kind-hearted, and charming person, then make sure your proposal uses warm and sincere language.

Mr. H's gift proposal in Appendix 5–C is somewhat similar to Mrs. G's. Mr. H, an alumnus from the business school, was a self-made businessman who worked his way up from manager to corporate executive officer for a chain of convenience stores. He was extremely proud that he made some "lucky" business decisions along the way and that he stayed with the same company. Like Mrs. G, Mr. H had been cultivated by the university long before I met him. After meeting with him a few times, he told me that he wanted to make a $50,000 gift to the business school spread over the next four years. He asked me if we could send him a pledge reminder each month or each quarter, whichever was more convenient for the university. This was music to a fundraiser's ears!

Knowing that Mr. H. was a very proud businessman, I suggested that his gift be a named scholarship gift and that it be directed to the dean's scholarship fund at the business school. I explained that we had a dean's scholarship fund whereby each year the dean would award scholarships from this fund.

Mr. H's gift proposal only had to be a letter outlining the details of our conversation. In this case, however, the tone is more businesslike because Mr. H is more businesslike. I thought he would like to see how his named scholarship fund would look in our publications and honor roll, so I dropped this in his letter in larger font, separated from the rest of the text. This gift was a done deal, and all we had to do was select the timing of his payments, either monthly or quarterly. In the letter I let him know that either way was just fine with the university. I closed the letter with a thank you and an acknowledgement of his loyalty to the university.

Mr. H chose to send his gift in quarterly payments. Two weeks after I sent this gift proposal we had our first pledge payment toward his $50,000 gift.

Appendix 5–D contains what I call the "blend donor," that is a donor who makes individual gifts and brings with them the possibility of a corporate or family foundation gift. Mrs. J is an example of this type of donor. As major gifts manager for Deborah Hospital Foundation, I came to know Mrs. J. While her yearly gifts were not in the major gifts range, her cumulative giving made her a major gifts prospect. After meeting with her several times, I found out that her brother and several other family members had been treated at Deborah Heart and Lung Center. She had a fondness for Deborah because of its mission. Deborah will treat adults and children with heart and lung problems, *regardless* of their ability to pay. She was impressed that the hospital could offer the latest surgical procedures to cure potentially fatal heart and lung disease and that the hospital had a "family feel" to it. Family was important to Mrs. J because she and her husband owned an extremely successful family-owned and operated car dealership in the area. The business had been in the family for several generations. Preserving family institutions was very important to Mrs. J.

During one of our meetings, Mrs. J told me that her neighbor's child was recently a patient in "some new area" at Deborah. I explained that we had just opened a new neonatal and pediatric cardiac unit to treat newborns with congenital heart disease. I invited her to see the unit and she accepted. The day of the tour, I arranged for the nurses in the unit to spend some time with Mrs. J explaining the different types of surgeries and post-operative care for the newborns. I also had a mother whose newborn had surgery and was recovering beautifully speak with Mrs. J.

After the tour, I asked Mrs. J if she would consider making a significant gift, in the nature of $150,000 to cover the costs involved in running the neonatal and pediatric unit. My research indicated that she could do a gift of this magnitude, but that it would have to be spread out over a number of years. To illustrate the need for an outright gift of this size, I told her about the costs for just two patients. One example was for an infant with an atrial defect requiring a five-day stay that would cost in the range of $25,000. The other was for an infant born in another hospital with an irregular heartbeat who had to be transported to Deborah and required immediate surgery and a 21-day stay that would cost in the range of $90,000. I then told her that since the opening of the unit, every bed had been filled and that there was a waiting list of newborns to get into the unit. Her gift of $150,000 would provide immediate care for several critically ill newborns and would bring a lifetime of joy to their families for generations to come.

Mrs. J thought about it for a minute or two, and then said that she really could not afford to make a gift of this size. She had no doubt it would be a wonderful gift, but there was just no way she could do it. Our conversation focused on her interest in the gift and how we could make it happen. Knowing she was the co-owner of a business, I asked her if the company had a corporate giving program, and if so, who were some of the past recipients. She told me that the company does make gifts, but over the past few years, all the gifts have gone to one organization that supports local children in need. Since the unit was exclusively for newborns and children in need of vital care, I asked if I could submit a proposal to her company to support the unit. She agreed and said the best way was to send a letter to her stating just what we had just spoken about, and she would present it to the board at the next meeting.

Appendix 5–D contains the letter I sent to Mrs. J. While my initial instinct was to make this more formal and to give it the feel and look of a detailed corporate proposal, I chose to keep it short, personal, and to the point. It was a gamble on my part, but sometimes you just have to go with your instincts on which type of proposal will win over your prospects and the decision makers. I chose this format for several reasons. First, Mrs. J told me to put it in a letter and to just reiterate our conversation. If I had made this longer or more formal, I would not have listened to the donor and violated one of the important rules in fundraising—"always listen to the donor and follow up with her requests." Second, Mrs. J was extremely educated about Deborah. She had seen first hand the quality care the hospital provided and experienced the "family" atmosphere that the nurses, doctors, staff, and patients created at the hospital. My proposal did not need background information or filler information. All she needed at this time was a brief description of the new unit with the examples I gave her for the cost to care for our newborn patients. Third, I knew that Mrs. J would be presenting this for the first time to the board and that the board's first impression of Deborah was critical to receiving the gift. I had great faith that Mrs. J would speak very well of Deborah and its unique mission. I also knew that she would drive home the point that Deborah is one of the few hospitals that can treat these severely ill newborns and that the company should support this neighboring "family" institution. Mrs. J's words would be so much more powerful and persuasive than anything I could write.

Just to make sure I was on the right track, I hand delivered the letter to Mrs. J at her office one week before the board meeting. I asked her to let me know if this was what she had in mind and to let me know if I should add or supplement any portion. Mrs. J told me this was all she needed for now. She would be "introducing" the proposal at the next meeting and in all likelihood, the board would vote on it at their next meeting.

This gift proposal example raises a few important points to keep in mind during this phase of the major gifts process. Even if you believe your prospect has the ability, motivation, and interest in making a major gift, there may be a "deeper pocket" or better yet, a "dual pocket" possibility. In this case, Mrs. J in time may have made a gift to support the neonatal and pediatric unit, but it probably would not have been a gift in the $150,000 range. Her company had the corporate program to make this gift happen. As an added bonus, Mrs. J made a major gift to support the unit, and all her future gifts were targeted for this area. Her gifts to this unit were an expression of her personal and professional commitment to help local children in need. It sent the message to her board that if she supports this unit, it is worthy of the company's support. Additionally, her future gifts to the unit showed her board that they made the right decision in making a major gift for Deborah's new unit. Remember the adage, "People like to give to forward moving trains." Mrs. J's continued support proved to the board that their investment in Deborah's neonatal and pediatric program would continue to yield great results, well into the future.

Tip: During the gift proposal stage, consider whether the prospect has a connection with a larger funding source, such as a corporate giving program or family foundation. Work with the prospect to secure both an individual major gift as well as a corporate/family foundation major gift.

GIFT PROPOSALS FORMAL, YET PERSONAL

Up until this point, the gift proposal illustrations have been in the form of a personal and specific letter. The next set of illustrations contained in Appendixes 5–E through 5–H demonstrate the more formal approach to gift proposals. These proposals are more formal and detailed for several reasons. First, they mirror the personalities of the prospects. Each prospect that I presented these proposals to would have expected the gift proposals to have the look, feel, and tone of an official document. Second, the ask is much higher. These illustrations are for gifts of $250,000 and above. Third, the gift vehicle and benefits of the gift required explanation. Most high-end gift proposals contain tiers of benefits as well as suggestions on how and when the gift can be made. These important gift factors cannot be glossed over. It is crucial to obtaining the gift that the prospect be fully apprised *in writing* of the benefits of the gift as well as the benefits the suggested gift vehicles can bring to the prospect.

The first example of this type of proposal is in Appendix 5–E. Mr. and Mrs. V lived several states away from Deborah. They were extremely proud of their Greek heritage and loved the fact that our board president had Greek ancestral roots. I had visited with them many times at their home, which was situated in a Greek community. I found out that many years ago, they lived in New Jersey, fairly close to Deborah, and owned a diner for 19 years. They knew about Deborah from family, friends, and customers and began making yearly gifts.

It was very easy and enjoyable to cultivate Mr. and Mrs. V. Every time I visited them, I brought them something from Deborah. Mr. V told me that for all the years he owned the diner, he never had a picture of it. I found a newspaper article that featured businesses that were opened during a recent snowstorm and sent it to him. The story pictured and featured his diner. He loved this so much I thought I really have to get a color photograph of the diner. A coworker and I took a Deborah poster with our logo and drove to the diner. I stood on the stairs of the diner holding up the poster while she took the picture. I had it framed and brought it with me on my next visit. When he unwrapped the gift, he cried and thanked me. He then set out to tell me hilarious stories about some of his customers and the variety of foods they would order. When I left, he said he would never forget that Deborah gave him this great gift. Sure enough, the next time I returned, there it was, hung on his wall, directly across from his favorite seat in the living room.

Since Mr. and Mrs. V still had family in New Jersey, I got them to agree to take a tour of Deborah during one of these family visits. I knew that the one person they had to spend time with was our board president. I met with our board president and told him all about Mr. and Mrs. V. The gift proposal I had in mind for them was to support our Visiting Greek Nursing Program. Each year, Deborah sponsored four to five nurses to study and observe under Deborah's doctors and nurses so that they could take these new medical skills and apply them to their hospitals in Greece. It was designed to improve the healthcare system in Greece. It was a natural fit to ask these prospects, who were so proud of their Greek heritage, to help us improve the quality of medical care in their ancestral country. The board president suggested that we describe the program to them during their visit to test their interest.

After the hospital tour, we gathered in our board president's office. I can honestly say that I only grasped half of the conversation because for the most part they were speaking Greek—literally, not figuratively. I knew things were going well because they were smiling, laughing, and pointing to the several Greek artifacts in the president's office. Twenty minutes or so went by, when my board president launched into a description of our Visiting Greek Nursing Program. The whole time our board president was describing the program, Mr. and Mrs. V were nodding their heads saying, "Yes, yes I can see that." He told them they were one of the few Deborah family members who would understand the importance of the program and that we would like them to consider making a leadership gift of $50,000/year for the next five years to ensure the continued success of the program. As we walked them to the door, the board president suggested that we send them something in writing that would describe the details of the program. They agreed.

Appendix 5–E contains that gift proposal. It lists how the Greek nurses are selected, how they are educated at Deborah, and most important, how their experience at Deborah would improve the patient care services in Greece. It sets forth the timing of the yearly gift payments and suggests a way to recognize their gift. This is something that almost any fundraiser can do with the aid of computer software. I merely did a draft of a plaque that we would make for them if they made the gift. I suggested some language, but stated in the proposal that we would be happy to work with them to compose a message for their plaque. I used this technique because I sensed that Mr. and Mrs. V would want something in Deborah that would show their support for Deborah and the Greek community. The plaque mock-up is a good tool to use to get your prospects thinking about how they would like their gift to be recognized. It also adds a little "push" for them to make the gift, which is exactly what you want.

This next statement bears repeating, just one more time. *Let the prospect's personality guide the gift proposal process.* In this instance, Mr. and Mrs. V had instant bonding with our board president. He was the key to getting this gift. We thought they would like a commemorative plaque, but the icing on the cake was the suggestion to have the plaque displayed in our board president's office. We knew how "at home" they felt in his office, and we guessed that it would mean so much more to them to have the plaque there, rather than in the hallway. It turned out to be a good guess. That is exactly where the plaque hangs today.

While this proposal is not in letter form as the previous illustrations, it still contains the personalization that must be present in every gift proposal. It weaves in Mr. and Mrs. V's strong connection to Deborah, references our "shared mission" to improve health care in Greece, and addresses them as prospective "founding leaders" of the program. All proposals must capture the essence of the importance of the gift and tug at the prospect's heartstrings at the same time.

The next proposal in Appendix 5–F illustrates how a formal proposal can be a simple one. In this case, Ms. E had been the chair of the university's vocal department for many years. She had a long and distinguished career and was known as one of the "visionaries" for the music college. She orchestrated several new programs, including an international internship program. Each year she made a major gift to support a music scholarship fund. When I met her, she had been cultivated for many years by the dean and development members. In addition, other faculty members and alumni held her in high esteem. She often traveled to see her former students' concerts and never ceased to be strong mentor and role model for her students.

I made it a point to attend several concerts of performers that she coached so that I could be brought up to speed on the vocal department. During this time, the dean restructured the college's concert series to include a Vocal Master Class Series. I met with the dean and asked if the college would consider sponsorship levels for each of these newly formed series. The one I was most concerned with at that time was the Vocal Master Class Series. I thought if Ms. E were going to target her gift toward any program at the college, this would be it. After a few meetings, it was decided that the series could be named for a gift of $250,000 or more.

The gift for this prospect would not have to be a hard sell. Ms. E had already been a loyal and dedicated department chair who loved to teach and sing. She helped build international acclaim for the college, and it was only fitting that her name be associated with the best and most talented vocalists. Her gift proposal, in Appendix 5–F, is no more than a cover sheet and a one-page description of all her accomplishments, plus a few bullet points on how her endowed gift of $250,000 would be used. We agreed that the gift should be endowed so that the college could invite two to four renowned artists per year to provide master classes for the college's vocal students. Since Ms. E was extreme-

ly knowledgeable about this program, the proposal did not call for any lengthy description.

Furthermore, this was the type of gift proposal that had to be delivered in person. Ms. E was the type of person who would make all the time in the world for you, so the proposal had to be presented in person. I brought this proposal with me when I asked her to make the gift. It never came out of my briefcase. She knew every aspect about the master class series and was flattered and honored that we would want her name to be forever equated with this "prestigious" program.

Even though I did not use the gift proposal I prepared, I was grateful to have it with me. It helped me to learn as much as I could about the program and gave me the security to talk fluidly about it. If I never prepared the formal gift proposal, I would have been ill prepared to make the ask. I did not want to be in the position of having Ms. E say, "Do you have something in writing you can leave with me now so I can think about it?" The last thing you want to do is appear unprepared during the gift proposal process. This will surely decrease your chances of securing major gifts.

> ***Tip:*** *Do not let the prospect's knowledge about the prospective gift deter you from preparing a written gift proposal. Always have at least a one-page summary of the benefits of the gift as well as the payment structure prepared to leave with the knowledgeable prospect.*

GIFT PROPOSALS THAT INCLUDE A PLANNED GIFT

Many of your major gifts proposals will include a planned gift. Planned gifts, especially charitable gift annuities and charitable trusts, can offer substantial income, estate, and capital gains tax benefits that will attract your wealthy prospects. When you are working with prospects that want to make a gift using a planned giving vehicle, or if you think that considering the prospect's financial circumstances, a planned gift would be more appropriate than an outright gift, your gift proposal should include a planned gift illustration.

Appendix 5–G is an example of a planned giving illustration. Mr. K, a business graduate in his 80s who never married or had children, wanted to make a major gift to the business school. He had just completed his last pledge payment on a prior major gift when he told us that he wanted to do something with the stock he had held since 1950. Mr. E worked as an accountant for the same firm for 37 years and had sizeable pension and retirement benefits.

He was fascinated with computers and joked how he would never have a job today because he did all his accounting with pen and paper, and now it is all done by computer. We talked to him about the business school's international honors' laptop program, whereby the top 20 business students in their freshman year would be given the latest laptop computer and software to work in cohort teams both here and abroad. The laptops would be upgraded in their junior year, and at graduation the students would be given the options to lease the computers from the business school. The cost to run this program was in excess of $1 million. We knew that Mr. K would not agree to a gift this size, but that a $500,000 gift was well within his range. He was delighted and fascinated.

Mr. K lived in a retirement community; so on occasion we brought business students and faculty to meet him. They talked about the international honors' laptop program and other technological advances, such as our e-commerce program and online courses. We had the students bring their laptops to show Mr. K how they could work on entrepreneurial projects with students and faculty both here and abroad.

Over several lunches, we discussed with Mr. K the benefits of a charitable remainder unitrust. It was a great opportunity for him to roll his stock into the trust, avoid capital gains, receive yearly income, and most important, to make a leadership gift toward the international honors' laptop program. After we felt comfortable that Mr. K liked the concept of the charitable trust, we asked if we could meet with him to show him an illustration on the financial benefits of his prospective gift.

At this meeting, I brought hard copy of the illustration contained in Appendix 5–G, as well as my laptop where I had saved the illustration. I showed him on the computer how I calculated his $500,000 gift. Given his age and the fact that he was using stock with a low cost basis, his $500,000 charitable remainder unitrust would give him an income tax deduction of $328,730, avoidance of capital gains on the appreciated stock, and a yearly income of $25,000 or more. Based on Mr. K's age and life expectancy, the business school was projected to receive $814,447. The illustration on the last page of the proposal made it very easy for him to graphically see how his investment would yield big financial benefits for him and for the business school. It shows the donor, Mr. K, putting his $500,000 stock

with a $50,000 cost basis into a 5 percent unitrust, which gives him a sizeable income tax deduction, avoidance of $450,000 capital gains, and a sizeable remainder gift to the business school.

Mr. K sat and stared at the illustration for a very long time. He said he would put the proposal on the top of his "to do" pile. Before we left, I folded up the laptop. I told him that his gift would make it possible for many business students to have a laptop just like this one. The laptop turned out to be a good selling feature to sell the benefits of this gift.

> **Tip:** Whenever possible, give your prospect whose gift proposal includes a planned gift an illustration tailored to the prospect's specific information, which contains his or her age, assets funding the gift, tax benefits for the prospect, and remainder benefits to the charity.

Generally, top major gifts asks will involve the top leadership from your organization. This creates a peer-to-peer dynamic that can carry the most leverage during the solicitation process (Sturtevant 1997, 72). In these instances, the top leadership has been involved with some aspect of the cultivation process and presolicitation process and will be involved in the ask. It is important, and often critical, to the gift proposal process that the top leadership be involved.

In many instances, top major gifts proposals will offer a naming opportunity. For instance, a local library may offer to name a reading room after a top donor; a children's advocacy center may offer to name a summer camp program after a top donor; or a cancer research center may offer to name a new laboratory after a top donor. Usually naming opportunities are discussed with the top leadership prior to any solicitation so that the suggested gift, gift level, and naming opportunity have the organization's approval.

During the course of your major gifts fundraising career, your organization will no doubt target a major gifts prospect for a top gift that entails a naming opportunity. The last gift proposal example, contained in Appendix 5–H, is an example of this type of proposal.

Dr. Q was a long-time trustee of the School of Medicine at a midwestern university. He dedicated his entire career to medicine and research. As a trustee for the school, he knew the leaders of the school as well as the university. He was invited by the president of the university to attend athletic events, alumni receptions, and dedication dinners and generally accepted all invitations. As he became more involved, it was clear that he cared deeply about attracting the best research fellows and prospective students for the school. He wanted to increase the number of scholarship opportunities and have the latest technological tools available for students and faculty.

Based on Dr. Q's loyalty to the school, it was decided that Dr. Q might be interested in naming the school for a gift of $30 million. As with many major naming opportunities, this would require a resolution approved by a committee of trustees. The president secured their approval and met several times with Dr. Q. At each meeting they discussed different ways Dr. Q could fund the gift. Gifts of this magnitude would require time and attention. Dr. Q met with retained counsel to explore the best outright and planned gift opportunities to make his gift.

Appendix 5–H contains some suggestions for Dr. Q to make his gift. Since he was meeting frequently with the president, there was no need to add pages and pages of the benefits of the gift. Dr. Q knew that if he made the gift, the money would be used for endowed chairs, professorships, fellowships, scholarships, and upgrades. Unlike the gift proposal in Appendix 5–G, there was no need to include a planned giving illustration because Dr. Q had gone over that thoroughly with retained counsel. She had given him several planned giving illustrations.

Dr. Q was very proud of his family name. Essential to this gift was showing Dr. Q how wonderful his family name would look on all sides of the school. An artist sketched the building showing his name on it. Powerful visual images can really enhance a gift proposal. They allow the prospect to "experience" what it will be like once the gift is made.

> **Tip:** *Whenever possible, include photographs, computer-generated pictures, or artist's renditions in your top major gifts proposals that include naming opportunities. It will create a tremendous visual impact on the prospect and will move the prospect one step closer to making the gift.*

Lastly, gift recognition was discussed. Dr. Q had a large extended family, many colleagues at the school and the university, and many friends. The proposal closed with a note suggesting that a dedication ceremony be held including all the important people in his life.

RECAP AND REVIEW

1. Every major gifts proposal is specific, unique, and personal.

2. It must match the prospect's interest in the organization with an existing or newly created gift opportunity.

3. When deciding on the prospect's gift range, err on the high end.

4. Make sure you know the prospect's assets intended to make the gift; his or her desire to reduce income, estate, and capital gains taxes; and his or her need for any additional income before suggesting a gift vehicle.

5. Consider whether there is a dual gift—the prospect's major gift as well as any corporate giving program or family foundation—then work on drafting two major gifts proposals.

6. Always communicate to your development office your prospect's anticipated timing to make the gift so that institutional funding goals are kept on track.

7. Within your organization, check to see if there is a competing prospect proposal and if others have targeted your prospect for a special gift.

8. Major gifts proposals usually include the amount of the gift, purpose of the gift, when the gift will be made, how the gift will be made, and how the gift will be recognized.

9. Almost every major gifts proposal is in writing.

10. Major gifts proposals should reflect the tone, demeanor, and personality of the prospect.

11. Major gifts proposals range from the simple letter to a board-approved, detailed, and illustrated document.

12. Major gifts proposals should always be reviewed by your boss as well as by any others who have cultivated your prospect.

13. If the major gifts proposal includes a planned gift, include a planned gift illustration.

14. Major gifts proposals can be hand-delivered or mailed when the time is right to solicit the prospect.

15. After the proposal has been presented, be sure to establish how and when you can continue your discussion on the gift proposal, then follow through.

REFERENCES

Andersen, A. 1999. *Tax economics of charitable giving.* 13th ed. Sarasota, FL: Arthur Andersen.

Barrett, R., and M. Ware. 1997. *Planned giving essentials.* Gaithersburg, MD: Aspen Publishers, Inc.

Clifford, D., and C. Jordon. 1996. *Plan your estate.* 3d ed. Berkeley, CA: Nolo Press, Inc.

Dunlop, D. 1993. Major gift programs. In *Educational fund raising: Principles and practice,* ed. M.J. Worth. Phoenix, AZ: Onyx Press/American Council on Education.

Lawson, D. 1996. The artful asker. *Fund Raising Management,* April.

Mammone, B. 1996. Giving with the best intentions. *AHP Journal,* Fall.

Stevenson, S. 1996. *Solicitation skills builder.* Sioux City, IA: Stevenson Consultants, Inc.

Sturtevant, W. 1997. *The artful journey.* Chicago: Bonus Books, Inc.

Williams, J. 1991. *Big gifts.* Rockville, MD: Taft Group.

SUGGESTED READINGS—PLANNED GIVING

Andersen, A. 1999. *Tax economics of charitable giving.* 13th ed. Sarasota, FL: Arthur Andersen.

Ashton, D. 1991. *The complete guide to planned giving.* 2d ed. Cambridge, MA: JLA Publications.

Barrett, R., and M. Ware. 1997. *Planned giving essentials.* Gaithersburg, MD: Aspen Publishers, Inc.

Clifford, D., and C. Jordan 1996. *Plan your estate.* 3d ed. Berkeley, CA: Nolo Press, Inc.

Gregg, K. 1996. *Doing well by doing good.* Chicago: Bonus Books.

Sharpe, R. 1999. *Planned giving simplified.* New York: John Wiley and Sons, Inc.

Tromble, W. 1998. Planned giving. In *Excellence in advancement,* 181–209. Gaithersburg, MD: Aspen Publishers, Inc.

Appendix 5–A

Sample Gift Proposal—By Letter—Conversational, Covering All the Details

Mr. R
10 South Orange Street
Philadelphia, PA 19107-3818

Dear Mr. R:

Thank you for taking the time last week to meet with us. We truly enjoyed getting to know you better and learning more about your family's strong ties with Temple University. It was particularly moving to hear you say that one of the best experiences you had in your distinguished career was teaching seventh and eighth grade students in disadvantaged areas of Philadelphia.

At our last meeting we discussed your interest in supporting our highly successful literacy program, Experience Corps, coordinated by Temple University's Center for Intergenerational Learning. Knowing how much you and your family care about the quality of Philadelphia public education in elementary schools, we thought this would be a great opportunity for you to make a real difference in the reading skills of many deserving Philadelphia children. We are delighted that you have an interest in Experience Corps, and we are submitting this proposal to you now at your request.

Experience Corps began in 1996 as a national pilot program to mobilize teams of older volunteers to work in elementary schools to improve children's reading skills. More than 15 cities were targeted for the project. Here in Philadelphia, three schools participated in the program: Olney, Taylor, and Morrison Elementary Schools. The program was coordinated by Temple University's Center for Intergenerational Learning, in collaboration with the government-funded National Senior Service Corps program. During the 18-month pilot program period, more than 72 trained elder volunteers provided one-to-one tutoring, two to three times a week, for more than 360 Philadelphia children in grades K–2. These students were tested to be most at-risk to fail at reading. The volunteers conducted small group literacy activities with the children and held numerous parent outreach programs, such as parent book club meetings.

The results of the pilot program in Philadelphia were outstanding, and in fact, Philadelphia emerged as one of the most successful of the national programs for three key reasons:

1. The elder volunteers realized an enhanced sense of purpose. By working directly with the children through tutoring and mentoring, they served as leaders in developing new service projects to benefit children and their parents.
2. The children showed marked improvement in academic performance, attendance, classroom behavior, and overall self-confidence.
3. The classroom teachers witnessed improved academic performance in the students' basic literacy and numeracy concepts, reading and math skills, and language development.

At the present time, there are nine Philadelphia elementary schools participating in Experience Corps that have been funded primarily by public foundations and the U.S. government. While our current funders have committed their support for the existing nine schools, we cannot expand our literacy project to reach even more at-risk children in Philadelphia without the help of private support. We turn to you now, Mr. R, and ask you and your family to consider a $50,000 gift to Temple University's Center for Intergenerational Learning so that we can expand our Experience Corps literacy program in two more North Philadelphia elementary schools.

Your $50,000 investment is needed to cover the costs of screening, training, placing, monitoring, and evaluating volunteers, as well as the costs for the small-group literacy activities and parental outreach programs for two new sites for the program. Your investment would represent your commitment to improve the reading skills for many deserving Philadelphia children and to change the lives of many families in Philadelphia.

Mr. R, you shared with us how meaningful and rewarding it was for you during your teaching experience to work with inner-city children. You found the right words and the right teaching style to reach them. They respected you because you believed in them, and in turn, they did learn. In that spirit, we ask you now to help our neediest inner-city children through our Experience Corps program.

Thank you for your consideration and time. Please feel free to contact us if you have any questions about this proposal. We look forward to hearing from you soon.

Sincerely,

Laura Fredricks
Senior Director of Major Gifts

Encl.

A. ***Volunteer Stipends***
    1. 10 Volunteers @ $150/mo. $\times$ 9 mos.   13,500.00
    2. 1 Volunteer @ $200/mo. $\times$ 9 mos.   1,800.00

B. ***Staff Expenses***
    1. 1 Part-time Coordinator 10-12 hrs/wk. $\times$ 9 mos.   7,000.00
    2. 1 Part-time Support Staff 2-5 hrs/wk. $\times$ 9 mos.   700.00

C. ***Supplies***
    1. Photocopies   150.00
    2. Postage   100.00
    3. Curriculum Instruction Manuals   750.00
    4. Books   450.00
    5. Volunteer Uniforms (name badges, shirts)   150.00
    6. Materials for Testing   400.00

TOTAL COSTS PER SCHOOL   25,000.00

TOTAL COSTS $\times$ 2 SCHOOLS   **50,000.00**

Appendix 5–B
Sample Gift Proposal—By Letter—Personal

Mrs. G
455 Bridge Road
San Diego, CA 92117

Dear Mrs. G:

Thank you for the pleasure of your enjoyable company yesterday. I truly enjoyed getting to know you and learning about your fondness for our school of art. Your artwork reflects your warmth, open-mindedness, and free-spirited nature. We are very privileged to have you as a distinguished and talented alumna.

I wanted to discuss with you further the gift opportunity of an endowed scholarship that we mentioned during lunch. It would be called:

The Mrs. G Scholarship

Your scholarship would be awarded each year to a talented art student in need of financial assistance. The Dean and a committee of faculty members would select the scholarship recipient each year.

You asked about the greatest need at the art school. The greatest need we have is to increase our scholarship fund so that we can attract and retain the best talent for our world-renowned art school. Your gift of $100,000, which can be funded with appreciated stock, would benefit numerous art students, now and for years to come. The interest income your endowment generates each year would be used to fund the scholarship. Just imagine the joy and relief the award recipients will feel when they can put their financial worries behind and just concentrate on their craft! Your generous and thoughtful gift, Mrs. G, will make that possible.

Mrs. G, thank you again for your time and your genuine interest in helping future school of art students. I will call you in a few days so that we can talk further about your exciting prospective gift to the school.

Most cordially,

Laura Fredricks
Senior Director of Major Gifts

Appendix 5–C
Sample Gift Proposal—By Letter—Structured and Formal

Mr. H
22 Bensalem Lane
Seminole, FL 34642

Dear Mr. H:

It has been a pleasure to speak with you so frequently over the past few weeks. We are delighted and impressed that you devoted a great deal of time to consider the type of gift you wish to make to Temple University.

During our last conversation, you said that you would like to make a $50,000 gift of cash over a period of time and suggested a 50-month period. Your gift would be used for scholarships at the Fox School of Business and Management. We would like to call it:

The Mr. H Dean's Scholarship Fund at the Business School

The Dean would have the discretion to use your gifts immediately for the most pressing scholarship needs for our students.

Since you suggested a 50-month time frame, a convenient way to make your pledge payments would be on a quarterly basis. For the next four years, you would send to me in the self-addressed envelopes, quarterly gifts of $3,125 each. You would make your check out to "Temple University" and in the memo section write "Mr. H Dean's Scholarship Fund at the Business School." The gifts would come to me directly, and I would make sure that they are deposited in your scholarship fund. Your gifts could come every January, April, August, and December. The first gift could be made this April or sooner.

This is just a suggestion for your gift pledge payments. If you feel more comfortable, you can send $1,000 per month, for the next 50 months. I did not know if it would be more convenient for you to write a check four times a year, as opposed to every month. Either way, you will be making a significant difference for many business students.

Just let me know which pledge payment method is better for you and send your first gift in one of the envelopes. I will then set up your scholarship fund.

Mr. H, we don't say this often enough, but we really do appreciate your support and loyalty to Temple. I look forward to speaking with you soon.

Most cordially,

Laura Fredricks
Senior Director of Major Gifts

Appendix 5–D
Sample Gift Proposal—The Blend Donor

Mrs. J
55 Lindy Lane
Medford Lakes, NJ 08055

Dear Mrs. J:

Thank you for taking the time last week to meet with me. I really appreciated that you gave me the opportunity to share with you Deborah Heart and Lung Center's new patient care programs.

During our discussion, it became clear that you and your company would be interested in supporting our new Neonatal and Pediatric Cardiac Surgical Unit. We would like to provide you with some important information that you can share with your Board of Directors at your next meeting.

In May 1997 we opened the William G. Rohrer Neonatal and Pediatric Cardiac Surgical Unit, which was funded by the memorial foundation of one our executive board members. This state-of-the-art eight-bed unit was designed specifically for critically ill newborns, infants, and children with congenital heart disease. We have a transport unit that brings the neonates just hours after birth from neighboring hospitals directly to Deborah. Through the expertise of our renowned pediatric surgeons, these tiniest of patients receive lifesaving surgery for their rare congenital heart defects.

All children in the Neonatal and Pediatric Cardiac Surgical Unit receive one-on-one nursing care, 24 hours a day. Our team of pediatric cardiologists and surgeons make rounds on all pediatric patients twice each day. In addition, we have an attending pediatric cardiologist or surgeon, who specializes in repairing the hearts of neonates with single ventricle problems, such as hypoplastic left heart syndrome. Our pediatric cardiothoracic surgeon is one of only a few physicians in the entire country who can perform these surgeries on neonates.

To illustrate the importance of this unit, since our opening day in May 1997, the unit has been filled at or near capacity. As you can imagine, there are many high costs involved with performing these highly specialized surgeries and with providing skilled physician and nursing care.

A two-year-old infant with atrial septal defect repair would require surgery and five days in the unit at a cost of well over $25,000. A neonate transported to Deborah at two-days old with hypoplastic left heart syndrome would require surgery and 21 days in the unit. This would cost approximately $90,000.

It is only through the support from our loyal Deborah family members like you, Mrs. J, and your company that Deborah is able to provide these lifesaving services to newborns, infants, and children in our community. Your company has supported Deborah over the years, and for that we are eternally grateful. We turn to you now and ask you and your company to consider a gift of $150,000 to support our Neonatal and Pediatric Cardiac Surgical Unit.

Courtesy of the Deborah Hospital Foundation.

Mrs. J, we thank you for taking this important proposal to your Board of Directors. I am available at your convenience to answer any questions you may have about this prospective gift.

Your board members are very lucky to have you as such a strong and dedicated leader. We at Deborah are also lucky to have you as a leader and a friend.

Most cordially,

Laura Fredricks
Major Gifts Manager

Appendix 5–E
Sample Gift Proposal—Formal, Illustrative, and Personal

**GIFT OPPORTUNITY FOR MR. AND MRS. V
TO SPONSOR DEBORAH'S
VISITING GREEK NURSING PROGRAM**

Deborah Heart and Lung Center, in conjunction with AHEPA General Hospital, Thessaloniki, Greece, have developed the Visiting Greek Nursing Program at Deborah. Since 1993, teams of four to five Greek nurses study and observe under the leadership of Deborah's medical professionals, in an effort to improve the patient care services at AHEPA General Hospital.

To date, 75 Greek nurses have been educated at Deborah in the following critical areas:

- Nursing management
- Patient assessment
- Pre- and post-operative care
- Intensive care
- Equipment maintenance
- Hospital administration

To qualify for the program, each nurse must complete an application, undergo an interview, and write an essay about his or her interests and objectives. Only nurses with superior credentials are selected. Those chosen for the program meet regularly with Deborah's Director of Nursing. During their three-month residency, the nurses either rotate their schedules from department to department, which broadens their medical knowledge, or they are assigned to one department, which gives them the opportunity to study specifically within their area of expertise.

The visiting nurses are given a $250 monthly stipend, an apartment on the grounds of Deborah, and access to transportation. On weekends, the visiting nurses have the opportunity to expand their cultural experiences by traveling to neighboring cities, such as New York, Washington, DC, and Baltimore.

Upon their return to Greece, each nurse works closely with other nurses who have participated in the program. Their combined knowledge and newly acquired skills play a major role in the ongoing effort to improve the health care system in Greece.

Deborah has a long and rich history in the Greek community, both here and abroad. For over 75 years, Deborah has stood ready to serve those in need from as close to home as adults and children from your neighborhood and as far away as children in Greece. We come to you now, our loyal Deborah supporters, and ask you to be our proud sponsors of our **Deborah Heart and Lung Center's Visiting Greek Nursing Program**.

Courtesy of the Deborah Hospital Foundation.

It would be our honor and privilege to name you, Mr. and Mrs. V, as our *founding leaders* for this important program. Your commitment to support this project will be instrumental to the success of our shared mission to improve patient care services in Greece.

We ask you to consider making this significant impact by making a $50,000 yearly gift, for the next five years, to sponsor this unique and worthy program. Your first gift can be made anytime by the end of this calendar year. We would like to commemorate your gift with a plaque that would be proudly presented to you in the presence of your family, friends, and colleagues. You may keep the commemorative plaque, or if your prefer, we would gladly display it in the prestigious office of Deborah's President. Attached is some sample language for your plaque. We would be happy to discuss the details of the type and style plaque you prefer to recognize your prospective gift.

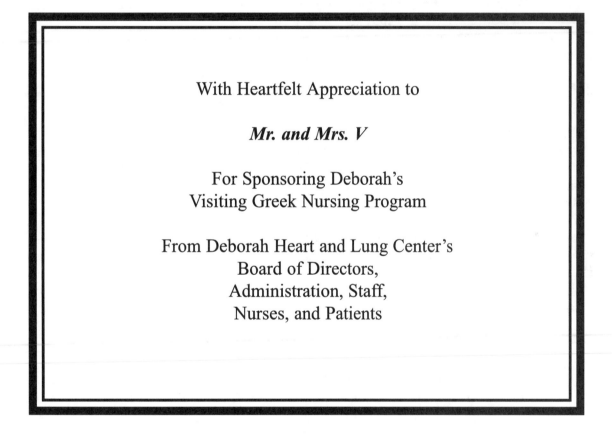

With Heartfelt Appreciation to

Mr. and Mrs. V

For Sponsoring Deborah's
Visiting Greek Nursing Program

From Deborah Heart and Lung Center's
Board of Directors,
Administration, Staff,
Nurses, and Patients

Appendix 5–F
Sample Gift Proposal—Simple and Persuasive

College of Music and Dance

Proposal for:

Ms. E
Chair, Vocal Department
Vocal Master Class Series

The Ms. E Vocal Master Class Series

The list of accomplishments is long and distinguished: the renaming of the College to honor the generosity of a distinguished alumna; the merging of the New School of Music with the College; the implementation of the Doctor of Musical Arts and Doctor of Philosophy degrees; the emergence of the Music Preparatory Division's Center for Gifted Young Musicians; and the establishment of the Friends of the College of Music, to name only a few. Your tenure as chair of the vocal department at the College included some of the most profound changes in its musical history. Now as the College embarks on an aggressive fundraising campaign, we invite you to join us in our efforts.

As you are well aware, master classes are a vital part of every musician's education. Master classes provide students with a unique practical and professional educational experience that cannot be duplicated in the traditional classroom. Because of your continued commitment to the College of Music, we ask you to endow the Ms. E Vocal Master Class Series. Your contribution will ensure that this program will remain intact for future generations of students at the College of Music.

Specifically, the master class series will:

- *Attract* a group of the most respected musicians who are presently performing on stages internationally.
- *Ensure* the future of the program in perpetuity, so that music students for generations to come will benefit from this invaluable educational experience.
- *Strengthen* the College's vocal programs by fostering a dialogue between students and internationally renowned musicians.

An endowed $250,000 gift would make it possible for us to invite between two and four artists per year to the College to provide master classes to our vocal students.

Your development accomplishments have been instrumental in the growth of the College and its programs. We ask you to join us again now with your leadership gift.

Appendix 5–G

Sample Gift Proposal—Using a Planned Gift

Temple University School of Business and Management

Prepared for: Mr. K
November 29, 1999

Life Income Projections
Summary of Benefits

ASSUMPTIONS:
Projection begins in 1999 and runs for 10 years.
Measuring life age 78 [2/2/1922].
Date of gift is 11/9/1999.
Original principal is $500,000. Cost basis is 10%.
Donor income tax bracket is 39.6%, 20% for capital gains.
Beneficiary income tax bracket is 39.6%, 20% for capital gains.

	Charitable Unitrust 5%
Gross Principal	$500,000
Charitable Deduction	$328,730
Tax Savings	$130,177
Cost of Gift	$369,823
Income	5%
Capital Appreciation	5%
Total Before-Tax Benefit To Income Recipient	$314,447
Total After-Tax Benefit To Income Recipient	**$189,926**
Benefit to Charity	**$814,447**
Total Benefit	**$1,004,373**
Prepared by: Laura Fredricks	IRS Discount Rate: 7.4%

Note: This chart is for illustration purposes only.

Courtesy of Temple University.

Life Income Projections

Detailed Cash Flow Analysis

ASSUMPTIONS:
Projection begins in 1999 and runs for 10 years.
Measuring life age 78 [2/2/1922].
Date of gift is 11/9/1999.
Original principal is $500,000. Cost basis is 10%.
Donor income tax bracket is 39.6%, 20% for capital gains.
Beneficiary income tax bracket is 39.6%, 20% for capital gains.

5% Charitable Unitrust

YR	Year-End Principal	Capital Apprec. (5%)	Income (5%)	Before-Tax Ben. Inc	After-Tax Ben. Inc. (39.6%)
1999	$500,000				
2000	525,000	$25,000	$25,000	$25,000	$15,100
2001	551,250	26,250	26,250	26,250	15,855
2002	578,813	27,563	27,563	27,563	16,648
2003	607,753	28,941	28,941	28,941	17,480
2004	638,141	30,388	30,388	30,388	18,354
2005	670,048	31,907	31,907	31,907	19,272
2006	703,550	33,502	33,502	33,502	20,235
2007	738,728	35,178	35,178	35,178	21,247
2008	775,664	36,936	36,936	36,936	22,310
2009	814,447	38,783	38,783	38,783	23,425
TOT	**$814,447**	**$314,447**	**$314,447**	**$314,447**	**$189,926**

Prepared by: Laura Fredricks   IRS Discount Rate: 7.4%

Note: This chart is for illustration purposes only.

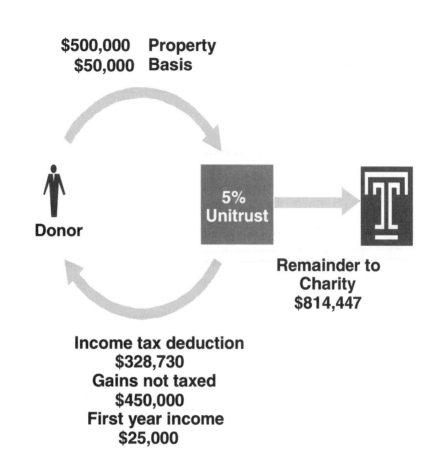

$500,000 Property
$50,000 Basis

Donor

5% Unitrust

Remainder to
Charity
$814,447

Income tax deduction
$328,730
Gains not taxed
$450,000
First year income
$25,000

Benefit

Immediate
Income tax deduction of $328,730. May save up to $130,177.
Pay no capital gains tax. May save up to $90,000.

Annual
First year income of $25,000. Income will vary in future.
Projected total before-tax income of $314,447 over 10 years.

Future
Charity projected to receive $814,447 in 10 years.
Reduced estate taxes and costs.

Appendix 5–H
Sample Gift Proposal—The Large Naming Opportunity

Resolved. The Board of Trustees approves the following recommendation of the Committee of Trustees:

The Dr. Q School of Medicine

In consideration of Dr. Q's outstanding contributions as Trustee at the School of Medicine and his distinguished contributions to the profession of medicine, including his magnanimous gift of $30 million for the benefit of the School of Medicine, the Board of Trustees hereby names the School of Medicine in honor of Dr. Q. The School in perpetuity will henceforth be known as "The Dr. Q School of Medicine."

Payment Schedule for this gift is as follows:

1. $20 million outright payable over the next five fiscal years.
2. $10 million in a 5% Charitable Remainder Unitrust with the University named as remainder beneficiary.

Gift Designation

The President of the University, the Dean of the School of Medicine, and select faculty from the School of Medicine, will determine appropriate uses for this unrestricted gift in the following areas:

1. Endowed chairs
2. Professorships
3. Term professorships
4. Research fellowships
5. Full scholarships
6. Technology upgrades

Gift Recognition

The School of Medicine Building will be forever named, "The Dr. Q School of Medicine." A dedication ceremony will take place at a date and time to be determined. We would like you to feel free to invite as many family, friends, and colleagues as you desire. With your approval, we would like to invite University Trustees, cabinet members, deans, administrators, faculty members, together with the School of Medicine Trustees, dean, doctors, faculty, administration, and staff.

Chapter 6
Asking for Major Gifts

I like the ask to be simple and direct. State clearly and consistently the purpose of the gift and the amount of the gift. Ask the question—will you! Do as many personal visits as required to complete the cultivation before asking for the gift. It always helps to have someone who gave, a peer, ask for support.

H.F. Lenfest, billionaire, former president and
owner, Lenfest Communications Inc.

DECIDING ON A SOLO SOLICITATION

Asking for major gifts can be one of the most difficult steps to the major gifts fundraising process. Many fundraisers enjoy getting to know their prospects and cultivating them to the point of the ask. But when it comes time to do the ask, they think that unless they say the right magic words, at the right moment, and all the stars in the sky are aligned in the right position, the prospect will say "no" to the gift.

While we know this is not true, doing the ask can certainly feel like a moment of pressure and can create tension and anxiety. Luckily, we can put some structure on this process to help you do many effective and successful asks.

The first step is to decide whether a solo solicitor or a double team should do the ask (Donovan 1994, 22). There are a number of factors that can influence the strategy of whether to have a solo solicitor or a double team:

1. The size of the nonprofit.
2. The number of fundraising staff.
3. The budget for fundraising expenses.
4. The time devoted by top management to solicit gifts.

Generally, the smaller the nonprofit the more likely most of the asks will be done by one person. Many small-to-medium size organizations simply do not have enough staff to have two people on each solicitation. This is especially true in offices that have an executive director, CEO, or president, with one or two fundraisers and one assistant/support staff. It is often the case that limited numbers of fundraisers at these nonprofits are responsible for multiple tasks. Asking for major gifts is just one part of their responsibilities. Under these circumstances, most of the asks, other than the top high-end asks, would be done by the fundraiser. Top asks would be done by the executive leadership.

Many small-to-medium size organizations may not have the fundraising budgets to send two people on the ask. Some organizations may feel that precious fundraising expense dollars can be put to better use by having one person solicit one prospect. This way, more prospects can be covered with fewer dollars spent.

Time is yet another factor to consider, especially the time allotted by the senior management to solicit gifts. For example, the executive director may not have enough time to go on every solicitation. In these situations, the front line fundraisers should do most of the asks, leaving the senior management to handle the top asks from the top prospects.

If you find yourself fitting into the circumstances I just described above, and you are not sure when to ask senior management or a volunteer to accompany you on the solicitation, then use the next set of guidelines in Exhibit 6–1 to help you decide when to do the ask alone and when to use the double team approach.

Exhibit 6–1 Using a Solo Solicitor

A solo solicitor can be used when:

1. The fundraiser has been the only one or the primary person working with the prospect.
2. The ask will not be one of the organization's top asks.
3. The fundraiser is extremely confident he or she can address the prospect's questions and concerns.
4. The prospect would feel more comfortable being asked by the fundraiser than anyone else from the organization.

Let's use an example to illustrate the points made in Exhibit 6–1. Over the past year, Major Gifts Officer Sam has been working with prospect E to secure a major gift for the aquarium. He has met with prospect E several times at her office and has brought her and her family several times to the aquarium's special events. Major Gifts Officer Sam has been with the aquarium for over six years, and during that time he has developed strong relationships with senior management, the board, the aquarium's executive committees, and staff. He feels the time is right to ask prospect E for a $30,000 unrestricted gift to maintain the new tropical fish exhibit that will remain a permanent feature for the aquarium. Top major gifts for the aquarium would be in the $150,000 and above range. In this situation, having Major Gifts Officer Sam ask prospect E for the gift would be a good strategy. His six-year tenure at the aquarium would give him the confidence to address any question or concern that prospect E may have about the gift or the organization. Since he is not asking for a top major gift, having him do the ask would be perfectly acceptable. Last, since prospect E knows Major Gifts Officer Sam the best, chances are she would be more comfortable with having him ask her for the gift than anyone else from the aquarium.

USING THE TEAM APPROACH

The ideal situation when asking for major gifts is to use *the team approach*. This is by far the best way to major gifts fundraise (Walton 1999, 18). Why? Soliciting in teams can be more effective than asking for the gift alone. Team members can use individual strengths to present the case for support and can gain energy and competence from each other during the process. One member of the team can speak, while the other team member can listen and observe the prospect's body language. With a team approach, there is less chance that you will miss something the prospect has said, or has shown through body language, than if you did the ask alone.

I never really appreciated the value of having a partner assist me during the solicitation until I started doing every ask in a team. Even if the solicitation was for a modest increase of the donor's gift from his or her previous year's gift, I always took someone from the organization with me. Later, after the ask, my solicitation partner and I would compare notes. We would carefully go over what each person heard and saw during the visit. You would be amazed at the number of things each of us would have missed if we did not have each other as a backup listener and observer.

The team approach serves to let the solicited prospect know that he or she is important enough to merit two people from the organization when it comes time to ask for the gift. It elevates the prospect to the top tier of supporters for the group. It sends the message that the organization values this prospect and that the organization does not take this type of solicitation lightly. This moment has been well thought out, well planned. The solicitation team can bring to light all the prospect's involvement with the organization and the benefits of his or her past support. The prospect now feels much time and attention has been paid to him or her by the organization and that sets the stage for a very effective ask.

Selecting the Right Team Solicitors

The team approach requires that the solicitors be carefully chosen. Exhibit 6–2 contains the ideal characteristics of a good solicitor.

Exhibit 6–2 Ideal Characteristics of a Good Solicitor

1. Possesses a strong, personal relationship with the prospect.
2. Knows everything about the prospect, his or her interests and involvement with the organization.
3. Is easy going, relaxed, and confident.
4. Is well versed and knowledgeable about the gift opportunity.
5. Is a top organizational leader—for high-end gifts.
6. Is a volunteer/peer who has made a gift of similar size requested.
7. Demonstrates a strong commitment to the organization.
8. Has a willingness to spend time before, during, and after the solicitation to ensure receipt of gift.

Any solicitation team should include someone who can naturally and comfortably relate to the prospect (Dickey 1997, 29). This usually includes someone who has worked the most with the prospect and has a strong prospect-fundraiser relationship with him or her. More often than not, this will be the organization's development/major gifts staff member. The fundraiser is usually the one who makes the calls, sees the prospect, brings the prospect to events, sends the prospect targeted mailings, and keeps the prospect fully informed about the organization's progress. By this point in time, the fundraiser should feel extremely at ease and relaxed with the prospect, such that asking for the gift will be the logical and natural next step to the prospect-fundraiser relationship. The prospect in turn should also feel very "at home" with the fundraiser. There must be good chemistry between the prospect and the fundraiser, otherwise the ask will not go well.

One solicitation member must be well versed and knowledgeable about the gift opportunity. This is par-ticularly important if the gift proposal is complex, contains detailed financial planning options, or includes a planned gift. For instance, fundraiser N prepared a $250,000 charitable remainder unitrust proposal for his prospect. During their presolicitation discussions about the prospect's gift, the prospect said that if he were going to make a gift of this size, he would probably use his stock. Fundraiser N felt pretty confident about the details of his proposal and how it would work using stock to fund the gift. When fundraiser N presented the proposal to the prospect, the prospect asked the following questions:

- "Can I fund the trust using half cash and half stock?"
- "I have a property in the mountains that I have always wanted to sell. Can the charity sell it for me and use the proceeds to fund the trust?"
- "Who will be the trustee of the trust?"
- "If the organization serves as trustee, does it charge a management fee?"
- "How many years can I carry forward this income tax deduction you just showed me?"
- "Can I fund it this year but have it start next year? I really don't need the deduction this year."

Fundraiser N did not have the answers to these questions. This example shows that while fundraisers may think they know enough about the gift proposal, it is advisable to bring someone who has the special skills that may be called upon during the solicitation (Burke and Reardon 1994, 14). In this instance, someone with planned giving knowledge or financial planning would have been ideal to accompany fundraiser N on the solicitation. That person could have quickly addressed the prospect's questions and kept the prospect's enthusiasm about the gift and the financial benefits of the gift alive. Instead, fundraiser N now has to get back to the prospect with the answers. Much of the momentum and rhythm of the gift solicitation has been lost. This is not to suggest that the gift will not happen if the fundraiser does not have all the answers to the prospect's questions during the solicitation. Rather, it is to suggest that the more prepared you are, with careful thought into who would be best to accompany you on the solicitation, the smoother the solicitation process will be. Your preparation will give you the confidence you need for future solicitations.

Tip: *When selecting a cosolicitor, make sure you consider whether or not you will need someone with special skills to address any questions the prospect may have about the nature of the gift or the financial benefits of the gift.*

Complex gifts or gifts that will create or fund highly technical projects, programs, or equipment may call for a volunteer or staff person in your organization who has that expertise to accompany you on the solicitation. This is especially true in the health care field. Physicians, nurses, clinicians, and laboratory technicians, if they have the time and are willing to go with you on the solicitation, can make excellent solicitors. These folks have the energy, intelligence, and aura of authority when they describe the features and benefits of a program or service.

For instance, Major Gifts Manager Chris had a $2.1 million gift proposal for two brothers to fund a new emergency room in a local Catholic hospital. Both brothers had surgery in the old emergency room, and they were ready to make a gift to the hospital that took such good care of them. Major Gifts Manager Chris knew that the brothers enjoyed watching all the television shows that involved some aspect of medicine. One brother even went to medical school for two years but never completed his degree. Major Gifts Manager Chris knew that the brothers would have numerous questions about the new emergency room. While she could answer most of the questions pertaining to the physical structure of the new unit, she was unsure she could address all the patient care questions the brothers may have.

Major Gifts Manager Chris asked a physician assigned to the emergency unit to accompany her on the solicitation. She felt that a gift of this magnitude required someone with extreme knowledge of the new unit and someone who would speak with convincing authority. All areas of potential questions could be covered by either member of this solicitation team.

This example also shows the need to bring the top leadership from your organization on your top solicitations. Major Gifts Manager Chris' gift proposal for the two brothers was a top ask for the hospital. Selecting a physician in perhaps the hospital's most vital area, the emergency room, was an appropriate decision because the physician constituted organizational leadership. Solicitations of top asks are almost always done with either someone in a leadership position, such as an executive director, president, board member, trustee, dean, faculty member, or a volunteer or peer who has made a gift of a similar size (Goettler 1998, 17). Their presence sends the signal to the prospect that this is a very important moment and the top leadership or a top donor must be part of this significant meeting.

It also sends the signal to the prospect that if the prospect does make the gift, he or she can feel secure that the organization will use the gift wisely. Most prospects have positive impressions of the top leaders of the organization. If they didn't, you would have heard about it during the cultivation period. They would not be at this point, considering whether to make a major investment with your group if they did not think highly of the organization's leaders. Remember, fundraisers up to this point have spent a long time with the prospect building up the good reputation of the organization. When it comes time for the ask, chances are the prospect has met, spoken with, or corresponded with someone of authority in the organization. Having an organizational leader co-present an ask will send the message that the prospect is important, the gift is needed, and the leadership will be around a long time to oversee the prospect's investment.

Many solicitation teams consist of the fundraiser and someone who has made a gift of similar size as the one requested of the prospect. These types of peers are marvelous historians and storytellers for the organization. I use this characterization because they can relate to the prospect's initial concerns, hesitancies, and sometimes fears about making the gift. They speak from experience, and the prospects want to hear their stories. These donors were in the prospect's shoes once, and they can in a very warm-hearted yet persuasive way, alleviate the prospect's worries or concerns and focus the prospect on the benefits of giving.

These peers then go on relaying delightful stories of how the gift changed their lives and the lives of their families. It helped to instill in their children and grandchildren the importance of giving back and helping those who cannot help themselves. Many times these folks speak about how they became more involved with the organization, volunteering to help events, fundraisers, and outreach programs. They name people at the top of the organization who have taken the time to call and meet with them just to let them know all the great things that are happening because of their gifts. Having a peer speak from the heart and serving as a beacon of light to the benefits of gift giving can create a powerful solicitation for your prospect.

> *Tip: Consider selecting someone, a peer, who has given to your organization on the same scale as the gift amount requested to accompany you on your solicitation. Your prospects may feel more reassured about making the gift once they have heard from the peer how well your organization continues to manage the gift and how your organization continues to include them in all the organization's activities.*

The last characteristic of a good solicitor must apply to at least one member of the solicitation team. Someone must demonstrate a strong commitment to the organization and have the time and desire to spend on the prospect before, during, and after the gift is received. Why are these factors so important? Just think what would happen if in the example of the peer solicitation above, the prospect said to the peer, "Gee, you really do know how hard it is to want to make the gift, because we just don't know how long we'll live and how much money we'll need. Mind if I call you if I need to talk this through with someone other than my family?" Now let's say the peer says yes and gives his or her telephone number. A few days later, the prospect calls the peer. The peer is out of town but will call next week. One week goes by, two weeks go by, and by now the prospect begins to distrust the peer's sincerity. The prospect then calls the fundraiser who was on the solicitation team, but she, too, can't get a hold of the peer. The prospect was led to believe by the team that the prospect's interests came first and that the prospect was important to the organization. Whatever faith in the solicitation team the prospect might have had is surely lost.

All your solicitation preparation and efforts will be of no use if the members of the solicitation team appear as if they are not committed to your organization or cannot commit the time to follow through with the prospect once the gift has been solicited. Some fundraisers think that they have this covered by asking their executive directors, presidents, chiefs of staff, or any paid top administrator for the organization to accompany them on the solicitation. I assure you this is not always the case. There are instances in nonprofits where top leaders and administrators feel that it is the fundraiser's job, not their job, to raise money. They may come with you for the solicitation, but from that point on, it is the fundraiser's job to carry through. This is not necessarily a bad dynamic, and it is not meant to suggest that during the solicitation these solicitors will

not demonstrate a strong commitment to the organization or to the prospect. It is, however, a word of caution that if this is the case, then the fundraiser must be prepared after the solicitation to carry the ball. Your boss or the top leaders may inquire about the gift, but it is up to the fundraiser to follow up with the prospect and to section out time in his or her schedule to be available to address any of the prospect's concerns or need for additional information.

> *Tip: If you select a top official from your organization to be a cosolicitor, make sure you know before the solicitation if that leader will have the time to spend with the prospect after the solicitation. If the answer is no, make sure you section out time in your schedule to stay proactive with the prospect and to keep the gift proposal in the forefront of the prospect's mind.*

Preparing the Solicitation Team

Once you know who is going to solicit the prospect, then it's time to thoroughly prepare the team for the solicitation. This preparation stage takes two parts. The first part entails making sure that the team knows all the facts about the prospect, such as the prospect's involvement with the organization and giving history with the organization, and has complete understanding of the gift proposal. The second part entails scripting the ask for each solicitor, so that each member knows the gift proposal inside out and knows what they are expected to say and do during the solicitation.

Painting the Total Prospect Picture

Part one of the preparation stage is where the fundraiser gathers all the prospect information for the solicitation team. Most of this information should be readily available in the donor's profile discussed in Chapter 2, "Creating Donor Profiles." Exhibit 2–1 in that chapter lists 14 items that should be part of every donor profile. Be sure to review that information and make sure that it is up to date. It is good to have this information readily available for your team; however, a suggested approach is to prioritize the data. This way you will not overwhelm your solicitors with reports and files. You can concentrate on the most important features of the donor profile that are key to the solicitation. Exhibit 6–3 is a list of priority prospect information that should be shared with the solicitation team.

Exhibit 6–3 Priority Prospect Information for the Solicitation Team

1. Prospect's involvement with the organization.
2. Prospect's gift history.
3. Prospect's visits and meetings with anyone from the organization.
4. Prospect's contacts with organizational leaders/volunteers/peers.
5. Prospect's wealth—including the types of assets the prospect will most likely use to fund the gift.
6. Prospect's motivation to make the gift.

Armed with these facts, the solicitation team will have a good idea of the type of person they are about to solicit. Keep in mind that in most instances, the solicitor will have met the prospect previously and may even know the prospect on a personal/professional basis. Even if this is the case, make sure the solicitor knows the details listed in Exhibit 6–3. It will set the solicitor in the right frame of mind to ask for the gift. Pay particular attention to past contact reports. These should reveal any presolicitation discussions that occurred. It will give the solicitors a keen insight into any obstacles that may be presented during the solicitation.

For example, let's suppose that during a solicitation team preparatory meeting with a fundraiser and peer, the fundraiser showed the peer seven prior contact reports. While describing those meetings, the peer was reading over each report. The peer questioned why on four occasions the prospect always mentioned the cruises he just took. The fundraiser responded that the prospect in his later years enjoys travel and likes to share his vacation memories when the fundraiser visits. The next question is key—the peer asked, "Is there any way the prospect will turn us down because he wants to save his money for his future vacations?" This is a great question. It shows insight and forethought into the solicitation process. No doubt the fundraiser thought this might come up during the solicitation. Now the team can work on their combined response to the prospect if he uses this as an obstacle to the gift. The team can strategize on the phrases they will use that will recognize the prospect's zest for travel, while

promoting the rewards the prospect will feel when he makes the gift.

The next step to the initial preparation stage is to make sure that the solicitation team knows every aspect about the gift proposal. The solicitation team should be given a copy of the gift proposal and should carefully go over the details of the proposal (Kelly 1998, 494). Try to prevent what I call the "team glossing over the plan" syndrome, which can happen during this meeting. This is the scenario where one or more team members will try to deflect the importance of knowing all the aspects of the proposal by making the following remarks:

- "I've been with this organization for years."
- "I've known the prospect for ages, she'll really like this offer."
- "I founded this program."
- "The prospect has enough wealth to make this gift and live two more lifetimes."

Statements like these can set the wrong tone for your team because it gives them a false sense of security. Implied in each of these remarks is the sense that the solicitor, through tenure with the organization or personal knowledge about the prospect, can field whatever question the prospect may have. This is exactly what you are seeking to avoid. You want your team members sharp, thinking of possible prospect questions and concerns. You want them asking questions about the proposal so that they will have confidence and commitment in their voices when they make the pitch. You do not want to lose sight that the purpose of this meeting is to educate your solicitation team on the gift proposal facts contained in Exhibit 6–4.

Tip: Try to prevent members of the solicitation team from "glossing over" the details of the gift proposal. Make sure they know all the facts about the proposal and feel confident that they can answer the prospect's anticipated questions.

SCRIPTING THE ASK

When scripting the ask for your solicitation team, keep in mind that you should count on no more than 25 minutes for the total solicitation. Of course you want to be able to spend more time with your prospect during

Exhibit 6–4 Gift Proposal Facts Each Solicitor Must Know

1. The purpose of the gift.
2. Why this gift proposal is the perfect match for this prospect.
3. How and when the gift can be funded.
4. The income and tax benefits for this prospect if the proposal includes a planned gift.
5. Who is going to benefit from the gift.
6. How the organization came to place this dollar figure on this gift opportunity.
7. Why the gift is needed.
8. Why the organization cannot take a lesser amount for this gift proposal.
9. Other donors who have made gifts of this size.
10. The proposed recognition if the gift is made.

the solicitation, however, it is wise to script the ask for this time frame. It will focus the prospect's attention on the purpose of your visit. It will also prepare you in case you get to your appointment and the prospect tells you he or she has a limited amount of time to spend with you.

Your solicitation team must be aware of the four basic components to the major gifts ask as well as the time limits for each component:

1. The warm-up—5 minutes
2. The ask—6 minutes
3. The response—10 minutes
4. The close—4 minutes

The Warm-Up

Once the solicitation team is in the door with your prospect, you want the prospect to feel at ease with each solicitor. This is sometimes referred to as making casual preliminaries with your prospect (Kelly 1998, 494). It is the role of the solicitor who has had the most contact with the prospect to set the friendly tone of the visit by asking the prospect questions about the prospect's family, work, activities, and hobbies (Sturtevant 1997, 93). For instance, if you know the prospect's daughter just had a baby, ask how the newest member of the family is doing. You might even see some new pictures of the baby in the prospect's home or ask the prospect if he or she has any pictures of the latest grandchild. If your prospect has returned to school to get an advanced degree, ask the prospect how

he or she is doing at juggling a full-time job or full-time family responsibilities and taking a course.

The most important thing is that you *bond* with your prospect. You do not want to look too serious or too stiff. This can happen because the solicitors have the ask on their minds and their body language may be revealing that they are just a bit anxious to ask for the gift. Five minutes will give you enough time for the solicitors to bond with the prospect and to ease into the presentation of the ask. If the solicitors have chatted with the prospect about some enjoyable aspect of the prospect's life, then everyone in the room at this point should be smiling and comfortable. This is exactly what you want as you launch into the second component of the solicitation—the ask.

The Ask

The transition from the warm-up to the ask should be as smooth as glass. You do not want everyone joking and laughing during the warm-up, then like a ton of bricks, blurt out, "We're here to ask you for a half a million dollar gift for our child day care program." While you do want to get to the specific dollar amount of the gift, *how you lead up to the ask* is critical.

The way to make a smooth transition from the warm-up to the gift proposal presentation and to gain the focused attention of your prospect is to reference the prospect's connection and/or activity with your organization (Sturtevant 1998, 95). Exhibit 6–5 contains a list of transitional phrases you can use to focus your prospect's attention on the upcoming gift proposal presentation.

Phrases like the ones suggested in Exhibit 6–5 will put your prospect in the right frame of mind to lead up to the ask. It invites the prospect to reflect over the years of service to your group, the prior monetary investments he or she has made, and the friends and colleagues from your group he or she has come to know and enjoy. It guides the prospect down the path to think about the next step he or she can take with your organization to do something *more*. And more is exactly what the solicitation team is going to suggest.

Two key points to keep in mind for your solicitation team as they make their way from the warm-up to the ask. First, make sure the solicitors have *high energy*. This is an enthusiastic moment and requires the solicitors to be upbeat and positive. Prospects will pick up on the solicitors' demeanor. If the solicitors present the gift opportunity in a quiet, reserved, and soft-spo-

Exhibit 6–5 Transitional Phrases—From the Warm-Up to the Ask

- "You have been an exemplary donor over the past three years. Your gifts have inspired others to support us."
- "We are blessed to have you as such a faithful and loyal donor. Your generosity has made it possible for us to feed the homeless, to give weekly reading classes to the partially blind..."
- "As a trustee for a number of years, I think you can appreciate and celebrate with us how far we have come in the past seven years."
- "Volunteers are our best cheerleaders for the organization, and we would not have been able to grow and thrive as a leading national charity without your leadership and your dedication to us."
- "We have known each other for quite some time, and we at the organization feel very close to you as a trusted friend, an inspiring volunteer, and a generous donor."

ken manner, all the energy and the build up to the ask will be depleted. After all, solicitation is marketing. To really sell the gift, the solicitors must be enthusiastic about the organization's mission, its direction, its leadership, and the prospect's participation in this exciting process.

The second point is that the solicitors must be mindful of their *body language*. In most situations, the prospect and the solicitors are sitting in an office, living room, or dining room. Be careful how you are sitting in the chair. I have seen some solicitors slouched in an easy chair, rocking nervously in a rocking chair, lost in a mountain of pillows in a large couch, rhythmically tapping their fingers on the kitchen table, and sitting what appears like a football field away from the prospect. All these nonverbal communications can send distracting signals to your prospect. Solicitors should sit in an upright position in a chair, close to the prospect, with their eyes focused on the prospect. This will send the right message to the prospect that the solicitors have something very important that they want to *share* with the prospect.

Now the team is ready to ask for the gift. Since preparation is 90 percent of the solicitation process, this is the part where the team's preparation will really pay off (Williams 1997, 366). Lead by referencing the prospect's known interest in a particular program or area in your organization. Some examples would be:

- "Jim, your support for our mentoring program has put us on the map as the model for these types of programs."
- "Leslie, your suggestions on how to expand our membership for our science center have been invaluable."
- "Scott, without the help from your local business, we would not have been able to provide the food and clothing for our shelters last winter."

The solicitation team can also reference any prior comments the prospect may have made regarding the importance of a particular project or program (Stevenson 1996, 26). This is a natural lead-in to let the prospect know that the organization has matched his or her interests with the perfect gift opportunity. For instance, the solicitor could say:

- "Amy, when we met the last few times, you expressed an interest in helping us acquire better equipped vans to transport our disabled residents. We have a plan in mind, and we need your help."
- "Richard, you have spoken on several occasions about your desire to someday help us have a more powerful voice in government. With your help, we can achieve this. Let us explain."
- "June, we share your concern for not having a large enough facility to help the number of homeless people in our city. We have a way to expand our facility to provide for every homeless man, woman, and child, and we turn to you now and ask us to make this dream a reality. Let us explain."

Phrases like these will let the prospect know that the organization has listened to his or her interest and that the organization has thought long and hard about matching the right gift opportunity to meet the prospect's desire to support that area of interest. You have the prospect's attention now, which is perfect! The prospect is curious to know exactly what the organization has in mind. Now it is time for the team to state the particulars about the gift.

The solicitors need to share the following details in this order about the gift with the prospect:

1. A description of the gift.
2. The benefits of the gift.

3. How this gift will achieve the prospect's personal/financial goals.
4. The gift amount requested.

It may seem painfully obvious that the gift needs to be described; however, there have been occasions when solicitors assume the prospect will know all about the gift. For instance, the solicitor says, "We wanted to see you today because we would like you to consider making a significant gift to support our scholarship fund." That sounds like a great start, but the solicitors need to expand a bit on the details of how the scholarship fund works. Too many solicitors jump to the benefits of the gift before describing what the gift is all about. It does not have to be an elaborate discussion, just a sentence or two about how the scholarship fund works, the number of past students who received scholarships, and how the recipients are chosen.

One way to ensure that the gift is sufficiently described is to tell it like a story. Have the solicitors tell in their own words and in their own experience the importance and significance of the gift. It is important that the solicitors bring their own personalities into the process. The stronger they feel about the gift, the stronger the prospect will feel. Using the scholarship fund example, if the solicitor or family member or friend ever received a scholarship, have the solicitor talk about those experiences. The more personal the solicitors make this process, the more convincing they will be that this gift is worthy of the prospect's support.

The solicitors are then in the prime position to launch into the benefits of the gift. Notice that the team at this juncture is speaking about the *benefits of the gift, not the financial needs of the organization.* Prospects want to hear how the gift will help people, not how the organization will reach its funding goals (Stevenson 1996, 26). In the example of asking the prospect to support the scholarship fund, the solicitors could cite an example or two of how recent scholarship students landed terrific jobs. This is much more effective than telling the prospect that the college has a goal to increase its scholarship fund. Remember, even if the ask is to construct a new wing, add an additional studio, or pay for new computers, the gift will ultimately help *people.* This will be a much easier sell than emphasizing how well the organization will look with a new unit or how high tech the organization will be with the latest computer capabilities.

This is also the time the solicitors need to mention the benefits the gift will bring for the prospect. If the prospect said previously that he or she always wanted

Tip: When the solicitation team introduces the gift idea to the prospect, they should mention no more than three benefits the gift will bring. Otherwise, the prospect may be overwhelmed with facts and figures and may lose enthusiasm for the "core" reasons to support the gift.

to help the organization out in a more meaningful way, make sure the solicitors tell the prospect that this gift will achieve the *prospect's desire* to do something rewarding. If the gift will help the prospect meet his or her financial goals, make sure the solicitors highlight this point. This is especially true if the prospect has been concerned with avoiding taxes yet maintaining enough assets to live on and to pass on to family members. If the gift as presented can achieve those goals, the solicitation team must share this good news with the prospect.

At this point, the prospect knows about the gift and its benefits and has a good idea why the organization has offered him or her this particular gift idea. Now it's time for the solicitors to ask for the specific dollar amount. Up until this point the prospect has felt that the organization has devoted careful time and attention to his or her individual interests. The solicitors' role is to make sure the prospect continues to feel this way, even when being asked to make a large investment.

Asking for a specific amount can be an uncomfortable task for some solicitors. No one likes rejection, and the fear, of course, is that the prospect will reject the solicitors' gift proposal. One way to get by this potential stumbling block is to have the solicitation team practice the way they will ask the prospect for a specific amount. The words the solicitation team uses to ask the prospect are crucial because you want them to keep the solicitation as personal and sincere as possible. Prospects will really listen and give careful consideration to the gift offer, if they are asked from the heart. Exhibit 6–6 lists suggested ways the solicitors can ask for the gift that will keep the solicitation on a personal and sincere basis.

Notice how the words are carefully selected. They "invite" the prospect to become active, to "join" with them and the leaders of the organization to climb aboard this forward moving train. The prospect has the opportunity to do something he or she has always wanted to do, whether that be to help others in a tremendous way or to make a gift that will last for generations to come. Everything is upbeat, full steam ahead. The prospect does not want to be left behind.

Exhibit 6–6 How To Ask for the Gift

- "We would like you to consider…"
- "We invite you to consider an investment of…"
- "We only ask this of our top donors."
- "As a loyal and devoted donor, we turn to you now and ask you to think about how meaningful your ____ will be."
- "Your gift of ____ will be the cornerstone to our students' future."
- "By your previous conversations, it is clear that you share our vision to ____. We turn to you now and ask you to make a commitment of ____."
- "Your ____ investment with us will be the leadership gift that will spark this exciting project."
- "You have always given from the heart and have set the example for others to support us. In that spirit, we would be grateful if you would consider making a ____ investment."
- "We think you feel as passionately as we do about ____, which is why we would like you to consider a ____ gift to ____."
- "This is an invitation to make a real difference for ____. Your ____ investment will fulfill that dream."
- "We are turning to you now, and to a few of our other special friends, to ask you to consider making a leadership gift of ____ to ____."
- "I think you agree and our leaders agree that ____ is an exciting project and worthy of support. Your gift of ____ will get us there."
- "My commitment of ____ has helped start this project that you, I, and the leaders at ____ think is vital to our future. We ask you now to join with others and show your support for the campaign by making a similar commitment of ____."

The momentum is at an all time high, and all that is left is to sit back and listen to the prospect's thoughts.

These suggested phrases do not include words like "contribution" or "donation." To me these words sound stagnant, ordinary, and dull. They neither inspire nor capture the prospect's attention. The solicitors need to speak to the prospect as if he or she were part of a winning team. Use words like "we" not "I." Make sure you bring in whenever possible the fact that this is something the *prospect* always wanted to do and that the

leadership of the organization *joins* the prospect and shares his or her vision. The prospect will feel the strength in numbers. No one likes to think that they are making this huge monetary commitment all alone. If the solicitor has made a similar size gift, bring it to light right away. It shows that the prospect will not be alone in this investment. His or her gift will be joined by that of others, and together it will build the school, assist the elderly, clothe the poor, or save the wildlife.

> *Tip: When asking for the specific dollar amount, make sure the solicitors speak passionately about the gift and ask the prospect to join the leadership of the organization to make the gift happen. Make the prospect feel special by stating that he or she is one of a handful of select leaders the organization can invite to make this important commitment.*

The Response

After the solicitors have asked for the specific dollar amount, they must sit back and *say nothing*. This can be painfully difficult. We all have a tendency to want to jump into the conversation, keep it on a roll, until everyone is in agreement. Silence is key at this point (Stevenson 1996, 26). You want to give the prospect this moment to think about the gift and to respond and react. The prospect's response, verbal and non-verbal, will let the solicitation team know what they should do next. By listening effectively, then addressing the prospect's concerns, the solicitation team will gain the prospect's trust and respect. It will also increase the chances of securing the gift.

The prospect can react in a number of ways, and the solicitation team has to prepare for any and all responses the prospect may have. Many fundraising books, journals, and articles refer to this as overcoming objections, turning objections around, or making the objection the opportunity. But the prospect is not objecting to the ask when he or she says, "That sounds like a lot of money." The prospect is voicing a concern—a concern that the solicitation team with preparation will be able to discuss and lend support, so that the prospect feels the solicitors do care about his or her individual circumstances. This process is really about listening to the prospect's response and addressing the prospect's concerns and questions so that the gift proposal will be given great consideration.

To start, every solicitor should use the fundamental strategies listed in Exhibit 6–7 once the prospect has voiced a concern about the gift.

Exhibit 6–7 Fundamental Strategies To Address the Prospect's Concerns about the Gift

1. Clarify the concern by asking the prospect a question.
2. Restate the concern.
3. Do not argue with the prospect—just listen.
4. Use examples of others who had similar thoughts and how they were resolved.
5. Try to keep the discussion positive.
6. Recognize in some instances you may not be able to change the prospect's mind.

Let's discuss these strategies by using the example of a solicitor representing a public radio station, who just asked Roger to make a $100,000 investment for additional studio space. Roger turns to the solicitor and says, "I've been a fan and a supporter for years. But now, I really don't like the guy you have on the morning show." The solicitor at this point needs to get the gift proposal back in front of Roger by saying, "Roger, if I understand you, you like our station, and we know you've been a great supporter. But at the current time you don't care for this one announcer. Is your feeling about that announcer preventing you from considering this very special gift?" This shows that the solicitor has listened to Roger's concerns. The solicitor needs to understand the exact nature of the concern and discuss the issues directly and honestly with the prospect (Edwards and Benefield 1997, 57). The solicitor will gain more ground with Roger if Roger's feelings are not discarded.

This also helps to steer the conversation back to the gift proposal. Addressing the concern by asking a question and restating the concern does not mean that the solicitor loses sight of solicitation. If this step is done properly, it will serve to bring the gift proposal back into the conversation. Notice how the solicitor asked Roger, "Is this preventing you from considering the gift?" This question must be asked because it has two outcomes. Roger could say, "No, I didn't say that at all." If the solicitor did not ask Roger this question, she could have wrongly assumed that Roger's feeling for the morning announcer was a major stumbling block to the gift. Instead, she learned that it isn't. She can acknowledge Roger's concern while returning to the

gift discussion by saying, "Roger, we always encourage our supporters to let us know what they like and dislike about the station. We are very grateful you shared that with us today. I will make sure that the managers at the station know how you feel about this announcer. Your input means that you are genuinely concerned about the future of the station. We share your enthusiasm and want to share with you more details about this very exciting gift opportunity for *your* station."

Roger's alternative response to this question could be, "Yes, I won't think about another gift to the radio station until that guy is off the air." If this is the case, the solicitor needs to let Roger vent. Obviously, he has strong feelings about this announcer, and it will do the solicitor no good to argue with him. After the solicitor has listened to why Roger dislikes the announcer, the solicitor needs to keep the conversation on a positive note. She can say, "Well, Roger, I understand you may not care for this one particular announcer, but I think you will agree, for over 17 years our station has been a constant source of education and entertainment for you and folks just like you in our listening area. You said that the show "On-Air Live" is your favorite, and it's mine too. We would not be able to produce shows like this one without the help of our good friends like you." This will get Roger into thinking about the positive aspects of the station, which motivated him to make his previous gifts. The solicitor must listen to the concern and try to put a positive spin on the situation whenever possible.

Another approach the solicitor could try with Roger is giving examples of others who may have had a similar feeling about an announcer, program area, or music selection and how that person still made a gift. For instance, the solicitor could say to Roger, "We had a similar instance when we asked an avid listener and special donor for a similar gift, and she responded by telling us she did not like a few ads that we ran during a political primary. We told her, as we are telling you now, that if we don't hear this feedback from our loyal supporters, like her and you, we have no way of knowing how we can better serve our audience. She felt better that we listened to her and that we promised to carry that message to our owner and manager. After giving our gift proposal some thought, she did make the gift." This approach will go a long way in winning back your prospect. Examples of other donors with similar concerns can lead the prospect down a more positive path. It shows the prospect that the organization will listen to this concern and any other concern the prospect may have. In some instances, if enough donors have the same concern, it may even motivate the organization to find a constructive solution to resolve the issue (Stevenson 1996, 27). After citing similar donor concerns with positive outcomes, the prospect's negative feelings may dissipate. The prospect at that point may be ready to hear more about the gift and the benefits it will bring.

There will be instances when the prospect's concerns cannot be turned around. The solicitors need to be aware of this fact. Sometimes, a prospect will let the concern prevent him or her from even listening to one more word about the gift. It is very disappointing, but it happens. The solicitors should implement the first five strategies in Exhibit 6–7 first, and then if it is evident that the prospect has no intention of giving the gift proposal any consideration, the solicitor should just listen to the prospect's concerns. Once the prospect is finished, the solicitor should let the prospect know that his or her concern will be passed on to the leadership of the organization. As with any other visit, the solicitor should set up the next meeting or way to keep the prospect active. The worst thing the solicitor could do at this point is to discontinue working with the prospect. *A "no" response now does not mean the prospect will never make a gift.* Even though the gift is turned down or put on hold for awhile, the solicitors have given the prospect a greater understanding of the institution. The solicitation, despite the outcome, has brought the prospect one step closer to the organization. Continued cultivation will keep the door open for a future solicitation.

> *Tip: If the prospect has a deep-seated concern that prevents him or her from considering the gift proposal, the solicitor should listen to the prospect, promise to bring the concern to the organization's attention, and continue to cultivate the prospect for a future solicitation.*

Turning Stumbling Blocks into Building Blocks

The best preparation any solicitor can have going into the solicitation is to prepare for the most likely response the prospect will give after the ask. Preparing and rehearsing with other development professionals on staff and with family members and friends can ensure that the words flow smoothly and that there are as few surprises as possible. I encourage fundraisers to practice with family members and friends because those folks generally do not know the prospect inside and out like the solicitors do, and oftentimes they can come up with responses that might throw the solicitor off if that were truly the prospect's response. It is much harder to get the words out when they are said live in front of a neutral person, than it is when they are said silently to yourself.

The following is a list of responses that prospects have made to asks for various gifts. This list is by no means the entire universe of what any prospect would say to any ask. It is, however, a good road map to use when soliciting gifts. Without preparation, the prospect's responses could seem like major roadblocks to obtaining the gift. With the awareness of these potential responses, some practice, and knowing that the prospect may have a response not listed here that the solicitor will have to address openly and honestly, the solicitor's response to the prospect's concern will be a building block, not a stumbling block, to getting the gift.

1. ***That's too much money you're asking me to give.***
   - We understand perfectly, and believe us, we do not ask for this everyday.
   - You are but one of the very few people we can turn to and ask for this very important gift.
   - Is it the size of the gift or the fact that we asked you now for the gift that seems most troubling?

To many fundraisers, this is the most common response they anticipate the prospect will have to the ask. The apprehension is that the prospect is telling the solicitor that he or she has asked for too much, but if the solicitor asked for a lesser amount, the prospect would still be interested. *Resist all temptation* to lower the gift level. It is very natural to want to ask the prospect, "What level can you give at this time?" You can get to this answer, but you will get much further if you start with the approach suggested above of stating right up front that yes, this is a very large amount asked, something not done everyday. The last impression you wish to give the prospect is that the organization asks for this level gift quite often or that the organization has many prospects and donors to ask for this size gift. That would leave the prospect feeling that if he or she didn't make the gift, it would be no big deal—the organization would move on to someone else. By stating, right up front, "We know it is, and we do not ask for this everyday" will let the prospect know that he or she is on the top of the organization's list for this size support. The next response, "You are one of the few people we can turn to ask for this important gift," will bolster your original statement and will let the prospect know that the organization views him or her as a treasured and model donor.

The solicitor should next clarify the prospect's concern that the ask is too high. This is done by simply asking the prospect, "Is the amount the part that seems most troubling, or is it the fact that we asked at this particular time?" Again, it is very easy to make assumptions when the prospect responds to an ask, but resist, resist. When this happens, ask questions to make sure you know exactly why the prospect responded this way. By asking this type of question, the solicitor will have a clear idea if the prospect feels the solicitor asked for too much money or whether there is some other issue at hand, which would make this size gift out of the question. You may find out that the prospect is saving for a child's education, paying for a parent's continuing care costs or his or her own medical bills, to name a few.

2. ***I wish I had as much money as you people think I have.***
   - Yes, this gift is extremely important, because it will transform the lives of so many families for generations to come.
   - Gifts like this one are once in a lifetime opportunities. Knowing your strong ties with the organization, we had to come to you first. We would not be here today were it not for the strength and generosity of our many supporters, particularly you.

The tendency here is to think that the prospect may not have as much wealth as the prospect research and personal meetings have led the organization to believe. Before jumping to this conclusion, the solicitor should make the importance of the gift the focal point of the discussion. Let the prospect know that this is a "once in a lifetime chance" and that you and others could not possibly ask anyone else first, knowing how much the prospect cares about the organization's future. Now is the time the solicitor needs to weave in the prospect's interests in the organization and say why this gift matches perfectly the prospect's desire to do something significant for the organization.

This is also the time to remind the prospect that this is not a "stand-alone gift." The organization has the backing of many supporters, and the gift the prospect is about to consider will be a solid investment. You want to make sure the prospect knows, and is reminded at this crucial time, that your organization is on solid ground. The prospect's anticipated gift is at the top tier of this support, and it will attract additional solid support from many donors for years to come. Telling the prospect, "We would not be here today but for the strength and generosity of our many supporters, particularly you," will send this message loud and clear.

3. ***I'm really not interested in supporting this project.***
   - From our previous conversations and your questions and comments about the project, we thought this gift idea would match your interest for this project. Can you tell us where your main interest lies in our organization? We want to hear more from you.
   - Now that we know you are really enthusiastic about supporting the overall good work, as opposed to one specific project, we would be happy to share with you how others have made similar gifts to support the organization.
   - Thank you for being so candid with us today. Our goal is to always know our friends like you as best we can.
   - Since we are being perfectly frank here today, how do you feel about making a gift of this size that would ensure the success of the organization for years to come?

Sometimes, no matter how much time has been spent cultivating and getting to know the prospect, a gift idea will be suggested that the prospect has no interest in supporting. The organization may have thought by the prospect's active interest and participation in a particular project or program that the prospect would naturally make a gift in this particular area when the time was right. Solicitors who encounter this type of response need to let the prospect know why this type of gift was suggested and must ask what the prospect's primary area of interest would be if he or she were to make a gift of this size. This exercise will accomplish several goals. First, it will let the prospect know that the people who have been cultivating him or her have listened to him or her and these are the reasons why the organization thought this would be a good gift opportunity for him or her. Second, it will give the solicitors a chance to hear directly from the prospect his or her primary interest in the organization. Third, it will keep the gift solicitation on track. Now the solicitors can talk about other supporters who have made gifts of this size and for the same purpose. This will give the prospect confidence to know that again, there is solid support for your group, and that he or she would join that small circle of top supporters. Fourth, it keeps a gift opportunity for this prospect alive. What if the solicitors said, "Gee, we had no idea you really liked this area and not that area," and then did not follow through with questions about the prospect's interests? The solicitation would go dead in the water, and it would take many more visits to get the prospect back to the position of considering a major gift. By asking the prospect questions about his or her main organizational interest, then reviving his or her enthusiasm to make a gift that matches that interest, the solicitors will be ever so close to securing a major gift from that prospect.

4. ***I can't give you an answer now, and I really can't say when I'll know.***
   - Important decisions take time, and we want you to take your time deciding this very important opportunity.
   - As we described the gift opportunity, what are your feelings right now about it?
   - How can we help you while you are making your decision? Do you need more information? Would it help if we speak with others who may have a say in this very important and rewarding gift opportunity?
   - There are many factors you probably want to spend some time thinking about. During this reflective time, we would like you to keep in mind the joy your gift will bring to all those people you have said you really wanted to help out someday.
   - We will be in touch very shortly, just to listen to your thoughts and to see if we can answer any questions you may have.

No doubt the solicitation team will get the response from the prospect that he or she simply cannot commit at this time and that a decision may be far off in the distant future. The solicitors cannot let the end of this rope go, by simply saying, "Thank you for your consideration. We appreciate all you have done in the past, and let us know when you reach your decision." Rather, the solicitors should emphasize the importance of the gift and recognize that it may take some time. The solicitors at this point need to get the gift idea back into the conversation to see if the prospect has a genuine interest in the proposal. Like the prior example, this prospect may not be head over heels about the gift opportunity, which is why he or she will not commit. You must uncover this important fact before you can move on.

It is important to offer the prospect the solicitor's services to provide additional information and meet with the other people who may have a say in this decision. Prospects do not always tell you that they want to discuss it with their spouse, significant other, child, lawyer, or accountant, which is why the solicitors must take the initial step to meet with others. Even if the prospect turns down the offer, at least he or she knows that this must be an important gift since the organization is willing to meet the people closest to the prospect.

The solicitors need to end the meeting in two ways. First, they must leave the prospect thinking about the benefits of the gift because if the meeting is left on this note, chances are the prospect will want to ponder the gift idea. Remind the prospect of all the good that will come from his or her generosity. This is a wonderful thing that the prospect can do—helping those people the prospect has always wanted to help. If you leave the prospect with these thoughts, he or she will give the gift idea greater consideration, than if the prospect was left thinking that he or she must decide this in a week or two. Second, always have the solicitors be proactive in setting up the next step with the prospect. Otherwise, the prospect may never get back to the solicitors. Too much valuable time will be lost between the solicitation and the decision. Have the solicitors say, "We will call you in a few days, just to check in and listen to your thoughts." This will ensure that the prospect continues to consider the gift and does not put in on the eternal "to do" list.

5. ***I have to consult with my spouse/daughter/ attorney/accountant, but I don't think he or she will want me to do it.***
   - Naturally we would want you to share these facts with others you wish to confide in.
   - What is important here today is that you would like this gift to happen.
   - We found that anytime someone is really enthused about an idea, "jazzed-up" about it, others take that approach as well. We bet if you share your eagerness for this gift, your advisor will feel the same way as well.
   - We would be delighted to meet with your advisor with you, or alone, so that we can provide first-hand information about the gift.

- We could put the proposal with some additional materials in the mail to the advisor and follow up with a telephone call. How does that sound?

This is the flip side to the previous example where the prospect could not commit to an answer. Now we have an instance where the prospect appears to want to continue discussing the gift but has let the solicitors know that it will not be a solo decision. The solicitors must first acknowledge that it is only a natural desire to want to consult with others when considering a large gift. They must continue by getting the prospect to say that he or she would like the gift to happen. The prospect's positive feelings about the gift can then be carried over when he or she meets with the other decision maker. You do not want the prospect going to meet with the other decision maker half-heartedly or feeling 50–50 about the gift because it will most assuredly be met with the response, "It sounds like you are not crazy about this idea, so say no for now." While the solicitors cannot control how the prospect will be when he or she meets the other person, they can try to set the stage for this meeting by getting the prospect in a positive frame of mind and feeling upbeat about the opportunity.

The solicitors should always offer to personally meet the other decision maker. I suggest that the solicitors offer to meet collectively first, then offer to meet with the other person alone. Most prospects would feel extremely uncomfortable having the solicitor meet alone with a family member, but they may not mind if the solicitor saw a more neutral party, such as their financial planner, accountant, or attorney. A fallback position is to offer to write to the other decision maker, detailing the proposal and adding information about the organization (Sturtevant 1997, 113). Most outside decision makers will need to be educated about your organization, so the solicitors must include all background information and information specific to the proposal. Now the solicitors can market the charity to the outside decision maker and sell the features of the particular gift proposal. It is a good idea to include in these materials information about the prospect's leadership with the organization; how he or she shaped the future direction for the group; or some special point about the prospect. This will let the outside decision maker know that the organization thinks well of the prospect and that the prospect's past relationship with the organization merits consideration of this gift.

If something is sent in writing to the other decision maker, the solicitors need to send a copy to the prospect to "keep the prospect in the loop." No prospect wants to feel like an outsider, especially now. This will inevitably lead to lost ground with your prospect. Also, make sure the solicitors suggest that they will call the other decision maker after the materials are sent. This will give the prospect the chance to let the solicitors know if they have his or her permission to contact the outside decision maker. Again, the prospect can feel "out of the loop" if the solicitors make the assumption that they can call the other decision maker after sending material. If they get approval, then the solicitors can keep the gift on track by calling the outsider decision maker. If they do not, then they should suggest that they will call the prospect right after they send the material to the outside decision maker so that the prospect and the advisor can discuss the gift. In this instance, it will be the solicitors' responsibility to stay in contact with the prospect to make sure he or she discusses the gift with the other decision maker. If you allow the prospect to control the timing of following up on the ask, the solicitors will have a difficult time judging when they should contact the prospect to keep the proposal alive (Hartsook 1998, 83).

6. *You couldn't have picked a worse time to ask. (My business is down/I just got laid-off/I lost a major investment.)*
   - Thank you for being so honest with us. I'm sure that was not an easy thing to say.
   - Obviously this is not a good time to discuss the gift idea so why don't we agree to keep in close contact and to revisit this idea when things turn around.
   - We are extremely grateful that you gave us the time to introduce you to this gift idea.
   - Please know that all of us at the organization are on your side, and you are a very special friend to us.

This is the hard one—one where your heart goes out to your prospect because no one wants to see a person suffering hard times. The solicitors must be as empathetic as possible right up front. They must thank the prospect for his or her honestly in sharing this very painful information. After all, it is not an easy thing to admit to anyone, let alone people who just asked you for money, that life is really not going your way now. The prospect could have told the solicitors an excuse for not making the gift, and in fact, could have said "no" instantly. Instead, the prospect chose to be honest and forthright. The solicitors, therefore, must acknowledge and respect the prospect's honesty.

Next, state that this really is not a good time to discuss details of the gift. Any attempt to do so at this point would be futile. The prospect would not be listening, and it would make the solicitors appear cold and callous. The solicitors should, however, say that they want to keep in close contact with the prospect. It will let the prospect know that they are not about to drop the prospect simply because he or she cannot make the gift at this time. Rather, it keeps the door open to the future date when the prospect will be in a position to discuss the gift.

The solicitors need to remind the prospect that the organization is extremely grateful for all he or she has done in the past. You will earn big points if the prospect feels appreciated, especially now when things are not so good and the prospect's confidence is probably very low. It also is very important for the solicitors to speak with the voice of the entire organization, the leadership, staff, volunteers, and beneficiaries of the organization, when thanking the prospect for his or her past support and vested interest in your group. This will make the prospect feel that there are many people on his or her side, pulling for him or her, and that your organization really does think about the prospect in a specialized and individual way.

7. *I don't think I can do this. My son wants to go to a private school next year, and my wife and I are considering placing her mother in a nursing home.*

- Selecting the right school is a big decision. Congratulations to you and your son.
- We try to think of our parents as the ones we can always count on, but there comes a time when they need us. That's a difficult decision to make, but knowing you, you'll make the right one.
- Put those two things aside for just a moment. Tell us what you think about the gift idea we just described.
- Maybe making this gift can actually help, rather than interfere with some future financial commitments. Let's brainstorm about this for a minute.

This is a very common response. Your prospects do have other financial commitments, especially if they are still raising families or have elderly parents who may need their financial help. The first thing the solicitors need to do is to congratulate or be sympathetic with the prospect, depending on the information just revealed. If the prospect has a son, daughter, or stepchild who is about to enter college, congratulate the prospect. This is a big moment for the family, and the solicitors want to be a small part of this happy time. If the news is not so good, such as a family member in the hospital, an elderly parent who may be placed in a nursing home or continuing care facility, then be sympathetic. The point here is to get closer to the prospect by speaking as if you were a family member.

Next the solicitors need to steer the prospect back to the gift idea, gently. They do this by saying, "Putting those things aside just for a moment, tell us how you feel about the gift." The solicitors need to get a good read on the prospect's interest in the gift proposal. Even if the prospect is not able to make the financial commitment now, he or she may be able to do so in the future. This is also the time to see if the solicitors have matched the prospect's interest with the right gift proposal.

The information the solicitors have just revealed is very telling. The prospect sees the gift proposal as another thing that may deplete his or her wealth, and for this period of time, it is out of the question. Here is the chance for the solicitors to turn it around, by informing the prospect about the organization's various planned giving vehicles that may help alleviate some of the financial burdens that he or she may incur with upcoming commitments. Have the solicitors explain how a structured charitable trust agreement may solve all the concerns. If the solicitors do not feel comfortable enough describing the planned giving vehicles, they can introduce the concept to the prospect at this meeting. Later, they can follow up with a planned giving illustration, showing how the prospect could use the income from the trust to pay for the college tuition or retirement care costs. This keeps the gift proposal a possibility with the prospect, when it could have turned out to be a definite "no" for a long period of time.

8. *With a charitable trust, what are the maximum payments I can get each year? How many trusts does your group manage? Can I select the trustee? Why can't I make it revocable now, and then later make it irrevocable? Can I switch beneficiaries once the trust is formed?*

- These are all excellent questions. We do not have all the answers for you today. We would like to gather these facts and come back in a few days with the complete information.
- It sounds like you are well informed about the numerous benefits a charitable trust can bring. Why don't we go over each of your questions one by one right now?

I use this example to illustrate two scenarios. The first is where the solicitors may not have all the answers to the prospect's questions. In the first scenario, there will be times that no matter how well the solicitors may prepare prior to the solicitation, they may not know all the answers to the prospect's questions. The questions may be centered on the mechanics of a planned gift. Many of your prospects will be very knowledgeable about planned gifts. They receive numerous mailings and invitations to attend financial planning sessions and planned giving seminars. Some may know a few facts and will look to the solicitors to answer questions they have had for a long time. Other questions may be about specific details about the organization or about the proposal that the solicitors cannot answer in full.

If the solicitors cannot address the questions on the spot, rather than have the solicitors guess or "fudge" the answers to the questions, they should tell the prospect that they are excellent questions and set a date and time when they can meet the prospect again with the answers. It is much better to give full and complete information at a later time. Otherwise, the solicitors will lose credibility with the prospect. The solicitation will begin to fall apart, and the gift will become less and less important to the prospect.

In the second scenario, the solicitors may well be able to answer the prospect's questions. One or both of the solicitors may be very knowledgeable about the organization's planned giving program. Under those circumstances, it is always a good idea to have the solicitors acknowledge that the prospect has done homework and that he or she has many very good questions. This is great energy for any solicitation. You have the prospect engaged and ready to discuss the fine points of the proposal. Keep this energy going by complimenting the prospect in this way, and then stating that the questions will be answered one at a time. This puts structure into the solicitation process. You want to keep your prospect focused at this point, because he or she may have the tendency to keep asking questions, rather than taking one point at a time, then moving on to the next question. The goal is to have your prospect listening to your answers, and then asking follow up questions. You will not make any progress with your prospect by jumping from question to question, without the prospect fully comprehending both the mechanics and the benefits of the gift.

9. ***I'd like to do something more, but I don't think I can go that high.***

- Your past support has been a model for other supporters to emulate. We are confident that your past, present, and anticipated future dedication to our organization will lead you in the right direction.
- We really appreciate that you want to do something that will be worthwhile and fulfilling for you. Tell us how you feel about this one-time chance to make a real difference.
- I'm sure you have a lot to think about at this point, and we want you to think about this very exciting opportunity carefully. Why don't we call you in a few days so that we can discuss this further?

Here we have a situation where the prospect has been a loyal donor and has thought about a major gift before the solicitation. From the outset, this should give the solicitation team great confidence that their timing for the ask is right on target. Armed with this confidence, the solicitors should not fall into the temptation to take a gift of a smaller amount before exploring all possibilities that the prospect could make this size gift. To start, have the solicitors thank the prospect for his or her past support. This gets the prospect to reflect on past gifts. Fundraisers have the tendency to think that if a prospect thinks too much about past gifts, he or she will say, "I've already given x amount, isn't that enough?" What many prospects are really thinking is, "I could have given a little more each time." Solicitors want the prospect to think about his or her past giving history with the organization because it is a natural lead in to discuss a major gift. Every gift brings the prospect closer to the organization. The prospect experiences a sense of ownership of and responsibility to the organization. Since the prospect in this instance is hesitant, the solicitor needs to remind the prospect of this bond with the organization and should state something to the effect that, "It will lead her to the right decision" about the gift proposal.

Sometimes the prospect may be extremely hesitant to talk about a gift of the size suggested. In that case, the solicitors must echo the prospect's words that he or she "wants to do something more" and get back to the gift at hand. Let the prospect tell the solicitors that he or she likes the gift idea; it's the money that is getting in the way for now. This is also the time the solicitors need to emphasize the benefits of the gift and stress that it is a once in a lifetime chance to do something really meaningful that will affect so many people.

Last, the solicitors should resist the temptation to lower the gift price. The natural tendency with this type of response from the prospect is to ask what level major gift the prospect could make. This may indeed come later, but not now. The solicitors must pursue the gift offer all the way through, by giving the prospect some time to think it over and meeting again to discuss it further. If the prospect says at that later time that he or she cannot make a gift of that size, then it would be an appropriate time to help the prospect decide on the right gift level (Williams 1991, 40).

10. *What made you think I have this kind of money?*
    - You have been an outstanding supporter, and the leaders of our organization wanted to turn to you first and ask you to consider this wonderful opportunity.
    - We respect you highly and hold you in our highest regard. A project this important, one that will shape our organization for years to come, is a fantastic opportunity. We wanted you to be the first to know about it.
    - I think you will agree that this is a terrific project. We are not looking for an answer today. Instead we would like you to give it some thought, and we can discuss it more next week.

This can be an embarrassing moment for the solicitors, but by focusing the response on the prospect's outstanding contribution to the organization, any embarrassment will quickly disappear. The solicitors cannot say, "Well we did our prospect research, and by all factors, we know you have the assets to make this size gift." I guarantee you the prospect will not consider the gift with this response. The best way to handle this is to have the solicitors get off the subject of money and get on to the subject of why they asked the prospect. Prospects who give this type of response generally want to hear that they have been good supporters and that they are at the top tier of givers. Use phrases like "outstanding supporter," "model donor," "true leader," "one of the few we could turn to," and "gifts of this kind come seldom—we had to come to you first." This serves as a huge pat on the back for the prospect and changes the tone of the meeting from edgy to warm and friendly. It is very important that the solicitors set the right tone in these instances; otherwise, they will be left justifying why they asked for this level gift.

Once that has been established, the solicitors can then move to discussing the gift. During the discussion,

the solicitors need to observe if the prospect likes the idea and is willing to talk about it or whether the prospect has dismissed the idea completely because the price is just too high. As with the example above, the solicitors have to resist negotiating the price of the gift (Sturtevant 1997, 118). Give the prospect some time to consider the offer, and then plan to meet again to follow up.

11. *We like to give to many charities, and if we make this gift, there will not be enough to give to others.*
    - We understand perfectly. Many of our top supporters give to more than one charity. That's what makes people like you so special.
    - We do not want to mislead you. Our purpose here today is to introduce you to this exciting opportunity and to hear your thoughts about it. We are not looking for you to decide right away.
    - How do you feel about the gift opportunity we just described?

Most of your prospects probably do give to more than one charity; therefore, you need to be ready to handle this type of response. The suggested approach is to compliment the prospect for being so generous to so many groups and thanking him or her for supporting your organization. State up front that you are not looking for an answer today. Rather, you want the prospect to take time and think it over. The prospect has just stated that he or she is unsure and that he or she needs some time to think. If the prospect makes a sizeable gift to your charity, it will impinge on the size of the gifts he or she can give to other groups. Pushing the prospect at this point will not help the solicitation process.

A word of caution to the solicitors about this type of prospect response: Solicitors should not downplay the importance of the other charities that the prospect may support. Sometimes solicitors get a little overzealous about their group, and their words and body language send negative signals to the prospect about other charities. Since the prospect has just made them aware that they are competing for donor dollars, the solicitors may want to convince the prospect that their charity is more deserving of a major gift than the other charities. If this happens, the solicitors will appear unprofessional. It will bring more harm than good to this process if they try to discredit other groups. Keep in mind that your prospect selected these other charities and supports them because he or she believes in them.

How will the prospect feel if the solicitors speak disapprovingly about these charities or try to convince the prospect that their charity is more worthy of a major gift than the other charities? The solicitors will not gain any ground with this approach. In fact, it has the potential to really backfire, leaving your group without a gift.

The solicitors at this point should glean from the prospect his or her feelings about the gift. If the prospect continues to reiterate concern that by making the gift, he or she will not have enough to give the other charities, then the solicitors should close the meeting graciously and continue to cultivate and involve the prospect in the organization's activities (Sturtevant 1997, 115). This prospect may need more time and education about your group before feeling comfortable with supporting it in a major way.

12. ***Prior to you coming, I already made out my check. It's on the table.***
   - Thank you for this generous gift. Before we accept it, why don't we tell you more about this great opportunity? Then at the end of the meeting you can decide if you still would like to give it at this time.
   - You are such a loyal donor; our organization is so lucky to have you. Think about what we just talked about. If you still would like us to take your gift, we would be happy to. But let's keep the door open to this opportunity we just described.
   - If you decide you would like to make the gift we just described, we can use this as your first payment/credit toward that terrific opportunity.

Your organization should consider itself fortunate if your solicitors receive this type of response. Here we have a loyal donor who is showing how much he or she cares about your group that the prospect is giving before being asked. What is difficult for the solicitors in this instance is not to look disappointed and not to accept the gift without pursuing the larger gift. A "bird in the hand" theory does not work here. The solicitors should immediately thank the prospect and then quickly get back to the major gift proposal they just described. Key phrases like, "before we accept it," "your loyal gifts make you the perfect person to consider this great gift," and "let's keep the door open" will clue the prospect into thinking about the gift. Solicitors need to resist the temptation to accept the prospect's first offer and should continue to pursue the gift proposal (Williams 1991, 41).

The hard part is the thought that by not accepting the gift the prospect has made prior to the ask, the prospect will be insulted, hurt, or feel that his or her "smaller gift" will not be appreciated or needed by the organization. The way to get around this is to have the solicitors acknowledge that he or she is such a thoughtful person and to suggest the possibility that if he or she does make the major gift, this check can be used as the first payment or credit toward the larger gift. This will bring several benefits:
   - It will get the prospect to think more about the major gift.
   - It will put the solicitors at ease that they have not said or done anything that would indicate the organization is not grateful for the gift the prospect has just given.
   - It may entice the prospect to make the major gift if this gift can be the first installment.

13. ***Sounds great, when do you want the money?***
   - As soon as possible! (Try not to smile too hard!)

The Close

Regardless of the prospect's response to the ask, every solicitation must end with a close. Exhibit 6–8 contains the elements of an effective close.

Exhibit 6–8 Elements of an Effective Close

1. Thank the prospect for his or her time.
2. Restate the gift and purpose of the gift.
3. Bring up one or two benefits that attracted the prospect during the solicitation.
4. Give the prospect a date when you will get back to him or her with answers to any questions raised.
5. Pause to see if the prospect has any additional comments or questions.
6. Speak to the prospect as if he or she said yes to the gift.
7. Maintain strong eye contact and positive body language.
8. Talk about the possible ways the prospect's gift can be recognized and celebrated.
9. Ask the prospect how he or she would like the gift recognized.
10. Do not leave until you have a tentative date to meet again.

Thanking the prospect for his or her time is a gentle way to bring closure to the meeting. The prospect will know that the meeting is about to end with this simple statement. Before it does end, the solicitors must, with enthusiasm in their voices, restate the nature and purpose of the gift, and then talk about one or two benefits mentioned earlier that caught the prospect's attention. For instance, if during the solicitation for a $150,000 leadership gift for an after-school program, the prospect seemed to really like the fact that the program will be instrumental in reducing drug abuse and crime, the solicitors should expound on this benefit. During the close, you want to hone in on the salient points of the gift, not repeat every point previously made. This will hold the prospect's attention during the close, and it will leave the prospect with the best points to think about once the solicitation is over.

If the prospect has raised a question or concern that needs to be addressed, pledge during the close that you will get this information for the prospect. This will show the prospect that you did listen to his or her every word and that he or she has your promise that you will get back with answers. This is why it is so important that the solicitors give the prospect an approximate date to anticipate hearing from the organization again. You do not want the prospect guessing or wondering how long this can take. By saying to the prospect, "We'll get back to you in a few days with the details you requested," the prospect will have a clear idea when he or she will have the answers.

> **Tip:** *After each solicitation, make sure you record in your personal calendar system the date you are to contact the solicited prospect again so that the solicitation continues to move forward.*

The solicitors then need to pause and say nothing. This will give the prospect the chance to ask more questions or make any further comments. It is necessary at this point to do this "silent period" again as was done right after the ask because you want to be sure you have not been doing all the talking and the prospect has been doing all the listening. Your silence will invite the prospect to speak. If the prospect says nothing, ask if there is anything else the solicitors can share with the prospect at this time and if the solicitors have explained to the prospect's satisfaction the pur-

pose and the benefits of the gift. If the prospect has no further comments or questions and understands the gift proposal, the solicitors have done their job well.

At this point, it always helps the close if the solicitors speak to the prospect as if he or she has said "yes" to the gift (Hartsook 1998, 22–23). They can do this by using the following phrases:

- *Your* named scholarship fund
- *Your* state-of-the-art studio
- *Your* name on the atrium
- *Your* children and youth camp
- The joy *your* gift will bring to our patients

This has the powerful effect of bringing the prospect into the moment as if he or she said "yes" (Sturtevant 1997, 122). At this point, the prospect can experience how good he or she will feel by making the gift. Once you have the prospect in this mind frame, you will be closer to obtaining the gift.

It is very easy at this point for the solicitors to lose steam and to be less conscious of their eye contact and body language. After all, asking for gifts is a very emotional experience. It requires energy to look sharp and to sound convincing. During the close, it is important for the solicitors to maintain their enthusiasm, their strong eye contact, and positive body language. These are the types of lasting impressions you want to leave with your prospect. They connote the strength and reliability of the organization.

At the close, the solicitors should briefly mention ways the gift could be recognized. Relay examples of the ways your organization recognized donors who made similar size gifts in the past. For instance, if you asked the prospect for a leadership gift for a campaign, tell the prospect how your group recognized previous leadership gifts. Ideas could include a front-page article in the organization's newsletter; a special plaque at the facility; and a quarterly luncheon for everyone who made leadership gifts. The solicitors should make sure that they ask the prospect his or her ideas on recognition. The prospect may have a unique and special request that neither the solicitors nor the organization ever thought about.

> **Tip:** *When discussing gift recognition during the close, be sure to ask the prospect for any ideas on how he or she would like the gift recognized.*

This is a presumptive approach because you are speaking to the prospect as if he or she is going to make the gift (Wood 1996–1997, 43). This approach may give an extra push for your prospect to give greater consideration to the gift. It will also clue the solicitation team into the prospect's degree of readiness to make the gift. If the prospect joins the conversation by giving his or her views about how he or she would want or not want the gift to be recognized, this is a good sign. It means the prospect will seriously consider the request. If, on the other hand, it is met with the response, "That's getting ahead of us now," or "This is really premature to discuss now," the solicitors know the prospect is not ready to commit and will need more time.

Every close should end with a next step to see or contact the prospect. This may have been already established when the solicitors set a time to get back to the prospect with answers to his or her questions. If the prospect just needs more time to consider the gift or wishes to consult other decision makers, make sure the solicitors set a tentative date to meet or speak on the telephone. A simple, "We will call you next week" or "Can we set up a time to meet next week" will cover this step.

WHEN THE RESPONSE IS "NO"

Solicitors need to be prepared if the prospect responds to the ask with a firm "no." Sometimes no matter how perfectly the solicitors have executed their answers to the prospect's responses, the prospect simply will not make the gift. It is hard to hear the word "no" because a lot of time, thought, and energy have gone into the solicitation process. No one likes to be rejected, and this certainly can feel like rejection.

A few thoughts to keep in mind when this happens: First, the prospect is not saying "no" to the solicitors, he or she is saying, "I do not want to make this gift," or "I cannot afford to give at this level at this time." Try not to internalize the "no" or to take it personally. Easier said than done. However, the more solicitations you do, the more you will anticipate a "no" or two. It will become part of your job once you hear the firm "no" to keep working with the prospect. The prospect has said no to this gift, at this time. The prospect has not said that he or she wants nothing to do with the organization or that he or she would not consider this gift or a new proposal at another time.

Which brings up the second point. *"No" now does not mean "no" later.* Do not discontinue your cultivation efforts with this prospect. The prospect will feel dropped, neglected, and rejected by the organization if this happens. A cultivated, solicited prospect is a much better candidate to make a major gift than is a new, uncultivated prospect. The tendency with some fundraising organizations is to put the solicited prospect at the bottom of the prospect list. This would not be a wise method of fundraising. Many solicited prospects will find it harder to say "no" at a later time if the organization continues to educate and involve the prospects in the organization's activities and if the prospects have a genuine desire to support the group (Williams 1991, 41).

A change in the prospect's circumstances at a later time could lead to a future gift. For example, the prospect could get a big promotion at work, inherit money, or make some wise income-producing investments. Under these new circumstances, the prospect may be in a position to consider the gift. What a missed opportunity it would be if the solicitors gave up on the prospect with the first ask and never knew that the prospect was ready at a later time to make the gift. This illustrates the need to stay with your prospects and not to give up on them. Fundraising will test your patience and endurance. But those that persevere get the major gifts.

The third point is that even if the prospect gives a firm "no," the prospect has a much deeper understanding and appreciation of the institution. The solicitors have brought the prospect one step up on the involvement and education ladder. Additionally, prospects are always flattered that they have been asked to make a significant gift, even if they cannot do so at this time. The important factor is that the door has been left open for a future gift opportunity.

Reasons Why Prospects Say "No"

There are several reasons why prospects may say "no" to the gift opportunity. It is helpful to look over the list of reasons in Exhibit 6–9, so that the solicitors will not take the "no" personally and will have a better understanding of what the prospects are thinking about when they have turned down the gift.

It is hard to imagine spending a great deal of time with your prospects, getting to know their likes and dislikes, and then proposing a gift opportunity that the

Exhibit 6–9 Reasons Why Prospects Say "No" to the Gift

1. Wrong gift opportunity
2. Wrong timing
3. Wrong gift vehicle
4. Ask was too high
5. Specific amount was never requested
6. Ask was too low
7. Personality conflict with a solicitor or institutional leader
8. Not enough involvement with the organization
9. Immediate need for the gift was not conveyed
10. Sometimes it just happens

prospects have no interest in whatsoever. Believe it or not, it happens. Prospects' interests do shift from time to time, and they may have talked at length about one project, when all along they always wanted to support another.

Asking at the wrong time is very common. Your prospects are not one-dimensional people. They have families, businesses, friends, and social and recreational activities. They get ill, lose their jobs, and incur unexpected expenses. There is never an ideal time to solicit a gift. The solicitors must be aware that these are factors that they can encounter during the solicitation, and sometimes they will be unable, for now, to get by these major stumbling blocks.

If the solicitors have not suggested the gift vehicle that best suits the prospect, the prospect may reject the gift offer. Some prospects know exactly how they will fund the gift, if and when they decide to make a gift. They do not always share this information with the solicitors no matter how much the prospects have been cultivated. Money and investments can be very private topics for some folks, and these are usually the ones that know exactly what they will do when they are good and ready. This type of "no" is much easier to convert to a "yes" at a later time. The solicitors just need to continue to work with the prospects once they know how they would like to fund the gift. They are really only a footstep away from securing the gift.

To no one's surprise, asking for too much can lead to a "no." All the prospect research in the world and all the prospect-fundraiser meetings cannot produce the exact dollar amount the prospect is ready to give at a particular time. Knowing that the solicitors have done their research and made their personal visits and that the proposal was reviewed by the leadership of the organization should give the solicitors confidence that

they made the right decision to ask for this amount. The far worse scenario is if they did not ask at all.

Even if the solicitors have practiced and rehearsed the ask, there are times when the ask is never made, or it is made in a confusing and muddled way. Some solicitors may have thought they asked for the gift when in fact they never did. How many times have you heard that someone was just so nervous they could not ask for the gift? How many times have you heard that the solicitation was done over a long meeting or over dinner, and "there just wasn't the appropriate moment to ask for the gift?" Some solicitors may ask for it in such a confusing way that the prospect is left thinking, "Did you just ask me for $100,000 now and $100,000 later, or $200,000 over a few years?" It makes the solicitation team appear unpolished and unsure of themselves, which most assuredly will lead to "no" for the response.

Do not fall off your chair if the prospect says that he or she had something "larger" in mind. Some prospects may know that naming a wing at this hospital costs x amount, so why are you asking them to make a similar gift for a lesser amount? Not every prospect is a bargain hunter, looking to get the biggest gift for the least amount from the organization. High-level major gifts maintain their luster and appeal by maintaining their high price (Sturtevant 1997, 128).

Keep in mind when this happens that the prospect may have in mind a larger, planned gift when the solicitors asked for a smaller, outright gift. The solicitors in this instance should work both gifts at the same time. The prospect can put on hold the solicitors' gift idea while the larger gift from a bequest, charitable trust, or annuity is being drafted and executed. After that, the solicitors should continue conversations about the gift proposal. This is a classic example of a "no" now does not mean "no" later.

Be aware that the prospect might not "gel" with one of the solicitors, a board member, or institutional leader. This dynamic has nothing to do with the gift idea, the prospect's interest in the gift, or how the gift will be made. It has everything to do with clashing personalities. I was in the middle of a solicitation when the prospect said that he wouldn't give to the organization right now because he did not care for the leader's view on a certain political issue. After listening to the prospect, I said that it was only natural that some people would be in disagreement over some issues. Many leaders shape an institution. Leaders come and go, but the institution lives on in perpetuity. His gift would ensure our group's successful future. If this happens, try to steer your prospect into thinking about the "big picture" of the organization and not one leader.

The prospect may not like one of the solicitors, and that can really sour the solicitation. Even with great preparation, there is the chance that the prospect may feel competitive with one of the solicitors, particularly if you have asked a peer to join you on the solicitation. The best you can do at this point is to recognize that the peer was not the best person to solicit the prospect and to continue cultivating the prospect without this person's assistance.

If the prospect has not been sufficiently involved with the group, it is highly likely that the prospect will turn down the gift. The ask is premature. Each prospect requires a different degree of involvement and education. With some, it takes months; with others years, and there is always that group that seems like a lifetime will go by before they make a major gift. This makes it difficult to judge the prospect's readiness, as discussed in Chapter 4. Even if the ask was early, at least you have planted the seeds for the prospect to consider the gift at a time when he or she feels more attached to and educated about the organization.

Some solicitors fail to convey a sense of urgency for the gift. The prospect gets the idea that it really does not matter if he or she makes the gift now or next year. Once the prospect feels this way, he or she will say "no" for now. While this is a "soft no" it is still a "no," which is disappointing. This emphasizes why the solicitors should keep their energy high and convey clearly and convincingly why the gift is needed now and the immediate impact it will have on so many deserving people.

Last, sometimes a prospect will just say "no." In time you will learn why the prospect said no, and then you will be in a position to actively overcome any question or concern he or she may have. That's inspiration all by itself to keep working with your prospects, even if their first answer was "no."

WHEN THE RESPONSE IS "YES"

Usually prospects will need some time to think things over carefully before they render a yes response, but there are instances where a prospect has said yes on the spot. If the prospect says yes right away, the solicitors may think they did not ask for enough money. After all, if a positive response came this quickly, maybe they could have gotten a larger gift if they asked for more money. Maybe yes, and maybe no. The point

is that the solicitors and the organization put together a terrific gift idea that the prospect liked and is willing to fund. There will be plenty of time, after the prospect has received proper stewardship of the gift, to ask for the next larger major gift.

Exhibit 6–10 contains a checklist for solicitors to use once the prospect first tells them that he or she will make the gift.

Exhibit 6–10 Checklist When the Prospect Says "Yes" to the Gift

1. Thank the prospect on behalf of your organization.
2. Reconfirm the importance of the gift.
3. Reconfirm the benefits of the gift.
4. Discuss the details of how and when the gift will be made.
5. Discuss gift recognition.
6. Set up the next meeting to keep gift payment and recognition on track.
7. Do a contact report on the solicitation and outcome.

The first thank you the prospect receives should be on behalf of the organization. The solicitor needs to use phrases such as "we thank you" and "from all of us at the institution, thank you." After all, the prospect has just committed to a major gift to the institution, so the thank you needs to be on behalf of your entire group.

Next, reconfirm in a sentence or two the importance of the gift and the top few benefits that attracted the prospect to make the gift. This will be a natural lead in to discuss how and when the gift will be made. Devote as much time to this discussion as necessary. If the solicitors asked for an outright gift of $500,000 and the understanding is that the prospect would fund the gift with stock, the solicitors need to know when the prospect can transfer the stock to the organization. Other important details include information on the type of stock being transferred and the name of the prospect's stockbroker or brokerage.

Gift recognition may have been discussed in presolicitation meetings as well as during the solicitation. If so, the details need to be fine-tuned to everyone's satisfaction. If recognition has not been discussed, then it must be discussed now. To some donors, recognition is a large part of making a gift, and if it is, then the solicitors need to work with the prospect on the prospect's recognition package. Some donors will want to remain anonymous, and if so, this is the time to discuss private and personal recognition. If the donor wishes to remain anonymous, I always recommend that the solicitors tell the prospect that they will honor the prospect's wishes at the same time they tell the prospect the benefits to the institution if they can announce the gift. The prospect's gift can be used as a model to attract other major gifts from other prospects. As said before, "People give to forward moving trains," and if no one knows about the gift, it will be more difficult to convince new prospects that your organization is indeed a forward moving train. I also recommend that the solicitors use a gentle approach when introducing this idea. Many donors who want to remain anonymous usually have good reasons, and their personal reasons may outweigh the organization's desire to attract new gifts.

> *Tip:* If the prospect who has said yes to the gift wishes to remain anonymous and have no public recognition for the gift, let the prospect know that the gift will attract other major gifts and that it will bring multiple benefits to the organization. If the prospect declines publicity, honor the prospect's wishes for anonymity.

Saying yes to the gift brings with it many details that need to be addressed until the gift is funded and recognized. Be sure to strike while the iron is hot by setting up the next meeting. When you get back to the office, apprise your institutional leaders and coworkers about the gift, record your wonderful results in a contact report, and give yourself a big "congratulations."

RECAP AND REVIEW

1. For every solicitation, decide whether it would be better to have one solicitor or a solicitation team.
2. The best way to raise major gifts is to use the team approach.
3. The solicitation team members can include someone who has cultivated the prospect, someone who has special skills or expertise pertinent to the gift proposal, an institutional leader, or a volunteer or peer who has made a gift similar in size to the one requested.
4. Prior to the solicitation, each solicitor must know the total donor profile, understand every part of the gift proposal, and know his or her part and the cosolicitor's part in asking for the gift.
5. Every major gifts ask includes four parts: the warm-up, the ask, the response, and the close.
6. Throughout the entire solicitation, each solicitor must have high energy, speak with a clear and convincing voice, listen to all the prospect's questions and concerns, and use body language that will mirror the positive and persuasive presentation.
7. When asking for the gift, the solicitors should select words such as "consider," "invite," "commitment," and "investment" and phrases such as "this exciting project," "leadership gift," and "as a treasured friend and loyal donor" that will let the prospect know this is a very important gift offer, worthy of great consideration.
8. After the ask has been made, be silent. Give the prospect the chance to ask questions, ask for further information, or voice a concern about the organization.

9. If the solicitors need to get back to the prospect with additional information, set a time frame for when the solicitors will have the information for the prospect and follow through.

10. The best way to prepare for the prospect's response is to be aware of the common prospect responses and to have the solicitation team practice their style for turning a potential stumbling block into a building block to get the gift.

11. At the close, the solicitors should thank the prospect for his or her time, restate the purpose of the gift, restate one or two benefits that attracted the prospect to the offer, use presumptive phrases like "your name on the atrium" to put the prospect in the mindset as if he or she said "yes" to the gift, and set a date to meet again to further discuss the gift offer.

12. There are many reasons why a prospect will turn down a gift; however, "no" now does not mean "no" later.

13. After the prospect has turned down the gift, the solicitor MUST continue to cultivate the prospect.

14. Most prospects who agree to make a gift will do so after they have time to think it over.

15. When the prospect has agreed to make the gift, the solicitors must thank the prospect on the organization's behalf, reconfirm the importance and benefits of the gift, discuss how and when the gift will be made, discuss gift recognition, set up the next meeting, apprise institutional leaders and coworkers, and do a contact report.

REFERENCES

Burke, K., and R. Reardon. 1994. Competition or collaboration: Redefining success. *NSFRE's Advancing Philanthropy*, Fall.

Dickey, M. 1997. Taking time to secure large gifts. *Chronicle of Philanthropy*, July 24.

Donovan, J. 1994. Take the fear out of asking. The asking process: The APOC method. *Fundraising Management*, June.

Edwards, R., and E. Benefield. 1997. *Building a strong foundation for non profits*. Washington, DC: NASW Press.

Goettler, R. 1998. Excerpts from major gifts: Developing strategies for success. *Nonprofit World 16*, no.3:18.

Hartsook, R. 1998. *Closing that gift*. Wichita, KS: ASR Philanthropic Publishing.

Kelly, K. 1998. *Effective fund-raising management*. Mahwah, NJ: Lawrence Erlbaum Associates, Inc.

Stevenson, S. 1996. *Making the ask. Solicitation skills builder*. Sioux City, IA: Stevenson Consultants, Inc.

Sturtevant, W. 1997. *The artful journey*. Chicago: Bonus Books, Inc.

Walton, C. 1999. The psychology of major gifts. *Fund Raising Management*, February.

Williams, J. 1991. *Big gifts*. Rockville, MD: Taft Group.

Williams, J. 1997. Overview of major giving. In *The nonprofit handbook: Fundraising*, ed. J.M. Greenfield, 366. New York: John Wiley & Sons.

Wood, E. 1996–1997. The art of securing major gifts. *NSFRE's Advancing Philanthropy*, Winter.

Chapter 7

Thanking and Recognizing Your Major Donors

CHAPTER OUTLINE

- The Importance of the Initial Thank You
- What Makes a Good Thank You?
- Thanking Your Donors
- Gift Acceptance Policies
- Recap and Review

Once the gift is made, no thanks is needed.

Bruce E. Toll, Vice Chairman, Toll Brothers Inc., and Philanthropist

If the gift is significant, I liked to be thanked with either a naming opportunity or a resolution adopted by the institution's governing board.

H.F. Lenfest

I like to be thanked personally. The greatest "thank you" is to get involved and participate in the change . . . see first hand the benefits to children and families that the gift is making.

Bonnie McElveen-Hunter, President, Pace Communications, Fundraiser, Philanthropist and Volunteer

---

THE IMPORTANCE OF THE INITIAL THANK YOU

One of the most critical aspects of a successful development program is how you thank your donors. Up until this point, you have spent a great deal of time identifying, cultivating, educating, involving, and soliciting your prospects. When they finally give you the green light and say "yes" to the gift proposal, you want the thank you and the acknowledgment to be at the same high quality level as your previous activities with your prospects. This is not the time to lose steam by just writing a thank you letter and then moving on to the next list of top prospects. Rather, it is the time to showcase your organization's thoughtfulness and sincerity by making sure the donor's gift is properly acknowledged.

There are several reasons, listed in Exhibit 7–1, why the initial thank you is so important to the donor relations process.

It is not a cliché to say that your next gift will more than likely come from your last donor. It is a reality. It is painfully obvious to some and overlooked by others. This is where proper acknowledgment of the gift comes into play. Just think if you spent months and sometimes years cultivating a prospect, and finally, he or she makes the gift. You and your organization send a letter, maybe make a phone call, when all along the donor felt your organization could have done something more. Many months go by, and you think it's time that the donor should make another major gift. What are your chances this donor will say no? Pretty good, because the acknowledgment did not go well.

Exhibit 7–1 The Significance of the Initial Thank You

1. The best next gift is from the last major donor.
2. The best next larger major gift is from the last major donor.
3. It is a reflection on the institution.
4. It will establish a lasting bond between the donor and the institution.
5. It sets the right tone and paves the way for stewardship.

If the donor feels appreciated and elevated to high donor status by the organization, there is all the promise and likelihood that this donor will make another major gift and that it will be an increase over his or her last gift. Donors feel more and more attached to an organization once they have made this big decision to invest in the future well-being of your group. You will really score "big points" with your donors if they feel even better about making this investment after you thank them. This in turn sets the stage for them to make another gift. If you continue to work with your donors well after the gift is made, they will surely be primed to make another gift and at an enhanced level.

The right thank you can also erase any doubts your donors may have about making the gift. It is common for some donors to second-guess their decisions to give this amount at this time. They have faith at this point through their previous involvement with your group that the gift will be used for its intended purpose and that they will be kept updated by the organization of its developments. A personal, sincere, and well-planned thank you will give your donors a security blanket that will melt any hesitation they may have had about making the gift. It will make them feel great that they made this gift, and they will look forward to continued good relations with your group.

The right thank you can have a tremendous impact on how your donors view your organization for years to come. This ties into the concept that the next gift will come from your last donor. If your donors think that your organization did a wonderful job thanking them to the point where they are telling their families, friends, and colleagues all about it, then these donors think very highly of your organization. This in turn will lead to a next gift from these donors (Kirkman 1995, 38). Furthermore, many donors like to talk to others about how well they are treated by your group and the great things your group does to help people. These types of donors are perhaps your best public relations friends. If they are treated well by your organization, they will share this good feeling with many people. Your organization will be held in high esteem not only with your donors, but also now with the people who are very close to your donors. It is hard to think that any newsletter, brochure, or video could carry the message about your group more effectively than enthusiastic and appreciative donors telling their friends, families, and colleagues in person great things about your group. Once you have your donors feeling this way, you will have established a long-lasting bond between those donors and your institution. It is this bond that will help you get your next gift.

Last, the right thank you sets the tone and paves the way for you and your organization to steward your donors to the point of asking them for their next gift (Kihlstedt and Schwartz 1997, 169). Chapter 8 will explain in detail how proper stewardship is necessary to capture future gifts, but it is important to see how stewardship fits along this continuum line. If donors feel that the organization really cares about them because of the way their gifts have been recognized, then they are more likely to say yes to future visits by the organization, accept more invitations to special events, volunteer for committees and projects, and stay apprised of the organization's activities. This is effective stewardship, made possible by an earlier proper thank you. Think of it as a two-act play. Act One is thanking and recognizing your donors. If the donors like the first act, they will stay for Act Two, which is stewardship. If they do not like Act One, they will leave or be half-hearted about sticking around for the second act. You will have a harder time trying to keep your donors active and interested in your group if you do not do the right thank you.

WHAT MAKES A GOOD THANK YOU?

There are some guidelines contained in Exhibit 7–2 for you to use when thinking about how to thank each of your donors.

Every major gift must be acknowledged with a letter from the organization and a telephone call from someone in the organization. Nothing can turn off a donor more than making a gift and then waiting days, weeks, or even worse months before the gift is acknowledged. This can really sour any good feelings the donor had about making the gift. Moreover, if the gift is not acknowledged timely, it leaves the donor wondering if the institution ever received his or her

Exhibit 7–2 Guidelines for Thanking Your Donors

1. Every gift must be recognized at a minimum by a letter and a telephone call.
2. The size of the gift should guide the type of thank you.
3. The size of the gift should guide who should be doing the thank you.
4. Each thank you must be tailored to each donor.
5. Use donor information obtained during cultivation to fashion the thank you.
6. The donor's wishes on how he or she would like to be thanked must be honored.
7. The more creative the thank you, the more appreciative the donor.

money. You do not want to be in the position of having one of your donors call you after a significant period of time has gone by since he or she made the gift and ask you, "Did you ever get my check/stock? I haven't heard anything from you." You will be left in a position of defending a losing and damaging argument that the thank you is on its way. You will have lost significant ground and credibility with your donor. Do not think for a minute that he or she will not remember this moment the next time he or she is asked by your group for a gift. Donors have very vivid recollections of how they were treated by your organization. You do not want this to be one of their recollections.

A good rule of thumb to use is that a written acknowledgment should be sent within 48 hours of receiving the gift, pledge, or firm commitment for the major gift (Weinstein 1999, 107). This should be followed up with a telephone call within 72 hours of receiving the gift, pledge, or firm commitment (Warwick 2000, 243). This is fundamental fundraising, and every organization must make this a priority, no matter how large or small the nonprofit.

The size of the gift will help to shape the type of thank you as well as who should be doing the thank you (Harrison 1996, 37). All major gifts should be acknowledged in writing and by telephone by the fundraiser who has had significant contact with the donor and who has established a strong relationship with the donor. The donor will expect it, and it is a logical extension of the donor-fundraiser relationship to have at least one of the acknowledgments from the fundraiser. For high-end major gifts, the leadership of the organization, such as the chief executive officer,

president, vice president, executive director, board member, or trustee, should send a written thank you. The more personal this letter can be the better. You want to give the donor the impression that he or she is singled out as the most philanthropic person alive, that his or her generosity will help many people, and that it will attract new gifts for the charity. Exhibit 7–3 lists some suggested phrases you can use for your leadership's thank you letter.

Exhibit 7–3 Suggested Phrases for a Thank You Letter by the Institution's Leader

- Your compassion and remarkable generosity will (send seven children to camp/staff our food bank/ preserve our precious wildlife).
- Special people make special gifts, and you, Ms. Donor, are a very special person.
- You are truly counted as one of our most cherished friends.
- Your commitment here today tells us that you want to make a significant difference in the people we help.
- You have our word and our pledge that we will use your outstanding gift to make a difference in the lives of the people we serve.
- Because of you, (a child can be tutored/ we can expand our scout program for two more counties/we will have two new blood bank mobiles).
- We hold you in our highest esteem, and we admire your spirit of helping us help others.
- Your gift will make it possible for us to ask others to follow in your footsteps and pledge their significant commitment to our organization.
- It is clear that your unique care and compassion has helped to make us a stronger and better organization.
- Your thoughtful generosity has given us the wonderful opportunity to ask others to join with you by showing their dedication and commitment to our group.

Suggested phrases like the ones contained in Exhibit 7–3 will enhance your donors' perceptions of your organization and will bring your donors closer to those in leadership roles. These top gifts command the attention of the top leaders. They should be acknowledged by the leadership of the organization.

To the extent your leaders feel comfortable, they should also be encouraged to include a handwritten note at the bottom or the side of the typed letter. This shows your donors that the leader spent the time to draft, write, and personalize the letter. By doing this, you will quickly eliminate any suspicion that the same letter is sent to every donor at this level. Remember, the more personal the thank you, the more likely the donor will want to stay active and involved with your organization.

Whenever possible, these leaders should follow up their letter with a telephone call to reinforce the importance of the gift and to express the gratitude of the entire organization. This is especially true if one of the leaders solicited the gift, knows the donor well, or has met the donor on several occasions at special events. A top donor will expect that the person he or she knows the best within the leadership of the organization will acknowledge the gift in some way. A letter will serve this purpose fine, but a follow-up telephone call will be even better. It will show the donor that the leader is fully aware of his or her gift and that it will have a tremendous impact on the constituency it serves.

> *Tip: It is the fundraiser's job to make sure that the leadership of the organization sends a personal thank you letter and makes the follow-up telephone call to the top major donors. Do not expect that the leadership of your organization will automatically do these tasks upon notice of the gift. The fundraiser must work with the leadership of the organization until these tasks are completed.*

Many organizations have gift clubs, membership clubs, and donor recognition levels that detail the type of recognition the donor will receive for giving at a certain level. For instance, at an art institute, for a gift of $100,000 or more the donor would receive a free yearly membership to all exhibits, events, and lectures; a signed watercolor painting from a resident artist; the institute's quarterly newsletter; special discounts at select art supply stores; and discounts at the institute's café. A gift of $250,000 or more would include everything at the $100,000 level plus having the donor's name engraved in the hall of honor, biannual invites with visiting artists, and invitations to all pre-opening receptions. A gift of $500,000 or more would include everything at the $250,000 level plus five private art instruction sessions, a framed oil painting from a local artist, an invitation to the chairman's annual reception, tours to tri-county museums, and a special discount for the institute's art abroad program. These programs can be a very effective way to bring in major gifts because the donors know exactly what they are going to receive from the institution once the gift is made. For prospects who like social events, openings, receptions, and named recognition, these gift clubs are a great way to keep your donors active and involved.

Major gifts fundraisers need to make sure their donors receive these gift club benefits, but their work does not end there. To keep the donor-fundraiser relationship on a personal level, they must come up with ways to thank each donor in a creative and individualistic way. Gift clubs and donor recognition levels are a *start, not the end*, to effective donor recognition.

Much like the gift proposal, each thank you should be tailored to fit the personality and style of each donor. Once again, draw upon the knowledge of the donor that you and others obtained during the cultivation period, presolicitation discussions, and solicitation. Think about what you saw in the donor's home and office. Were there many plaques, family pictures, or works of art hanging on the walls? Were there crystal pieces or fine china from other organizations thanking the donor for his or her generosity? These are all good indicators of the type of recognition your donors like and enjoy and, most important, may expect they will receive from your organization once the gift is made (Harrison 1996, 37).

Think about what the donors have talked about in the past. Did they like to discuss how they were president of their sororities; on the board of several charities; honored by a civic organization for their volunteer efforts; or did they seem reserved to discuss any prior accomplishments and honors? The key is to know your donors' personalities and to have the recognition mirror their personal styles and their philosophy on giving. If they have said in the past that they like to give and the gift itself brings them the most joy and satisfaction, then you know this type of donor deserves a very simple but special thank you. If on the other hand, they have accepted all your invitations to special events, love to meet the leaders of your group, and have been to your site on many occasions, then you know they would probably like to have a reception at your organization or some public recognition for their gift.

Once you have some ideas on how your donors should be thanked, make sure you have the approval of your superiors. Tell them how and when you want to recognize your donors and how much it will cost the institution. Only after you have the institution's approval, should you approach the donors with suggested ways the organization would like to thank them for their gift.

Asking the donors how they would like to be thanked is extremely important. While it may seem like the obvious and logical thing to do, many organizations plow ahead with their recognition plans without consulting the donors. If you do, I assure you something at some point will go wrong. Donors do have very definite ideas about how they would like to be thanked. They range from "I'll take it all" to "I want nothing." The next section of this chapter will describe the various ways you can thank donors no matter what their preferences may be on gift recognition. The important thing is that you ask the donors how they would like to be thanked and that you have as many meetings as it takes with the donors until you understand their views about recognition.

> *Tip: The most important factor in donor recognition is that you ask the donor how he or she would like to be thanked, then honor those wishes.*

A word about creativity and thanking the donor: The more creative the thank you, the more appreciative the donor. Now that you know how the donor would like to be thanked, as well as what your organization is willing to do to thank the donor, the fundraiser and development team members should come up with some creative ways to thank the donor. This goes beyond the initial thank you letter and telephone calls from the fundraiser or institutional leader and beyond the gift club benefits. This is the time to showcase how your organization has gone the extra mile to let the donor know how much he or she is appreciated.

A creative thank you does not have to be a costly thank you. Think about what you, your staff, volunteers, and constituents can do for donors. If you represent a child advocacy center, have some of the children write letters to your donors, so that they have a pen pal. If you represent a zoo, send them an autographed picture book or video of rare animals. If you represent an air and space museum, send them a model airplane with your group's name on the airplane wing. Small, thoughtful gestures go a long, long way (Kihlstedt and Schwartz 1997, 169).

These creative ways of saying thank you do not necessarily have to be done right after the gift is made. In fact, they may have more impact if they are received

shortly after the initial thank you. For instance, once the donor has made the gift, he or she will be receiving a thank you letter and telephone call within one week of the gift. Let some time go by, say a few weeks, and then ask to see the donor because you want to bring something to him or her. At that visit, present him or her with your thoughtful and unique gift. It will let the donor know that your initial thank you was not a one-time occurrence and that the organization intends to stay in contact with him or her. It tells the donor that he or she is now, and will be for years to come, appreciated and valued by the organization.

THANKING YOUR DONORS

Since each thank you should be tailored to meet the individual preferences of each donor, it is important to know the most common types of donor preferences for recognition. Exhibit 7–4 contains the five most common types.

Exhibit 7–4 Five Most Common Donor Preferences for Recognition

1. The Expectants—As much publicity and recognition as you can offer.
2. The Moderates—Some, but not too much.
3. The Frugal—Some, but don't spend any money.
4. The Secretive—Privately, yes, publicly, no.
5. The Anonymous—No one can know I made the gift.

The best way to show how to thank each of these types of donors is by example. Let's use the examples of donors who support a school, a hospital, and a symphony and how fundraisers working for these groups could thank the donors from each of the five donor preferences for recognition categories. Keep in mind that the suggestions that follow are in addition to the initial thank you letter and telephone call from the fundraiser and institutional leader.

Some of the gift recognition ideas for the first category—as much publicity and recognition as you can offer—may resemble things that are offered in donor recognition programs or capital campaigns. I thought it would be useful to include these ideas and weave in a few other recognition ideas to give the "complete picture" to thanking this group of donors.

The Expectants—As Much Publicity and Recognition as You Can Offer

These types of donors truly enjoy being in the limelight. Most organizations have a few donors who could fit this category. Usually they are people who support other organizations, attend social events, and enjoy seeing their names in print. I call this type of donors the Expectants because they expect that for the size gift they have just made, your group will offer to make the gift known publicly. If the gifts are the highest gifts your organization has received to date, or if the donors have committed significant leadership gifts that will spark a campaign and will attract other gifts, then you should be prepared to offer these donors as much public attention as possible within your budget. For this group of people, they will probably expect that you will name something after them, so here is a list of areas and programs and events within each institution that offer naming opportunities as well as some special ways of saying "thanks."

The School

1. Named school
2. Named endowed chair
3. Named endowed fund
4. Named scholarship fund
5. Named research fellow
6. Named program
7. Named project
8. Dedication ceremony
9. Bronze framed picture in hall of honor
10. Engraved plaque on a promenade
11. Named building
12. Named foyer to a building
13. Named recreation center
14. Named athletic field
15. Named laboratory
16. Named library/study hall
17. Named lecture series
18. Named awards dinner
19. External media releases
20. Internal publications—newsletters, brochures, or annual report

The Hospital

1. Named hospital
2. Named wing
3. Named unit
4. Named department
5. Named laboratory
6. Named patients' center
7. Bronze framed picture outside head physician's office
8. Named garden or resting area outside the hospital
9. Named equipment
10. Named research unit
11. Named patient care program
12. Named internal place of worship
13. Named health fair
14. Named wellness program
15. Special dinner with top physicians and head nurses
16. External media releases
17. Internal publications

The Symphony

1. Named symphony
2. Named concert
3. Named concert series
4. Named pre-event gala
5. Named stage
6. Named circle of seats
7. Named concert hall
8. Named concert foyer
9. Named conductor's circle
10. Special dinner with the maestro
11. Exclusive invitation to a pre-concert rehearsal
12. Invitation to tour abroad with symphony
13. Guest of honor at a music banquet
14. External media releases
15. Internal publicity

The Moderates—Some, But Not Too Much

These types of donors feel very good about their gifts and like some form of recognition. The recognition cannot be too lavish or too extravagant, otherwise they will feel embarrassed. They generally like to have their families, friends, and colleagues included in whatever ceremony or event the organization suggests as a way to honor them. They will agree to give a quote or two for any external media release or internal publication, but they will probably like to review it first. These folks I call the Moderates because they will want public recognition within their comfort zone. The organization must strike that delicate balance of giving them just the right amount of publicity and recognition—but not too much.

The School

1. Recognition luncheon on campus with school president, dean, select faculty, and guests chosen by the donor
2. Small get-together with honor students
3. Invitation to speak in a class or at an awards dinner
4. Seating near the board of trustees for graduation
5. Plaque or picture hung inside a hallway/auditorium/classroom of the donor's choice
6. If it's a naming opportunity, name in three-inch letters, not eight-inch letters
7. Special parking on campus
8. Special seats to all campus scholastic and athletic events
9. Upon the donor's permission and review, featured article in school publication
10. External media releases—reviewed and approved by the donor

The Hospital

1. Recognition luncheon with hospital CEO, leading surgeons, head nurses, and guests chosen by the donor
2. Special plaque or dedication sign inside a patient unit, emergency room, or physician's office
3. Invitation to physicians' lectures
4. Invitation to presentation of research studies
5. Special parking
6. Special interview by hospital staff for internal magazine—reviewed and approved by the donor
7. Feature in hospital's promotional video—reviewed and approved by the donor
8. External media releases—reviewed and approved by the donor

The Symphony

1. Orchestra seating to all concerts
2. Special invitation for donor and family to attend pre-concert rehearsal
3. Recognition from the podium prior to the concert
4. Framed picture of the donor in the rehearsal room
5. Dinner for donor and family to join the maestro and lead musicians
6. Special note of thanks on a CD
7. Permission and review for internal and external media releases

The Frugal—Some, But Don't Spend Any Money

These next three categories, "The Frugal," "The Secretive," and "The Anonymous," are where you really need to rely on the personal touch. These folks have very definite ideas that either the organization should not spend "their gift" on recognition or that they do not want the public to know about their gift. This is not to say that the previous two categories, "The Expectants" and "The Moderates," should not also receive these personal gestures, in fact I encourage you to include the following suggestions with those two groups where appropriate. The fact is that with people who want no money spent on their thank you and want to keep it private, you need to come up with thoughtful and creative ways to thank them that do not cost money and will not be made public.

For "The Frugal" folks, the emphasis is on the *time spent* by representatives from the organization, not the organization's money. These people are quite admirable because they want every penny of their gift to go toward your charity's mission. Public recognition, dinners, and luncheons are unimportant to them. They will feel better if you skip all that and just let them know from time to time that the people or interests your group serves are benefiting from their gifts.

The School

1. Telephone calls from your beneficiaries
2. Telephone calls from staff members who work in the area the donor has supported
3. Student artwork in a special frame with a thank you note
4. Visit by students and/or faculty in the area they have supported
5. Invitation to audit or attend, at no cost, classes or seminars of interest
6. Ask them to become student mentors
7. Ask them to speak before a class on a topic of expertise or pure experience
8. Bring a handmade item with school logo on the next visit

9. Bake cookies, brownies, or a cake and bring on the next visit
10. Ask them to serve on an advisory committee
11. Feature in an internal publication and external media release

The Hospital

1. Invitation for a guided tour of the facility by the CEO or leading physician
2. Thank you letters written by patients
3. Thank you letters written by medical staff, nurses, and administrators
4. Handmade quilt or pillow with hospital logo
5. Ask them to serve on advisory/auxiliary board
6. Send advance copies of hospital's internal publications with handwritten note
7. Make a videotape that features the whole staff saying thank you and showing special patient care areas
8. Feature them in internal publication and external media release

The Symphony

1. The best seats to the best concerts
2. Backstage tours
3. Internal publications signed by the maestro/leading musicians
4. Meet the members of the orchestra
5. Invite them to tour, at their expense, with the orchestra
6. Make a scrapbook of the orchestra's tours signed by orchestra members
7. Exclusive invitation to be present during a recording session
8. Feature them in an internal publication and external media release

The Secretive—Privately Yes, Publicly No

This group of donors does not mind if the institution thanks them privately, perhaps a luncheon with the leadership of the group and some of the beneficiaries, but they do not want their gifts to draw outside publicity. They feel that any outside publicity will bring on a flood of unwanted and unwelcome solicitors. They have carefully chosen your charity to support, and they do not want other charities, through publicity, to come after them for gifts.

For these donors, I would suggest you keep your thank you very simple and personal. You can use any of the suggested ways previously mentioned in thanking the "The Frugal" donors with a few caveats:

1. Keep the publicity to your internal publications, such as newsletters, brochures, and annual reports.
2. Always ask the donors' permission to write about them and their gifts in any internal publication.
3. Explain to the donors that you want to respect their privacy—that is the reason you are honoring them internal and not external.
4. Ask if you can honor/thank them in some other venue that is personal and special to them.

By privately honoring these donors, you will be respecting their wishes. It is easy to assume, however, that by keeping all the publicity "in house" that these donors will automatically agree to publicize the gift internally. Always err on the other side, and ask the donors' permission to write about their gifts in your newsletter or brochure and if you can list their names in your annual report. Even though the communication pieces are produced by your organization and are mailed to your constituency, your organization cannot control that fact that they may be read by "outsiders." For example, what if the donor left the annual report on his or her coffee table at home and a friend or neighbor happened to read it and see that the donor gave at the top level of your organization? What if the donor brought the newsletter to work not knowing there was an article about him or her and the gift, and he or she lent it to a coworker to read? News about gifts travels fast, and if one person knows, surely others are soon to find out. If you have the donors' permission to write about their gifts in your publications, the donors, in reasonably good faith, cannot be upset with your group.

> **Tip:** Even if you think the donor will not mind that you publicize the gift in the organization's internal publications, always ask for the donor's permission first.

It is important that you explain to these donors that your organization is thanking them privately and internally because that is their wish. You do not want to give these donors the impression that you are slighting them or giving them less recognition than you would give someone else for this level gift. Sometimes even though these donors want their gifts out of the public eye, they may think that the organization could do something more for them. This is where asking the donor if you can honor them someplace that is special to the donor comes into play. For instance, I knew a donor who did not mind if the organization held a small get-together for him, but I could sense that it just wasn't quite enough. I thought that he might feel disappointed if that were his one and only celebration. I asked him if he wanted a small group of our leaders to come to his home, where he could be surrounded by his family and chosen friends, to celebrate his gift. He liked that idea, and we catered a small brunch for him at his home to honor him.

The Anonymous—No One Can Know I Made This Gift

Not everyone who makes a major gift wants to be known. Some donors go out of their way to prevent anyone at any time from knowing about their gifts or their wealth. Before we can begin to think of ways we can thank this group of people, while respecting their need for anonymity, it is important to know why these people do not want anyone to know about their philanthropy. Exhibit 7–5 lists various reasons why some donors choose to remain anonymous.

As you can see from the list of reasons in Exhibit 7–5, donors have very different motives for their desire to remain anonymous. Some are altruistic and humble. Some are purely business and financial. It is important to understand their reasons for anonymity because that will guide you on the style and type of thank you your organization can do for these donors.

I suggest that for this group in particular, it does not matter the type of organization doing the thank you, it matters the type of anonymous donor you are trying to thank. Again, the emphasis on the personal is true for any donor you are trying to thank, but for this group of people thoughtful, private, one-on-one personal gestures are the only things you can do to thank them. For instance, you can't host an in-house luncheon, write about them in your newsletter, or have beneficiaries write them letters. You can, however, do very simple and thoughtful things periodically to let them know

Exhibit 7–5 Reasons Why Some Donors Want To Remain Anonymous

1. They do not want to burden the institution or beneficiary of the gift with a sense of indebtedness.
2. They want volunteers and those performing the services to be given the credit.
3. They think it would be ostentatious to be given large praises.
4. They do not want anyone to know they have this much wealth.
5. They may have received a windfall (inheritance, lawsuit settlement, bonus, lottery win, exercised stock option), and this is the only large gift they will be able to make.
6. They fear exposure to their wealth may have repercussions, such as enhanced damage awards against them if there were ever a lawsuit for any reason.
7. They crave privacy and their solitude to be left alone.
8. They prefer their stockbrokers or brokerage houses handle all the details, including dealing with the charity on any level.
9. They need to hide their wealth from their family, friends, business, or coworkers.
10. They want to hide their wealth from their family, friends, business, or coworkers.

how much your organization and your beneficiaries appreciate their kindness.

It is important to know that there are two kinds of anonymous donors: (1) people who are known by the organization and who requested total anonymity about their gift; and (2) people who are unknown, and the organization has no idea who made this wonderful gift. The thank you options for each of these groups varies. For the first group, the organization should know these anonymous donors pretty well. You and/or leaders of your group have met with the donors, and you have learned about their hobbies, interests, family life, and activities. Use that information to craft your thank you. For instance, if your donors love to garden, send them a packet of flower seeds with a special note by you or your executive leadership that thanks them for helping to make your organization "grow" (Kirkman 1995, 40).

Some organizations send a bouquet of flowers to their top-level anonymous donors once a month. If your donors love horses and/or hunting, send a photograph or note cards depicting these hobbies, with a note of thanks. Some groups shy away from this for fear it may not be the style of art that the donors prefer. If you do not know for sure if the donors will like it, I encourage fundraisers to send it anyway. You know for sure that the donors love horses and/or hunting so sending this type of thank you will show that your organization remembered they have this hobby and interest and that the thank you ties into their special interest.

With this first group of anonymous donors, periodic communication and recognition are key. Send them everything you can about the progress of your group. That would include annual reports, newsletters, brochures, videos, and board-approved public strategic plans. This will keep them educated and involved, albeit from a distance, with your group. It will show them who benefited from their gifts and will reconfirm that your institution is well managed.

For the second group of anonymous people, your organization has few options. If the gift "arrived from heaven" and cannot be traced in any manner, then it can be publicized internally and externally that an "anonymous gift" was received. This gives the organization great leverage to attract new gifts. It may even attract others to give anonymously. Keep in mind, the chances are very good that these anonymous donors will be watching and listening to see how your organization announces the gift. Even if they do not want anyone to know who they are, not even the receiving organization, they will surely be listening for the news; and if they receive your communications, they will be looking for the announcement.

> *Tip: If the gift cannot be traced to any person in any manner, make sure the gift is announced in the organization's internal communications as well as external media. This anonymous donor may be monitoring the organization from a distance to see how the organization announces the gift.*

If the gift has come via a stockbroker or an intermediary, the organization should ask this contact if they might send a letter of thanks and some personal thank you gestures to the contact to be forwarded to the anonymous donor. If they agree to be the go-between, it will be a great way to get the message of thanks to that otherwise "unreachable" donor.

GIFT ACCEPTANCE POLICIES

A gift acceptance policy is a well-thought, board-approved institutional policy that every fundraising entity should have and should follow (Breckon and Snapp 1995, 14). Think of a gift acceptance policy as a set of directions that is going to keep your organization on the proper route to soliciting, accepting, and acknowledging gifts and managing and overseeing gift funds. The size of the organization is of no importance when it comes to gift acceptance polices. Even if you are a one-person operation, you need one. Exhibit 7–6 lists the numerous reasons why any organization should have this policy.

Exhibit 7–6 Important Reasons for a Gift Acceptance Policy

1. Ensures equal treatment of donors.
2. Avoids any misunderstanding.
3. Spares everyone embarrassment.
4. Serves as an agreement between the donors and the institution.
5. Avoids public relations disasters.
6. Makes the organization more accountable.
7. Ensures sound fiscal management for the organization's funds.
8. Serves as a protection for the organization's charitable status.
9. Causes the organization to have a committee to oversee implementation of the policy.
10. Makes everyone in the institution aware of the gift guidelines.

The first three reasons listed in Exhibit 7–6 address the need to have something in writing that the organization can point to and rely on to avoid any potential ill will between the donor and the institution. For example, donor Doris wanted to give a conservation charity a gift-in-kind of collector comic books. This organization has no use for this gift, and comic books do not have a related use to the charity's mission. The conservation charity does not want to offend donor Doris because she has been a loyal and faithful donor, one who is prime to make a major outright gift. What can the conservation charity do? They could have a series of conversations with her trying to explain why they cannot accept this gift. How will that make donor Doris feel? What if she heard that the conservation charity accepted rare books on wildlife and that she can see no difference between that gift and her perspective gift? The leadership of the conservation charity would feel a bit on the defensive side, and donor Doris would feel she is getting "slighted" by the charity because other donors are able to make in-kind gifts. This all could have been avoided if the conservation charity had a gift acceptance policy that stated clearly the type of gifts it could accept and those it could not accept. The leadership could simply point to the section in the policy that explains why the gift could not be accepted and rely on it to prevent situations like this one from occurring.

Gift acceptance policies really come in handy *while the gift is being solicited*. For instance, if you are in the process of soliciting a $50,000 gift from prospect Doug for a local Big Brothers/Big Sisters Association and the gift is to be used by the association to recruit and counsel more volunteers to become big brothers or big sisters, now is the time to show prospect Doug your gift acceptance policy. You want to show it to him at this time so that he will know exactly what the association will do with the gift once it is made. Since the policy is a written and board-approved document, it will serve as an agreement between the donor and the association. In this example, prospect Doug, now that he is aware of the policy, has a clear idea how the association is going to manage and distribute the gift to the intended beneficiaries.

> *Tip:* Use gift acceptance policies during gift solicitation so that the prospect has a clear idea before the gift is made, how the gift will be managed and distributed to the beneficiaries. It will help to avoid any misunderstandings about the gift.

Nonprofit organizations are always trying to get publicity for their groups to make their donors feel good about their gifts and to attract new prospects to their causes. Nonprofit organizations want to avoid at all cost publicity that puts their groups in a bad spotlight or questions the source of solicited funds or management and use of the funds. A gift acceptance policy can be a security blanket for the organization to prevent these public relations disasters from occurring. It tells the organization what it needs to consider before the gift is solicited, accepted, or managed. If everything was carried out in terms of the policy, then the organization can prevent a public relations nightmare (Shehane 1995, 18).

Donors invest in charities that they feel will manage their gifts wisely. Gift acceptance policies can be a wonderful tool to show donors, during and after the solicitation process, who will be responsible for proper investment and distribution of their gifts and how the money will be invested and managed. Think of it as selecting the right bank for your savings. You would not put your money into a savings account that was not federally insured and that was not going to get an acceptable rate of interest. You would want to see from the bank officer some documentation that states the guaranteed rate of interest and its seal of protection from the government. Similarly, donors will feel more secure if you show them in writing that your group has a gift acceptance committee that will ensure the gift will be used for its intended purposes and that the funds are invested and managed prudently. But for the policy, many groups would avoid or put off having such a gift acceptance committee, which could lead to very undesirable results.

Using the gift acceptance policy to reinforce your donors' perception of your group's sound fiscal management has many benefits. First, it increases the faith and trust the donors have for your group. Second, it makes the organization more accountable to the donors (McClintock 1996, 12). Third, it ensures proper stewardship for any gift to the organization (Shehane 1995, 19).

A gift acceptance policy that is widely distributed and known among the leadership, board, trustees, committees, staff, volunteers, and peer solicitors keeps everyone involved with the organization on the "same page." You want to avoid sitting in a board meeting hearing a peer solicitor say, "I didn't think our campaign gift levels were etched in granite. I just told my friend that he could have his name on the entrance for $2 million, not $3.5 million," or a board member say, "I already told that donor we did not need an appraisal for his gift-in-kind and that we would take care of it." The way to prevent these types of situations is to have everyone who works or volunteers for your group fully knowledgeable about the policy. It should be permanently placed in board and trustee notebooks and staff manuals and should be readily accessible in visible places throughout the organization (Beyel 1997, 57).

It is suggested that the organization devote one staff meeting a year to the policy contents and any additions or deletions so that everyone in the organization is made aware. This will avoid any potential discrepancy that someone had "no idea" the organization had a gift acceptance policy. Support staff should be included in these meetings. Support staff interact with donors sometimes more than fundraisers do. They answer telephones, take messages, send information in the mail, and in general try to be a resource for the donors on the organization's behalf. If they know about the policy, it will avoid any mixed messages or confusion regarding whether or not your organization has a policy. The last thing you want is someone unaware of the policy telling the donor that he or she has no idea if the organization has one, and that he or she has never seen it.

Fundraisers should carry the updated policy with them when they are making calls and soliciting gifts, so that they are prepared to show the prospect the policy where appropriate. It is yet another preparation tool in the fundraiser's toolkit that can steer the prospect in the direction to make the gift.

> *Tip: Fundraisers should carry a copy of the organization's gift acceptance policy when making calls and soliciting gifts. This will add credibility for the organization and may be a persuading factor for the prospect to make the gift.*

What Should a Good Gift Acceptance Policy Include?

Gift acceptance policies range from the very succinct form to the very elaborate form. Some groups feel that they only need a few basic points to protect the organization, while others want to include every element possible to cover all the bases. It will be up to the leadership of your organization to decide how much or how little they feel is necessary for your group. Exhibit 7–7 contains a list of suggested gift acceptance policy issues that should be explored while drafting the policy or reviewing and updating an existing policy.

While this seems at first like too much to tackle, I assure you it is well worth the time and effort. The best way to show you how this all comes together is by example. Appendixes 7–A through 7–E contain examples of various organization's gift acceptance policies. As we go through the list of issues to consider when forming or reviewing a gift acceptance policy, I will refer to these examples to give you a good idea of how some groups thought through these issues and set forth a policy.

Exhibit 7–7 Suggested Gift Acceptance Policy Issues

1. What type of gift (outright, life income, deferred, in-kind) will the organization accept?
2. Under what circumstances will a gift be declined?
3. Are there established gift levels and gift amounts for named funds/facilities/programs/projects/services/equipment?
4. Who will be responsible for soliciting different gifts at different levels?
5. Who will be responsible for accepting different gifts at different levels?
6. Who will acknowledge different gifts at different levels?
7. How will gifts at each level be recognized?
8. Will cumulative gifts/past gifts be credited for larger gift levels?
9. How will matching gifts be recognized for overall gift levels?
10. How will the gifts be tracked?
11. What banks and financial services do the organization use to invest/manage its funds?
12. How does the organization invest its named funds?
13. What are the guidelines on how gifts are valued?
14. What are the minimum amounts to establish the various planned gifts?
15. What are the guidelines for life income and deferred gifts, such as minimum/maximum pay out, number of beneficiaries, and term of years?
16. Under what circumstances will the organization serve as trustee for charitable trusts?
17. Will the organization require written proof before it will recognize a bequest or gift via a will?
18. How does the organization recognize/credit gifts that are revocable?
19. What are the guidelines for accepting gifts of real estate, life insurance policies, and retirement benefits?
20. Who pays the costs for the real estate transfer, land surveys, appraisals, title search, bills, and taxes?
21. Will a gift acceptance policy committee be formed to oversee and carry out the terms of the policy?
22. Under what circumstances will the organization use outside counsel?
23. Will the organization consider exceptions to the policy and, if so, under what circumstances?
24. How and under what circumstances will gift agreements be dissolved?

Right from the start, your group needs to state the types of gifts it will and will not accept. It seems obvious, but it needs to be written. At a minimum, all gifts of any kind need to be related to the group's mission. Another way of saying this is that the gift needs to be compatible with your cause (Breckon and Snapp 1995, 15). This is particularly important for gifts-in-kind. It is a good idea to spell out in your gift acceptance policy the types of gifts-in-kind your organization will accept to give the potential donor some idea of non-monetary gifts that advance the mission of your organization. For instance, The Curtis Institute of Music in Philadelphia, Pennsylvania, will accept in-kind gifts such as musical instruments and works of art (see Appendix 7–A). Other gifts-in-kind for a music institute or music school might include sheet music, rare books on music or musicians, music cases, or music stands. Cornell University in Ithaca, New York, includes real estate, equipment, art, antiques, rare books, livestock, mortgages, and copyrights as gifts-in-kind (see Appendix 7–B). Cornell's Gift Processing Policy goes one step further and includes a statement that it will accept an in-kind gift if it can be put to a "related used by the university or can be sold" (see Appendix 7–B).

If you are working for a social service agency that provides clothes, furniture, and other personal property for disadvantaged or displaced adults and children, your gift acceptance policy should contain language about gifts-in-kind. The policy and procedures manual of Southern Homes Services in Philadelphia, Pennsylvania, contains a lengthy list of the types of gifts that they will accept: clothing, food, toys, household goods, office equipment and furniture, transportation vehicles, entertainment tickets, computer equipment and supplies, personal hygiene supplies, and appliances (see Appendix 7–C). Since Southern Homes' mission is to stabilize children and families in the community, their list of in-kind gifts gives the potential donor a clear idea of the items that are related to the mission of the organization.

Stating that the gift must advance the organization's mission has another advantage. It protects the organization from the situation where a donor may request that the gift be used in some way that is incompatible with an existing policy, program, or philosophy of the institution. For example, what if a donor wanted to give a large outright or planned gift to the college of environmental studies within a university, provided that the college of forestry would be merged into the college of environmental studies? The donor would be asking for something that may jeopardize the integrity or reputation of the institution, and the gift may be viewed as undermining the authority vested with the university president and board of trustees. You can avoid situations like these in two ways. First, spell out the organization's mission, purpose, and philosophy in the gift acceptance policy. For example, at Stephens College in Columbia, Missouri, the gift policy on the first page states that the college encourages gifts with a "genuine donative intent" and that are "beneficial to the donor while protecting the fiscal and legal integrity of the institution" (see Appendix 7–D). It is a good idea right up front to reference other board-approved policies or bylaws in other manuals that may bolster this point. Second, state in the gift acceptance policy how and under what circumstances your groups will decline a gift. Stephens College declines gifts that "would jeopardize the financial, legal, or moral integrity or reputation of the institution, or where the gift would cause embarrassment to the donor or her/his family" (see Appendix 7–D).

Some organizations have a separate section in the policy that spells out when gifts will be declined. Cornell University has a separate section in their gift acceptance policy called "Declining Gifts" that illustrates four conditions under which Cornell will not accept a gift (see Appendix 7–B). Note that the introductory paragraph to this section contains the clarifying language, "including, but not limited to, the following" four conditions. It is important that your group use similar language to give it the broadest protection possible. You cannot know now every circumstance under which your organization will decline a gift, so make sure your policy protection is not limited to the stated examples.

> **Tip:** *Gift acceptance policies should state the organization's mission as foundation for the type of gifts it will accept and decline. While it is a good idea to give examples of the types of gifts the group will accept and decline, be sure there is language in the policy that states these are examples and that they do not represent an all-inclusive list of acceptable or nonacceptable gifts.*

Every organization should have set gift level amounts to establish special funds (Nichols 1999, 128). For instance, these special funds can be for endowments, scholarships, chairs, facilities, programs, projects, equipment, rooms, wings, foyers, and services. Once these are established and board-approved, they should be incorporated into the gift acceptance policy (see Appendixes 7–A and 7–D). This will protect your organization from letting one donor establish a scholarship fund with $50,000, while another donor is allowed to do so with only a $25,000 gift.

The next issue, who is responsible for soliciting gifts, is often not part of many gift acceptance policies. It may seem too obvious to some groups that the development team, along with the leadership and key volunteers and peers, are responsible for soliciting gifts. It is wise to include this element, even if it only takes a sentence or two. Cornell University's policy lists "Fund Raising Responsibilities" and "Soliciting Gifts" at the very beginning, which makes very good sense (see Appendix 7–B). You want your organization and potential donors to know right away who bears the fundraising responsibility.

The next logical issues to include in the policy are who is responsible for accepting different gifts at different levels and who will acknowledge them (Nichols 1999, 127). What if one of your volunteers came to you and said, "I just got a business colleague to kick in $500,000 toward the campaign, only if she can add a new program that sounds really exciting. For that amount, I think we should do it." Did the volunteer have the authority to solicit and/or accept this gift? A well-drafted policy would put this situation into perspective. Cornell University under "Accepting New Commitments" states who is authorized to accept gifts on behalf of the university and details steps to follow for those people who are not authorized, yet have received a "verbal or written commitment of a gift" (see Appendix 7–B).

Who acknowledges the gift is as equally important as who accepts the gift. Along with your gift levels and who can accept gifts at what level, it is a good idea to include who acknowledges gifts at different levels into your policy. PresbyHomes Foundation in Lafayette Hill, Pennsylvania, sets aside one page of its Policy Statement to explain its procedure for gift acknowledgment (see Appendix 7–E).

Gift recognition is the next logical item to include. If your organization has established gift levels and established funds, it may want to set forth, albeit in broad terms, who determines how donors will be recognized (see Appendixes 7–B and 7–D). This will really come in handy as a great resource when dealing with naming opportunities and campaign gifts.

How an organization credits prior gifts will surely have an impact on whether or not the potential donor will make a future larger gift. Many organizations use cumulated prior gifts as a selling feature for the potential donor to make the larger gift. For instance, if donor Kirsten knew that her previous gifts of $50,000 for the past two years plus her stock gift of $100,000 would be credited toward the $750,000 gift to build a new facility for abused women, she may be more inclined to make the gift. This is why it always helps to articulate under what circumstances your organization will credit prior gifts. The same principle applies to matching gifts. What if donor Kirsten's two $50,000 gifts were matching gifts, and in fact, she gave the organization $25,000 for two years that was equally matched by her company? Now the organization needs to tell her whether $100,000 or $50,000 cash gifts will be counted toward her prospective gift.

Crediting prior gifts is not restricted to gifts of cash or stock. Many donors make life income and deferred gifts, which an organization may or may not count toward a larger gift, which is why this too must be spelled out in the policy. For example, The Curtis Institute of Music gives "recognition credit" for all irrevocable deferred gifts "provided that the present value of the gift exceeds 25 percent of face value" (see Appendix 7–A).

Gift tracking is key for any organization to keep tabs on the status of gift proposals, gift solicitations, gift commitments, pledges, and payments for gift commitments and pledges. Gift tracking will be thoroughly covered in Chapter 9 as a tool to use for determining when to keep a prospect on your top list and when to add new prospects to your top list. While the tracking of gifts in many instances is an administrative task, an organization can lose many gifts if it does not keep a good system for tracking gifts. It is for this reason that the organization's system for tracking gifts should be part of the gift acceptance policy. The policy at this point should include the process of gifts solicitation to gift receipt, acknowledgment, and recognition. Putting in a paragraph about gift tracking will complete this process (see Appendix 7–B).

Now it's time for the policy to address the investment of its funds. Some policies detail the banking or financial services the organization uses to invest and manage the funds. Others choose not to do so because that information is contained in another board-approved document. Even if the policy does not state where the funds are invested in a particular financial institution, it should state how the funds are invested, particularly restricted funds and special funds. Named funds, life income funds, and endowed funds, to name a few, need to be put into separate accounts so that the organization knows the principal and interest earned for each fund. For instance, at Stephens College, if a potential donor wants to establish an endowed chair, it will require a commitment of $1 million or more, with an initial gift of $375,000 or more, "to be held and invested separately from the college's endowment portfolio" (see Appendix 7–D).

> **Tip:** *If the organization has special funds or restricted funds, its gift acceptance policy should include the procedures on how the organization invests those funds.*

Valuation of gifts comes into play particularly when a potential donor wants to make a non-cash gift of personal, tangible, or real property. These non-cash gifts need a value for tax purposes. For the donor to take an income tax deduction for the gift, he or she will need a "qualified appraisal" for a gift of non-cash property, other than publicly traded securities, if the claimed value exceeds $5,000 (Internal Revenue Code, Section 1.170A–13(c)). Regardless of the claimed value, it is always recommended that the organization put into the policy that non-cash gifts be valued by a credited, third-party appraiser (see Appendixes 7–A and 7–B). This is to ensure proper and neutral evaluation of the gift and to avoid any allegation that the organization overvalued the gift for its own purposes.

The next set of issues centers around life income and deferred gifts, such as charitable remainder trusts, charitable annuities, pooled income funds, wills, and bequests. Each organization should establish minimum levels for establishing a charitable trust, charitable annuity, or pooled income fund. For example, at Stephens College a donor would need an initial investment of $25,000 to establish a gift annuity, $100,000 to establish a charitable remainder trust, and $10,000 to establish a pooled income fund (see Appendix 7–D). Once minimum thresholds are set, the guidelines should be further refined by stating the organization's policy on:

- Rate of payout for life income gifts
- Limitations on the number of beneficiaries for charitable trusts
- Number of generations across which beneficiaries can span

- Age limitations for life income beneficiaries (see Appendixes 7–B and 7–D).

Who will serve as trustee of a charitable trust should also be included at this point in the policy. Some organizations will agree to serve as trustee provided that the trust is over a certain amount, say $250,000, and that the trust is invested and managed with the financial institution selected or used by the organization. This can be a very attractive selling feature for the potential charitable trust donor because under this situation, the potential donor would not pay trustee fees. Whatever trustee options your organization decides to offer your donors, make sure it is in the gift acceptance policy.

Regarding wills and bequests, the institution needs to have a policy on how it will recognize and accept these types of gifts. For instance, some groups require the donor to sign a card, or sign and notarize a testamentary pledge, describing the type and size of the gift that the donor is giving via a will or bequest. The Curtis Institute of Music requires that it be "confirmed in writing with a letter of intent" (see Appendix 7–A). Others will accept a verbal commitment. Unless the donor has specifically made an irrevocable provision in the will, or an irrevocable bequest, the donor could change his or her mind and the gift may never come to the charity. The charity will have to decide, therefore, how it is going to recognize and credit this type of gift and put it into the policy (see Appendix 7–A).

Minimum amounts for gifts of real estate, life insurance policies, and retirement benefits also should be set forth in the policy. For instance, Stephens College will accept a gift of real estate that is "mortgage free" and has a "minimum value of $50,000." Gifts of life insurance, where the college is designated a future beneficiary, are acceptable "with a minimum face value of $50,000 so long as the college is not required to expend funds from sources other than the donor to maintain the contract" (see Appendix 7–D). The Curtis Institute of Music will give full recognition credit for "the face value of life insurance policies given to The Institute if the policy is fully paid up and the insured is age 55 or older" (see Appendix 7–A).

In addition to threshold amounts, the organization needs to state if there are any conditions for accepting these types of gifts and who bears the costs related to these gifts. For instance, Stephens College will accept a real estate gift at the stated minimum value, if the property is salable and if the donor agrees to:

- Pay all property taxes.
- Maintain the property.
- Provide adequate insurance.

Stephens College adds that conditions for accepting the real estate include:
- Annual maintenance costs, including evaluation of any liens
- Real estate taxes
- Previous and current environmental conditions (see Appendix 7–D).

Another point the charity may want to include is who pays for the real estate transfer fee.

One of the most overlooked elements in a gift acceptance policy is establishing a governing body that will have the responsibility to oversee and implement the policy. If you have a gift acceptance policy, then your organization needs to have a gift acceptance committee (Breckon and Snapp 1995, 16). The committee is usually comprised of a select group of board members or an executive committee, which will represent the constituency of the organization. It is suggested that your policy state:
- The composition of the committee
- The committee's responsibilities
- The committee's reporting requirements
- When the committee meets
- How decisions are ratified
- When outside legal counsel should be consulted (see Appendixes 7–A and 7–D).

Many organizations have retained legal counsel to handle certain matters for the organization. If your organization has legal counsel, it is a good idea to list in your gift acceptance policy how and under what circumstances legal counsel will be used. For instance, Stephens College's Board gives its president or presidential advisor and legal counsel when "deemed necessary" the authority to negotiate life income gifts, and potentially controversial gifts are to be reviewed by legal counsel (see Appendix 7–D).

Issues and concerns that affect donors today may not be the "hot topics" of tomorrow. In fact, it cannot be predicted what donor and gift issues might arise for any group in the future. It is for that reason that your gift acceptance policy needs to include some guidelines for how and under what circumstances exceptions to the policy will be considered. This can be as simple as stating that the gift acceptance committee has the authority to consider and decide on exceptions to the

policy, or it can list some factors that the committee will use to consider an exception (see Appendix 7–A).

Last, a statement needs to be included in the policy that addresses how and when gift agreements can be dissolved (Shehane 1995, 20). Certain gift funds may outlive the gift's intended use, or the gift may no longer be pertinent to the mission of the organization. For instance, what if a donor made an endowed gift "to build and maintain a field house" and the organization no longer has a field house? The gift acceptance policy should state that gift acceptance by the organization may rely on inclusion into the gift agreement that the gift designation represents a "preferred use" and that the organization will seek an "alternative use" consistent with the general intent of the gift before dissolving the gift agreement (see Appendix 7–D). This will give the organization a chance to discuss with the donor some options on how to use the gift at the present time and leave dissolution of the gift as a last resort.

Now that you know why gift acceptance policies are important and what they should contain, think about how the following scenarios could have either been avoided with a policy in place at the organization or could be used to handle these awkward gift situations:
1. A donor who will make a mega-gift to a hospital near a retirement community, provided that the hospital only admits patients over the age of 55.
2. A donor who wants a charitable gift annuity to give her a 9 percent annuity payment when your organization follows the rates established by the American Council on Gift Annuities that would give her a 6.9 percent annuity payment.
3. A donor who wants to give the charity an abandoned farmhouse that is located near an oil refinery that had a leakage within the past year.
4. A donor who wants to give a conservation group a rare and highly valued gun collection.
5. A donor who wants to endow a chair at a medical school for $1 million, not the $1.5 million requested in the gift proposal.
6. A donor who makes an endowed gift and agrees that the gift will be invested with the organization's selected investment firm, and then is dissatisfied with the amount of interest the gift is generating and wants to invest the gift at his investment firm.

7. A donor who is about to make a mega-gift but wants his brother to be placed immediately on the organization's board.

8. A donor who is considered among the top leaders of a tobacco company that wants to make a gift to a cancer charity.

9. A peer solicitor tells a prospect during a solicitation that if she makes the gift, her company logo could be attached to the charity's Web site.

10. A board member gives a "top prospect" permission to use the charity's logo in the prospect's corporate publications.

RECAP AND REVIEW

1. Each thank you needs to be tailored to fit the donor's personality and style.

2. The right thank you will lead to the next enhanced major gift from the same donor.

3. The right thank you sets the stage for proper stewardship.

4. Benefits contained in gift and membership clubs are a start, not an end to effective donor recognition.

5. The donor must be asked how he or she would like to be recognized for the gift, and then it must be discussed and approved by the leadership of the organization.

6. The more creative the thank you, the more appreciative the donor.

7. There are five common donor preferences for recognition, and each one has a special set of ways to say thank you.

8. Always get the donor's permission before publicizing the gift in any external or internal media.

9. Every fundraising organization should have a board-approved gift acceptance policy that sets forth guidelines to solicit, accept, acknowledge, recognize, manage, and distribute all gifts and gift funds.

10. A gift acceptance policy should describe the types of gifts it will accept and decline; minimum levels to establish special funds, life income gifts, and planned gifts; how gifts and pledges are tracked; how gifts are invested and managed; who bears the costs and fees related to prospective gifts; who sets the values for gifts; how past and current gifts are credited for larger gifts and campaign pledges; and how wills and bequests are recognized.

11. Gift acceptance policies can be used during solicitations so prospects have a clear understanding of who will be responsible for proper investment and distribution of the gift.

12. Gift acceptance committees should be formed so that there is a governing body that will be responsible to oversee, implement, update, and revise the policy.

13. Gift acceptance policies should include when outside counsel will be used.

14. Gift acceptance policies should include how to handle exceptions and challenges to the policy.

15. Gift acceptance policies should include how and under what circumstances gift agreements will be dissolved.

REFERENCES

Beyel, J. 1997. Ethics and major gifts. *New Directions for Philanthropic Fund Raising,* no. 16: 50–57.

Breckon, D., and T. Snapp. 1995. Gift acceptance policies: Is it the source or use that matters. *Fund Raising Management,* April, 14–15.

Harrison, B. 1996. When a plaque isn't enough…how do you thank major donors? *Fund Raising Management,* July, 36–39.

Kihlstedt, A., and C.P. Schwartz. 1997. *Capital campaigns: Strategies that work.* Gaithersburg, MD: Aspen Publishers, Inc.

Kirkman, K. 1995. Thanks again—and again. *Case Currents,* September, 38–40.

McClintock, N. 1996. Why you need a sponsorship policy and how to get one. *Front & Center,* September, 12–13.

Nichols, J. 1999. *Transforming fundraising.* San Francisco: Jossey-Bass Publishers.

Shehane, J. 1995. Development policies: Protect your image. *Fund Raising Management,* July, 18–20.

Warwick, M. 2000. *The five strategies for fundraising success.* San Francisco: Jossey-Bass Publishers.

Weinstein, S. 1999. *The complete guide to fund raising management.* New York: John Wiley & Sons.

Appendix 7–A

The Curtis Institute of Music

Gift Crediting Policies

Courtesy of the Curtis Institute of Music.

The Curtis Institute of Music
Gift Crediting Policies: February 12, 1997

The following policies are intended to achieve crediting equity among donors and an appropriate administrative framework for The Institute's development efforts.

1. A gift of $25,000 or more may be used to establish an endowment fund named by the donor, with income designated for student instruction, student financial assistance or other use approved by The Institute's Board of Trustees. A gift of $5,000 or more may be used to establish an endowment fund named by the donor, with income unrestricted.

2. Pledges may be fulfilled on a schedule established by the donor over a specified period, up to a maximum of five years from the date of the pledge. Irrevocable deferred gift arrangements are exceptions, governed by the terms of the trust.

3. Upon acceptance by The Institute, real estate and other gifts-in-kind (e.g., musical instruments, works of art, etc.) will be credited at an appraised value set by a qualified third party accepted by Curtis.

4. The donor's name, or choice of name will be applied formally to a chair, fellowship, program or space when half of the published price of that chair, fellowship, program or space is funded in cash or by an irrevocable deferred gift arrangement.

5. The Institute will give full recognition credit for all irrevocable deferred gift arrangements (e.g., charitable remainder unitrusts, charitable annuity trusts, gifts to the Curtis Pooled Income Fund and gift annuities) provided that the present value of the gift exceeds 25% of face value. Recognition credit for naming a chair, an active program or space for revocable trusts or bequests will be granted upon receipt of the funds.

6. The Institute will give full recognition credit for the face value of life insurance policies given to The Institute if the policy is fully paid up and the insured is age 55 or older. Curtis reserves the right to determine what constitutes "fully paid-up" policy status.

7. Membership in the Founder's Society will be granted to individuals who have provided for The Institute in their will or through irrevocable or revocable deferred gift arrangements, which can be confirmed in writing with a letter of intent.

8. Any departures from the above policies require approval of The Institute's Gift Acceptance Committee.

The Curtis Institute of Music
Guidelines for Exceptions to Gift Crediting Policies
Adopted by the Gift Acceptance Committee, December 15, 1998

As set forth in The Institute's Gift Acceptance Policy:

> The Institute will give full recognition credit for all irrevocable deferred gift arrangements (e.g., charitable remainder unitrusts, charitable annuity trusts, gifts to the Curtis Pooled Income Fund and gift annuities) provided that the present value of the gift exceeds 25%. Recognition credit for naming a chair, an active program or space for revocable trusts or bequests will be granted upon receipt of the funds.

"Recognition credit" is the dollar value of the gift which can be applied towards an endowment or naming opportunity. During the *Sound for the Century Campaign*, the requirements for "campaign credit" are similar, but may not be the same as those for "recognition credit." For example, endowment of The Common Room requires "recognition credit" of $1 million. A $1 million deferred gift with a $230,000 present value would not be sufficient to endow The Common Room.

To obtain recognition or campaign credit, exceptions to the above policy may be requested for one or more of the following reasons:

- The deferred giving arrangement is not completely irrevocable. For example, the donor has named Curtis to receive a bequest under a will, or funds through the exercise of a power of appointment that can be changed by will.

- The present value of the (deferred) gift is less than 25% (in such cases, an adjustment of the amount of campaign or recognition credit may be sought).

- The donor requests the naming be done, before 100% of the funds pledged are received by The Institute.

Before making exceptions that will give the donor recognition or campaign credit, the Gift Acceptance Committee will consider the following facts and circumstances pertaining to the gift:

a. Certainty of the assets to be donated and their future value to Curtis
b. Likelihood of the donor having a "change of heart"
c. Estimated present value of the gift
d. Donor's connections to The Institute
e. Giving history of the donor – annual fund and capital gifts
f. Donor's record of volunteer service to The Institute

Appendix 7–B
Cornell University
Gift Acceptance Policy

Courtesy of Cornell University.

Cornell Policy Library
Volume 3, Financial Management
Chapter 1, Gift Processing
Responsible Office : Alumni Affairs and Development
Originally Issued November 1983
Revised December 1992

Policy 3.1
Gift Processing Policy

PROCEDURES

Fund Raising Responsibilities

The responsibilities for fund raising are shared among administration, Deans, and Alumni Affairs and Development staff. During university campaigns, all development efforts will be in support of the defined goals of the campaigns and will be directed and coordinated through the Vice President for Alumni Affairs and Development.

Soliciting Gifts

All gift solicitations should be made in support of university priorities as determined by the Provost and college and unit Deans and Directors. During university campaigns, gift solicitations should be in support of campaign priorities. Written approval from the Provost must be obtained before any solicitations outside of campaign priorities can be made.

Pledge Cards and Commitment Tracking Forms

Gifts are generally obtained through fund-raising activities organized around annual and special efforts. These activities include direct mailings, phonathons, and personal solicitations. To document a monetary or gift in kind commitment, you must use either a pledge card or a Commitment Tracking form.

When not using a pledge card, use the appropriate Commitment Tracking Form. The Commitment Tracking form is also used to record commitments that will be received by the university over a period of years.

Accepting New Commitments

Only authorized Alumni Affairs and Development staff or their designees can accept new commitments on behalf of the university. Gifts should be in amounts appropriate to carry out their specified use. Monetary gifts to be used for restricted purposes and gifts in kind should receive approval in advance by college, unit, or department offices of the university most concerned with carrying out the donor's specifications. These requirements are to protect the interests of both the university and its donors.

During gift solicitation and acceptance, it is vital that the university's tax-exempt status be maintained and protected. Gift requirements must support the university's mission, and any restricted use stipulated for a gift must be consistent with prevailing laws and public policies.

• **Caution:** Written approval of the Provost is required prior to making any solicitations of significant new programs, new positions, new facilities, or any other long term add-on obligations to the university.

Special procedures associated with accepting gifts that require a financial commitment from the university, the circumstances under which gifts may be declined or returned, gifts of service, matured bequests, and publicly honoring an individual who has made extraordinary contributions to the university are explained in the *"Special Situations"* Section of this document. Current minimum endowment levels and the "Gift Versus Sponsored Project Designation Chart," detailing what is a gift and what is a sponsored project, are found in the *"Appendix"* Section of this document.

• **Option A**

If you are not on the Alumni Affairs and Development Staff:

1. Contact your college or unit AA&D Office of the University Development Office as soon as you receive a verbal or written commitment of a gift.

The AA&D Officer is responsible for reviewing, accepting and reporting the commitment to the Development Office.

• **Option B**

If you are on the Alumni Affairs and Development Staff:

1. Complete the appropriate Commitment Tracking form and submit it to the Development Office.
2. If you accept a verbal commitment, you are responsible for doing the follow-up work to make sure the written commitment is received as soon as possible.
3. When accepting a verbal commitment, be sure to include the date you expect the written confirmation to be received on the Commitment Tracking form.

Page 1

Reporting Monetary Commitments

All new monetary commitments must be reported immediately through the University Development Office to Information Services. Alumni Affairs and Development Officers or their designees normally report the required information using a donor pledge card, and Individual Commitment Tracking form, or a Corporation or Foundation Commitment Tracking form.

Alumni Affairs. and Development staff should observe the following two options.

• Option A
When using a Pledge Card:

1. Review the commitment to make certain it complies with the provisions of the Gift Processing Policy.
2. Review the information on the pledge card to make certain it is accurate and complete.
3. Return the pledge card to Information Services in accordance with the instructions provided by your Alumni Affairs and Development Officer.

• Option B
When using a Commitment Tracking form:

1. If the commitment is for an individual, use the white Commitment Tracking form; if it is for a corporation or foundation, use the yellow one.
2. When the commitment is from a donor who is not coded by the Prospect Tracking System, complete the appropriate commitment form and forward it to the Director of Cornell Development.
3. When the commitment is from a donor who is coded by the Prospect Tracking System, you must immediately contact the appropriate Individual Giving Officer or Program Director who will complete the appropriate form and forward it to the Director of Cornell Development.
4. When the commitment is from a corporation or foundation, complete the appropriate form and forward it to the Director of Cornell Development, with copies to the Corporate and Foundation Relations Office.

• **Caution:** Always attach any written documentation you receive to the Commitment Tracking form.

Reporting Gift in Kind Commitments

All gifts of tangible and intangible assets and property must be reported immediately to Information Services. Gifts in kind include real estate. equipment. art. antiques. rare books, livestock, mortgages. and copyrights, all of which must be recorded in Information Services and the university accounting systems.

Individual Giving Officers or their designees normally report the required information to Information Services and to the Real Estate and Property Gifts Office or the Planned Giving Office using an Individual Commitment Tracking form, or a Corporation or Foundation Commitment Tracking form.

During the process of accepting and reporting a gift in kind. the following considerations must be observed:

- Gifts in kind should not be accepted unless they can and will be put to a related use by the university or can be sold.
- When a gift is tangible personal property, the person accepting the gift must inform the donor how the university intends
- to use or dispose of it.
- The university will accept gifts in kind and non-marketable securities but will not assign a value for acknowledgement purposes.
- When a value is placed on a gift for internal reporting purposes, it must conform to regulations of the Internal Revenue Code and university policies.
- Any value assigned to a gift accepted by the university is based on the current market value to the university.

Operating Unit Written Procedures

Individual operating units are responsible for developing written internal procedures to ensure gift checks received at college. unit, or department offices are processed in a timely and appropriate fashion. A copy of each operating unit's written procedures must be provided to Information Services for review and approval.

The operating unit procedures should be designed to provide an adequate review for compliance with the Gift Processing Policy, to satisfy the informational needs of the college or unit business and public affairs offices, and to ensure the timely depositing of checks. These procedures should incorporate the following elements:

- A statement from the Dean or Director of the unit informing faculty and staff of the policy requirements for accepting gifts, accompanied by a copy of the Gift Processing Policy;
- Delegation of responsibility for review of commitments and gifts received for compliance with the Gift Processing Policy;

Page 2

- Instructions to deliver all gift checks and source material received locally to the college or unit AA&D office;
- Internal procedures for providing information to the college or unit business office as appropriate;
- Instructions regarding gift acknowledgement letters; and
- Instructions on insuring gifts of equipment and other gifts in kind.

Processing Monetary Gifts Received

Information Services must be used to record and control all transactions of monetary gifts received by the university. Every effort must be made to deposit checks on the same day they are received.

• **Caution:** All checks in the amount of $50,000 or more must be deposited the same day they are received.

Follow your college or unit written procedures for processing monetary gifts received. If you do not have a copy of these procedures, obtain one from your department's administrative office, AA&D Officer, or college/unit business office.

Checks may be deposited through Information Services, the Cash Management Office in Day Hall, or the Statutory Finance and Business Services Office in Mann Library.

• **Option A** (Preferred)
Depositing checks through Information Services:

1. All checks should be endorsed immediately upon receipt. The endorsement should state "For Deposit Only to Cornell University." Write or stamp the Gift Clearing Account Number below the endorsement.
2. When a check is not accompanied by a pledge card or letter, you should complete the Standard Gift Information form, available from Information Services.
3. Place the check, letter, pledge card or Standard Gift Information form, and matching gift form (if received), in the original envelope. This ensures accurate processing of the gift by the bank.
4. Write the amount of the check in the lower right-hand corner of the envelope.
5. Sort through the envelopes and place those with checks of $5,000 or more at the top of the batch.
6. Complete the Gift Transmittal form provided by Information Services.
7. Run a double adding machine tape of all envelopes in the batch and attach it to the Gift Transmittal form.

• **Caution:** To make certain the checks are deposited to the correct project or program, use the AA&D fund code or the Accounting Office general ledger account number in the "Account #" section on the Gift Transmittal form. If you need to establish a new account, contact the Endowed or Statutory Accounting Office.

8. The Gift Transmittal form and gift checks, along with the appropriate tracking form must be sent to the Information Services Office using one of the following methods:
   - Send deposits of less than $1,000 via campus mail.
   - Hand carry larger deposits to Information Services at 55 Brown Road or to the AA&D Office at 245 Day Hall.

• **Option B**
Depositing checks at the Cash Management Office or the Statutory Finance and Business Services Office:

1. All checks should be endorsed immediately upon receipt. The endorsement should state "For Deposit Only to Cornell University" with your department's general ledger account number, including object code.
2. Follow the University Bank Deposit Procedures (available from Information Services or the Cash Management Office).
3. On the same day as the deposit, provide the original letter, pledge card or Standard Gift Information form, a matching gift form (if received), and a copy of the deposit slip to Information Services.

Processing Gifts of Securities Received

Process gifts of securities by directing the donor or their agent to the Office of Trusts and Estates, which will work with the donor to transfer ownership of the securities to the university. Gifts of unregistered, restricted, or closely held stock, or gifts of securities with limited marketability require the prior approval of the Investment Office, the Vice President for Alumni Affairs and Development, and the Controller.

If actual securities certificates are received, do not send them via campus mail. Immediately call the Office of Trusts and Estates to arrange for proper handling. All supporting documentation accompany gifts of securities, including the mailing envelope, should be included when securities are delivered.

Processing Gifts in Kind Received

The university receives many gifts in kind. The following options describe how to process the most frequent types of gifts in kind received. When you are unsure of how to handle a particular gift in kind, call Information Services.

• **Caution:** Gifts of art, equipment, and library materials will have tax considerations. Therefore, you need to contact both the appropriate office and the Office of Real Estate and Property Gifts.

If you must protect against loss of any gift in kind received, immediately contact the Department of Risk Management and Insurance to obtain appropriate insurance coverage.

• **Caution:** When a gift in kind has not been previously recorded as a commitment, you must receive approval to accept the gift in accordance with your operating unit's written procedures before processing it.

• **Option A—Art**

1. Contact the Johnson Museum AA&D Office for instructions on processing gifts of art.
2. In all circumstances, contact the Office of Real Estate and Property Gifts for processing instructions to ensure that tax considerations are properly handled.

• **Option B—Equipment**

All gifts of equipment must be reported to Information Services and the Office of Real Estate and Property Gifts. Information Services will record the gift and forward required information to the Accounting Office for recording in the general ledger. Items of $500 and over and with a useful life of over two years must also be recorded in the capital equipment inventory system maintained by the Accounting Office. The Office of Real Estate and Property Gifts will provide processing instructions to ensure that all tax considerations are properly handled.

1. When processing gifts of equipment, you should first complete the gift in kind information form, available from Information Services. Attach invoices, packing slips, and any other supporting documentation.
2. When necessary, complete the original Equipment Inventory Control Acquisition Report, available Information Services. Any value placed on a gift must be based on its accompanying invoice. If the invoice does not list the cost, contact the supplier in order to ascertain the value to the university.
3. Forward the above information to Information Services.
4. Donors may supply you with their acceptance form and Internal Revenue form 8283. Complete the required information on these forms and send them to Information Services for review, approval, and mailing to donor. All Forms 8283 will be forwarded by Information Services to the Office of Trusts and Estates for review and signature.

• **Option C—Life Insurance**

1. Contact the Office of Trusts and Estates or the Planned Giving Office in University Development for instructions on processing gifts of life insurance.

• **Option D—Livestock**

1. Contact the College of Veterinary Medicine's AA&D Office, or the College of Agriculture and Life Science's Department of Animal Sciences for instructions on processing gifts of livestock.
2. In all circumstances, contact the Office of Real Estate and Property Gifts for processing instructions to ensure that tax considerations are properly handled.

• **Option E—Rare Books and other gifts of Library Materials**

1. Contact Cornell Library's AA&D Office or the Library Department of Rare Books for instructions on processing a gift of rare books.
2. Contact the Assistant University Librarian for Collection Development and Preservation or the Office of Real Estate and Property Gifts for instructions on processing other gifts of library materials.
3. In all circumstances, contact the Office of Real Estate and Property Gifts for processing instructions to ensure that tax considerations are properly handled.

• **Option F—Real Estate**

The university accepts gifts of real estate if they can be sold or put to good use by the university and/or if the management of the properties won't be a burden. Only the Vice President for Alumni Affairs and Development and the Vice President for Finance and Treasurer have the authority to accept real estate gifts. After acceptance, real estate gifts are categorized as academic, investment, or non-investment real estate.

1. Contact the Office of Real Estate and Property Gifts for instructions on processing real estate gifts.

Page 4

• Option G—Real Estate Trusts

The Vice President for Alumni Affairs and Development, after consultation with the Associate Treasurer for Investments and the University Counsel, is the only person authorized to accept gifts of real estate trusts. After acceptance, real estate trusts are treated as investment real estate.

1. Contact the Planned Giving Office in University Development for instructions on processing gifts of real estate trusts.

• Option H—Devised Real Estate

The Senior Vice President and CFO represents the university's interests in devises until title has been transferred to the university. After title has transferred, devises are categorized as academic, investment, or non-investment real estate. Devised trusts are treated as investment real estate.

1. Contact the Office of Trusts and Estates for instructions on processing devised real estate.

• Option I—Trusts

1. Contact the Planned Giving Office in University Development which will work with the Office of Trusts and Estates and the donors to establish trusts, including charitable remainder trusts, pooled life income funds, and charitable gift annuities.
2. Payout rates for charitable remainder unitrusts and annuity trusts will be provided by the Investment Office. The Senior Vice President and CFO must approve any special circumstances of rates different from those set by the Investment Office.

• Option J—Other Gifts in Kind

1. Contact Information Services for instructions on processing other gifts in kind such as copyright interests, mortgage rights, notes, patents, royalties, and software licenses.

Disposing of Gifts in Kind

The disposition of gifts in kind must be handled on an individual basis, as special IRS rules related to the donor apply when the disposition occurs within the first two years of acceptance of the gift. Follow your department's normal procedures for disposing of equipment.

You must contact the capital equipment section of the appropriate accounting office (Endowed or Statutory) for instructions on removing equipment from the Central Equipment Inventory list. The accounting office will determine if there are any IRS considerations involved, and, as appropriate, provide guidance for complying with those considerations.

Issuing Gift Receipts

Information Services is responsible for the production and issuance of all official university gift receipts, except for payments made to trusts where official gift receipts are issued by the Office of Trusts and Estates.

Receipts for gift payments will be produced and mailed to the donor except in situations where the donor has requested to not receive a receipt.

Issuing Acknowledgement Letters

The University Development Office normally sends acknowledgement letters for all gifts of $500 or more. Colleges or units may also send acknowledgement letters and provide instructions on issuing them in each of their individual written procedures.

Writing Off Pledges

The University Development Office is responsible for the annual review of the list of unpaid pledges to ensure it accurately reflects the outstanding commitments to the university as of the June 30th fiscal year-end.

Pledges with unspecified payment dates will be reviewed by the Director of University Development who will make a determination as to whether or not to continue recording them on the list of outstanding pledges.

At fiscal year-end, Information Services, in consultation with the Development Office, will cancel all unpaid current year pledges.

The University Development Office will review the list of pledges canceled at fiscal year-end to determine which, if any, should be carried forward into the new fiscal year and to identify the revised schedule of payments.

Declining Gifts

Gifts may have to be declined under certain conditions including, but not limited to, the following:

- The gift is restricted and would require support from other resources which are unavailable, inadequate, or may be needed for other institutional purposes.
- The gift is restricted and would support a purpose or program peripheral to existing principal purposes of the institution, or create or perpetuate programs or obligations which would dissipate resources or deflect energies from other programs or purposes.
- The gift would limit, or tend to limit, the academic freedom of the university.
- The gift would injure the reputation or standing of the university, or generate such controversy as to substantially frustrate and defeat the educational purpose to be served.

1. Contact the Director of University Development for questions or considerations regarding declining gifts.

Gifts of Service

Gift receipts are not issued for gifts of service. The Director of University Development may assign a value to a gift of service for donor recognition purposes only.

Gifts Requiring Financial Commitment from the University

Sometimes gifts require a present or future financial commitment from the university over and above the amount pledged.

• **Caution:** Before soliciting or accepting any gift which requires a present or future financial commitment from the university, you must obtain written approval from the President or Provost.

The Vice President for Finance and Treasurer and the University Counsel should be apprised of such approval negotiations at an early stage to assist if necessary. Examples of some university gift-related commitments are:

1. To provide matching funds.
2. To continue a project after the gift has terminated or been exhausted.
3. To finance a construction project.
4. To establish a permanent, interest-bearing fund when the gift amount is not large enough to carry out its specified purpose.
5. To finance and/or administer a project outside of the routine functioning and operation of the university.

Matured Bequests

Matured bequests are accepted and administered by the Office of Trusts and Estates, subject to the bylaws and policies of the university.

1. Contact the Office of Trusts and Estates for instructions on accepting and processing gifts of matured bequests.

Naming a Building or Other Facility

Under special circumstances, the university may publicly honor an individual or organization by the naming of a building or a facility. Certain procedures must be followed for this kind of honor to be bestowed.

The Committee on Memorials and Named Facilities is charged by the President with the responsibility of reviewing and recommending to him all proposals to name any building or facility for any individual or organization. This committee is appointed by the President, chaired by the Vice President for Alumni Affairs and Development, and consists of at least two members of the faculty, nominated by the Dean of the Faculty, and others as the President deems appropriate.

The procedures which appear below apply to all buildings and facilities of the university at its main campus in Ithaca, New York; the Geneva Experiment Station in Geneva, New York; the Medical College in New York City, New York; as well as facilities located elsewhere.

1. The naming of any building, part of a building, road or facility for a person or organization is a high honor and should not be done casually. This honor should be reserved for those who have made extraordinary contributions to the university and its life through their achievements in the service of the university or in other ways.
2. Buildings or other facilities or parts thereof, whether new or existing, are named or renamed only by action of the Board of Trustees on recommendation of the President.
3. The State University of New York must be notified of action of the Board of Trustees in naming any building or facility of a statutory college before the building is publicly identified by the name or before any sign with the name is attached to the building.
4. The proposed naming of any building or facility or the memorializing of any individual or organization by a plaque or any other physical device is referred to the Committee on Memorials and Named Facilities which reports its decision on the propriety of the proposed name or memorial to the President.

Page 6

In the instance of a proposed plaque, the Committee on Memorials and Named Facilities must be given a recommendation for plaque wording, size, material, and method of attachment as suggested by the supervisory university department. Approval of these matters is at the discretion of the Committee on Memorials and Named Facilities.

To qualify for consideration of an honorific plaque, the Committee stipulates a minimum of a $25,000 gift to the university or to benefit a building, structure, room, or other unit of a building.

To qualify for consideration of an honorific plaque, the Committee stipulates a minimum of a $10,000 gift to the university for items such as a bench or an honorific plaque to be mounted on a stone boulder, a marker, a wall, or fencing material.

5. Contact the Committee on Memorials and Named Facilities through the Office of the Vice President for Alumni Affairs and Development for all issues related to naming a building or other facility.

• **Caution:** Approval for the naming of any building or facility must be secured from the Committee on Memorials and Named Facilities prior to any discussions with donors concerning the naming opportunity. The Committee on Memorials and Named Facilities will not accept any obligation to honor commitments made by faculty, staff, or members of the administration without its prior consent and approval.

Returning Gifts

In certain situations it may be necessary to return a gift to a donor. In these circumstances you must contact the Director of Cornell Development before returning the gift. The Director, working with the Vice President for Alumni Affairs and Development, the Vice President for University Relations, and University Counsel will advise you on the strategy and procedures for returning a gift.

Appendix 7–C

Southern Homes Services

Policy and Procedures—Acceptance of Gifts-In-Kind

Courtesy of Southern Home Services.

SOUTHERN HOME SERVICES
Organization-wide Policy

POLICY: ACCEPTANCE OF GIFTS-IN-KIND	# DEV 021
APPROVED: _____ _____ Executive Director President, Board of Trustees	REVISED: 1/19/2000 Original Date: 6/5/97

PURPOSE
Southern Home Services (SHS) recognizes the valuable contribution of Gifts-in-Kind (GIK) to the effective and cost-efficient delivery of services to our clients.

POLICY
The Administrative Assistant to the Director of Development is responsible for managing the Gifts-in-Kind program.

DEFINITION
Gifts-in-Kind refer to the donation of non-asset goods and services. Examples include donated clothing, food, toys, household goods, office equipment and furniture, transportation vehicles and tickets to sporting and entertainment events.

STANDARDS
Gifts-in-Kind shall be acknowledged in a timely fashion and will be cited in the SHS Annual Report.

PROCEDURE: RECEIVING GIFTS-IN-KIND

Please take the following steps when a gift-in-kind contribution is received at South Branch or CSC:

A. CLOTHING/TOYS/HOUSEHOLD ITEMS

1. Sort the items.

2. Fill the Gifts-in-Kind Acknowledgement Form (see attached sample form): If the gift is received at South Branch, send it to the Development Department; if it is received at CSC, send the form to South Branch within 2 (two) business days. Attn: Development Department: Be sure to date and sign the form.

3. If an item is received at South Branch, determine if it can be used there. If so, contact the AA to the Development Department so that distribution can be arranged. If it can't be used at South Branch, contact Margarita Vera at CSC to find out if it can be used there. If it can, arrange for a delivery through the Development Department and Rosemarie Mascuilli.

4. If the gift is received at CSC, first determine if it can be used at South Branch (i.e., clothing, toys for children in the residential program). If so, contact the Development Department so that a pickup/delivery can be arranged. If the gifts can't be used at South Branch or if it is determined that there is greater need for the gift at CSC, contact the CSC Outreach Coordinator so that she may arrange for distribution.

B. FURNITURE

1. People will usually call if they have furniture that they would like to have picked up. All Gifts-in-Kind furniture pick-ups should be arranged only through the Development Department.

2. If the furniture is simply dropped at South Branch or CSC, fill out the Gifts-in-Kind Acknowledgment Form, making sure to note the condition of the furniture — Southern Home Services only accepts furniture in good condition. Be sure to date and sign the form and send it to South Branch, to the attention of the Development Department, within 2 (two) business days.

3. Contact the Outreach Coordinator to find out if there is a need for the furniture at CSC. If so, and the furniture was dropped at South Branch, arrange through Building Services and the AA to the Development Department a delivery to CSC.

   Note: If a gift is given anonymously, a Gifts-in-Kind Acknowledgement Form should still be filled out and sent to the Development Department.

ADDITIONAL THINGS TO CONSIDER

- If a large (more than 5 bags) donation of clothing is received, it is generally not necessary to be EXACT with the item count. For example, instead of counting each item of clothing, you might write something like, "4 bags of sweaters, and pants" and "3 bags of shoes — women's size 8 and 9."

- If the items are fairly new, then a more exact description should be given because the donor will be more likely to give a $ value to the donation for tax purposes. However, the size of the donation should still be taken into account.

- When a GIK donation is received from a company or foundation, the name of the company or foundation, not the name of contact or the individual who left the items, should be on the Gifts-in-Kind Acknowledgment Form.

- No donations are accepted on the weekends due to secure storage issues.

C. DEFINITION(S)

- **Gifts-in-Kind** refer to the donation of non-asset goods and services.

- Gifts-in-Kind: Examples include donated clothing, food, toys, household goods, office equipment and furniture, transportation vehicles, tickets to sporting and entertainment events, computer equipment and supplies, toys, appliances, personal hygiene items, etc.

D. RESPONSIBILITY:

RESPONSIBILITY	ACTION
Dev. Dep't. AA	1. Record GIK on GIK Acknowledge Form
Dev. Dep't. AA	2. Input GIK into Donor Perfect database
Dev. Dep't. AA	3. Send acknowledgment letter to the donor

E. FORMS TO ACCOMPANY THIS PROCEDURE: (attach forms)
Gifts-in-Kind Acknowledgment Form

Appendix 7–D
Stephens College
Gift Policy

Courtesy of Stephens College.

Stephens College

Columbia, Missouri 65215 • (573) 442-2211 • FAX (573) 876-7248

I. OVERVIEW STATEMENTS

A. Board Commitment

It is the policy of the Board of Trustees of Stephens College to offer the donor the opportunity to make gifts to the College, both of cash and non-cash assets in a manner beneficial to the donor while protecting the fiscal and legal integrity of the institution. It is also the policy of the Board to give the opportunity to the donor to make gifts reserving life income for the donor and other beneficiaries through their wills or through current giving. This board is committed to aggressively seek such gifts and to provide adequate staff and resources for a full and effective program.

This policy replaces sections 9.1.4, 9.1.6, 9.1.13, Appendix A, B, C, 9.3 and suggested policy 9.1 (all the material behind the blue divider) of the Stephens College Codification, July 19, 1994, and as revised February 1997.

B. Ethics in Receiving Gifts

This Board authorizes the acceptance of gifts to Stephens College only where there is genuine donative intent, where there has been full disclosure between the donor and Stephens College including, to the best of Stephens' ability, full disclosure of any tax or other ramifications to the donor, where the donor has been encouraged to seek her/his own counsel on legal and financial matters, and where the gift is in the best interest of both parties. This Board does not authorize the acceptance of gifts that would jeopardize the financial, legal or moral integrity or reputation of the institution, or where the gift would cause embarrassment to the donor or her/his family.

C. Valuing Gifts

This Board authorizes the Office of Advancement to value gifts (other than cash, which should be valued at dollar face value) in an appropriate manner for the campaign or fund drive, and in consonance with sound accounting principles. Full disclosure must be made to the donor when the gift is valued higher than the value placed on the gift by the Internal Revenue Code in determining the amount of the deduction for the donor's income gift or estate taxes. When necessary, this Board authorizes the Office of Advancement or other appropriate office to adjust the value given to a gift in case of revaluation by the IRS.

Full responsibility rests on the donor for claiming any deductions including filing form 8283, and any appraisals or other documentation. Full responsibility also rests on the donor for the value given to tangible personal property or services, and donors will be expected to give the College a written statement of value for these types of gifts.

II. ASSETS ACCEPTABLE AS GIFTS

The following assets are acceptable as described, as outright gifts, as bequests or devises (estate gifts), or when appropriate, as funding for a charitable remainder trust, gift annuity, pooled income fund gift or lead trust as determined by the Internal Revenue Code.

A. Cash

Cash is acceptable.

B. Securities

Listed securities, or securities actively traded over-the-counter are acceptable. Securities in closely held corporations, S corporations, or otherwise privately held securities are acceptable upon the approval of Stephens College legal counsel.

C. Real Estate

Real property that is mortgage free is acceptable of a minimum value of $50,000. Full interests, partial interests and remainder interests in real property are all acceptable. Remainder interests are contracts. In the case of such gifts, the donor will be expected to agree to pay all property taxes, maintain the property, and provide adequate insurance on the property.

Conditions for acceptance shall include salability and annual maintenance costs including evaluation of any liens against the property and any real estate taxes. Donor may be asked to sign a statement regarding liability for previous and current environmental or other conditions if the College deems it appropriate.

D. Bargain Sales

Definition: A bargain sale is one in which the College is provided the opportunity to purchase property at less than its fair market value. The gift is usually the difference between the sale price and the market value.

Bargain sales are not acceptable unless submitted by the Gift Acceptance Committee and passed by the Executive Board before acceptance.

E. Tangible Personal Property

Gifts of tangible personal property are acceptable. Conditions for accepting gifts include salability or as-is usability and current College needs for the type of property offered, physical condition of the property, cost of any storage or insurance needed and any other unusual feature or condition involved in the transfer.

F. Insurance

Gifts by contract, particularly life insurance, through which the College will receive a future benefit, are acceptable with a minimum face value of $50,000, so long as the College is not required to expend funds from sources other than the donor to maintain the contract. Stephens College may be named as a percentage or contingent beneficiary of any life insurance policy.

Paid-up life insurance policy gifts in which the College is the owner and irrevocable beneficiary are acceptable. The College cannot accept a gift of term insurance.

G. Services and Volunteer Expenses

Gifts of professional or volunteer services as requested by the College are acceptable. Donors are expected to discuss with the recipient department the nature and value of the service in advance of giving it.

Volunteers may receive gift credit for expense reimbursements donated to the College.

H. Other Assets and Forms Gift May Take

Other types of gifts not mentioned in this policy may be acceptable within reason for the purpose given and in an amount appropriate for the gift type. The Gift Acceptance Committee is expected to use fiscally and legally sound rationale for acceptance and to defer to the Executive Committee of this Board when appropriate. This policy should serve as a general guideline under such circumstances.

III. LIFE INCOME VEHICLES

The following life income agreements are acceptable when in compliance with the Internal Revenue Code at the time the gift is established and are subject to reformation as tax laws change. Stephens College willingly acts as trustee and/or gift manager for these life income vehicles where Stephens is to receive no less than 25 percent of the remainder interest.

A. Gift Annuity

A gift annuity contract may be established for a minimum gift of $10,000. As of January 1, 2000, the minimum amount to establish a gift annuity will increase to $25,000. Annuitants must be 60 years of age or older when payments begin. Annuities may have no more than two annuitants.

B. Charitable Remainder Trusts

Both charitable remainder annuity trusts and charitable remainder unitrusts are acceptable. A minimum funding amount of $100,000 is required to establish these gifts. The number of life income beneficiaries and the generations across which beneficiaries may span are negotiable based on meeting the Internal Revenue Code for remainder values, generation skipping tax implications for the donor and the funding amount. Minimally funded trusts are limited to two income beneficiaries of the same generation.

C. Pooled Income Fund

Stephens College maintains a pooled income fund to which gifts of at least $5,000 per transfer are accepted. As of January 1, 2000, the minimum amount will increase to $10,000 for the initial transfer and $5,000 for subsequent transfers. Life income beneficiaries must be at least 50 years of age, and no more than two life income beneficiaries who must be of the same generation are accepted per transfer.

IV. ENDOWED FUNDS

A. General Guidelines

Stephens College encourages donors to establish permanent endowed funds and allows donors to name these. The College accepts unrestricted endowed funds, preferred use endowed funds and restricted endowed funds. Funds must be $500,000 or more at the time of establishment to be held and invested separately from Stephens' endowment portfolio. (Donations of any size for endowed funds or life income gifts may be held and invested separately from the endowment portfolio on a temporary basis without conflicting with this policy.)

Restricted endowments must contain the following language: "Should the provisions for the use of the income from this endowment cease to be effective or practicable, the Board is authorized to use such income in a manner consistent with the general intent of such provisions."

Establishing a term-of-years endowed fund is permitted when recommended by the Office of Advancement and approved by the Gift Acceptance Committee.

All endowment agreements with funding of $100,000 or more must be reviewed and approved by Stephens College. Agreements funded with less than $100,000 may be reviewed by counsel as deemed appropriate by the College.

B. Types of Endowed Funds

1. Scholarships

Endowed scholarships may be established with a minimum gift of $30,000. Beginning January 1, 2000, scholarships may be established with a minimum gift of $50,000. (Cash and cash equivalent gifts below the minimum, which are designated for scholarships, will be placed in the general scholarship endowment, unless a pre-existing scholarship is designated.)

Donors may accumulate gifts toward minimum funding of an endowed scholarship with a gift of one fourth the required minimum and a signed scholarship agreement. Accumulations toward the minimum must be completed within 10 years from the date of the agreement. When accumulation is not completed, the agreement will be considered terminated, and gift amounts received will be placed in the College's general endowed scholarship fund.

Scholarship payments to student recipients will not be made until the minimum for the endowment has been received, the scholarship agreement is signed and approved by the Gift Acceptance Committee, and sufficient income has been generated for distribution. Donors accumulating gifts toward minimums may provide for an annual stipend in the agreement when that stipend is supported by an annual gift.

Scholarships may be established with estate or planned gifts. Scholarship moneys received by the College through a will or other planned gift, which is less than the required minimum funding at the time of distribution, will be placed in the College's general endowed scholarship fund, unless legally impossible, in which case, the College reserves the right to decline the gift.

Scholarship agreements shall be signed by the donor and by a member of the Gift Acceptance Committee.

2. Endowed Academic Chairs

Endowed chairs may be established with a minimum funding negotiated with the College as determined by the purpose of the chair, the program it will support, and the amount of income desired to be generated annually, but with no less than $750,000. Funding must be one million dollars or more (with an initial gift of $375,000 or more) to be held and invested separately from the College's endowment portfolio.

Donors may accumulate gifts toward an endowed chair with a gift of one-fourth the required minimum and a signed agreement. The agreement must specify the date within which minimum funding must be completed. Unless otherwise specified, where accumulation is not completed, the agreement will be considered terminated, and gift amounts received will be placed in the College's general endowment fund and be used for the program named in the endowed chair agreement while that program is extant.

Distribution of income from the endowed chair may be made before minimum funding has been reached if the agreement so provides.

Endowed chairs may be established with estate or planned gifts. The College reserves the right to negotiate, through the probate process, the use of any moneys received through a will or other planned gift that have been designated for use as an endowed chair and that will not generate sufficient income to support the purpose of the academic chair named in the agreement.

Endowed chair agreements shall be signed by the donor and by the president, and show the date on which the gift was approved by the Gift Acceptance Committee. The Gift Acceptance Committee shall note in its record approval as well as comments by the Vice President for Academic and Student Affairs.

3. Other Endowed Funds

Unrestricted endowed funds may be established with a minimum gift of $30,000. Beginning January 1, 2000, unrestricted endowed funds may be established with a minimum gift of $50,000. Restricted endowed funds (other than scholarships) may be established with minimum gifts of $100,000.

Donors may accumulate gifts toward minimum funding of an endowed fund with a gift of one-half the required minimum and a signed agreement. Accumulations toward the minimum must be completed within 10 years from the date of the agreement. When accumulation is not completed the agreement will be considered terminated, and gift amounts received will be placed in the College's general endowment fund.

Payments to the recipient purpose/program will not be made until the minimum for the endowment has been received, the endowment agreement is signed and approved by the Gift Acceptance Committee, and sufficient income has been generated for distribution.

Endowed funds may be established with estate or planned gifts. Endowment fund moneys received by the College through a will or other planned gift, which is less than the required minimum funding at the time of distribution, will be placed in the College's general endowment fund, unless legally impossible.

Endowed fund agreements shall be signed by the donor and by a member of the Gift Acceptance Committee.

V. DESIGNATING GIFTS

A. Restricted Current Gifts

1. Gifts Under $1,000

Cash and Securities

The College will accept restricted gifts when the restriction already exists in the form of a gift fund at the time the gift is made. The fund may be an endowed fund, an annual fund or a campaign fund. Restricted gifts will also be accepted where the gift is usable by the College at the time the gift is made, even though a fund does not exist.

Non-cash Gifts

Once accepted under this policy, non-cash gifts may be restricted under the same guidelines as cash and securities. Donors must be advised before making the gift whether the gift will be sold, held for eventual use or put to a "related use" as defined by the Internal Revenue Code.

2. Gifts of $1,000 or Greater

Cash and Securities

Donors may make restricted gifts to the College where the restricted fund exists or where the Gift Acceptance Committee agrees to the restriction.

Non-cash Gifts

Restricted gifts are acceptable as above. Donors must be advised before making the gift whether the gift will be sold, held for eventual use or put to a "related use" as defined by the Internal Revenue Code.

B. Restricted Deferred Gifts

1. Estate Gifts (wills, trusts, life insurance, other instruments)

The College will encourage unrestricted estate gifts to the College or unrestricted estate gifts to the endowment fund, since specific designations become inactive or non-existent over time. The College reserves the right to decline restricted estate gifts.

Upon the donor's request, the College will provide language to assist in establishing a restricted estate gift. The sample language will include the following: "This designation represents a preferred use for these funds and is not an absolute restriction. Should the exact designation cease to be effective or practicable before or after the gift is received by Stephens College, the Board is authorized to use this gift in an alternative way consistent with the general intent of this designation."

Gifts received where the College had no prior knowledge of the amount or nature of the gift will be treated as if the language above had been included, unless legally impossible. Gifts of $10,000 or less will be placed in the General Endowment Fund when the restriction no longer exists.

2. Other Planned Gifts (charitable remainder trusts, gift annuities, pooled income fund gifts, etc.)

Gifts established through the planned giving program at Stephens College may be restricted with the approval of the Gift Acceptance Committee. Acceptance will rely in part on inclusion of the language in the instrument, which reads: "This designation represents a preferred use for these funds and is not an absolute restriction. Should the exact designation cease to be effective or practicable before or after the gift is received by Stephens College, the Board is authorized to use this gift in an alternative way consistent with the general intent of this designation."

Gifts distributed to Stephens College where the College had no prior knowledge of the gift instrument or its restriction will be handled on a case-by-case basis. Stephens reserves the right to decline restricted gifts from planned giving instruments.

VI. NAMING OPPORTUNITIES

A. Naming New Construction

Negotiations may be initiated with donors who wish to name the building(s) of new construction or of existing buildings under renovation with a current gift of two-thirds of the construction cost announced at the beginning of a campaign, construction or renovation project. The College encourages donors naming buildings to consider endowing the maintenance of the building to prevent the need for renovation and possible renaming.

B. Naming Through Planned Gifts

1. General Policy

Stephens College reserves naming opportunities for current gifts and living donors. Use of an estate or planned gift to name campus property is not preferred but will be considered on a case-by-case basis.

Unless legally impossible, the College will treat estate and planned gifts with naming elements as a request. The College will honor the request at the final distribution of the gift when the name is appropriate and where the gift meets minimum funding for the naming opportunity at the time of distribution. The College reserves the right to decline gifts with naming restrictions.

2. Campaign Policy

Donors wishing to name an item during a campaign may use the present value of a planned gift only if a) the gift is established during the campaign in which planned gifts are counted, b) the gift is irrevocable, c) the College is given a copy of the gift instrument, and d) the present value of the gift equals the minimum funding amount or the naming opportunity.

C. Honorary Naming

The College reserves the right to honor, through appropriate naming opportunities, any individual or family irrespective of the individual or family's giving record. Such honors will generally be made posthumously.

D. Donor Recognition Policy

The Office of Advancement donor recognition policy, including any current campaign guidelines, will govern naming opportunities in all instances not covered by this policy. The donor recognition policy and all campaign guidelines shall conform to this policy and may not supersede it without Board approval.

VII. POLICY EXCEPTIONS

A. General Exceptions

Exceptions to this policy must receive the recommendation of the Advancement Committee of this Board and the approval of the Gift Acceptance Committee. The Board's Executive Committee shall be asked to ratify the Gift Acceptance Committee's action at regular board meetings.

B. Exceptions for Completed Gifts and Gifts Under Negotiation

Gifts made through estate plans that have been properly executed prior to the date of this policy, and gifts already received by the College are grandfathered in under this policy. Gifts under negotiation at the time this policy is adopted need not conform to the policy but will be accepted based upon the spirit of this policy and the specific terms negotiated with the donor.

C. Reviewing Gifts for Conformity

Gifts established with a written agreement shall be reviewed periodically, and action taken to conform the gift agreement to current law and College policy when necessary or appropriate for the well being of the College. Donors are responsible for conforming gifts where the College is not the trustee or gift manager.

VIII. GIFT ACCEPTANCE PROCEDURE

A. Authority to Negotiate

This Board authorizes the President and his or her delegates to negotiate on behalf of Stephens College acceptable gifts (other than cash and listed securities). Gifts negotiated by the delegate must be in consonance with this policy.

The Board authorizes the President or any presidential delegate working through the planned giving program, and any advisor or outside counsel deemed necessary, to negotiate life income gifts—charitable remainder trusts, charitable lead trusts, pooled income fund gifts, gift annuities—both *inter vivos* and through estate planning.

B. The Gift Acceptance Committee

Negotiated gifts shall be submitted to the Gift Acceptance Committee for approval. The committee shall consist of the Vice President for Administration, the Associate Vice President for Administration and Finance, the Vice President for Advancement and the Associate Vice President for Advancement.

The Associate Vice President for Advancement shall be responsible for the committee agenda and for calling the committee to session. Anyone with authority to negotiate (including delegates) may request a session.

The committee shall meet before each Board of Trustees meeting, and as needed, to formally accept or reject negotiated gifts. They may seek the advice or input of any party they deem appropriate to make a fiscally, legally and morally sound decision. The committee shall report its actions to the president and to the Advancement Committee of this Board. The Gift Acceptance Committee may request that this Board, in regular session, ratify its committee decisions when appropriate.

Potentially controversial gifts are to receive a recommendation for action by the Gift Acceptance Committee, to be reviewed by legal counsel, and to be deferred to the Executive Committee of this Board for acceptance or rejection.

Appendix 7–E
PresbyHomes Foundation
Policy Statement

Courtesy of Presbytery Homes Foundation.

PresbyHomes Foundation

2000 Joshua Road

Lafayette Hill, PA 19444-2430

Phone (610) 834-1001

Fax (610) 260-0947

www.presbyhomes.org

Section: 7

Policy: 7._

G-2

PHILADELPHIA PRESBYTERY HOMES and SERVICES FOR THE AGING
POLICY STATEMENT

SUBJECT: Gift Substantiation and Acknowledgment
SCOPE: Philadelphia Presbytery Homes Foundation
EFFECTIVE DATE: January 25, 1995

POLICY STATEMENT:

Philadelphia Presbytery Homes Foundation will ensure uniform and accurate substantiation and acknowledgment of gifts.

Implementation:

SUBSTANTIATION

A.   GIFTS

In accordance with IRS regulations and its own commitment to good stewardship of benevolence giving churches, corporations, groups and individuals, Philadelphia Presbytery Homes Foundation (PPHF) prepares and promptly mails written acknowledgments of all gifts. Gifts received on behalf of Philadelphia Presbytery Homes and Services for the Aging, and its affiliates will be forwarded to the Corporate Office for acknowledgment, except by the Auxiliary and Church Representatives. They are requested to provide copies of their gift acknowledgments of $250 or more. Written acknowledgments will contain: The donor's name as it appears on the check or letter of transmittal, the date of gift (or of receipt by PPHF if gift date is unknown), amount of gift, or nature of the gift if other than cash, conditions of the gift, such as: donor-imposed restrictions; anonymity; memorial or honorific status; term of gift, statement as required by IRS regarding donor's receipt of goods or services in consideration of the gift (if over $75), signature of an appropriate staff member.

For gifts designated to a facility/program by a donor, gift logs and copies of checks will be sent to facility administrators.

B.   GRANTS

Reports on the use of grant funds will be created in conjunction with the Treasurer's office, which will prepare all financial reports. The final report will be signed by the President or Vice President.

NOTE: All grant applications will be signed by an officer of the corporation, as they are contractual documents of the corporation.

Presbytery Homes Foundation supports innovative and continuing services for older adults. The official registration and financial information of PresbyHomes & Services and its affiliates may be obtained by calling toll free within Pennsylvania (800)732-0999. Registration does not imply endorsement

Section: 7
Policy: G-2-7
Gift Substantiation and Acknowledgment
page 2

Implementation:

ACKNOWLEDGMENT
Gift acknowledgments will be prepared by the PPHF staff and signed for PPHSA and its affiliates by the following persons:

PRESIDENT

1) Gifts and grants of $100 or more for any purpose

2) Gifts under $100 from Board Members, staff, and Pastors, Churches, or Presbytery.

3) Bequests and the remainders of other deferred gifts.

PPHF EXECUTIVE DIRECTOR

1) All gifts of less than $100 to all funds except those made by Board Members, staff, Churches, Pastors or Presbytery.

ACKNOWLEDGMENT OF GIFTS TO PPH AUXILIARY AND 58TH STREET HOME CHURCH REPRESENTATIVES.

1. The officers of the Auxiliary and Church Representatives acknowledge all gifts of cash (by currency, check, or electronic transfer) they receive, in writing, and keep a record of gift receipt and date of acknowledgment.

2. They will provide PPHF's office with copies of the acknowledgment letters they write to all donors of $250 or more where there is no return of gifts or services, and of $75 or more where a return is made.

3. It is the responsibility of the donor to value all non-cash gifts. The Auxiliary and Church Representatives will provide the donor a dated receipt that describes property received by them, and will forward copies of any receipt for gifts likely to be of substantial value.

4. PPHF's office will prepare an additional acknowledgment for gifts over the $250/$75 limit, and may acknowledge substantial gifts of property as well.

Presbytery Homes Foundation supports innovative and continuing services for older adults. The official registration and financial information of PresbyHomes & Services and its affiliates may be obtained by calling toll free within Pennsylvania (800)732-0999. Registration does not imply endorsement

PresbyHomes & Services

Chapter 8
Stewarding Your Donors for Their Next Enhanced Gift

CHAPTER OUTLINE

- Stewardship—What Is It? How Does It Work?
- Judging the Donor's Readiness To Make the Next Major Gift
- Individual Stewardship Strategies
- Intergenerational Stewardship
- Recap and Review

We expect the organization to keep us advised of the use of the funds and the organization's overall progress in meeting goals.

John C. Haas

I will make more than one gift to the same group if I see positive results.

Bruce E. Toll

Continued cultivation is important if I am going to give again to the same group.

H. F. Lenfest

When I support a charity, I will stay active and involved with that organization by committing my time and my resources. If I'm not passionate, I cannot produce!

Bonnie McElveen-Hunter

STEWARDSHIP—WHAT IS IT? HOW DOES IT WORK?

Treat donors well, and they will make additional gifts. Treat donors very well, and they will make additional larger gifts. Treat donors superbly, and not only will they make additional larger gifts, they will also get their families, friends, and business contacts interested and involved in your organization, sometimes to the point of making gifts of their own.

It is one of the oldest and most fundamental rules in fundraising that if donors feel appreciated, respected, and well informed on the use of their gifts, they will give again and again, usually in larger and larger amounts (Tromble 1998, 88). Organizations that spend the time and personal attention thanking their donors and showing them the numerous benefits that each gift has brought to each beneficiary will most assuredly have a solid base of multigift major donors. A well-treated donor is an extremely satisfied donor, one who will "reward" the organization with larger future gifts (Greenfield 1994, 128).

Major gifts stewardship is the continuous personal interaction and information exchange that you and others from your organization have with your donors. Stewardship paves the way for your donors to make repeat larger gifts. This sounds like cultivation, right? Well, indeed, *stewardship is a form of cultivation. It takes cultivation to the next level.* Chapter 4 "Cultivation—What Is It? How Does It Work?" detailed the numerous ways you could cultivate your prospects, such as inviting them to be a speaker, introducing them to the leadership of the organization, asking their advice on a special program, sending them holiday and birthday cards, and taking them to an outside event such as a music concert. Through your cultivation efforts, you were able to learn as much as you could about your prospects, in preparation of asking them for the right gift at the right time for the right amount for the right purpose.

Once they agree to make the gift, cultivation transforms into stewardship. Stewardship begins with the first thank you the donors receive from you and the leadership of the organization, and it remains a timeless process of involving, educating, and reporting to the donors not only about the gift, but also about the lives it has changed and the projects it has made possible. Stewardship requires not only that you and others from your organization regularly report on the use and benefits of their gifts, but also that you and your organization continue to cultivate your donors in preparation for their next major gifts. Exhibit 8–1 details the requirements for good stewardship.

Exhibit 8–1 Elements of Good Stewardship

1. Proper gift acknowledgment and recognition throughout the course of the entire donor relationship.
2. Proper use of the gift funds for the intended purpose.
3. Yearly reports and updates to the donor or the donor's family/heirs on the use of the gift funds.
4. Yearly reports and updates to the donor or the donor's family/heirs about the benefits of the gift.
5. Yearly reports and updates to the donor or the donor's family/heirs about the status of the fund, particularly endowed gifts and life income gifts.
6. Continuous communication, education, and involvement with the donor to preserve and strengthen his or her ties with the organization.
7. Maximum attention and focus on keeping the donor extremely pleased with the direction and progress of the organization.
8. Individual strategies for each donor to make the next enhanced major gift.

Proper gift acknowledgment is key to any major gifts stewardship program. As covered in Chapter 7, "Thanking and Recognizing Your Major Donors," if the organization creates a special thank you package for each donor, tailored to suit the unique ways the donor would like to be thanked, and uses every creative means to thank the donor on repeated occasions, the organization will have jump started its way to solid stewardship with that donor. Remember, you cannot thank the donor enough times or in enough ways. Every donor in some way likes to feel appreciated, stroked, and rewarded for his or her selfless philanthropic gift to help others. The right thank you package sprinkled periodically over time is the foundation of good stewardship. Thank them now, thank them in a month, thank them in a year—keep it going!

> *Tip: Stewardship starts the moment the donor agrees to make the gift and is thanked personally and individually by several people from the organization over the entire course of the donor relationship with the organization.*

The next stewardship step is an ethical obligation that the organization has to ensure that the donor's gift will be used for its intended purpose (Nichols 1997, 260). This is sometimes referred to as gift accountability or gift management (Beyel 1997–1998, 57). Several professional fundraising associations have adopted a Donor Bill of Rights that prescribes that donors have the right "(t)o be assured their gifts will be used for the purposes for which they were given" (see Appendix 8–A). This ethical principle reinforces the sum of the points raised in "Gift Acceptance Policies" and "What Should a Good Gift Acceptance Policy Include?" in Chapter 7. Your organization has the obligation of exercising sound fiscal management over the donor's gift; namely, making sure that if the donor made a gift for a specific purpose or designed to a specific fund that the donor's wishes are fulfilled (Ciconte and Jacob 1997, 134). For instance, if a donor made a gift to support the organization's endowment, the gift must be placed in the organization's endowed fund. A donor who makes this type of gift is well aware of the need for the organization to have a strong base of support through its endowment and knows that the organization will only use the interest that the endowed fund generates yearly for general operating purposes. It may sound beyond obvious that an organization must use the gift for its intended purpose, but there have been instances where organizations with sloppy fiscal managers, poor recordkeepers, or tremendous staff turnover have caused donors' gifts to be misdirected from their intended use. Sometime these acts are even overt, such as when a board "dips" into the endowed funds to pay for outstanding expenses or to prevent bankruptcy. No organization should find itself in this situation. It is simply unethical and in most instances violates the terms of the original gift agreement.

Donors have the right to expect that the organization will use their gifts as they have designated (Nichols 1997, 260). If the gift or gift fund has outlived its intended use or the donor wants the gift to be used for something the organization does not have and cannot accommodate, then it is incumbent upon the organization to immediately inform the donor and to suggest alternative ways the gift can be used or alternative funds where the gift can be invested. The organization cannot, however, make this decision for the donor or shift the donor's money from an established or designated fund to another without the donor's consent. This is not a unilateral decision on the organization's part; rather, the donor or the donor's family or heirs must agree to the gift designation or the gift's alternative use.

Key to any stewardship program is reporting to the donors on a regular basis on the use of the funds, particularly the good results achieved with the donor's funds (Greenfield 1999, 30). Their gifts are their expressions of how deeply they feel about your organization. You and your organization have the obligation to be the keepers of their trust and loyalty and to give them *at a minimum* yearly reports and updates about the wonderful tangible and intangible results their gifts made possible. Use telephone calls, mailings, and invitations to let the donors know just how important their gifts are to your institution.

Take, for example, the donor who made a gift to a community development project that would establish the community as an "enterprise zone" providing low-cost loans to the community's small businesses and preserving community gardens and open spaces. The donor should receive updates and reports on how the gift was instrumental to the growth and progress of these community projects. This can be done by telephone calls from business owners, mailings that contain articles from local newspapers about the growth and revitalization of the community, and meeting the donor at a local coffee shop to "absorb" the good feeling about the neighborhood. Think of how appreciated that donor will feel when he or she sees how meaningful his or her gift is and continues to be for the revitalization of a community that means the most to him or her. Think of how great he or she will feel when the community development group lets him or her know that the gift has transformed the lives of not only the business owners, but also of the residents that live, and patrons that shop, in that community. Show your donors the wonders of their gifts and they will most assuredly be inspired to give again and again.

Donors who make endowed gifts should receive yearly reports on the status of their gifts. Most donors expect that the organization will send them, sometime between September and December, a report that shows the growth in principal and interest. This accomplishes two things. First, donors who make endowed gifts like to know that their gifts are the "core" of the institution. They appreciate these reports because it lets them know that the institution will not "go under" and that it has a solid base from which a steady stream of income can be generated and used to keep the institution on strong footing. Second, they like to see how much interest the fund has generated because it is the interest that will be put to good use each year by the organization. I knew a donor who gave an endowed gift to the hospital foundation and designated that the interest be spent on medical research for heart disease. It was very important to him to know the amount of interest the fund generated each year because he felt with each dollar "he was one step closer to curing fatal heart disease." These are very meaningful gifts your donors have chosen to make, and you and your organization owe it to these donors to let them know how much they are appreciated and how important their gifts are to your organization.

Donors who make life income planned gifts such as a charitable gift annuity, pooled income fund, or charitable remainder trust should receive from your organization, or the financial institution that oversees the management of these life income gifts, a year-end account of any payment that was made by the charity to the beneficiary of the charitable gifts. In most instances your donors will need these statements for state and federal income taxes (Estes 2000, 30). These statements can be great tools for stewardship. I suggest that when these year-end statements are given to your donors, you include a thank you from the beneficiaries of the gifts (a handwritten note card would really go a long way) or a general letter from the CEO, executive director, or vice president of your organization thanking them for their gifts. NSFRE in its Code of Ethical Principles and Standards of Practice encourages its members to "take care to ensure proper stewardship of charitable contributions, including timely reports on the use and management of funds" (see Appendix 2–D, Standard #10). From the donors' point of view, they have made investments with your group, and they want to see the total return of their investment both in dollars and in benefits to your group's beneficiaries. What better way to stay in touch with your donors then to show them not only the monetary return they are receiving from their life income gift, but also to show them the lives they have changed, the land and wildlife they have preserved, and the structures that will attract wider and more diversified audiences.

Gift reporting both in numbers and in benefits is an excellent way to steward your donors for their next gift. Many well-stewarded life income donors make additional life income gifts if they like the "total return" they see in their investment. This is not just the annuity payment or pooled income gift they receive. Rather it is the "total benefits picture" they get when they receive a letter of thanks from a child who is able to go to camp, a call from a women who is now able to receive cancer treatment, or a picture from nursing home residents sitting in their new sun porch holding a great big "thank you" sign.

> *Tip:* Use gift reporting on the status and benefits of the gift to steward your donors towards their next major gift.

A point must be made about the fundraiser's and the organization's responsibilities that go beyond the donors and that involve the donors' families and/or heirs. In many instances, donors do not outlive their gifts, particularly if they made endowed gifts or planned gifts. When this is the case, the fundraiser and the organization have the duty to inform the donors' families and/or heirs about the use, benefits, and status of the gifts. These stewardship steps do not end upon the death of the donor when the donor has family or heirs. In fulfilling this obligation, your organization will actually be expanding its base of support because now it has new donors to educate, involve, inform, and cultivate. If your organization is diligent in its stewardship efforts to report on the exciting use, benefits, and status of the donors' gifts to the donors' families/heirs and cultivates them as "new prospects," your organization will be well positioned to capture new gifts from the donors' families and heirs.

Since stewardship is the continuation of cultivation, you must continue to communicate with your donors *in person* as well as through internal and external media. This is not the time you want to "drop" your donor and spend your time on your new group of prospects. You have to juggle your time between your previous givers, soon-to-be donors, and new prospects. Easier said than done; however, it is a MUST. Your stewardship efforts should include an enhanced version of your previous education and involvement with your donors. Why enhanced?—because now you know your donors better. When you were first cultivating them, you were learning all you could about their philosophy on giving, wealth, family, interests, hobbies, education, and profession. Now in stewardship, you have that body of research behind you, and you can tailor your movements, communication, and involvement using all that you have learned during cultivation (Kelly 1998, 433). It is critical that you bring all this knowledge gained during cultivation and use it throughout your course of stewarding each major donor.

The fundraiser's goal is to make sure that each major donor remains positive about your organization's progress and future. Remember, up until the gift, you and others were spending a great deal of time and attention on your top prospects. These prospects come to enjoy and then expect that you and others will continue to keep them involved after they have made their investments with your group. You want to keep them as pleased and involved with your group as they were when they made their gifts, because in all likelihood they will give again. By now the theme "the next best gift will come from the last donor" should be echoing in your mind. It's true, it happens, and that is why you need to keep these donors in clear view on your radar screen if you intend to secure another major gift from them.

> *Tip:* Since your next big gift will in all likelihood come from a previous donor, it is the fundraiser's responsibility to make sure that previous donors are stewarded with the same time and energy it took to secure the first gift.

JUDGING THE DONOR'S READINESS TO MAKE THE NEXT MAJOR GIFT

Similar to judging the prospect's readiness to make the first gift, the fundraiser has to be prepared to judge the timing of when to ask the donor for the next gift. Since the overriding goal of stewardship is to motivate your donors to make repeat major gifts, the fundraiser throughout the course of stewardship must form individual strategies for each donor to make the next major gift. This should be the mirror image of the steps you took cultivating and asking for the first gift. It is no different from employing the initial strategies the fundraiser used to craft the right initial gift opportunity (see Chapter 5), except this time the fundraiser has more complete information about the donor. At this point, the fundraiser should know the donor's key areas of interest to target for a gift, the type of assets that can and in the future will be available for the next gift, and any potential stumbling blocks or concerns that may influence the donor's decision to make another gift. All this information was initially gathered during cultivation and presolicitation conversations. It was fully discussed during the initial solicitation and was further refined when the donor had questions and the solicitor or team of solicitors addressed the donor's concerns. The fundraiser must use all this stored knowledge and interpersonal connection with the donor to judge the donor's readiness to make the next gift.

This is where stewardship can be a big help. Since stewardship is the ongoing exchange of information with the donor and includes the donor's active involvement with the organization, the fundraiser should be gathering further information about the donor to craft the next gift opportunity. Take, for instance, a donor who made an initial major gift of $25,000 for overall support of a before-school child-care program. After proper acknowledgment and recognition, the fundraiser did the following stewardship activities:

1. Had the children write the donor thank you letters.
2. Invited the donor to tour the school and meet the children.
3. Introduced the donor to the teachers, school board, and the children's parents.
4. Featured the donor in an internal publication.
5. Called the donor periodically to share stories about the children's activities during the before-school program.

In the course of these stewardship activities, the fundraiser learned that the donor never had children of his own and always wanted to do something to help "just one child." While he was happy that his first gift helped many children, he wanted to see real results in making a difference in the life of one child. He always

thought he would be a good father but never had the opportunity to have children. Helping one child would take away some of his regret of not having children. The fundraiser asked him if he would be interested in supporting an individual tutor/mentor for a student who was most in need of academic attention. The tutor/mentor would be assigned to the child for the entire time the child was in elementary school. They had a successful tutor/mentor program in place; however, there were not enough funds to accommodate all the children. As is typically the case, they had a wait list for children who needed a tutor/mentor.

To match the donor's interest in wanting to help "one child" with an existing funding need at the school, the fundraiser mentioned that there was a particular child who had a complicated and troubled family life that was preventing him from doing well in school. A tutor/mentor could help the child with his studies before and after school and serve as a role model for the child. The school had used tutors before for a child who needed individual attention and saw marked results in the child's self-esteem and academic achievement. The donor liked the idea, but he wanted to visit the school again to meet with one of the tutors/mentors to see how the program worked before he would commit.

This example illustrates how stewardship can be used to gain further insight into your donors so that the fundraiser can plan the next major gifts opportunity. Think of what would have happened if the fundraiser did not do any stewardship activities or did not gather more information about the donor during stewardship. The donor may have given again to the overall support of the before-school program, but chances are he will make an even larger gift for the tutor/mentor program because the fundraiser was able to "tap" into an even deeper and more meaningful interest the donor had to help one child.

> *Tip:* During stewardship, the fundraiser should gather additional information about the donor and the donor's views about the first gift to craft the best next gift opportunity.

INDIVIDUAL STEWARDSHIP STRATEGIES

Each donor is like a crystal, unique and precious to your institution. Each has individual interests, needs, and requires different handling (Iversen 1997). While the same types of stewardship activities may be used for several donors, such as taking donors to events, inviting them to meet the board, or sending them personal notes on annual reports, it is the *type, timing, and frequency of activities* that varies from donor to donor. This is why the fundraiser and others from the development team must plan individual stewardship activities for each donor. The best way to see how this works is by example. Here are several examples of donors who may require some added thought and creativity to steward properly. These examples include donors who are:

- Hard to reach by telephone or mail
- Difficult to keep informed and involved because they decline meetings and invitations
- Difficult to pin down to talk about their next major gift
- Content to give only by bequest
- Geographically distant from your organization
- Disgruntled over their first gift
- Eager to change/strengthen/shape the direction, focus, and output of the organization

If you do not already have a few examples of these types of donors, eventually you will encounter one or two. Let's go through the donor profiles for each and see how we can keep these donors informed and involved with the organization and on the road to considering the next best major gifts opportunity.

The "Hard-to-Reach" Donors

The easiest way to keep your major donors consistently educated, informed, and involved throughout the year is by:

1. Sending your internal publications such as newsletters, brochures, magazines, annual reports, and special invitations.
2. Sending external media pieces such as local or national newspapers, journals, and magazines about your organization or about the donor's interest.
3. Sending holiday and special occasion cards.
4. Sending invitations to special events.
5. Seeing the donors to update them on the organization's latest developments.
6. Calling the donors just to say "hello."

What if every time you call you the donor you get a message machine, and the donor does not return your call? You don't want to bombard the donor with telephone calls, but you want to keep in touch with the donor. How many telephone messages should you leave? How can you make an appointment to keep your stewardship on track if the donor never or seldom returns the call? What if the donor never responds to your mailings? No return telephone calls, no replies to your invitations, and no correspondence back to you equal no stewardship.

If this is the situation, you need to step back for a minute and consider that a number of things could be going on in the donor's life that are preventing or making it difficult for him or her to get back to you. Many donors do not think that they need to get back to you; in fact many think it is just a "nice gesture" that you called and that is enough for them. While it is on our minds as fundraisers that we have to stay in contact with our top donors, it is not their top priority to get back to us. I always use the phrase that donors do not wake up in the morning and say, "Gee, I haven't called my fundraiser today." It is foremost on our minds, not on theirs. Stewardship requires that you maintain your steady level of outreach with correspondence and telephone calls *regardless* of the lack or trickling of a response that you may get from your donors.

A few points need to be made about stewarding these hard-to-reach donors. First, make sure you have their right mailing addresses and their correct telephone numbers. It seems obvious, but this may be the reason why the donor is not responding to your communications. Second, presuming that all your records are correct, your telephone calls and correspondence are wonderful stewardship steps, and you should continue to make calls and send mail even though there has been no response. It is discouraging, yes, but keep in mind your donors may be reading all the mail you send them and may not like the burden that they have to return your call. In any event, you are doing your job to keep them informed. You really have no choice. Think of how the donor would feel if he or she made the gift, you called and sent mail for a few months, the donor did not respond, then your correspondence and calls ceased? The donor would feel that he or she was not worthy of your organization's time and would have grave reservations about giving again to your group.

Third, if your donors really do not want you to call, or they do not want you to send correspondence, brochures, and invitations, *you will be the first to know.* Major donors are not shy about letting fundraisers know what they want and what they do not want. The rule is unless your donors have told you not to call or send mailings, continue to do so regardless of the lack of response.

Fourth, do not presume that no response means that they are not reading the magazines and cards you are sending or that they do not appreciate a call from you from time to time. I had a donor that I did not see for over one year after he made his first major gift. I sent our quarterly newsletter, our annual report, and a birthday and several holiday cards. In addition I left messages on his answering machine once a month to say "hello" and intermittently asked if I could see him. It was just into the new year when he finally picked up the telephone when I called. He told me that his sister died suddenly the last year. He had to go take care of his two nieces and his sister's complicated estate. He had his mail forwarded to her house so he received everything I sent him. He told me that he had it on his mind to call me, but "there never seemed to be a good moment," to call me back. I was relieved to hear from him, and I felt terrible because all this time I thought he was "putting me off" or that this was truly a one-time major donor. Goes to show you that it is dangerous to presume that your donors are ignoring you or that they will only make one major gift. They generally have other things going on in their lives, and they seldom make only one major gift. Hang in there and do consistent outreach to your donors. You will see big and rewarding results.

> **Tip:** *Even if your donors do not return your telephone calls and do not respond to your mail, continue to call them periodically and to send them all the appropriate mail. Do not presume that they are not reading what you send or that they do not appreciate your telephone calls—especially if you are leaving a message just to say "hello."*

Exhibit 8–2 lists some suggested ways to steward the hard-to-reach donors.

E-mail is a great way to communicate with that hard-to-reach donor—provided that you have the donor's permission to communicate with him or her via e-mail. Remember, some donors view it as an invasion of their privacy or do not want to use their work time for their personal affairs. Furthermore, e-mails add up, and some donors may think of them as yet another thing on their "to do" list. The last thing you want to do is annoy the donor, but if you have his or her permis-

Exhibit 8–2 Suggested Ways To Steward the "Hard-to-Reach" Donors

1. Send e-mails—if you have previously received the donors' permission to do so.
2. Hand deliver a small gift with the organization's name/logo or a personal note.
3. Send a small handmade or homemade gift.
4. Ask a peer if he or she will help you contact the donor.

sion, use e-mail along with your telephone calls and mailings to get the donor's attention.

If your donors live or work within driving distance from your workplace or home, try hand delivering a small gift or personal note. Drop it off in their mailbox, or leave it with their assistant at work, so that the donors see there is no postage on it and that you must have taken the time to come by and drop it off. I don't disturb them by ringing the doorbell to see if they are home or asking to see them if I dropped by their office. I simply leave the gift or letter in the mailbox or with an assistant at work. I sometimes drop off a shirt, a cap, or note cards with the institution's logo just to keep the organization's name fresh in their minds. If often spurs them to give me a call or send me a note.

In some instances I leave a personal note that says:

> We really do miss you, and everyone at the organization sends their warmest regards. I do not mean to bother you or to overburden you with calls and letters, but I was concerned that something happened to you, a family member, or colleague. All of us at the organization are thinking of you, and we would be delighted *and relieved* to hear that you are all right. Please, when it is convenient for you, do give a brief call so we will know how best to stay in contact with you, our special friend.

I generally leave a note like this when it has been more than six months since I last communicated with the donor. Keep in mind the season in which you are trying to reach the donor. Many donors, especially elderly donors, travel either June to September to where it is cooler, or November to March to where it is warmer. The reason you may not be able to connect with them is purely a matter of a travel schedule. I use this note when I know their schedule, travel is not an issue, and I have not been able to reach them. It shows thoughtfulness on the part of the organization that you are thinking of the *donor's well being*. It's stewardship in its purest form.

Try sending a small handmade or homemade gift. If you work for a group that aids children, send something the children have made. If you work for a zoo, aquarium, or wildlife organization, send them a handmade gift or drawing of their favorite animal, fish, or wildlife species. If you work for a hospital, send them a pillow signed by the nurses. I often just drop off some homemade cookies. The possibilities are endless, and the cost is very low. Handmade and homemade gifts convey the message that your donors are valued donors. These gestures will spur them to call you and thank you for your thoughtfulness. Once they do, the door is open to set up your next appointment or to bring them to your organization.

As you work with more and more major donors, you will begin to see connections between some of them. Most major donors are friends with people who are your prospects and previous major donors. Find the connection and make it work for you. For instance, I was working with a prospect for many months. She was pretty well known in the philanthropic community, and during our cultivation visits she mentioned a name or two of people she "thought would already be contributing" to the organization. Turns out that one of the people she mentioned was a donor who I had been trying to reach for the past two months. The prospect was a tour guide at a historical museum, and I asked the prospect if she would give a private tour of the museum for this donor and me. She said yes. Then I asked her if she wouldn't mind calling the donor to invite her because that way they could pick a date that was convenient for both of them, and I would free my schedule no matter what date they picked. She agreed, and we all met at the museum. Turns out that my "hard-to-reach" donor was busy fixing up her summer home and that she had no time to meet with me, but the tour was too good to pass up. I asked her if I could see her summer home once it was completely redecorated and she said yes. I then had my next stewardship step with this "hard-to-reach" donor.

> **Tip:** *Take a creative approach to stewarding your donors by using other donors, prospects, peers, and volunteers to help you reach and involve your "hard-to-reach" donors in a variety of outside activities and events.*

The "Chronic Canceler, No-Show to Your Events" Donors

These donors are the extremely busy donors. They have a zillion things going on in their professional and personal lives, and it is next to impossible to get them to commit to an appointment or an event. They may take your telephone calls or have an assistant get back to you. The meeting is set, only to have them cancel it the day before or the day of the meeting. They may RSVP "yes" to an event, you confirm over the telephone that they will be attending, only to find out on the day of the event or at the event that they will not be attending. Frustrating, indeed, but you need to keep those telephone calls and invitations steady. You cannot make them show up at the appointment or get them to come to your event, so your telephone calls to set appointments and invitations must serve as your stewardship tools until you actually meet with them. Exhibit 8–3 lists some additional ways you can steward these donors.

Exhibit 8–3 Suggested Ways To Steward the "Chronic Canceler, No-Show to Events" Donors

1. Try to see them when and where they are traveling for business.
2. Try to see them when you are at an out-of-town seminar.
3. Let them know where you will be on vacation in case they will be in that area for business.
4. Ask them to host an event at work, business, or their club.
5. Attend outside events that they must attend.
6. Go to social or cultural events that they like to attend.

I find that travel, for business or pleasure, usually gets in the way of the fundraiser trying to see donors. Many of my donors travel for business, and they do not always know ahead of time where or when they will be out of town or out of the country. In this instance, I always try to set up the appointment anyway, knowing it may get canceled. At least you have made it to their calendars and it reminds them of your organization. Even though they may not get to see you through numerous cancellations, at least they know that the organization they have supported is doing its best to keep in touch with them.

If you travel to certain areas for work, let the donor or the donor's assistant know the territory you frequently cover in case the donor will be there at the same time. For instance, in several jobs, I covered the east coast from Maine to Florida. I let the donor's assistant know where I was going to be over several months. The assistant crossed my schedule with the donor's schedule and turns out we were going to be in Florida at the same time. The assistant set up a date when I could meet the donor for breakfast so that I would not be taking time from her work schedule.

Many donors are into exercise, and I have met donors while traveling to go for a long walk in the early hours of the day, as well as at sunset. If you know the donor likes a particular sport, like tennis, racquetball, basketball, or golf, and you like the same sport, try to set up a time when you both can play. Your donors will be more apt to meet you if you are tying into one of their daily routine events or if you tap into one of their key interests. Since you both are away, it makes it much more enjoyable to meet under these circumstances. If you do not travel for work now, keep this idea tucked away for a future position where you may travel for business. Remember, this is stewardship, and you need to get creative with the types of interpersonal connections you will be having with your donors. You should not aim to always meet formally, at an office or at an event. If you do, chances are they will put you off and put you off. The key is to make some of your visits enjoyable and *fun* so that your donors will look forward to your next get together. This sounds like a lot of planning, but you may find it easier to see some donors away from work than at work. You will get closer to your donors, because now you will be at the point where they feel more at ease with you. The more you know them and the more they know you, the closer the fundraiser-donor relationship will become. The closer the relationship, the easier it will be for you to judge the donor's readiness to make another major gift.

Seeing donors during travel can even work when you are at a seminar or on vacation. Many fundraisers attend seminars out of town, and it is very easy to set up a breakfast or dinner meeting with a donor before or after the seminar. If they say no, at least they know how serious you are about seeing them if you are willing to coordinate your schedule for them. When you do see them, it gives you the chance to let them know about the seminar and to compare notes about the area's restaurants and cultural events.

Seeing a donor during the fundraiser's vacation is a sacrifice. Fundraisers really get the gold medal for going this distance with their donors. While no one wants to give up a vacation day, it may turn out that your "chronic canceler, no-show to events" donor may be in the same place at the same time while you are on vacation. I recommend trying to see them ONLY if they are there on business. If it is their vacation, I never suggest seeing them because this is their free time, and I do not want to intrude on their private time.

Since these donors are your busy types, a great way to not only see them but to involve them further is to ask them to host an event. This idea does not appeal to all your donors, but it will for some. I have asked people to be the host of a small group of top supporters at their homes, offices, or private clubs. I bring a CEO, board member, dean, or faculty member to these events to meet with the guests one-on-one to let them know about the current and upcoming projects and programs for the organization. I always encourage the donors to invite some of their families, friends, and colleagues to join us. The organization pays the costs, but in some cases the donors want to take care of all the amenities. These events can be small and informal, such as a cocktail reception, brunch, or dessert party, or they can be more formal, with a sit-down dinner and program. In the more formal setting, the leadership can give a small talk and have a multi-media presentation.

These hosted events serve many purposes. First, *you will have your meeting* with your donors because they are hosting it. In all probability, they will not cancel because it is their event, and people are coming at their invitation. Second, *they will feel elevated* within the tiers of your organization because they are spending time with the top leadership of your institution. Many of them want continuous access to the organization's decision makers, and this is the perfect setting for your donors to share their views with your leadership. Third, if they bring family, friends, and colleagues to their home or office so that they can learn about your group, it is a strong sign that these donors *will be your long-standing major donors*. If they feel this good about your group that they are willing to share their good feelings with others, you have stewarded them well. Fourth, you will *have expanded your base of supporters* to include these guests who are close to your donors and who may be your next best prospects.

In formulating your stewardship strategies for this group of donors, take a look at their outside board memberships, committee responsibilities, or volunteer activities. If they will not meet you at your designated meeting, then meet them at an event that you know they will attend. For instance, one of my donors was on the board of a local food bank. The food bank held a yearly 10K run as a fundraiser. My donor mentioned that this event always takes place on the Saturday before Mother's Day. I made it a point to go to the event just so that I could say hello and let him know that I remembered this was an important day for him. Later that week I received an e-mail from him thanking me for being there, and we set a date to meet for lunch.

This type of stewardship requires that you draw upon all your previous conversations and refer back to their donor profiles so that you can find an outside event or activity that you can attend for the purpose of seeing your donors. Again, it is going the extra mile for your organization. It would be much easier to see these donors at your suggested time and place. But that strategy will not work with these very busy donors, so you need to add the outside event strategy to your stewardship plan. The more you meet them in "their arena" and follow their interests, the stronger their ties will be with your group.

> *Tip: Review the donor's profile and your contact reports to find an outside activity or event that your donor has an obligation to attend. Make a point to go to this event and meet the donor so that the donor knows you went out of your way to see him or her and to recognize his or her outside interests.*

If your donors do not have an outside obligation or volunteer activity, think of their hobbies and interests that may lead to a possible meeting. For example, one time I had a donor who loved to read mystery books. I saw in the newspaper that a mystery writer was coming to a local bookstore for a book signing and to read from her latest book. I called the donor and let her know I would be there. I went to the event, but she did not attend. I thought my perfect plan went bust. One week later, she called me to let me know she could not go because she had some out-of-town guests staying with her that night. I asked her if there were any other book signings she planned to attend, and she let me know about an event the following month. We set the date and time to meet at the bookstore.

Tap into your donors' interests and hobbies and find local events that match these interests and hobbies. Even if your donors say no to your invitation or fail to show up at the event, they know you made an extra effort to see them beyond the conventional ways an

organization generally keeps in touch with its benefactors. They will be impressed that you remembered these important details about their lives, and you have made it difficult for them to turn down your next invitation to meet. This is a significant stewardship step.

The "Not Now, Maybe Later" Donors

The goal of stewardship is to get your donors to the point where you want to start discussing the size, type, and purpose of their next major gift. What if you have a donor who always seems to avoid the next gift topic? What if no matter how you phrase it or no matter who conducts the presolicitation discussion, the donor tries to put the topic off until another day? Some fundraisers would probably like to put this type of donor on the bottom of the list of donors to steward. It is a tempting idea; after all, it feels like you are getting nowhere fast with this donor and that it will take forever before he or she will be ready to discuss it. But what do you do in the meantime with this type of donor? How much time should you spend on him or her and how frequently should you bring up the next gift topic? Exhibit 8–4 lists some suggested ways you can steward these types of donors.

Exhibit 8–4 Suggested Ways To Steward the "Not Now, Maybe Later" Donors

1. Intermittently discuss their next gift on every third or fourth visit.
2. Bring along a different person at each visit to meet the donors, such as the leadership of the organization, coworkers, volunteers, and beneficiaries.
3. Be sure to talk about other donors who have made major gifts.
4. Hand deliver articles about other donors' gifts.
5. Invite them as special guests to other donor recognition events.

These types of donors take much longer to steward than others do. There is no easy way to steward them, and it takes patience and tenacity to hang in with them. Realize that it will take longer to get their next gift than it will be to get the next major gift from other donors. The bottom line with these folks is that you have to intermittently discuss the next gift at every other meeting or every third meeting that you have with them. For instance, one time take them to lunch—and just have lunch. Talk about politics, travel, a few things going on at the organization, and nothing more. The next time you see them, talk about recent gifts your organization just received from other donors and hand deliver your most recent newsletter or annual report. After that meeting, bring them to your organization or meet with them at their home or office just to talk about their interest in making the next gift. Then sit back, let some time pass, like three to four weeks, after which you can invite them to a special event or outside event. The point is to mix up the focus of your meetings, but to be sure that the topic of their next gift is gently woven into the discussion every so often.

It is also very effective if you can bring a "new face" from your organization to meet your donors. I like to bring as many different leaders, board members, coworkers, new development staff, volunteers, and beneficiaries with me at each visit. It gives the visits a nice break from the routine, and it allows the donors to hear from others connected with the organization just how well the organization is doing and how important it is for the organization to have their private support. Most donors will feel flattered if the leadership of the organization takes the time to meet with them. Additionally, it can be a heartwarming experience for the donors to see and hear from someone who has benefited from their generosity. You want these donors to be totally immersed with every detail about your organization so that there is no doubt in their minds that this is the organization they should *continue* to support. Since they are procrastinating about making the next gift, you need to do all you can to convince them, using many voices from your organization, that they should be making another gift. Strength in numbers works here.

A very persuasive tool to get these types of donors to make another gift is letting them know every time a donor makes another major gift. You have to do it in such a way that it motivates them or at least gets them thinking about their next gift. You do not want it to sound like their gift was in the past and is now unimportant; rather you want them to know that their gift was instrumental in attracting new gifts. For instance, if your group just received a large gift, let the donor know about this new gift and remind the donor that past support, like the gift the donor made, works like a magnet to attract new gifts for the organization. Let the donor know that gifts to your group are like building blocks to a solid foundation. Each one serves as sup-

port for the other. This is why it is crucial to the growth and future of your organization that you have a steady stream of major gifts and *repeat and enhanced* gifts.

You may want to reinforce this concept by showing these donors any publicity pieces or written articles about these new gifts, especially if the "not now, maybe later" donors like public recognition. It will let the donors know that they have invested their first gift wisely because others believe in your cause and have followed suit by making similar investments. The donors may be attracted to the idea that they will receive further publicity and recognition if they make another gift. Showing them how well your organization gets the word out to the community about new gifts may give them a little "push" in the right direction to ponder their next gift.

If your organization has special recognition events where top donors are honored or donors who reach a certain giving level are thanked and recognized, consider inviting one of these "not now, maybe later" donors. I like to take one donor at a time to these events because these events are meant to be exclusive. Since the purpose of this event is to bring together people who have made gifts at top levels, you do not want to diminish the importance of this meeting by bringing several soon-to-be top givers. This would surely detract from the purpose of the event. Bringing one donor at a time will not detract from the purpose of the event and will lay the solid groundwork for that donor to make a next gift at a top level.

I let the donor know right up front that only donors at "x" level have been invited, but I wanted him or her there to meet the top supporters of the organization. I want to spend some time introducing him or her to top donors and letting him or her experience how good it feels to be surrounded by others who give at this level. Not all donors will feel comfortable going, but you will get a handful who will. Generally, donors like to "smooze" with each other, especially if it is a festive and celebratory occasion. This is a great time to let the donor know that your organization wants the number of donors at this level to increase next year and to lace into the conversation that you want him or her to consider making a gift at this level by next year. Now you have used a special event as the vehicle for getting your donor to consider making the next enhanced gift. Moreover, you have let him or her know the amount of the next gift your organization would like him or her to consider. You have sewn up several stewardship steps with one event and the right timing.

Tip: Make sure you let your "not now, maybe later" donors know about recent gifts your organization received and show the donors any publicity pieces announcing new gifts. Consider inviting one of these donors to a recognition event for donors who have given at higher levels to motivate him or her to make the next gift at a higher level.

The "Testamentary Gift Only" Donors

Almost every nonprofit organization has a group of donors who have given gifts through bequests or have made some testamentary gift that the organization will receive in the future. These are wonderful expressions of thoughtfulness and generosity on the part of the donors, yet organizations can only sit back and wait for these future gifts to materialize. The hard part for most groups is the reality that wills can be changed and revocable testamentary gifts can be changed so that there is no guarantee the organization will ever receive any money from these types of gifts.

Here is where stewardship is needed most. If your organization does not steward these donors well, you will be giving them a reason to shift the charitable beneficiary of their testamentary gifts. Moreover, you have to keep working with these donors because they may have the ability and the inclination to make an outright gift if you keep them well educated and involved with your group. Exhibit 8–5 lists suggested ways to steward your testamentary gift only donors.

Much like inviting the not now, maybe later donors to your top givers event, you want to take one donor

---

Exhibit 8–5 Suggested Ways To Steward the "Testamentary Gift Only" Donors

1. Have a special recognition event for donors who have given testamentary gifts AND an outright major gift.
2. Have the leadership meet with the donors periodically.
3. Have the beneficiaries of your organization call, write, and visit with the donors.
4. Bring the donors to your organization once a year.
5. Constantly send life income planned giving materials and offer planned giving sessions.

---

who has given a testamentary gift only to an event where other donors have made outright and testamentary gifts. Again, it gives that donor a "taste" and "feel" for being a multigiver in multi-ways to your organization. Let the donor talk to this new circle of friends, and let the event do the work. Usually the donor will have questions about how he or she can make an outright gift and the gift levels to support each program or area of his or her interest. If the donor does not have any questions or does not bring the topic up, then the fundraiser must recap the success of the event and state that the organization would be thrilled if he or she would consider making an outright gift. Let this donor know that if he or she does make an outright gift, he or she will be joining the new circle of friends just met and that it is important for your group to have outright gifts so that your organization can serve its constituency right away.

The most important way to steward these donors is by consistent interpersonal contact. These donors need more exposure and more involvement with your group before they will commit to an outright gift. This is why I suggest that you have the leadership of your organization meet with these donors in a one-on-one setting at least two times a year. Let them know how valued they are as donors and how meaningful it is to have their anticipated future gifts. The leadership can discuss your ongoing need for support for your projects and programs and detail the current success and future initiatives for your group. This will have a big impact on your donors and will pave the way for you during your next set of visits to talk about outright gift opportunities.

Intertwine these meetings with one-on-one meetings with the gift recipients of your charity so that they can see and hear how important it is to have outright support to help these people or your cause. To the extent that you can bring donors to your organization, have them come for a tour at least once a year to show them any new programs or physical enhancements and to meet your staff and volunteers. It is a tremendous advantage for you if you can have these donors meet and admire the hard work that these "behind the scenes people" do day after day just so those in need can live better lives. If these stewardship steps are carried out, you will have a better chance that these donors will make outright gifts well in advance of their testamentary gifts (Harstook 1998, 31).

If your donors are unwilling to make an outright gift, then suggest a life income gift such as a charitable gift annuity or charitable trust. Your donors may be interested in having some additional income at some point, so a charitable gift annuity or charitable trust may appeal to them. Your organization wants to be right there when it comes time to set up a life income gift, and sending them planned giving information periodically will not only pique their interest, it will get them to contact you when they are ready. Also, it gives you something to discuss and explain while you are stewarding these donors. Let them know the success of your program, how many donors you have that made life income gifts, and what your organization is able to accomplish with these gifts.

Even though your group may not realize the monetary benefits of the life income gifts for several years, it usually brings the donors one step closer toward making outright gifts. Once these donors receive some extra money each quarter or yearly from these life income gifts, they will be in a better position to entertain the idea of giving outright gifts. For example, a donor I knew gave through her will, then became interested in a charitable gift annuity. Once she started receiving a steady stream of payments, she found that she did have "a little extra cash" to make an outright gift. With each gift, her gift amount increased to the point she was making quarterly major gifts.

Planned giving seminars are also a very good way to let your "testamentary gift only" donors know that it may be better for purposes of income, capital gains, and estate taxes if they do make some life income and outright gifts. Many millionaire-plus donors are well aware that they need to make some well-thought charitable gifts before they die to avoid paying hefty estate taxes (Stanley and Danko 1996, 62). These accumulated asset donors will lose a substantial portion of their estate if they do not incorporate some charitable gift vehicles into their overall estate plans. Planned giving seminars are extremely helpful in this regard. A good seminar can show how charitable gift planning can make it possible for them to provide for their loved ones while avoiding excessive tax burdens. It is a good way to steward these "testamentary gift only" donors one step closer to making a life income and/or outright gift. Besides, if you do not stay with these donors, chances are they will select another great charity to receive their outright and life income major gifts.

The "Too Far Away" Donors

Many organizations have a group of major supporters that live across the country and abroad. Staying in contact with these donors and keeping their involvement level high can be challenging. Often, these donors go on the "back burner" because it is far easier, and usually less expensive, to steward donors who live near your organization than it is to steward the geographically distant donors. If you do, you will be missing out on some future major gifts to the detriment of your organization. This particular group requires that you plan your stewardship moves and that you and others review your budget to factor in the additional costs it will take to steward these donors. To the extent possible, on a yearly basis your organization should set aside some operating funds to spend on this group because you will probably want to visit with them at least once a year. Smaller organizations that cannot set aside the costs to travel should at least factor additional postage and telephone charges into their budgets. Exhibit 8–6 lists some suggested ways you can steward your too far away donors.

To the extent that you have the funds, you need to see these folks at least once a year. If you have the

Tip: *Steward your "testamentary gift only" donors by bringing them to your organization and meeting with the leadership of your organization and your gift recipients. Show them through life income planned giving materials as well as planned giving seminars how it may be beneficial for their estate plans if they make life income and outright gifts to your charity.*

Exhibit 8–6 Suggested Ways To Steward the "Too Far Away" Donors

1. Visit with them at least once a year.
2. Make sure all mailings and invitations have personal notes from you, the leadership, a volunteer, or a gift recipient.
3. Call at least once every six weeks and send e-mails when appropriate.
4. Send autographed pictures, sketches, posters, or note cards that depict your organization or token items that bear your organization's logo.
5. Remind them to visit your Web site to get the latest news about your group.
6. Let them know if there are other supporters who live near them.

funds, it would be ideal to see them four to six times a year. You need this personal interaction with them to learn more about them first hand. You need to gather research about their health, wealth, new interests, families, and business; and there is no better way than to sit down and spend time with them. They need to hear from you how your organization is doing, and they want to be reassured that the organization is progressing in the right direction.

Since these too far away donors cannot visit your site as often as they would like, they keep a sharp eye out for any word about your group in national or local media. Their ears pick up when your organization makes the news and that should clue you in that they have a real and lasting interest in your group. Many of my distant givers let me know when some news feature about the organization makes its way to their local news. Presuming that the story was a positive one, it is a great bonding moment when the distant donors want to be included in the successes of the organization. If you can get to see them shortly after this good news, do it. It will be the perfect time to ask them about their interest in making another gift. Remember, "people will give to forward moving trains."

Your mailings and invitations take on new meaning for these geographically distant donors. They are the consistent ties with your group so you need to make them as personal as possible. Always attach a note or post-it from you, the leadership, a volunteer, or a gift recipient even if it just says, "Thinking of you." You will get mileage out of this thoughtful gesture because you are not just sending a piece of paper, brochure, or invitation. You are sending your warmest wishes along with the correspondence.

It is important that you include these folks on all your special events invitations, even though there is a strong likelihood that they will be unable to attend. They like to know the events your group is conducting, and it gives you something to talk about when you see them or call them. You want them to feel like they are every bit as involved with your group as a donor living a few miles away from your group. Also, you never know what travel plans your donors may have, and they may be in your area during one of your events.

This may sound like a broken record, but you need to call these "too far away" donors every six weeks. Talk about your past and upcoming events, talk about your weather, or talk about any new gifts. Most distant donors will welcome your e-mails (provided you have their permission) so this is a cost-efficient way to keep them informed. E-mails and telephone calls will put them in the moment as if they were right there at your organization. That's exactly where you want them to be.

Every so often, budget permitting, send these donors something that either shows them what your organization looks like to date or bears your organization's logo. Gifts that can be permanently displayed, like a paperweight, letter opener, or framed poster, will serve as a constant reminder of your organization. Posters and note cards that depict any new physical changes or enhancements that occurred will make your donors feel that they are a part of your group's progress. Gifts that can be displayed on their coffee tables, desks, or walls will not only remind them of the organization, but they will also let everyone who enters their home or office know that they support your group.

If your group has a Web site, and it is well maintained and updated, be sure to remind your "too far away" donors to visit it every so often to get the latest news about your group. Web sites that include information about your new board members, your structural changes, your new major gifts, and stories about gift recipients are a great way for your donors to stay educated about your group. Most Web sites contain a link called "contact us" that will give your donors an easy way to stay connected with the institution (Johnston 1999, 143).

During my travels in visiting these "too far away" donors, I am often asked if there are other supporters who live in the area. Here's where strength in numbers takes on new meaning. Donors like to feel that they are surrounded by others who feel as strongly about the organization as they do. If you travel to their area frequently, you should be aware of other supporters in the area. You can handle this two ways. You can give the donors a general number of people who live in the area who support your group, or you can give the donors some names of people who support your group. If you do the latter, *you must first ask permission from each donor* if you can let others in the area know who they are and where they live. Once you have secured their permission, then you can let donors know about other donors in the area. It gives the donors a sense that there is a "local community of supporters" for your group and that they are not the only ones in the area that have a loyalty to your group.

If you have a group of people in the same geographic area, remember you can always gather them in a group setting for a lunch, brunch, or dinner. This will give them the opportunity to meet new friends and bond with other supporters. It will also allow you to see many supporters at one time, which can be a very efficient way to steward these distant donors.

> **Tip:** *If you have several distant donors in one location, gather them for a group event and give them a chance to meet other supporters who live in their community.*

The "Botched Gift" Donors

Not every gift goes well. There are countless stories of donors who for one reason or another are unsatisfied with the way their gifts were handled by an organization. It could be that the organization did not use the gift for the intended purpose or that the donor changed his or her mind after the gift was made and wants to support a different project. In some instances, the donor was dissatisfied with the way the gift was recognized and wants the gift returned immediately. In other circumstances, the organization simply waited too long to use the gift, such as when the donor makes a gift for a new structure, and the donor is angry that the building or addition may never be built. What does a fundraiser do in these situations? How can a fundraiser effectively conduct a stewardship plan with a donor who is angry and disappointed with the institution? Keep in mind that we are addressing situations where the organization could do something to make the donor feel pleased about the original gift. We are not addressing situations in which the donor wants to use the gift for an unethical purpose or one that would be counter to the organization's current mission. Exhibit 8–7 lists some suggested ways to steward the "botched gift" donors.

The ideal person that you want to get involved as quickly as possible is one of your organization's leaders. This can be your executive director, president, vice president, or board member. Gifts that go badly can be very damaging to your organization. You do not want one donor telling other people that your group mishandled his or her gift, did nothing to recognize it, or did not use the gift as was intended. While you have no foolproof way of preventing this from happening, you should get the leadership involved as soon as possible so that the donor feels the top people from the organization are paying attention to him or her. In my experience, the sooner this happens the quicker you will be

Exhibit 8–7 Suggested Ways To Steward the "Botched Gift" Donors

1. Get the organization's leadership to meet with the donor.
2. Spend as much time as possible reassuring the donor that you will do whatever it takes to get the gift back on track.
3. If things are going in the right direction, have a small event for this donor.
4. Ask the donor to serve on an advisory board or committee.
5. Ask the donor's advice on a particular issue that may shape the direction of the organization.

able to resolve whatever ill will this donor may presently feel for your group. Generally this will require that the fundraiser coordinate meetings and telephone calls for the leadership and the donor. It is well worth your time to get to this task as soon as you can. At the very least, get one leader to meet with your donor first, and then the fundraiser can do the follow-up.

Once the meeting with the leadership has taken place, the fundraiser needs to spend some time with the donor in person, followed by telephone calls and correspondence to reassure the donor. The fundraiser has to let the donor know that he or she will spend the time and energy overseeing the task to correct whatever mistake has taken place and to earn back the donor's confidence and trust. Usually this means that the fundraiser is the middle person between the donor and the organization. The fundraiser must meet and listen to the donor, then take those concerns back to the institution, share them with the leaders in charge, and get back to the donor. These are high-maintenance donors, but you have to spend the time until they feel good about your organization or at least have their negative feelings about your group slowly disappear.

> **Tip:** *It is the fundraiser's responsibility to make sure that some leader from the organization meets with the "botched gift" donor as soon as possible. After that time, the fundraiser needs to spend time listening to the donor's concerns and taking those concerns back to the organization until the "botched gift" issue is resolved.*

During the time the fundraiser is trying to "win back" the donor's trust, loyalty, and future support of the organization, the fundraiser may want to ask the donor for advice on some up and coming issue that is important to the organization. For instance, if the organization needs more volunteers to run a program or to help with staffing needs, the fundraiser may ask the donor if he or she knows anyone who may be interested in volunteering. If the organization is redesigning its Web site, the fundraiser could ask if the donor knows anyone who has expertise in that area. Asking the donor's advice will raise the donor's confidence in your organization. In effect you are saying to the donor, "Your opinion means a great deal to us," which should help overcome some past negative feelings the donor may have had about the prior gift.

Be sensitive to the timing of when you ask your donors for advice. You do not want to ask right after the donors let you know how unhappy they are about the way your organization handled their gift. If you do, the donors will probably lose even more confidence in your organization because they will think that you are ignoring the fact that the organization mishandled their gifts. The fundraiser should ask the donors for advice after they have met with one of your institution's leaders and after the fundraiser has spent some time reassuring the donors that any mistake on the organization's part will be corrected.

If things are mending along nicely with the donors, the fundraiser at this point could ask the organization's leaders if they approve of the idea of inviting the donors to serve on an advisory board or committee. This can get the "botched gift" donors over any prior negative feelings they may have had in the past. I have asked several donors who were not thrilled with the way the institution handled or recognized their gifts to serve on committees. I tell these types of donors that we need their help and expertise to ensure that we are doing our best to serve our supporters and our constituency. Many people would shy away from asking these types of donors to be on a committee for fear that they will "sour" the committee with stories of how the organization mishandled their gifts and other potentially damaging tales. My reply is that if the institution is behind the idea of placing the donors on a committee, then the institution has the foresight that getting all the "kinks out of the system" will only make that system better and stronger. Correcting past mistakes and moving beyond roadblocks is a wonderful way to showcase how your organization listens and responds to every donor and constituent. These botched gift donors can

help in that effort if they truly want to see your organization succeed.

> *Tip:* *"Botched gift" donors who are inclined to work with the organization to correct any prior mishap over their initial gifts should be asked for their opinions on some issue that affects the organization and with the organization's permission, to serve on an advisory board or committee.*

The "I Want Change" Donors

We are seeing more and more of a trend in fundraising that donors want to support nonprofit organizations that have the ability to bring about change and tackle important issues (Grace 2000, 18). Donors want to invest in results, and they want to see these results. They are called "transformational donors" because they seek to shape the future direction of the organization through their ideas, expertise, and hands-on approach (Grace 2000, 19). It is simply not good enough and not rewarding enough for them to give money or to have their names on buildings. Instead, they want to take their knowledge and the tools they have developed and use them to address social, political, environmental, and health problems. They want a base of power within the organization and the authority to exercise that power. So how can the fundraiser steward these types of donors who have very set opinions and goals on how your organization should be operating? Exhibit 8–8 lists some suggested ways you can capitalize on the expertise, energy, and dedication of these donors.

Exhibit 8–8 Suggested Ways To Steward the "I Want Change" Donors

1. Listen to each and every suggested idea and then seek ways to incorporate key concepts.
2. Involve these donors with strategic planning.
3. Get these donors on committees and spearheading projects.
4. Show them quantifiable results.
5. Ask these donors to lend technical support.
6. Encourage these donors to expand your organization's base of major givers, opinion leaders, and volunteers.

If you have donors like these, you are in a wonderful position. Up until this point we have been plotting and planning how to get your donors more educated and involved with your organization, and now you have a group of people who are eager and ready to help your organization. Yes, these folks are demanding and short on time and have a sense of urgency to move forward as quickly as possible. If your organization can adjust to this pace and adapt itself to meet their needs, your group will benefit in many ways, many times over. These are the donors who can really help your organization move forward. They are not the people who demand that you implement their every fundraising idea or walk away angry when the organization does not adopt all of their ideas. Rather these donors are motivated to help your organization meet the needs of the homeless, the ill, and the elderly; and they have the business savvy and proven success behind them to do it.

Of utmost importance is that the fundraiser, and preferably a leader from the institution, sit down over several meetings and listen to the donor's ideas, experience, and vision for your institution. This is a great brainstorming process from which many exciting, entrepreneurial ideas will flow. Usually the donor will have an idea that should be directed to the attention of someone overseeing a particular area, discipline, project, or program. It can take some time to line up the right people, but once you have all the right parties involved, it can be a very dynamic experience. In many instances nonprofits only have access to resources internally, and now there is the opportunity to have "new eyes with expertise" review and enhance current projects and programs.

If your group has a strategic plan or is thinking of formulating one, these donors are ideal to have on a strategic planning committee. They have the vision and the knowledge of how other nonprofit organizations and for-profit companies have succeeded and failed, and they can offer some sound advice on how your organization can position itself to make a marked difference in the philanthropic community (Allison and Kaye 1997, 86). These donors should also be invited to serve on a committee or help oversee a project or program that matches their area of expertise. If they do not have time to serve on a committee, meet with them one on one to glean their expertise and knowledge and share their ideas with the committee.

Many of these donors will be busy, successful business people, and many will have a solid technical background, such as high technology entrepreneurs,

founders of dot-com companies, and Internet executives. They will be used to seeing tangible, measurable results in reports as well as intangible results in a cohesive, team-effort workplace. It is very important that you cover both areas with these donors. With the leadership's approval, send them periodic reports on your progress in any campaign, project, or program. Ask them if these reports provide them with the right information or if there is any way the report could be improved. Remember, these donors have so many creative, successful ideas that you should want to hear them all. It does not mean you will use them all, but the fact that you asked and are considering each one is key to their stewardship.

You also want them to have the impression that your organization works as a team with team goals. Their businesses thrive on everyone pulling their weight and making a concerted effort so that team goals are met. This is particularly true for financial goals. The more you can show them the similarities between your group and their businesses, the more involved they will be and the more active they will become. Make them aware of your efficient operation, well-balanced budget, and yearly increase in dollars raised because those are tangible results that they are accustomed to seeing in their business sector. You can do this by having them meet with the leadership of your group, your constituency, and your volunteers and by their active committee participation.

If your donors have information technology expertise, then by all means ask them to lend time and knowledge to help your group with its technological needs. If you are in the process of selecting or upgrading a new computer system or data management system or if you want to select the right online research tools, ask these donors to help. Even if they cannot help, chances are they will know someone who can help. Moreover, they may offer to recruit volunteers or interns to help you at no cost or find the best, most cost-efficient way to get the technical support you need. They will be flattered that you asked and disappointed if you don't, so be sure you tap into their advanced technological knowledge and skills.

Another good way to steward these donors is to ask them to identify potential major givers, opinion leaders, and volunteers to support your organization. These donors want to get other influential people involved to bring about change (Grace 2000, 19). Nonprofit groups too often rely on their "internal stakeholders" to take care of the organization's every need, instead of asking its "external stakeholders" to bring people in who can strengthen the organization (Allison and Kaye 1997, 85). These donors can provide financial and technical expertise, connect your organization with influential people, and expand your funding sources.

> *Tip:* Be sure to ask your "I want change" donors for their financial, managerial, and technical advice and to bring in outside leaders and new sources of revenue.

INTERGENERATIONAL STEWARDSHIP

Within your organization you probably have what I call the "intergenerational givers" and the "intergenerational potential givers." The intergenerational givers have families that have a long history of involvement with your group. These intergenerational givers are often overlooked by organizations, and that is a mistake. Many times an organization will focus so heavily on recognizing the one person who made the most recent major gift, that they are blindsided to the fact that this donor comes from a long line of givers and potential givers to your group. While you want to devote time and attention to your donor who has just made that fabulous new gift, you want to include that donor's family in the recognition of the gift and in all your activities.

Your organization can expand its base of supporters simply by examining its current database of donors and sifting out those donors who have families who have given in the past and have the potential to give at a later time. This information is sometimes in the donor profile, such as a contact report that reveals that a donor started giving "because his father always gave." In many instances, facts about a donor's family are revealed during cultivation and stewardship, such as the donor letting you know about his or her parents, children, or grandchildren.

How you steward these intergenerational givers and potential givers is key to securing "intergenerational gifts." Intergenerational stewardship is the process of involving and educating your donor's family at the same time you are stewarding the donor individually. The mechanics of intergenerational stewardship are simple. If you are aware that there are family members who have given in the past, you continue to steward each individually and then host an event to recognize the "family gifts" or invite the whole family as

a group to a special event. It lets the family know that your group is well aware of their long history of giving and that you appreciate each member's gift. These types of intergenerational gifts are ideal to publicize in internal and external publications. Every nonprofit would love to boast that it has intergenerational givers. It shows the public that there are families who have known and trusted your group throughout the ages.

Intergenerational potential givers are family members who are new to your organization. They have the potential to give because one of their family members is so connected with your group that he or she made a major gift. These intergenerational potential givers will need time and attention. You need to involve them from the moment your donor makes the first major gift. While planning the donor's recognition event, make sure you ask the donor to invite family members to attend. At the event, have a guest book where the family members can sign their names and addresses. This can work even if the fundraiser and the CEO are going to the donor's home to thank him or her personally. To the extent the donor feels comfortable, tell the donor it would be an honor to meet his or her family so that you can recognize and thank the donor before his or her family. Take pictures and ask the family members for their names and addresses so that you can send them a picture. Start sending these family members all your mailings, including invitations to your events. If you have their telephone numbers, call them and try to get an appointment so that you can spend some time with them individually. This does not work for everyone, but it does for some, especially close families that feel their "combined gifts" can make a real difference to your organization.

For instance, I was working with a major donor who made steady major gifts to the hospital every year since his first open heart surgery. I knew he had two sons who lived far away, but I never met them. The donor had a second heart attack and was rushed to our hospital. He was there for two weeks, and his sons came to see him. During that time, I got to know his sons very well and had the chance to give them a tour of the hospital and introduce them to the doctors, nurses, and our foundation staff. The day my donor was discharged from the hospital, I asked the sons for their addresses so I could stay in touch. I sent them holiday cards and kept them on our mailing list. Several months later, one of the sons called me and asked how he could set up a fund at the hospital in honor of his father. I gave him the details, and the two sons made their steady major gifts to their dad's fund each year.

Intergenerational stewardship can unlock great sources of new wealth. Let's say that you were stewarding a husband and wife who just made their first major gift to your institution. During one of your top donor recognition events, they brought along their 27-year-old daughter to share in the festivities. You spend some time at the reception with the daughter, and it turns out that right out of college, she joined a start-up Internet company, and soon thereafter the company had its initial public offering of stock. She gained over $1.5 million. She says that her mom and dad love your organization, but she does not know too much about it. You invite her for a tour, and she meets your executive director and some volunteers. You have just discovered a great new prospect, and you're on your way to an intergenerational gift.

RECAP AND REVIEW

1. Stewardship is the continuous personal interaction and information exchange between the donors and the institution, which paves the way for the donors' next enhanced major gift.

2. Stewardship starts from the moment the donors make the major gift and continues for the entire duration of the donors' relationship with the organization.

3. Stewardship requires that the donors' gifts are properly acknowledged, that the gifts are used for the intended purpose, and that the donors receive reports and updates on the benefits of the gifts and the status of the gift funds.

4. During stewardship, the fundraiser needs to gather new and additional information about the donors and the donors' families, businesses, interests, and hobbies so that the fundraiser can judge the donors' readiness to make the next major gift.

5. All donors require an individual stewardship strategy.

6. "Hard-to-reach" donors can be stewarded by sending e-mails, hand delivering small gifts with the organization's logo, sending homemade and handmade gifts, and asking peers to help contact the donors.

7. "Chronic canceler, no-show to events" donors can be stewarded by seeing these donors when they are out of town, asking them to host an event, or meeting them at an event that they must attend or have an interest in attending.

8. "Not now, maybe later" donors can be stewarded by intermittently discussing their next gifts every third or fourth visit, bringing a new person along during your visits, discussing other donors who made repeat gifts, and inviting one "not now, maybe later" donor to an exclusive top donor recognition event.

9. "Testamentary gift only" donors can be stewarded by bringing one such donor to an outright gift recognition event, having the leadership meet with these donors, having the beneficiaries of your groups call and write these donors, sending life income gift materials, and targeting life income planned giving seminars targeted for these donors.

10. "Too far away" donors can be stewarded by visiting with them once a year, sending personalized mailings and invitations, calling every six weeks, sending e-mails, sending them autographed pictures and posters of your organization, reminding them to visit your Web site, and letting them know of other supporters who live nearby.

11. "Botched gift" donors can be stewarded by getting the leadership to meet with them immediately, having the fundraiser spend the time to win back their confidence and trust, asking them for advice, and with the organization's permission, offering them an advisory board or committee position.

12. "I want change" donors can be stewarded by listening and adopting their key ideas; involving them with your strategic planning; inviting them to work on committees; showing them quantifiable successes; lending their financial, managerial, and technical expertise and knowledge; and asking them to help expand your base of supporters and new sources of revenue.

13. Intergenerational stewardship is the process of stewarding each family member individually, while at the same time recognizing and rewarding the collective family gifts.

14. Intergenerational stewardship can expand your organization's base of support and can uncover new sources for major gifts.

REFERENCES

Allison, M., and J. Kaye. 1997. *Strategic planning for non-profit organizations.* New York: John Wiley and Sons.

Beyel, J. 1997–1998. Ethics and major gifts. *New Directions for philanthropic fund raising*, no. 16: 50–57.

Ciconte, B., and J. Jacob. 1997. *Fund raising basics.* Gaithersburg, MD: Aspen Publishers, Inc.

Estes, E. 2000. Planned giving clinic. *Contributions*, January–February.

Grace, K. 2000. Ten things you should know about…. *Contributions 14*, no. 1, January–February.

Greenfield, J. 1999. *Fund raising.* New York: John Wiley and Sons.

Greenfield, J. 1994. *Fundraising fundamentals.* New York: John Wiley and Sons.

Harstook, R. 1998. *Closing that gift.* Wichita, KS: ASR Philanthropic Publishing.

Iverson, J. 1997. Tips for your major gift program. *Fund Raising Institute Monthly Portfolio*, September.

Johnston, M. 1999. *The nonprofit guide to the Internet.* New York: John Wiley and Sons.

Kelly, K. 1998. *Effective fund raising management.* Mahwah, NJ: Lawrence Erlbaum Associates.

Nichols, J. 1997. *Pinpointing affluence.* Chicago: Precept Press.

Stanley, T., and W. Danko. 1996. *The millionaire next door.* New York: Pocket Books.

Tromble, W. 1998. *Excellence in advancement.* Gaithersburg, MD: Aspen Publishers, Inc.

Appendix 8–A
A Donor Bill of Rights

Source: Copyright NSFRE and others. Used with permission. All rights reserved.

A Donor Bill of Rights

PHILANTHROPY is based on voluntary action for the common good. It is a tradition of giving and sharing that is primary to the quality of life. To assure that philanthropy merits the respect and trust of the general public, and that donors and prospective donors can have full confidence in the not-for-profit organizations and causes they are asked to support, we declare that all donors have these rights:

I.

To be informed of the organization's mission, of the way the organization intends to use donated resources, and of its capacity to use donations effectively for their intended purposes.

II.

To be informed of the identity of those serving on the organization's governing board, and to expect the board to exercise prudent judgment in its stewardship responsibilities.

III.

To have access to the organization's most recent financial statements.

IV.

To be assured their gifts will be used for the purpose for which they were given.

V.

To receive appropriate acknowledgment and recognition.

VI.

To be assured that information about their donations is handled with respect and with confidentiality to the extent provided by law.

VII.

To expect that all relationships with individuals representing organizations of interest to the donor will be professional in nature.

VIII.

To be informed whether those seeking donations are volunteers, employees of the organization or hired solicitors.

IX.

To have the opportunity for their names to be deleted from mailing lists that an organization may intend to share.

X.

To feel free to ask questions when making a donation and to receive prompt, truthful and forthright answers.

DEVELOPED BY
American Association of Fund Raising Counsel (AAFRC)
Association for Healthcare Philanthropy (AHP)
Council for Advancement and Support of Education (CASE)
National Society of Fund Raising Executive (NSFRE)

ENDORSED BY
(information)
Independent Sector
National Catholic Development Conference (NCDC)
National Committee on Planned Giving (NCPG)
National Council for Resource Development (NCRD)
United Way of America

Chapter 9
Tracking Prospect Activities and Gifts

CHAPTER OUTLINE

- Managing Your Prospect List
- Selecting the Right Prospect Tracking Software
- Using a Word Processing System for Prospect Tracking
- Ranking Your Top and Next Tier Major Gifts Prospects
- Time Management and Prospect Tracking
- The Importance of Maintaining Hard Copies of Prospect Reports and Files
- Using Prospect Tracking Information for Biweekly Meetings
- Deciding When To Take Major Gifts Prospects off the Direct Mail/Annual Fund List
- Deleting Prospects from Your Top and Next Tier Major Gifts Lists
- Adding New Prospects to the Top and Next Tier Major Gifts Lists
- Recap and Review

I support organizations that offer fundamental leverage in enhancing mankind's condition.

William A. Porter, Founder and Director,
E*Trade, and Philanthropist

MANAGING YOUR PROSPECT LIST

Up to this point, you have been identifying, researching, cultivating, soliciting, thanking, and stewarding prospects from your top prospect list. This is a lot of activity even if you are only working with a small pool of 25–50 prospects. All your time and effort spent with each prospect will be lost if you do not have a system in place for keeping track of each prospect's activity and gifts. For example, what if fundraiser Jean over the course of one week visited with three prospects, called one prospect to follow up with a proposal she sent him last week, invited another to tour the organization's site, and learned in a staff meeting that during a benefit dinner the President spoke with one of fundraiser Jean's prospects and then fundraiser Jean did nothing to record this information? Think how this would hinder her relationships with her prospects and her progress in obtaining a major gift from any one of them. Even if you think you have a photographic mem-

ory and you can juggle it all, I assure you this is not the time you want to test your ability to recall every fact, figure, and date associated with your prospects.

How you organize and manage your prospect pool is key to major gifts fundraising. You need some structure to this process that will help you and those you work with get your arms around this vast amount of information that takes place every day with your prospects. Many people in addition to major gifts fundraisers, such as top management, coworkers, staff, and volunteers, need accurate information about your prospects for a variety of reasons that range from accurate addresses to solicitation strategies to gift acknowledgments. Exhibit 9–1 illustrates why prospect tracking is essential to any successful major gifts fundraising program.

Your role as a major gifts fundraiser entails organizing, planning, coordinating, directing, strategizing, and managing your pool of prospects. Prospect tracking is the system that ensures each prospect is receiv-

Exhibit 9–1 Importance of a Prospect Tracking System

1. Provides a system for organizing, planning, coordinating, directing, strategizing, and managing prospect activity.
2. Monitors each prospect's progress toward making the major gift.
3. Reviews the effectiveness of planned activities and meetings.
4. Reflects the quality of contact made with each prospect.
5. Serves as a tickler system to plan next steps with dates for each prospect.
6. Structures the fundraiser's time spent and time needed to be spent with each prospect.
7. Enhances communication with management, coworkers, other departments, volunteers, and staff.
8. Links information about each prospect from other departments within the organization.
9. Provides easy access to current prospect information for the entire organization.
10. Ensures accurate up-to-date records on each prospect.
11. Produces records for each major gifts fundraiser's assigned prospects.
12. Preserves institutional history for the organization.
13. Prevents the fundraiser from spending time with "select" prospects from the prospect list.
14. Evaluates the number and quality of contacts and activities that led to the major gift.
15. Shows how lack of contact and activity can forestall or prevent the gift.

ing the proper attention from you and your organization (Karsch 1993, 44). You need something that will enable you to monitor the progress of your prospects; otherwise, you will lose sight of what needs to be done with each prospect and where each prospect is in terms of readiness to make a gift. With a prospect tracking system, you will have that information right at your fingertips (Williams 1991, 32).

A prospect tracking system also serves to review the effectiveness of planned meetings and activities with your prospects. For example, I invited a prospect to an open house event as a cultivation move because I thought she might enjoy learning more about our group and meeting our leadership and other supporters for the institution. After the event, I called her to find out what she thought about our event. She told me that she really does not like going to these types of receptions and that this one event was enough. She had no desire to attend another event. I put this in my contact report, and it served as a reminder not to invite this prospect to open house-type of events where she would feel uncomfortable.

In addition to reviewing the effectiveness of activities and meetings, the prospect tracking system can reflect the *quality* of contacts made with your prospects. For example, what if a major gifts officer only called her prospects and rarely spent the time to visit with each one? What if a major gifts officer had worked with her five top prospects for more than one year without ever discussing their desire to make a major gift? A proper prospect tracking system would bring these situations to light and show that the major gifts officer was not managing her prospects to bring in potential major gifts.

No matter how organized you are, a "tickler" system that serves as a reminder to act can be invaluable. This is precisely what a prospect tracking system is all about. It serves as a tickler to remind you to see prospects, to ask them to volunteer, to get them to meet the top leaders of your group, and to follow up on a past solicitation. Every prospect needs an individual strategy that includes next steps and dates for action. A prospect tracking system will put this all in place. It will assist you in planning strategies and actions for each prospect (Karsch 1993, 45). Think of it as your personal organizer. It can help you organize your time and your calendar so that no prospect "slips through the cracks" and goes for several months without any contact from you or someone in your organization.

> *Tip: A prospect tracking system serves as a "tickler" system that prompts the fundraiser to maintain consistent contact with each prospect.*

A prospect tracking system should be designed to provide instant information for everyone in your organization, including volunteers (Nichols 1991, 65). Think about the daily operation in your organization. A new prospect calls your organization's general number, and the receptionist answers the telephone. The prospect says that he got "a call from someone wanting to see him," and he is returning the call. If the group has a good prospect tracking system in place, the receptionist or an assistant working for the development officers, can look up the prospect's name and see which development officer has been assigned to this new prospect. Without a system in place, the assistant would have to take the prospect's name and number and go around the office asking which development officer is working with this prospect. This would make your organization seem disjointed and would not be a very efficient use of the staff's time.

Additionally, a prospect tracking system can link information that other departments may have about your prospects. For instance, many organizations have other departments that handle special events, prospect research, alumni relations, public relations, and communications. What if your prospect received an invitation from the special events office to attend a murder mystery dinner benefit and attended, and you never knew? What if your prospect was featured in an internal publication, and you never knew? What if your prospect was honored by city council, and you never knew? These situations emphasize the importance of how each department needs to input their activity with the organization's prospects on a timely and routine basis so that everyone can easily access vital information (Schaff and Schaff 1999, 82).

Depending on how your prospect tracking system is set up, it should be designed to produce records on each major gifts fundraiser's assigned prospects. The executives and leaders of your organization will want this information for internal staff meetings, one-on-one meetings with the major gifts fundraiser, as well as board, trustee, and committee meetings. The key is to be able to easily retrieve information from the prospect tracking system so that anyone from the organization can access prospect information when needed. The more diligent everyone is about inputting information on a timely basis, the more up to date your prospect records will be.

Preserving institutional history is perhaps one of the most important features of a good prospect tracking system. Your organization needs to know from the moment a prospect has been identified how he or she has been active and involved with your organization and which staff members, leaders, or volunteers have been instrumental in cultivating and soliciting the prospect. The history with each prospect must be recorded and preserved. Current staff can then learn about a prospect's past activity with the organization so that they can chart out their next steps and plan of action with each prospect.

The prospect tracking system comes in handy when a major gifts fundraiser needs to accompany a coworker or fill in for a coworker on a visit. One time my boss asked me to join him on a short trip to see several donors in Florida. Some of the prospects were assigned to me, and some were assigned to him. I wanted to be prepared for all the meetings so I used our prospect tracking system to learn all I could about past visits and activities that my boss had with his prospects. He did the same for my prospects. When it came time to meet with each prospect, we were both "right in the moment" with each prospect, and we were able to jointly contribute to each conversation. It made the prospects feel that our organization had many people working for them, and they enjoyed the combined attention we gave them.

Another reason to preserve institutional history through prospect tracking is that many nonprofits experience high turnover in development staff. It is not uncommon for major gifts officers to change jobs, leaving behind their pool of prospects and their activities with each prospect for the next person to pick up and work with on behalf of the organization. If the organization does not have a good prospect tracking system in place, it can take months before the new person has a firm grasp on the assigned prospects. With a good system in place, it will take far less time and the new person can "dive right in" to ensure that the prospects receive uninterrupted time and attention from the organization.

> *Tip:* Preserving institutional history is the cornerstone to solid major gifts fundraising. A good prospect tracking system will ensure that all the information about each prospect is recorded and preserved for current and future use by the organization's fundraisers.

It is extremely tempting for a fundraiser to work with the "fun" and the "easy" prospects from the prospect pool, while leaving the more difficult or hard-to-reach prospects for another time. Our natural tendency is to gravitate to people we enjoy working with, those who are comfortable and personable (Dunlop 1993, 112). This is just the kind of activity you want to avoid. The last thing you want to do is to only work with your "select" prospects from the prospect list, while ignoring the rest of the folks on your list. A good prospect tracking system will prevent that from happening. It will flag the prospects who have not been contacted by you for several weeks, and it should motivate you to channel your time and attention to these previously forgotten prospects. This will ensure that you are spending *equal time* with all of your prospects and that you are setting up next steps and following through with each step for all your prospects.

Last, the prospect tracking system can evaluate how the right number of contacts and involvement led to securing the major gift, as well as how the lack of contact and involvement resulted in not getting the gift. It is important for the development team to assess what went right and what went wrong with each major gifts solicitation. It is important for everyone involved to see the series of steps that led to getting the gift and the lack of steps or follow through that forestalled the gift or distanced the prospect. The prospect tracking system can give the organization this information so that the development team members can capitalize on their successes and learn from their mistakes.

SELECTING THE RIGHT PROSPECT TRACKING SOFTWARE

It is essential that your organization have some form of computerized prospect tracking system to organize, manage, and sort all the information on your prospects. Ideally, you will want to store all your information in one central location where anyone from your organization can readily input new data and retrieve pertinent information. The most common way to track prospects is by using an integrated database system that uses specialized tracking software. An integrated database system simply means that there are multiple networked computer workstations using a common software program. Many nonprofit organizations use specialized software to store current prospect information, house prospect research, create gift and status reports, generate mailing lists, create ticklers for next contact, send pledge reminders, and list primary and secondary solicitors to each prospect. While this is the most common way to track prospects, some smaller development operations use a word processing system to create files, fields, and reports for each prospect.

In selecting the right prospect tracking system for your group you should consider:

- The number of prospects and donors
- Your existing computer capabilities
- Your budget for computer purchases, upgrades, maintenance, and warranties
- The types of features your organization requires from the system

- The number of people who will be using the system
- The computer learning curve for each user and the need for computer training
- The timing to implement a new system

The larger the organization and the larger the number of prospects and donors, the more your group will need special prospect tracking software. It is too large of a task to ask any organization with a large number of prospects and donors to keep track of every activity, gift, step, and contact with all these people. In making this decision, your group must also consider your existing computer capabilities. Does your organization have enough computers to accommodate the needs of your existing staff? If you are considering hiring additional development or support staff in the near future, you may need to purchase additional computers. Can your existing system support the type of software your group is considering using? Will you need first to upgrade your data processing "clock speed" (MHz), and memory capacity (RAM)? Does your hard drive provide enough storage space (GB) for the data you will store in your new system? Do you have a virus scan in place that has been updated and is capable of handling new viruses that can occur on your new system or will you need a completely new virus scan? These are all important questions that must be factored into your software selection decision.

The $6 million question is always do you have the funds for this new system? You may be in the situation where you have to undergo a few computer upgrades before you can apply your new software. In addition to the upgrades and initial purchase, your group should factor in the cost for maintenance and warranties. All this can really add up, and you have to do the math before you can be ready to make your selection.

It is highly recommended that your group spend some time and decide what it is you want the prospect tracking system to do. Get as much input from everyone in the organization as you can. For instance, your accounting/financial department may need several fields for inputting gifts, pledges, and acknowledgments; your prospect research department may need room for executive summaries and links to current and former employers; and the front-line fundraisers may need 15 lines or more to record contact reports and the ability to link donor records. All this needs to be worked out and agreed upon before your group can make the right decision on your prospect tracking system. Keep in mind that the system you choose should accommodate your needs, plus have room to grow (Karsch 1993, 46). You do not want to select a system that will not let you add on any new features that you may need in the future, otherwise you may have to get a whole new system.

Exhibit 9–2 lists the suggested functions that a good prospect tracking system should perform.

Exhibit 9–2 Suggested Functions for a Good Prospect Tracking System

1. Input all information in the donor profile [name(s), address(es), employment history, age, family members, association with organization, events invited and attended, interests, hobbies, honors, board memberships] for existing and new prospects.
2. Correct and update existing files.
3. Delete prospect files.
4. House all prospect research.
5. Code prospect files by ability and inclination to make gifts.
6. Sort prospect files.
7. Produce mailing lists and labels.
8. Display complete gift/pledge history with dates and list areas of support.
9. Link information and relational files.
10. List primary and secondary solicitors.
11. List anyone connected to the prospect.
12. Produce reports on selected fields for each solicitor's assigned prospects.
13. Store and date contact reports.
14. Store and date gift proposals.
15. List next steps with date of action.
16. Provide tickler system for scheduled contacts.
17. State target gift size, vehicle, purpose, and date for prospective gift.
18. Indicate the prospect's readiness to make the gift.

This may seem like much more that your group needs at this time. Remember, you want to choose and build a prospect tracking system that will be with your organization for several years. Select one that has the capacity to add on features as your organizational needs grow.

You must also consider the number of people in your office that will be using this system, factoring in perhaps new staff and additional staff. Exhibit 9–2 lists

many functions that your selected tracking system can perform. It is suggested that for several of these functions (such as inputting gifts and prospect research, adding and deleting prospect addresses and work history) designated people be responsible for these areas of data entry (Karsch 1993, 46). You want your system as up to date and accurate as possible, and you can achieve this by assigning data entry tasks to the appropriate staff member.

> *Tip: It is suggested that people with the expertise be assigned to input data such as updating prospect profiles, recording gifts, and storing prospect research to ensure accuracy of records and accountability for tasks.*

In considering the number of users on your system, you should take into consideration whether or not these people will need training for the new system. Chances are very good that you will want the software company or someone in-house to give all users a lesson on proper use of the system. For instance, at Temple University, we converted our database to a new system, and the head of our information services unit conducted several comprehensive training sessions. For several months after the conversion, we had update sessions just to make sure everyone was using the new system properly.

Using a new system takes time and patience. Often, existing computer systems are shut down for hours and days. You should consider the *timing of implementing your new system*. You do not want to be in the middle of acknowledging end-of-year gifts, weeks before a large special event, or in the middle of a capital campaign and not have access to your files.

One of the most important features for any prospect tracking system is the ability to produce simple reports on each front-line fundraiser's assigned prospects. This can be a simple sort of the fundraiser's name, assigned prospects, contacts made, next steps with dates, proposals discussed and/or delivered, and status of proposals (Sturtevant 1997, 200). This will benefit the organization in many ways. First, it will keep the fundraisers focused on what needs to be done with each prospect and by what date. Second, these reports can be the focus of discussion on prospects and next steps for staff meetings with the leadership and fundraisers of the organization. Third, right before a visit, fundraisers can review these reports to give them the most current information on the status of the prospect's involvement with the organization, as well as his or her readiness to make a gift. It is very hard to remember each prospect and what was said and discussed during each visit. These reports can "refresh" the fundraisers' recollections.

USING A WORD PROCESSING SYSTEM FOR PROSPECT TRACKING

If an organization does not use specialized software to track their prospects, then they must rely on a word processing system. There are many circumstances under which an organization would use a word processing system, rather than specialized software, to track prospects and donors:

1. The organization has decided that it can build and customize a prospect tracking system using the existing computer capabilities.
2. There may be no funds in the operating budget for the cost of the software, upgrades, training, and maintenance.
3. The organization may have to wait several months before the software is installed and the data are transferred from one system to the other.
4. The software selected cannot produce the charts and reports that are needed for staff meetings or fundraiser-prospect assignments.

Many organizations are able to successfully track their prospects and donors by using the existing resources in their computer programs. By using fields and sorts, they can input, update, delete, retrieve, and link data on their prospects and donors, which meets the needs of the organization. Other organizations may desire to acquire specialized software, but the costs involved are simply not in the foreseeable future for the organization. This is particularly true for small grassroots organizations, groups that utilize volunteers for much of their prospect/donor data maintenance, and groups that do not have the funds to increase the number of computers or to train the staff.

Some groups are caught in "limbo" for months, waiting for a new prospect tracking system to be installed, or waiting for the old system to be converted to a new and improved system. It can be very frustrating for the group because in many instances they can only use word processing capabilities during the installation or conversion to keep the major gift process on track.

Finally, even with the selected prospect tracking software in place, it may not have the capability to produce the necessary reports for:

- Rating prospects by ability and inclination to make a major gift.
- Assigning new prospects to each fundraiser.
- Charting fundraisers' assigned prospects with next steps.
- Listing outstanding gifts proposals with amount suggested and area to be funded.
- Ranking each fundraiser's assigned major gifts prospects.

Each prospect tracking system does not automatically come as a "deluxe model" fully powered to handle every institutional need. When institutional needs are greater than the specialized software can produce, the institution will need to extract the data to create the charts and reports that will keep the major gifts process running properly.

A word processing system can work just fine so long as it can provide *structure to the major gifts prospect tracking system* and can keep the system moving forward. This is achieved by creating monthly charts and reports that will apprise everyone in the organization about each fundraiser's contacts, next steps, proposals, and follow-through with each assigned prospect and donor. The first monthly chart you need to create is a list of contacts you have made and intend to make over that monthly period for your assigned top prospects and donors. Appendix 9–A contains two monthly reports. The first report lists the prospect/donor name, address, telephone number, and contact with date. The second lists the prospect/donor name, outstanding gifts proposal, and status of the proposal. It is suggested that you do this every month for all your assigned prospects. I like these types of reports for several reasons:

1. They are a visible, tangible reminder of which prospects you have worked with that month and which prospects need attention.
2. They are a visible, tangible reminder of which prospects should be receiving a proposal and which proposals need follow-up work.
3. In a page or two, there is ready access to all assigned prospects with their addresses, telephone numbers, and all monthly activity.
4. If the computer system should ever shut down or freeze, all the information needed to set up new appointments, confirm existing appoint-

ments, send letters, or call prospects is still available.

5. They avoid the need to go into the computer each time and check for your latest activity or gift proposal to a prospect.
6. They can be used during development meetings where strategies about prospect information are shared.
7. They can be used to show superiors and coworkers your activity with each prospect.

You can decide whether you want these reports arranged alphabetically by prospect/donor name as illustrated in Appendix 9–A, or you can rank your assigned prospects and list them in order of priority as illustrated in Appendix 9–B. Some fundraisers do it both ways. An alphabetical list has the advantage of giving anyone who wants information about prospect x an immediate answer because you can look the prospect up very quickly. A ranking list has the advantage of focusing your time and attention on your top prospects at the top of your list. These are the folks that your organization feels can make a major gift sooner than others, so it is wise that you concentrate on these prospects first. I find that I need both types of lists, so I do both.

RANKING YOUR TOP AND NEXT TIER MAJOR GIFTS PROSPECTS

Major gifts fundraisers must concentrate the majority of their time with their top prospects. The best way to accomplish this is by using reports that rank your top and next tier prospects (see Appendix 9–B). Certain specialized software has the capability of letting you rank each prospect and producing a report that lists the prospects in order by their rank, highest to lowest. If you do not have this type of system, create it through word processing. These types of ranking charts show which prospects should be receiving the bulk of a major gifts fundraiser's time and attention. This is not to say that fundraisers should ignore or put on the back burner the next tier of prospects. It is to say that this type of ranking chart keeps the fundraiser's eyes firmly focused on the prospects who have the most potential to make a major gift in the very near future.

Exhibit 9–3 shows how to rank your top prospects. Appendix 9–B shows how this ranking system works. For instance, prospect Baldwin is ranked number one because that prospect has a $150,000 outstand-

Exhibit 9–3 Ranking Your Top Major Gifts Prospects

1. Prospects with outstanding proposals in the highest amounts with likelihood of being funded.
2. Prospects with outstanding proposals with likelihood of being funded in next highest amounts.
3. Prospects who are well cultivated and involved and are ready for the major gifts ask.
4. Prospects who are cultivated and involved.
5. Prospects who need more cultivation and involvement.

ing proposal that is likely to be funded and is being followed up. Prospect Matika is next with a $100,000 outstanding proposal that also is likely to be funded and needs to be followed up. Rank prospects who you are actively pursuing with the highest outstanding gift proposal amount and work your way down the list. Notice that these are "live" proposals, ones that involve ongoing discussions. These are not the proposals that have been asked and delivered months ago and the prospects need time before they can decide. Those prospects would be ranked lower on your top prospect list, and in fact may be on your next tier list.

Tip: Do not rank all prospects with outstanding proposals at the top of the prospect list. Those with outstanding high-end asks where there is an ongoing dialogue about the proposal should be ranked in order of the proposal amount. Those prospects who have an outstanding proposal with less likelihood of being funded or where the prospects need time before they can decide should be ranked lower on the top prospect list or placed on the next tier list.

The next group of top prospects are those who have been cultivated and educated and are ready for the ask. In Appendix 9–B, prospect Gilbert is that type of prospect. The next step for prospect Gilbert is to have a presolicitation meeting to discuss a $10,000 endowed scholarship gift, so prospect Gilbert is ranked number 3. After that, rank your prospects in order by those most cultivated and involved to those who need more cultivation and involvement (see Appendix 9–B).

The next tier of major gifts prospects are those people you need more time with before you can determine

Exhibit 9–4 Prospects for Your Next Tier Major Gifts Prospect List

1. Prospects who are involved with your group but may be far off from committing to a major gift.
2. Prospects who travel or are very busy and with whom it is difficult to have consistent cultivation.
3. Prospects who you have been unable to reach by telephone or mail.
4. Prospects who have outstanding letters of appointment.
5. Prospects who declined initial visits but are well worth pursuing.
6. New prospects who need initial research before contacting.

if they should be moved to your top list, stay in the next tier list, or removed from your current major gifts prospect list altogether. Exhibit 9–4 lists the type of prospects who should be on your next tier list.

While Exhibit 9–4 lists the types of prospects who should be included in your next tier list, you will need to rank them giving priority to those who, in your judgment and perhaps with input from others at your organization, can make the biggest major gift in the shortest period of time. By and large the prospects in this next group need more cultivation and involvement with your group. As you begin to know them better and move them along the cultivation line, you will have a better feel for how they should be ranked. For instance, using prospect Ashton in Appendix 9–B, if after you have sent the initial letter, you were unable to reach her by telephone for weeks, and the weeks added up to a month or two, then in your following monthly major gifts report prospect Ashton would be ranked much lower than her current ranking at number 4.

Regardless of whether you are working with specialized software that can rank your prospects and produce reports or if you need to do these tasks with a word processing system, *ranking your major gifts prospects is a fluid process.* Each time you meet with a prospect or spend considerable time trying to contact your top prospects, their ranking may shift, and in some instances, they may move from your top list to your next tier list. For instance, you may have just met with the number 5 prospect on your top prospect list when she tells you that while the gift idea is really great, she simply cannot do it until next year. That

prospect may move down in ranking on your top list. Conversely, you may call someone for the first time from your next tier list, and that prospect tells you that she has been meaning to make a larger gift to your group, and she would be delighted to meet with you. That prospect would most assuredly rise to your top prospect list. This illustrates the importance of keeping up-to-date monthly reports on your top prospects. Each month, you can rearrange the ranking order on your top and next tier lists.

> *Tip:* One of the purposes of producing monthly reports for your major gifts prospects is to rank and re-rank top and next tier prospects. Be sure to keep these reports up to date so that they reflect accurate assessments of your prospects' timing and inclination to make a major gift.

TIME MANAGEMENT AND PROSPECT TRACKING

Similar to giving a list of names to prospect research without deadlines and then waiting weeks and months before contacting new prospects as mentioned in "Gathering Donor Information: Research—From a Distance" in Chapter 2, fundraisers and staff can get lost behind their computers, inputting data, checking files, and generating reports, before a telephone call or visit is made with a prospect. Tracking is a system to manage prospect activity. You have to be mindful of the proportion of time you spend tracking prospects as opposed to working with prospects. Avoid the temptation to spend most of your time working with your computer rather than working with your prospects (Karsch 1993, 47). Your major gifts operation depends

> *Tip:* Major gifts fundraisers must spend most of their time with their prospects and not most of their time with their computers tracking their prospects. While tracking is an important tool for major gifts fundraising, it does not substitute for the day-to-day personal interaction required for each major gifts prospect.

on you spending your time with your prospects. Use these tracking tools as wisely and efficiently as possible, and then move on to active cultivation and solicitation with each prospect.

THE IMPORTANCE OF MAINTAINING HARD COPIES OF PROSPECT REPORTS AND FILES

Regardless of the type of prospect tracking system you use, you should maintain some hard copies of reports and files. It is wonderful that all this information is maintained and updated in a computer system, but you will find it is very convenient to have hard copies of certain documents in addition to your computerized data. As illustrated in "Using a Word Processing System for Prospect Tracking" in this chapter, it is very useful to have hard copies of your monthly prospect contacts and monthly gift proposal reports, like the ones contained in Appendixes 9–A and 9–B.

In addition to contact and proposal reports, many organizations use hard copy as a backup to information stored in the computer. For instance, at Cornell University, even though they have customized a computer tracking system for all their prospects' and donors' activities, pledges, and gifts, they use a Commitment Tracking Form that lists the donor's information, payment information, commitment information, gift designation, commitment schedule, total amount paid/outstanding, acknowledgement, comments, and staff assignment and approval (see Appendix 9–C). While this information is stored in the donor's computer file, they now have hard copies to back up the gift information.

It is recommended that you keep separate file folders on your top prospects (Schaff and Schaff 1999, 84). Some people find this cumbersome or their office simply does not have the space to house these files. To the extent you can, you should maintain file folders on your top prospects. It will remind you that each prospect has a unique and individual personality, and the contents of the prospect's file folder will reflect that individuality. It will help you in your cultivation and stewardship efforts because you can review your prospect's file to see the types of notes they send you, the holiday cards you have exchanged, and maybe the postcards from vacations they took. No computer or file folder can store the personality of your prospects, but file folders that contain these types of tangible personal exchanges will remind you of each prospect's personality and style. For instance, if you had a prospect who traveled extensively, and sent you a postcard every time she went away, and you kept those postcards in her file, you would have a wealth of information to talk about every time you met. You could ask her about her upcoming trip and why she selected that vacation spot over others. You could bring the postcards and share her memories about the trip. All of this will bring you closer to your prospect, which is where you want to be. If you threw the postcards out after you read them, you would have missed this great opportunity to get to know your prospect better.

I keep in my file folder all the "tangible" notes, cards, and letters that either I send the prospect or the prospect sends me. The letters I keep are not the institution's thank you letters or introductory letters I did for new prospects. Rather, it is anything personal and individual sent by either the prospect or me, such as a thank you note from the prospects for taking them to lunch. Since our computer system lists all pertinent information about the prospect's gift, pledge, and acknowledgment, I do not include that in the file folder. But if I send a personal thank you, then a copy is kept in the file folder. Exhibit 9–5 lists the types of materials you will want to keep in each prospect's file folder.

Exhibit 9–5 Materials That Should Be Stored in the Prospect's File Folder

- Personal thank you letters
- Note cards
- Postcards
- Business cards
- Holiday cards
- Important notes taken during a telephone conversation
- Copies of articles sent to the prospect about his or her hobby or outside interest
- Personal correspondence from the organization's leadership, development officers, board members, trustees, volunteers, or peers
- Internal or external publications featuring the prospect or the prospect's area of interest
- Gift proposals
- Drafts of gift agreements
- Executed gift agreements

This type of information will give you a snapshot view of the type of prospect you are cultivating and soliciting, which is essential to your success in ultimately obtaining the gift. I generally keep note cards, postcards, and holiday cards in the file for one year, and then I make room in the file for new material.

USING PROSPECT TRACKING INFORMATION FOR BIWEEKLY MEETINGS

Now that you are storing and updating your prospect and donor information, and you are creating hard copy reports and files on each of your assigned prospects and donors, you should be having biweekly meetings with the organization's development team (Smith 1997, 38). The team should consist of all front-line fundraisers, prospect researchers, and the head of the development office. These meetings are designed to:

1. Keep all development team members up to date on the cultivation efforts for each assigned prospect and donor.
2. Discuss next steps with dates for each assigned prospect and donor.
3. Discuss any problem area that can be resolved by the development team.
4. Plan new strategies for prospects and donors who are not responding to current cultivation efforts.
5. Make the major gifts process a team effort and not a solo effort.

Development officers should bring to these meetings the reports or charts on their assigned top prospects and donors. Appendix 9–B is an example of the type of report that can be used for these meetings. Before each meeting, the development officer should record for each assigned prospect and donor a next step with a date to be completed. It is helpful if one person on the staff is assigned to run the meeting and to track the cultivation moves and outstanding proposals for the organization's prospects and donors. At Temple University, we have biweekly meetings where each vice president, assistant vice president, director of development, major gifts director, planned giving director, and prospect researcher discuss our top 25 prospects and next 25 prospects. Our prospect researcher brings current information on assigned prospects and donors and provides the team with newly identified prospects. We have one person in charge of these meetings who tracks our progress with each prospect and donor and charts our progress with respect to each gift proposal. These major gifts prospect meetings keep everyone apprised of who is working with which prospect and avoids situations where two development officers unknowingly could be working with the same prospect for different gift purposes.

These meetings motivate the development team to be constantly in contact with the assigned prospects and donors and to make sure cultivation moves are being made with each person. No one wants to show up at these meetings unprepared or reporting that they have made minimum or no contact with top prospects. Rather, it can be a real benefit to the organization if all front-line fundraisers are staying on top of their prospects in the combined effort to raise significant dollars for the organization. If all fundraisers share their experience and knowledge in working with prospects during these meetings, it will strengthen the organization's major gifts program (Smith 1997, 38). It is not wise to have any member of the development team working in a vacuum on prospects and donors. In fact it can really have a negative effect on the fundraising effort. The more ideas that are added to the cultivation and gift proposal tracking process, the stronger your major gifts program will be. Your organization will benefit greatly if the team is encouraged through these biweekly meetings to strategize on next steps and to provide solutions to problematic areas that forestall or prevent major gifts from happening.

DECIDING WHEN TO TAKE MAJOR GIFTS PROSPECTS OFF THE DIRECT MAIL/ANNUAL FUND LIST

You are at the point now where you have a firm grasp on each of your prospects. You have been cultivating, soliciting, and stewarding each for different purposes at different times. As you have seen, some prospects take months of cultivation while others only need a little stroking before they are ready to discuss and consider a major gift. When you and others from your development team have decided that a major gifts proposal should be given to a prospect who appears to be ready to make a gift, the question arises—should the prospect be taken off the direct/annual mailing and solicitation list?

This can be source of great tension for both the major gifts department and the direct mail/annual fund department. If the prospect is taken off the list, then it depletes the total dollars raised for the direct mail/annual fund. If the prospect is kept on the list, the major gifts department fears that the prospect will make the direct mail/annual fund gift first and postpone making the larger gift until a later point in time. There is no decisive right answer to this question. Instead, the organization has to weigh the pros and cons of the situation. Exhibit 9–6 lists the factors to be weighed while making this decision.

Exhibit 9–6 The Pros and Cons of Taking a Prospect off the Direct Mail/Annual Fund List

---

The Pros
1. The prospects can focus on deciding about the larger gift without being distracted or confused with additional solicitations from the direct mail/annual fund departments.
2. There are no mixed messages from the institution—it is clear that the major gift should be considered first.
3. It keeps the prospects on the "elevated" status because they have been targeted to support the institution in a significant way.
4. The prospective major gifts will be much larger than the direct mail/annual fund appeal; therefore, they should take precedence.
5. The prospects can always be asked to make a direct mail/annual gift after the major gifts have been agreed upon.

The Cons
1. The direct mail/annual fund will greatly diminish if select prospects are kept off the mailing and solicitation list.
2. In many instances, prospects are kept off the list too long or are never returned to the direct mail/annual fund list.
3. If the prospects have been properly educated by the institution for the need for both types of gifts, there will be no confusion and no mixed messages.
4. The prospects' decision not to make a major gift is rarely based on the fact that they are also receiving mail and solicitations from the direct mail/annual fund departments.
5. It should be the prospects' decision whether or not to make a direct mail/annual fund gift while considering a major gift, not the major gifts department's decision.

Different organizations handle this issue in a variety of ways, which further illustrates that there is no clear-cut answer. For instance, The Philadelphia Zoo, PresbyHomes Foundation, and Lehigh Valley Hospital *do not remove* major gifts prospects from the direct mail/annual fund list while they are being cultivated and solicited for major gifts. The Boys and Girls Club of Bentonville/Bella Vista Arizona *does not send* major gifts prospects direct mail appeals while they are being cultivated and solicited for major gifts. While Lehigh University's development team decides this on a *case-by-case basis*, all major donors are encouraged to include an annual gift in their support for the institution.

After your organization weighs the pros and cons of taking a major gifts prospect off the direct mail/annual fund list, it will need to select a strategy. While the leadership of the organization will ultimately select the strategy that is best for the organization, the major gifts officers working with the prospects and the direct mail/annual fund officers should have input in this overall decision. Exhibit 9–7 lists the strategic options available in deciding whether to take a major gifts prospect off the direct mail/annual fund list.

Your organization can select the appropriate strategic option and apply it uniformly to all major gifts

Exhibit 9–7 Strategic Options for Deciding Whether To Take a Major Gifts Prospect off the Direct Mail/Annual Fund List

---

1. *Leave all major gifts prospects on* the direct mail/annual fund list, even if they are considered ready to make a major gift.
2. Once major gifts prospects *are being cultivated* for a major gift, remove them from the list.
3. Only take major gifts prospects off the list once they *have been solicited* for a major gift, and return the prospects to the list once the prospects have made a decision on the major gifts proposal.
4. Keep the major gifts prospects *off the list until the prospects have decided* on the major gift. If the *prospects make the major gift, ask the prospects if they will consider a direct mail/annual gift.* If yes, then place the prospects back on the list.
5. Keep the major gifts prospects *off the list until the prospects have decided* on the major gift. If the prospects *do not make the gift, or if it will take more than six months for a decision to be made,* place the prospects back on the list.

prospects, or it can apply it on a prospect-by-prospect basis. In my experience, you should aim for the "have your cake and eat it too" approach. I take all my prospects and look at what I think they can and cannot do in terms of a major gift within either a calendar or fiscal year. In the first six months, all my prospects are on the direct mail/annual fund list. As mentioned in the section of Chapter 4 titled "Getting the Complete Information about Your Prospect on the First Visit," I make it a point to talk to my prospects about their views on our direct mailings. If the prospects have not voiced strong opposition to receiving direct mail or an annual appeal, I leave the prospects on the list. I let the prospects know that even though I am their main contact and link to the organization, they will continue to receive mail about our new programs as well as our annual appeals. This way there is a clear understanding and no mixed messages about the need for both types of gifts. I will concentrate my efforts on securing the major gift, while the direct mail/annual fund will use mailings and telephone calls to secure the annual gift.

If the prospects state that they do not want any of our mailings because they do not have time to read them or they think it is wasting the organization's money, then I take them off the list. This does not mean that I will not discuss or encourage them to make an annual gift. Now it is my responsibility to make sure they are aware of the importance of the yearly gift as well as a prospective larger gift. You have to wear two hats at the same time, but this is not uncommon. The most important thing to remember is that you have to keep steady communication with your prospects about the importance of both gifts. If the prospects decide to make an annual gift this year and continue to ponder the larger gift, you have done well to capture the annual gift while keeping the larger gift in focus. If you are the primary contact with that prospect and he or she does not want mail or telephone calls about the annual appeal, then it is up to you to ask that prospect throughout the course of your yearly cultivation for an annual gift.

> **Tip:** *If your major gifts prospects do not want direct mail or to be kept on the annual fund list, then it is up to the major gifts fundraiser to ask for both the annual and the major gift.*

Approximately six to eight months into the year, I look at all my prospects to assess the following:

1. Who has and has not made an annual gift.
2. Was the annual gift an increase over last year's gift.
3. Does the prospect have an outstanding major gifts proposal.
4. Will the prospect be receiving a major gifts proposal within the next two months.
5. In my best judgment, will the proposals be funded by the end of the year.
6. In my best judgment, do I think the annual ask would interfere with the major gifts proposal.

I use the charts contained in Appendixes 9–A and 9–B and updated information in our computer database to get this information. Appendix 9–A in the last column will give me information on any increase or decrease in the prospect's annual gift. For instance, prospect Gilbert increased the annual gift to $2,500. In Appendix 9–B the last column is called "Annual Gift" and has either a "yes" or "no" in this column for each prospect. For all prospects with a "no," I check the database to see if an annual gift has come in recently to make sure my chart is accurate. I then sit down with the director of the direct mail/annual fund and go over the list. At that point, those prospects who have outstanding major gifts proposals and those who will receive a proposal within the next two months from me are coded not to receive an annual ask or telephone appeal. I share this list with the director of direct mail/annual fund so that the director knows that I only want these select prospects removed from the list for the next two months while I follow up with a major gifts proposal or solicit them for a major gift. If the prospect has not made an increased annual gift, I make it clear that I will ask for the increased annual gift as well. We then share that coded list with the head of the development department. This is a joint effort led by the major gifts department, agreed upon by the direct mail/annual fund department, and approved by the leadership of the development department. It keeps everyone well aware of which prospects are being solicited for major gifts and annual gifts at each point in time throughout the year. It also lets everyone know whose responsibility it is to solicit each type of gift at each point in time throughout the year.

My reason for taking solicited and soon to be solicited prospects off the direct mail/annual fund list for a few months is that the major gifts officer has built a strong personal relationship with the prospect during the cultivation, solicitation, and closing phases. These prospects have come to know and trust the major gifts officer, and he or she is their primary link between the prospect and the organization. The major gifts officer will have more success securing an outstanding annual gift by asking the prospect he or she knows quite well for the gift while ongoing discussions are taking place regarding the larger gift. Note, however, that I only take the major gifts prospects *who I know I am going to see* off the direct mail/annual fund list. If there is a chance that I cannot see them, they remain on the list to be solicited for an annual gift.

Here is an example in which taking a major gifts prospect off the list who you know you are going to see can benefit both the major gifts department and the annual fund. I was soliciting a prospect for many months to make a $100,000 charitable remainder unitrust. During the course of the year, I kept checking the annual fund gift list to see if he had made his yearly gift. Eight months into our fiscal year, the prospect still did not make an annual gift. I sat down with our annual fund director and asked that his name be taken off the annual fund solicitation list for the next two months. I had a meeting with the prospect in three weeks and I intended to discuss the trust proposal and his annual gift.

At the meeting we discussed both gifts. He needed more time to decide on the trust, but he promised me he would make a $1,000 annual gift. I thanked him for his prospective annual gift and told him that I wanted to ask him in person for his annual gift because his gift is so important to our organization. It would help us to attract other annual gifts, and our students would be the ones to suffer if our annual fund declined. I let him know that if for some reason his annual gift did not come in within two months, our "trusty and ever vigilant" annual fund department would be sending him gentle reminders to get the annual gift in by the end of our fiscal year. He had no problem with that; in fact, he thought it was a good system of checks and balances for the organization. When I returned to the office, I gave our annual fund director a copy of my contact report and told her if the prospect had not made the $1,000 annual gift within two months, he should be solicited by their department for this gift.

There are several key factors that must be in place whenever an organization is systemizing its approach to taking major gifts prospects off the direct mail/annual fund list. First, there must be communication and agreement between the major gifts department and the direct mail/annual fund departments regarding which prospects should be left on or removed from the list. If there is "silent resentment" on either part that one department is "hoarding" prospects or is preventing it from raising more funds, the system will not work. Second, all decisions must be known and approved by the leadership of the development team. This guarantees that there is unity among departments, that prospects are not thought of as "exclusively major gifts or annual fund" prospects, and that your organization works as a team for organizational goals, not individual goals. Third, the direct mail/annual fund director must be extremely careful and organized in adding or deleting major gifts prospects from the list. Throughout the course of the year, major gifts can be added and deleted off the list several times. If one is not careful in placing the major gifts prospects on the list, it will lead to loss of many annual fund gifts. Similarly, if the major gifts director thinks the prospects are off the list and sees or hears that they just received a mailing or telephone call soliciting an annual gift, this can lead to bad relations between both departments and that is what you are seeking to avoid.

> **Tip:** *There must be open communication and agreement between the major gifts and direct mail/annual fund directors regarding which prospects remain or are temporarily removed from the list. Attention to detail in adding and removing prospects is critical. All decisions must be approved by the head of the development team.*

DELETING PROSPECTS FROM YOUR TOP AND NEXT TIER MAJOR GIFTS LISTS

As you continue to work with your prospects from your top and next tier lists, you undoubtedly will have to decide whether some should be removed from these lists. There will be prospects who you just have been unable to reach or those who have given clear signals that a major gift is not in the picture for a long, long time. Deciding which prospects should be removed and the timing for removing them is a matter that should be decided during the bimonthly meetings with your whole development team. This way everyone is well aware of the prospects who are no longer considered "top prospects" for the organization. Everyone will be on the same page, with a clear understanding of which prospects are and are not the top prospects for the organization.

Before you remove a prospect from the list, be aware that a prospect who is removed from the list today may be put back on the list at a later time. You are *not removing the prospect forever*, so all the information about the prospect that your organization possesses must be stored and ready to use at a later time. For instance, I had a prospect who I tried to reach by telephone and mail for one year. My calls were not returned, my letters went unanswered, and he never responded to special event invitations. I gave the prospect's name, information, and profile to my boss to see if he could establish contact. No luck. After all this effort, our group decided to take the prospect off the list and keep his files on hold. Several months later at a reception, a person walked up to the sign-in sheet, signed in, and went into the reception. I looked at the name and could not believe it. It was the prospect we had been trying to meet. I introduced myself and spent some time with him at the reception. I finally was able to connect with this top prospect, and eventually he allowed me to visit him. This is yet another example of how the top and next tier major gifts lists must stay fluid. To no one's surprise, that prospect was added to my top prospect list.

When you and members of your development team are deciding on which prospects should be deleted from the assigned top and next tier lists, you should look at all the effort that has been made by members of the organization to reach these prospects over the past year. Once you have that information, apply the guidelines for removing prospects off the lists shown in Exhibit 9–8.

Exhibit 9–8 Guidelines for Removing a Prospect from the Major Gifts List

1. Remove any prospect who you have been unable to contact after continuous efforts by telephone, mail, or invitations.
2. Remove any prospect who has declined to see you and does not want you or anyone from the organization to contact him or her.
3. Remove any prospect who has stated a major gift is really not likely for quite some time and does not want the organization "wasting" its time or money on him or her.

This is a very short list for removing prospects, and it is short for a reason. There are not many situations where your organization should remove your identified "top" prospects from the major gifts list until *all possi-*

bilities have been exhausted. Remember, in the section in Chapter 2 "Sorting It All Out," your group examined its entire prospect pool and sectioned out the top, then the next three tiers of top major gifts prospects. Right now you and other members of your development team have been working with that *top group*, those you and others have identified as the best candidates to make major gifts. You do not want to jump too quickly to delete these prospects from your top list.

The three guidelines in Exhibit 9–8 are short and simple. If after one year, with concerted effort by you and/or others from your group, the prospect has not responded to mail, telephone, or invitations, then take the prospect off the list *for now*. Once I take an "unreachable" prospect off the list, I keep an eye open to see if the prospect's name ever appears in newspapers, magazines, or trade journals. If it does, I will send a copy of the article with a handwritten note to the prospect in hopes that it would prompt the prospect to speak or meet with me.

If handwritten notes and cards have still produced no response, I take the hard copy file that I had on this prospect and place it in a larger file called "Inactive Prospects." I do this for all the prospects who are removed from my top and next tier lists. This helps me to remember the names and some pertinent information on these prospects in case they do respond and are added back on my lists.

I also remove prospects who I am unable to reach by telephone, who will not meet me, and who do not want anyone from the organization to contact them. These folks may just like to give to your group without seeing or speaking with anyone representing your organization. It sounds odd that someone who supports your group would not want to have any personal connection, but it is quite common. As we saw in the section of Chapter 7 "The Anonymous—No One Can Know I Made This Gift," some people want to keep their giving private and do not want anyone, sometimes even those in the organization, to know about them or their wealth. Others may decline contact from the organization because they may not want anyone to see them or their home/work surroundings for a variety of personal reasons.

The tips contained in "Staying in Touch with the Prospect When the Prospect Says 'No' to a Visit" in Chapter 3 unfortunately do not apply here because the prospect has told you that he or she does not want anyone contacting him or her. It would not be beneficial in this situation to use those suggested tips, such as calling the prospect just to say "hello" or sending holiday cards or some article or brochure produced by your group with a personal note. The prospect has told you quite clearly that he or she does not want to be contacted. You have no choice but to listen to that request and carry it out. I only delete this type of prospect when he or she has made it a point to let me know that he or she wants no contact, and "no contact" really means "NO CONTACT."

The last circumstance for removing a prospect from the top and next tier lists is when the prospect lets you know that a major gift really is not going to happen for quite some time, *and* the prospect feels uncomfortable with you and others spending the organization's time and money on him or her. Notice the connector "and" to this last guideline. You are not removing prospects who you have met, cultivated, and even solicited who are great prospects but just cannot make a major gift in what they feel is the "foreseeable future." That would go against the principles discussed in the section of Chapter 6 "When the Response is 'No'" because "no" now, may not be "no" forever. Major gifts fundraisers should hang in and continue to work with their prospects even when the prospects have said that they cannot make the gift at this time.

It is a different story if the prospect says he or she cannot make the gift for a very long time, *and* he or she feels uncomfortable having the organization spend time and money on him or her. If this has been expressed, do not give up right away. Rather, try to have a very frank conversation with the prospect. Let him or her know that he or she is valued, important, and well worth the time and energy. Let the prospect know that your organization owes it to him or her and other top supporters to maintain strong contact. If after your incredibly persuasive pitch, the prospect still does not want you or anyone else to visit or to invite him or her to anything, then at least ask if you can call from time to time or send a personal note or two. Most prospects will at least let you maintain "detached and inexpensive" contact via the telephone or mail.

If the prospect has stated firmly that he or she really does not want to hear from you and others, then I

Tip: Temporarily remove prospects from the top and next tier lists who cannot make a major gift within the foreseeable future AND do not want contact from the organization. After six to nine months, send a card or call to reconnect with the prospect.

take this prospect off the list *for awhile* because I am honoring his or her wishes. In my experience, this type of prospect just needs a break from the attention he or she has been receiving from the organization and in all likelihood will return to your top or next tier list in the very near future. Generally, I would take that prospect off the list for six to nine months, and then send a note and follow up with a telephone call to reconnect with the prospect.

ADDING NEW PROSPECTS TO THE TOP AND NEXT TIER MAJOR GIFTS LISTS

As you get into the flow of working with prospects from both lists, shifting them from one list to another, and deleting some where appropriate, you will be ready to add new prospects to your lists (Dunlop 1993, 113). There are two ways to add new prospects to your lists. First, new "hot" prospects will surface for your group on a regular basis. This includes a new prospect who:

- Sends a recent first-time high-end gift.
- Is just discovered by your prospect researcher or department.
- Meets you for the first time at a special event.
- Is introduced to you by a donor because the prospect is interested in making a gift.
- Has a connection to your group or has potential to be connected to your group based on a recent newspaper or trade journal article.

These types of prospects who come to the organization's attention should be brought up at the biweekly development meetings and assigned to the major gifts fundraisers. You can add them to either your top or next tier list. I add them to my top list for the following reason. These are "hot" new prospects who have been identified by some very recent event or research. My style is to move on these prospects very quickly so that I can capitalize on the recent information that these people have excellent potential to make a major gift. If I put them on my next tier list, I may not get to them as quickly as if they were on my top list. Adding newly identified "hot" prospects to your top list will motivate you to work with these solid top list prospects right away.

The other source of new prospects is the *next pool of prospects your group identified* in "Sorting It All Out" from Chapter 2. From that next pool of prospects, take the top people first from that identified list and add them to your next tier list. For instance, if you have worked with all your prospects from your first group of top prospects (those people who have made gifts of $10,000 or more within the last year), start working on the second group (those people who made gifts of $10,000 or more beyond a one-year period). Start with those prospects in the second group who made gifts of that size within 18 months and then within 2 years, and work your way back in time. As you and other members of your development team work with each new prospect, you will be determining whether each prospect should be:

1. Bumped up to the top list.
2. Left on the next tier list.
3. Removed temporarily from this list.
4. Researched further.
5. Removed from the list altogether because they are not major gifts prospects.

Every month new prospects from your next pool list should be added to your next tier list. For every prospect who is deleted from this list, a new prospect must be added. You will also need to infuse between 5 and 15 additional prospects to your next tier list on a monthly basis. Gauge the number of new prospects you add to the size of your organization and the experience level of the major gifts fundraiser. A small organization or a fundraiser with little major gifts fundraising experience would want to aim for 5 new prospects a month. A larger organization or a fundraiser with several years of major gifts fundraising experience would want to add 15 new prospects a month. This will "replenish" the supply of prospects who are no longer on your next tier list, plus add at least 5–15 more prospects.

The success of your major gifts program depends on you and others constantly adding and working with new prospects. You must constantly weave in new prospects so that there is new prospect activity occurring at the same time existing prospects are being cultivated and solicited. This is essential to securing future major gifts (*National Fund Raiser* 1998). For instance, if your group did not regularly add new prospects, it could only rely on gifts from that existing base of prospects. Once those folks gave to their capacity or decided not to make the gift at all, you would have no choice but to find new prospects. By then, it would be too late. Months, even years, could pass before your group would see another major gift because there was no one in the "pipeline" being cultivated to make a gift.

Not every prospect who is added to your next tier list will turn out to stay on that list. Some may turn out not to be great major gifts prospects, while others will

quickly elevate to your top list. This is why you need to add new prospects on a regular monthly basis. Adding a minimum of 5–15 new prospects each month will ensure that you have a solid next tier list.

As you need more prospects, select the next highest 5–15 prospects from your next pool list. *Now you can see how this whole process comes full cycle.* As you bump up prospects from the next tier list and delete prospects from your next tier list, you add new prospects to that list from your previously sorted and identified top prospect groups (see "Sorting It All Out" in Chapter 2). As new "hot" prospects are identified, they are added to your top list as well cultivated and soon to be solicited prospects. You are now working comfortably and productively on the right amount of prospects, focusing your time, attention, and resources on your top and next tier prospects. These are the people who have the best potential to make large gifts to your organization in the very near and reachable future.

Congratulations, you and your team have in place a solid major gifts program that will reap big gifts for years to come.

RECAP AND REVIEW

1. Every successful major gifts fundraising program needs a prospect tracking system that will organize, direct, monitor, review, and evaluate prospect activity.
2. A good prospect tracking system is needed to preserve institutional history.
3. A good prospect tracking system will serve as a "tickler" to remind the major gifts fundraiser of the prospects who need attention and will ensure that the fundraiser is spending equal time with all assigned prospects.
4. Selecting the right prospect tracking system entails an evaluation of the number of prospects and donors; existing computer capabilities; funds for computer stations, upgrades, maintenance, and warranties; number of people using the new system; and the need for computer training.
5. A prospect tracking system should meet your organization's current needs and have the capacity to add new features as your organization grows.
6. Whenever possible, select an integrated database system that uses specialized tracking software, tailored to meet the needs of your organization.

7. A word processing system can be used or designed to track prospect activity so long as all prospect information and activity can be stored and top and next tier major gifts prospect reports can be produced.

8. Remember that specialized software and word processing systems are tracking tools that need to be used wisely and efficiently. Major gifts fundraisers should be spending the bulk of their time with their prospects, not with their computers.

9. Regardless of the tracking system, make sure you keep hard copy files of "tangible" and important notes, cards, and letters for each of your top prospects.

10. Every major gifts development operation should have biweekly meetings with front-line fundraisers, prospect managers, and the leadership of the development team to make sure each assigned prospect is properly managed and that new strategies for prospect activity are discussed.

11. Deciding whether or not to remove a major gifts prospect from the direct mail/annual list should ideally be decided on a prospect-by-prospect basis, with input and approval by the major gifts and direct mail departments and the leadership of the development team.

12. If a major gifts prospect is removed temporarily from the direct mail/annual list, it is essential that at the agreed upon time the prospect is placed back on the list to capture future annual gifts.

13. In many instances, it will be the major gifts fundraiser's responsibility to get both the major and the annual gift.

14. Only remove a major gifts prospect from the major gifts lists if within one year the organization could not contact the prospect; the prospect expressly declines any and all contact; or if a major gift is highly unlikely for the foreseeable future and the prospect does not want to be contacted by the organization.

15. Major gifts prospects who the development team collectively decides to remove from the top and next tier lists are rarely removed forever; therefore, all prospect information must be stored and ready to be retrieved at a later time.

16. Newly identified "hot" prospects should be added to the top tier list.

17. Every month 5–15 additional prospects from the next highest group of previously identified major gifts prospects should be added to the next tier list.

18. Top and next tier lists are fluid and must be updated monthly by shifting prospects from one list to another and deleting and adding new prospects to each so that the fundraiser is constantly working with the organization's best prospects to secure big gifts.

REFERENCES

Building big gift potential. 1998. *National Fund Raiser*, June.

Dunlop, D. 1993. Major gift programs. In *Educational fund raising principles and practice*, ed. M.J. Worth. Phoenix, AZ: Onyx Press/American Council on Education.

Karsch, C. 1993. Prospect management: tracking and coordinating information. In *Developing an effective major gift program: From managing staff to soliciting gifts*, eds. R. Muir and J. May, 44. Washington, DC: Council for Advancement and Support of Education.

Nichols, J. 1991. *Targeted fund raising*. Chicago: Precept Press, Inc.

Schaff, T., and D. Schaff. 1999. *The fundraising planner*. San Francisco: Jossey-Bass Publishers.

Smith, P. 1997. *New directions for philanthropic fund raising*. San Francisco: Jossey-Bass Publishers.

Sturtevant, W. 1997. *The artful journey*. Chicago: Bonus Books, Inc.

Williams, J. 1991. *Big gifts*. Rockville, MD: The Taft Group.

Appendix 9–A
Sample Major Gifts Reports for Contacts and Gift Proposals

Major Gifts Report
Contacts with Prospects/Donors - March

NAME	ADDRESS	PHONE NUMBER	CONTACT with DATE
Ashton	111 Park Drive, Moneyland	(111) 111–1111	Appointment letter sent 3/1
Baldwin	222 Park Drive, Moneyland	(111) 111–2222	Still considering proposal—3/22
Cummings	333 Park Drive, Moneyland	(111) 111–3333	Left message with assistant 3/3, 3/9, 3/14. Will call at home by 3/30
Dimartino	444 Park Drive, Moneyland	(111) 111–4444	Will meet at her office 3/14
Enders	555 Park Drive, Moneyland	(111) 111–5555	Away until June—will call 6/4
Fillmore	666 Park Drive, Moneyland	(111) 111–6666	Met for lunch 3/19—will bring to campus in May
Gilbert	777 Park Drive, Moneyland	(111) 111–7777	Just increased her annual gift to $2,500/yr—will meet next week to thank, then in two months meet to discuss $10,000 endowed scholarship gift by end of year
Halpin	888 Park Drive, Moneyland	(111) 111–8888	Sent birthday card 3/23—will invite to lunch week of 3/25
Isler	999 Park Drive, Moneyland	(111) 111–9999	Will visit here in April—will call by 3/15 to set date
Juan	1000 Park Drive, Moneyland	(111) 111–0000	Said no to visit for now—will continue to pursue
Kakuto	1100 Park Drive, Moneyland	(111) 111–1100	Wants to mentor business students. Will bring him to meet the Dean by 3/30
Lin	1200 Park Drive, Moneyland	(111) 111–1200	Invited to music school's open house—4/24

Matika	1300 Park Drive, Moneyland	(111) 111–1300	Wants to meet with financial planner to discuss $100,000 charitable trust proposal
Nhim	1400 Park Drive, Moneyland	(111) 111–1400	Left several messages—3/4, 3/8, 3/15 at home—will call in the evening week of 3/25
Oyana	1500 Park Drive, Moneyland	(111) 111–1500	New prospect—will have research on her by 3/16—sent appointment letter 3/9—will call 3/17

Major Gifts Proposal Report
March

NAME	GIFT PROPOSAL WITH DATE	STATUS
Ashton		
Baldwin	$150,000/3 yr for internship program—delivered 3/12	Still considering
Cummings		
Dimartino	Will have presolicitation discussion 3/14 to find his area of interest to support	
Enders		
Fillmore		
Gilbert	Will meet by May and propose $10,000 endowed scholarship to be funded by the end of the year	
Halpin		
Isler		
Juan		
Katuto	During meeting with Dean by 3/30 will explore his interest in supporting the mentoring program	
Lin		
Matika	Proposal for $100,000 charitable trust delivered 2/23 for study abroad program	Still considering—will call by 3/30
Nhim		
Oyana		

DEVELOPING MAJOR GIFTS: TURNING SMALL DONORS INTO BIG CONTRIBUTORS

Appendix 9–B

Sample Major Gifts Reports for Top Prospects and Next Tier Prospects

Top Major Gifts Prospects Report
March

#	Name	College	Next Step with Date/Proposal	Annual Gift
1.	Baldwin	Music	Will call by 3/22 to follow up with $150,000 proposal	No
2.	Matika	Liberal Arts	Will call by 3/30 to follow up with $100,000 proposal	No
3.	Gilbert	Business	Will meet next week to discuss $10,000 endowed scholarship	Yes
4.	Katuto	Business	Will bring to campus to meet the Dean by 3/30	Yes
5.	Dimartino	Art	Will meet at her office 3/14	No
6.	Isler	Education	Wants to come for tour in April. Will set the date by 3/15	No
7.	Lin	Music	Invited to 4/24 open house	Yes
8.	Halpin	Engineering	Sent birthday card 3/23. Will invite to lunch week of 3/25	No

Next Tier of Major Gifts Prospects
March

#	Name	College	Next Step with Date/Proposal	Annual Gift
1.	Fillmore	Journalism	Met for lunch 3/19. Will bring to campus in May	Yes
2.	Enders	Business	Away until June. Will call 6/4	No
3.	Cummings	Forestry	Left several messages at work. Will call at home	No
4.	Ashton	Architecture	Sent initial letter 3/1. Will call week of 3/8	Yes
5.	Juan	Business	Did not want to meet. Will continue to pursue	No
6.	Oyana	Dance	New prospect. Will research by 3/16; send letter 3/9 and call week of 3/17	Yes
7.	Nhim	Engineering	Left messages 3/4, 3/8, 3/15 at home. Will call in evening week of 3/25	Yes

Appendix 9–C
Cornell University's Commitment Tracking Form

Courtesy of Cornell University.

1. DONOR CREDITING INFORMATION

- Donor Name & Class _____   Donor ID # _____
- Divide With Spouse? Name: _____   Spouse ID # _____
- Memo Credit to? _____   Memo ID # _____
- MG Company? Name: _____   MG Co. Code _____

                                              PTS Rating Code _____

2. PAYMENT INFORMATION

- *If this form reports a payment,* check here ❑ and attach a screen print of the donor gift history with the pledge circled.
- Payment Amount $_____   Please complete Sections 5 and 7. Use Sections 8 and 9 as needed.

3. COMMITMENT AMOUNT

- Individual Amount $_____   MG Amount $_____   Total Commitment $_____
                                                           (Ind. Amt + MG Amt)
                                                           Discounted Value $_____

4. COMMITMENT INFORMATION

- Is the commitment ❑ Written ❑ Oral? Date of Commitment _____
    If Oral Commitment, staff responsible for securing Statement of Intent _____
                                                  By When? _____

- Type of Pledge   ❑ Current year   ❑ Flex. Endowment (interest)   ❑ Revocable Trust (discounted)*
    (Check ONE)   ❑ Multi-year   ❑ Flex. Endowment (principal)   ❑ Advised Bequest (discounted)*
                       ❑ Lead Trust   ❑ Life Income Agreement*   ❑ Outside Trust*
                                          *Planned Giving approval   ❑ Gift In Kind
                                          required – see back

5. GIFT DESIGNATION

- Commitment to College/Unit/   Name/s: _____
    Department/Center?   _____

- Commitment Use: ❑ Current Use   ❑ Endowment
    Please detail how the gift is to be allocated.
    Specify the AMOUNTS designated to each fund, the FUND NAME, FUND NUMBER, or if a new fund is needed.
    For each amount identify the Campaign Priority (Gift Purpose) from the list at bottom.
    Use Comments (Section 9) for additional amounts or to detail complex designations.

- **1st Amt $**_____ to Gift Fund (Name) _____
            If New Fund, Check Here ❑ If Existing Fund, Fund # _____ Fund Purpose _____

- **2nd Amt $**_____ to Gift Fund (Name) _____
            If New Fund, Check Here ❑ If Existing Fund, Fund # _____ Fund Purpose _____

- **3rd Amt $**_____ to Gift Fund (Name) _____
            If New Fund, Check Here ❑ If Existing Fund, Fund # _____ Fund Purpose _____

GIFT PURPOSES

- Disposition Pending   • Unrestricted   • Professorships   • Undergrad Student Aid   • New Construction
- Library Acquisitions   • General Program   • Graduate Fellowships   • Renovation
              SPECIAL USE ONLY: • *Directorships*   • *Other Faculty Support*   • *Specific Programs*

6. COMMITMENT SCHEDULE

❑ Check here if payment schedule is undetermined.
❑ Check here if the donor is NOT to be billed against this commitment.

• Please indicate the dates when payments are expected, the amount to be paid by the individual, any amount to be paid by a Matching Gift Company, and the total/s of the individual and any matching payments.

	1st Payment	2nd Payment	3rd Payment	4th Payment	5th Payment
Date	_____	_____	_____	_____	_____
Ind. Amount	_____	_____	_____	_____	_____
MG Amount	_____	_____	_____	_____	_____
Total	_____	_____	_____	_____	_____

7. TOTAL PAID/AMOUNT OUTSTANDING

Payment #_____   Total Paid to Date Against This PL $_____   Amount Outstanding $_____

8. PRESIDENT'S ACKNOWLEDGEMENT

❑ Standard Letter   ❑ Special Letter   ❑ No Letter   Salutation: _____

9. COMMENTS

• Please provide any additional information pertaining to the gift designation and/or payment schedule:

_____
_____
_____
_____
_____
_____
_____
_____
_____
_____

Please attach ALL supporting documentation and forward to: the Office of the Director of Development, Suite 100, 55 Brown Rd.

10. STAFF SIGN OFF

Prepared by _____ Date _____ Telephone # _____

Responsible Staff _____ Prospect Mgr _____

Planned Giving Approval _____ Date _____

Planned Giving approval required for pledges and gifts related to trusts and bequests.

Director of Development Approval _____ Date _____

Info Services _____ Entered in PA System on _____

Notes: _____

Chapter 10
The Success Stories

CHAPTER OUTLINE

- Mr. Z
- Mr. B
- Mr. and Mrs. M

I'd like to show you now how this whole process comes together. What follows are three stories, which I call "the success stories." I've saved the best for last. These stories bring to life all the tips, tools, and techniques that are contained throughout this book. In the first story, Mr. Z, I cite the chapter and section or the appendix that applies to that particular moment in the major gifts process. I did this so you could see how this works "for real" not just in textbooks. As you read the next two stories, Mr. B and Mr. and Mrs. M, do the same exercise on your own and think which concept mentioned in the book applies to that part of the major gifts fundraising process. Once you do, you'll see that all these steps and strategies are well worth your time and effort. You'll also see how the fundraiser-prospect relationship develops. It is fluid, and on many occasions you will have to rely on your instincts and that "hidden voice" that lets you know what to say and when to move quickly on the solicitation. Most of all, I hope that these illustrations show you how professionally and personally satisfying this profession can be. Whether you have had some of these experiences (and I hope you have and will share them with me), or you are looking forward to them, the bottom line is that if you follow all the steps and sprinkle them with your own personality, major gifts will land on your organization's doorstep.

Remember, the rules of major gifts fundraising contained in this book apply if you work for yourself or if you work with 50+ fundraisers, if you represent a small missionary or if you represent an international research institute, and if you have a budget of $250,000 or a budget of $2.5 million. Take a careful look at the steps taken and the donors' responses in each of these three stories. The size of the organization, the organization's budget, and the number of fundraising staff were not factors in building and sustaining the relationships that sparked these major gifts.

Also keep in mind that these are success stories for a variety of reasons. *They are not successes solely because of their dollar amount.* While the sizes and increases of these major gifts are important, these stories are successes for the organization because the major donors:

- Remained loyal givers.
- Stayed educated, active, and involved.
- Shared their enthusiasm about the organization with others.
- Acted as "spokespeople" for the organization.
- Opened doors to new prospects.
- Asked to be considered for leadership and advisory roles.
- Encouraged their family and friends to give.

When you have all that, my friends, you have the most wonderful major donors.

MR. Z

I learned about Mr. Z by reading the business section of the local newspaper (Chapter 9, Adding New Prospects to the Top and Next Tier Major Gifts List). Every Monday, the paper would feature recently promoted people, new companies, and companies that increased their revenues beyond their wildest dreams. On the top of the page was a picture of Mr. Z in his new office. Here was a man in his early 40s, sitting very comfortably in his new office. It wasn't a stuffy business office picture; instead the picture portrayed a man of confidence, yet he was very relaxed. Mr. Z had just been promoted as senior vice president of the northeast region for an international bank. After getting through a few paragraphs about his new job, it stated that he received his undergraduate degree in business from our university and his MBA from a different school. For me, this was "a good reading day."

I quickly wrote him a letter, introducing myself and congratulating him on his new job on behalf of the university (Appendix 3–A). I asked if I could see him at his office, for no more than 20 minutes, so that I could congratulate him in person (Chapter 3, Writing to Prospects Initially). A few days later, his assistant called me, and I had the appointment.

During our first visit I learned that he had received a four-year out-of-state scholarship to our business school. He had a great experience and stays in touch with several college friends. He was married and has two children, a daughter, 16, and a son, 13. His wife, by the way, was an alumna of our university, and they met each other at our school. Although I did not want to leave, I said that I promised to keep it brief. He did not take that as a cue for me to go, instead he wanted to spend more time. This was music to my ears. He told me all about the bank, how he moved around the country for work, and how he now was glad to be back home. His office was a stone's throw away from the university. As we talked further, it turns out that Mr. Z lives two towns away from me. We began comparing restaurants, movie theaters, and, of course, our commute home and the traffic (Chapter 4, Making the Most of Your First Visit).

I noticed on his coffee table that he had a brochure from the college where he received his MBA (Chapter 4, Observing Everything You Can on the First Visit). I asked him if he received our mailings, and if he had divided loyalties between the two schools. He received some information about the business school but not on a regular basis. I told him I would take care of that. Mr. Z received his MBA from the other school by going part time in the evenings while working his full-time job. He didn't have the time to connect with faculty and students as he did in his undergraduate years. He said that he felt much stronger about our university. This was definitely getting better. He mentioned that the other school saw the same article about him in the newspaper and also wanted an appointment with him. Now I was really glad I moved quickly because it would have looked really bad for the university if we weren't right there in the moment when Mr. Z received his promotion. Just think how hard it would have been to get in the door with him months/years later if we missed this opportunity. I can just hear him say, "Well my MBA school was here a long time ago when I got promoted" and him thinking to himself "and where was my undergraduate school?"

While everything was going really well with our visit, I kept thinking what my next step would be with him (Chapter 4, Making the Most of Your First Visit). I could bring him in to meet the dean of the business school, but it was too soon for that move. I like to save that one for when I am further down the cultivation scale with my prospects and when I know the prospect's area of interest and the size of the gift. Instead, I invited him to an event the business school was hosting the next month. It was an open house run by the faculty and current students to recruit new students. Our corporate partners and business supporters would be invited. I thought it would be nice for him to come back to campus and meet some new peers in his business community. He agreed to come, and I had my next step before walking out his door.

On my way back to the office, I bought a congratulations card to send him when I got back to the office (Chapter 4, Cultivation—What Is It? How Does It Work?). Mr. Z's office was only a few subway stops away from campus so I was back from the appointment in no more than a half hour. From the time I left his office to the time I got back to my office, he had e-mailed me *thanking me* for taking the time to see him. He stole my thunder. I sent him back an e-mail that said, "You beat me to it" and that I was looking forward to seeing him next week (Chapter 3, Contacting Prospects by E-mail). I sent the card with a note reiterating the date, time, and place of the business school open house. I did a contact report on Mr. Z and added him to my top major gifts prospect list (Chapter 2, Gathering Donor Information; Chapter 9, Adding New Prospects to the Top and Next Tier Major Gifts Lists).

At the open-house event, I introduced Mr. Z to some students and faculty. As the dean was doing his whirlwind rounds trying to meet as many people as he could, I managed to introduce the dean to Mr. Z. They chatted for a few minutes, but it was an important few minutes. Everyone likes to meet the top leadership, and I think Mr. Z really appreciated it. After that, I suggested he tour around the school on his own and drop into a few informational classes to get reacquainted with our new business curriculum. That sounded good to him so he toured around the school for awhile. We later met up right before he was about to leave. He didn't have to say a word. His face said it all. He liked the people he met, the programs we were offering, and the students we were attracting. Most of all he looked like a student. He was back, reconnected, and looking forward to staying in contact with the school. While we were walking out the door I mentioned the topic of sports. From past experience I know how this can be a double-edged sword. Some alumni love it; others would rather watch paint dry than watch a game. I tried to "lace it in the conversation" and test the waters. I mentioned to Mr. Z that our basketball season was approaching, and that if he liked sports, it might be fun to take his family to a game in our new basketball arena. Mr. Z told me that he has followed our team since graduation and had gone to some games on his own but never in our new arena. Then he mentioned that his wife was in a commercial promoting our university and that it was filmed in our new arena. I said "Then it's settled. You have to come to see where your wife was acting, and your children should see the campus, new and improved, where mom and dad met." Pretty bold of me at the time, but it seemed like the perfect way to get the family to campus. It didn't take much to convince him so we cleared a date, and I had my next step (Chapter 4, Cultivation—What Is It? How Does It Work?).

The whole family came to the game, and it was a great family outing. We won the game, which always helps the alumni morale. During the game I spent some time getting to know his wife and teenage children. His wife told me all about the process of making a commercial. It looks simple, but it takes hours. She was there a few days on the shoot, and it seemed liked years. I knew she was a patient woman. The teenagers liked the game and the campus, and I knew they would have had an even better time if mom and dad weren't around. Well, at least I showed them the university and planted the seeds for them to consider our school for their education (Chapter 8, Intergenerational Stewardship).

Mr. Z and I kept in touch over the next few months strictly by e-mail. He traveled quite a bit for work and this was the best way to stay in touch. I felt it was time to ask Mr. Z to make a gift at the $5,000 level. He had no giving history with the university, and I wanted to get this *initial gift* while I learned more about him and his area of interest. Only then could I ask for his next larger gift for the right purpose, when the time was right (Chapter 4, Judging the Prospect's Readiness To Make a Major Gift). I sent him an e-mail and told him I wanted to meet him to talk about giving opportunities at the university. I was direct and to the point about the purpose of our meeting. He didn't try to put me off, and in fact, he welcomed the idea.

We met in his office, and I was just about to launch into my $5,000 ask when he told me that his company had a one-for-one matching gift program, *with no limit*. For every dollar the employee gives to charity, the company will match it. Now my wheels were spinning. I was about to increase my ask when he revealed his financial obligations. He was still paying off graduate school loans, and on several occasions he mentioned that he was saving as much as he could for his teenagers' college education. Considering this new information, a fallback position could be to do a $2,500 gift and have it matched, and he would be at the $5,000 level.

I began my warm up talking about the importance of supporting the business school, especially now since we had a new dean, a new direction, and a new curriculum, and everything was on an upswing for the business school (Chapter 6, Scripting the Ask). I talked about other alumni who made gifts of $5,000 or more and how our endowed funds begin at $5,000. I kept using the $5,000 figure to see his reaction. He was totally neutral. Then I asked him for a $5,000 gift to support the business school. I told him that we needed gifts like this to attract more gifts from more alumni. If he wanted, he could target his gift to support the business school's track in finance, where he majored (Chapter 5, Creating Hand-Tailored Gift Opportunities). He thought about it for two seconds, then shared with me how he had been thinking about giving a gift, but put it off because he wanted to make a larger gift at a later time. He asked about the different membership levels of our major gifts program, and I explained each one. He told me he was grateful I did not ask him for a larger gift, because it was simply out of the question. Now I was really glad I didn't ask for more than $5,000. He said he would love to be in the financial position to give $5,000, but he had other obligations as he just described and now was not a good time. He stated that someday he would like to make a $5,000 or more gift. He said that for now he could do a $1,000 gift. I asked him to consider making a $1,250 gift that could be matched by his company to put him in our $2,500 membership category (Chapter 6, Turning Stumbling Blocks into Building Blocks). He thought about that for a moment, and then said he could probably do $1,250. I then asked him how he felt about targeting the gift to finance, and he said that he respected our new dean, and he felt that the gift should be unrestricted so the dean could put the money to good use. I let him know the procedure for making his gift as well as the matched gift. As I was leaving, I thanked him for his gift and let him know how grateful I was that he shared his honesty about his current financial situation and his intentions to make a larger gift in the future (Chapter 6, The Close).

Two weeks later the university received his gift. He received thank you letters from the president of the university, the dean of the school of business, and me (Chapter 7, The Importance of the Initial Thank You). He received invitations to all the business school events and university events (Chapter 8, Stewardship—What Is It? How Does It Work?). He came to our annual dinner and several business school events. One event focused on investment strategies and risk management, which I felt was right on point with his international banking business. I made it a point to hand-deliver an invitation to him during one of our visits (Chapter 8, The "Hard-to-Reach" Donors). He could not attend, so I asked if his company would sponsor a $1,000 table. He could send some of his employees, and they could report back to him about the seminar. Sounded great to him and now Mr. Z was giving on an individual basis and on a corporate basis (Appendix 5–D, The Blend Donor).

While Mr. Z and I are continuing to send each other e-mails, Mr. Z let me know that he has a friend who is also an alumnus of the university who he would like me to meet. His friend is president and owner of a global technology company that recently went public. They were fraternity brothers and stayed in contact over the years. I e-mailed him back, "How soon can we meet?" Within two weeks, the three of us met for lunch (Chapter 3, Selecting a Contact To Open the Door for You). The friend was open to the suggestion of getting back in touch with the university, and now I was in the position of stewarding Mr. Z and cultivating the friend. The three of us met periodically at a basketball game or over lunch. It brought Mr. Z and me closer in the fundraiser-donor relationship. By stewarding him and cultivating his friend, Mr. Z came to realize how important it was for the university to reconnect with alumni, to gain their trust, to involve them in activities, to make a strong case for support, and to get individual support from them. I now had a new prospect, Mr. Z's friend, whom I added to my top prospect list (Chapter 9, Adding New Prospects to the Top and Next Tier Major Gifts Lists).

Some time had gone by, and I had not seen Mr. Z in person. I set up one of my "just want to drop by the office and say hello" meetings with him. I brought with me a sweatshirt with the business school logo to give him (Chapter 8, Stewardship—What Is It? How Does It Work?). While I was in the waiting area, his assistant told me that under Mr. Z's leadership, their region won "Region of the Year" award from the company for the first time. She pointed to this large, engraved crystal bowl on the credenza with Mr. Z's name on it and the name of the region. The assistant told me that Mr. Z has been flooded with letters and calls and that their region threw him a surprise breakfast this morning to congratulate him. This is clearly not what I was prepared for, and I thanked my lucky stars I had something in hand to give him on his big day.

We got into his office, and I congratulated him right away. It was a really significant honor for the region. He refused to take any of the credit and gave all the credit to his employees. He told me his region won this honor because they surpassed each stated goal by over 45 percent. I knew Mr. Z was a true leader, and this clearly proved it. I told him I had the good fortune of bringing something to him on his special day. He opened the bag and saw the sweatshirt and lit up like a Christmas tree. He said he would wear it at every basketball game and indeed he did. As he was folding the sweatshirt to place it back in the bag, he said *he wanted to talk about his next gift.* Yes, this was a good day for both of us! He said that it was just shy of a year ago that he made his initial gift, but for the next gift he wanted to do something else. He wasn't sure what it would be, but he was clear that the most he could do for the next several years would be $5,000 a year. I had been giving this some consideration, and I had a gift idea that I thought would match his connection to the university (Chapter 8, Judging the Donor's Readiness To Make the Next Major Gift; Chapter 5, Creating Hand-Tailored Gift Opportunities).

Since Mr. Z received a full four-year out-of-state student scholarship to attend our business school, I always thought that an endowed scholarship for an out-of-state student at the business school would be the ideal gift opportunity for him. I told him that our endowed scholarships start at $25,000 so that he could make $5,000 gifts for the next five years for the scholarship. With the corporate match, his total gift would be $50,000. While that amount would not cover a four-year out-of-state student scholarship, once the scholarship was set up, he could add to it at any time so that it would add up to a four-year scholarship. Even though the scholarship was not fully funded in year one, the dean and the faculty could use the interest from the fund each year to give to an out-of-state student to come to the business school. I asked him how he felt about the idea. He said as long as the school has a need for scholarship dollars he would be glad to make this type of gift. In fact, he said he always thought he would give something back by way of a scholarship, just like the one he received. We had the right match between Mr. Z's interest and a gift opportunity; now we needed to move on to the right gift vehicle (Chapter 5, Creating Hand-Tailored Gift Opportunities). I knew he was the financial expert and that he would have some questions about our investment policies. He did, and we went over his questions one by one. Since he had an expertise in finance, I wanted to connect him with our vice president for finance at the university so that the two of them could talk, peer to peer (Chapter 6, Using the Team Approach). I gave him the name and telephone number of the vice president for finance.

We then talked further about how he was going to fund the gift. He said he had some stock and that he would like to use the stock to fund the gift. Sounds like a plan to me. I gave him our stock transfer account number and didn't need to say anything more. He was the banking expert. Then I moved on to the naming opportunity for the gift (Chapter 7, Thanking and Recognizing Your Donors). I asked him how he wanted to name the scholarship fund, whether it would be in his name or his and his wife's names. He thought about it for a moment, and then said he would like it in both of their names. On that note he quickly interjected that he needed to discuss it with his wife first and that he would get back to me (Chapter 6, Turning Stumbling Blocks into Building Blocks). I said that I understood perfectly and that I expected that he would need to talk it over with his wife. We discussed recognition options, and he said that as long as their names were on the scholarship fund, that was all the recognition they required. I let Mr. Z know that we would love to have him meet the scholarship recipients. He said he would be definitely interested in meeting them (Chapter 7, Thanking and Recognizing Your Major Donors).

Two days later he e-mailed me and said his wife thought it was a great idea. He needed to meet with his attorney and would get back to me. Three weeks later he e-mailed me and said he was ready to make the stock transfer.

In less than one year, Mr. Z went from being a $2,500 major donor to being a $50,000 major donor. Mr. Z is a major donor *not only because he made generous and meaningful gifts* to the university, but because he also:

- Followed university news via our Web site.
- Attended the business school and university sponsored events.
- Agreed to be a mentor for business students.
- Spread the word about the university to his family, friends, and coworkers.
- Introduced the university to other potential alumni supporters.
- Enjoyed himself along the way.

Who could ask for a better major donor?

MR. B

I met Mr. B by mistake. A mistake I thought he made when he sent two checks for the same amount in December. Each year, Mr. and Mrs. B would make their annual gifts, in the nature of $500 a year, always in the month of December. On this occasion, one check came in on the first week of December, followed by a second check of the same amount one week later. Mr. and Mrs. B's cumulative gifts put them on the hospital's major donor radar screen as major gifts prospects, specifically the second tier list.

Even though the hospital thanked Mr. and Mrs. B by letter, I wanted to call them personally. Maybe the two gifts were not a mistake. I made the call, and Mr. B answered the telephone. He sounded like an elderly man, maybe in his 70s. I asked him about the two gifts back to back, and he said that he didn't recall sending two checks but he would check. He said that he thought the hospital "did good work" and that we had a reputation of "spending our money wisely on the patients." I was going to ask if I could visit with him before he did such a wonderful job of marketing our hospital; now I really had to see him. He said that he and his wife were in the process of selling his house and that they were moving up the road to a continuing care retirement community. He said that he was getting old and had bad knees, and the house was too big and too expensive to maintain. He gave me the number where I could reach him at his new home, and I said I would call after the holidays to set up a visit. I hung up the telephone and made a note in my calendar to call Mr. B in mid-January.

The third week of January I made my call to Mr. B. He answered the telephone crying. I told him who I was and reminded him of our past conversation. I don't think he heard a word I said. All he kept saying over and over was that his wife Christine had died. I wanted to hang up the telephone immediately and forget I ever called him at the worst possible moment. He then said, "You want to see me about the hospital, right?" I said, "Yes, but now did not seem like the right time." He said it would be all right to see him next week, even though he wasn't much company.

I went to the retirement community where he was living. Mr. B was in his mid-80s, and he walked with a cane. When he greeted me, he looked like a kid who had just been left at camp and didn't want to be there. He and Christine were going to live out their retirement years together in this new home. Three weeks into their new home, Christine had a sudden stroke and never recovered. Now Mr. B was left there all alone and didn't want to be there without her.

I spent the entire day with Mr. B. It was not what I had planned, but he really needed the company, and I thought it was the least I could do on behalf of the hospital since they had been such loyal donors. I told him about the origins of the hospital, how it started as a tuberculosis center and evolved into an international heart and lung center. He wanted to hear about all our programs, and I gave him the updates on everything. It turned out that Mr. B as a child used to go to the park and the lake near the hospital, and he always heard good things about the hospital.

I asked Mr. B why he and Christine supported the hospital. Christine was a career nurse. She worked for five hospitals in the area but not our hospital. She was a dedicated Red Cross volunteer and received their distinguished Clara Barton Award for Nursing. It was their joint decision to support the hospital, but Christine had a heavy hand in making sure that the hospital received most of their charitable dollars. Mr. and Mrs. B supported over 10 charities each year, and our hospital was in the top tier of their giving list.

During the visit I found out quite a bit about Mr. B. He and Christine had no children, but they have many nieces and nephews. Mr. B worked for the same family-owned automobile franchise for over 42 years. He worked his way up the ladder until he became regional sales manager and distributor. He still keeps in touch with the family, and they still own the franchise. Then he told me another important fact. He didn't make his money through his job. He made some "extra cash" by investing in oil fields in Texas a long time ago. He didn't want to go in on the investment, but a friend convinced him to do it. He did, and I was looking at a man who was a millionaire.

I asked Mr. B if I could come and get him and bring him to the hospital. He had never seen the hospital, and I wanted to give him a tour to "show him the value of his dollar." While Mr. B may have had a comfortable nest egg, I assure you he minded every penny. He agreed to visit the hospital, and I arranged for him to meet first with our executive director and then for our head nurse to give him a private tour.

Our executive director and Mr. B really connected. They liked each other's dry sense of humor, and Mr. B was accustomed to being around the top leadership of an organization. I then brought him to the hospital, and since he had "weak knees," I thought a wheel chair would be the best way to cover the entire hospital. Our head nurse came to meet us, and at the sight of her he broke down. Our head nurse, being as skilled and compassionate as she was, just held his hand until he could speak. When he did he said, "I wish Christine could be here to see this."

As we approached the pediatric intensive care unit, the head nurse's first assistant came up to Mr. B to say hello. He recognized right away a pin she was wearing. It was the Clara Barton Award pin. She said she heard that his late wife also received that high honor and that she had something in common with the B family. He put his head down, and I knew exactly what he was thinking. He wanted Christine back to meet this nurse and to compare nurse stories and how they had so much in common. Now I was starting to cry.

A month passed, and I gave Mr. B a call just to see how he was doing. He said since the notice of Christine's death was publicized in the newspaper, he had been barraged with telephone calls and solicitations from charities looking for "donations." One charity that they supported was looking for a large memorial gift. This gave me a wake up call. I had to move quickly with Mr. B and begin discussing a major gift, but I wanted to make sure enough time passed for him to heal from the death of his wife. I discussed this with my executive director, and we agreed that we should ask him for a major gift within the next several weeks. We did not want to let too much time pass, or he may be asked by another charity. We came up with a gift proposal that we felt would match his interest in the hospital. We also had a gift amount and ways to fund the gift included in the proposal. The best strategy would be to have the executive director and me take him out to breakfast and use the team approach to ask him for the gift.

When I called Mr. B he knew something "was up." I asked him to meet with our executive director and me because we had a gift idea to share and discuss with him. After teasing me endlessly that I was "after his money," he agreed to meet with us. The night before our breakfast, my executive director called me at home to let me know that his daughter was in the hospital and that he could not make our breakfast. We talked about rescheduling, but we both agreed that we had to ask now. I was to do the ask solo.

Mr. B arrived in his spiffy, maroon Cadillac. I explained our executive director's absence, and he understood. He told me to let him know how the daughter was doing when I got back to the office. I promised I would. After breakfast and before I could glide my way into asking for the gift, he said to me, "You want my money right?" I told him that we had thought long and hard about coming up with the right gift opportunity for him and Christine. I always spoke about her as if she were in the room with us. I told him that we knew Christine lived her life as a dedicated and admired nurse and that together they had made such loyal and meaningful gifts. Then I moved into the ask. I asked Mr. B if he would consider making a $500,000 gift to name the department of nursing *in honor of Christine*. It was important that we offered a gift opportunity that would be a *celebration of her nursing career*, not a memorial gift. The first thing he did was thank me for not asking him for a memorial gift. She would never be dead in his heart. At that moment I knew we had made the right type of ask. As for the money, even though he could well afford to make this gift, Mr. B lived by and counted his every penny. This was an enormous amount to give in his eyes. He kept reiterating over and over, "This is a lot of money you are asking for." I told him we knew it was, and we had never asked anyone before him to name the department of nursing, which was absolutely true. We were waiting for that special donor to make this special offer. We only had one department of nursing and one naming opportunity. This would forever be named in honor of the right individual. We wanted a donor who had some strong ties with nursing because we felt it would be the "crown and glory" for our outstanding nursing department. Christine, with all her years of nursing service and her years of volunteer nursing, was the perfect choice.

We got back to the issue of money. I told him that we anticipated that he could fund the gift using his stock and avoid hefty capital gains. He said there was no question he would use his stock—it was just that he didn't want to make the gift in one year. I was ready for this, in fact, my executive director and I discussed previously that we thought he would agree to make the gift if he could do it over five years. We sensed that he might be afraid that if he made it all in one year, the

hospital would get his gift and then ignore him. He clearly enjoyed our contact, and he liked being around the hospital and the nurses. Furthermore, Mr. B had never given a charity more than a five-figure gift at one time. This would be a huge leap for him. He had a giving philosophy that he lived by. Give charity small gifts and make sure the charity spends the money wisely. If we structured the gift so that he could pay it over time, it would fit in with his giving philosophy and distill any fears that we would not continue our stewardship efforts.

I told him that he could make the gift over five years. Since this was September, we would like his first gift by the end of the year. He said he would think about it, and I told him I would call him the next week. I told him that we would like to have a special dedication ceremony and that he could invite his family, friends, and business partners. I could see a light bulb went on. He clearly liked this idea and started asking me if he could invite people from his church and his neighbors. He asked me when the dedication would be, and I said I would work out whatever type of party he wanted on whatever date he wanted. As I walked him to the car, he told me to go back to work and tell my executive director that I "earned my money today."

The next day Mr. B called his stockbroker, and we had our first $100,000 toward his $500,000 gift.

I like to use the example of Mr. B's gift for several reasons. First, it illustrates the need to stay on top of incoming gifts and not to be afraid to pick up the telephone and call a donor when you think there has been a mistake about the gift. In many instances, it can get you in the door and on your way to cultivating a major gifts prospect. Second, making a cold call can pay off, so do as many as your schedule will allow and continue to work with your top and next major gifts prospect lists. Third, don't tell the prospect you will call next month and then push it off to the next two or three months. You just may miss a $500,000 gift. Use your personal calendar system to help you stay on track with your prospects. Fourth, sometimes you just have to move quickly. I wanted more cultivation time with Mr. B, but the reality was if we waited to do the ask, we may have missed our chance to capture this type of gift. Finally, this example shows how imperative it is to have the gift opportunity match the donor's interest. I firmly believe the hospital got this gift because we asked Mr. B to name the department of nursing *in honor of* his late wife. If we had asked to name it in memory of her, I do not think we would have gotten the gift, or if we did, it would have taken a much longer time to get. It was so important to him that Christine's years of dedication to the nursing profession be honored forever and this was the perfect gift opportunity to make that dream come true.

Postscript: Mr. B fulfilled his pledge payments in less than five years and continues to be a major donor for the hospital.

MR. AND MRS. M

I found out about Mr. and Mrs. M by doing a cold call. They had made steady end-of-year gifts, just like Mr. B, in the nature of $250–$500, and their cumulative gifts put them on my major gifts prospect list. They lived several states away, and I knew it would not be easy to make the road trip to see them, but they were my next prospects to contact. I sent them a letter saying I wanted to see them and followed that up with the telephone call. Mr. M answered the telephone. I made my usual pitch that I wanted to come see them and give them personal updates about the hospital when Mr. M blurted out, "Yeah, come see us. We have $5 million to give the hospital." My first reaction was that he was making a joke, or maybe he was getting too many telephone solicitations, and he thought that I was a telemarketer. I didn't know what to say so I asked him, "Are you serious or are you making a joke?" Mr. M said, "No, I'm serious. We won the state lottery, and we're going to get our lump-sum payment in a few months." Now I was stunned and speechless for a few seconds, as a matter of fact, which rarely happens to me. I heard that these types of prospects do exist in fundraising, but I never had the experience. And here it was, happening to me. What did I have to lose in seeing him? I asked him if he could give me more information, but he didn't want to say anything more over the telephone. He told me the news about the family hitting the lottery made his town's papers, and he was getting too many telephone calls. He didn't like the publicity or the hype. He was a local businessman who liked to do business in person. I figured turnaround was fair play. If I wouldn't give him any details over the telephone as a way to get in the door to see him, why should he? He wanted to see me the next day.

I discussed the telephone call with my executive director, and I asked him to take a leap of faith and come with me. I knew it was a lot to ask and that it would be a four-hour drive each way, but Mr. M sounded pretty serious and what if he really had $5 million to give the hospital? Shouldn't the executive director of the hospital be there so that we could discuss the details

of this rather significant gift? He trusted my judgment and instinct and agreed to join me on the road trip to see Mr. and Mrs. M. I knew I owed my executive director one.

We pulled up to Mr. and Mrs. M's house. It was a very well-maintained ranch-style home. Mr. and Mrs. M greeted us warmly. They were a down-to-earth couple—very soft spoken and kind hearted. They treated us like family from the moment we walked in their home. As I looked around, all I could see was a sea of pictures. Their home was a picture gallery. All the walls and bookshelves were lined with family photos. I asked Mrs. M to tell me about each one, and she did. They have 8 children and 17 grandchildren. Most of the family lives nearby, and they stay in very close contact. Mr. M directed us to the kitchen, and we sat at a picnic table where I could tell many a family discussion was had. We started out thanking them for their loyal and generous gifts and asked them how they came to support our hospital. Mrs. M said that their daughter, age 11 at the time, was brought to the hospital with a congenital heart defect. Our surgeons performed an operation to cure the defect, and their daughter has been making regular yearly visits to our hospital ever since. Their daughter was now 44, strong and healthy, and a mother of 2 children. Mrs. M told us that right after her daughter's surgery, they started supporting the hospital because as she said, "I know where the money goes. It goes to help people." Could we bottle this moment and have Mrs. M speak on behalf of our hospital to all our prospects?

Mrs. M went on to tell us that she had such loyalty and faith in our hospital that she wanted her grandson to come in for diagnostic testing. He was born with very small veins that kept collapsing. Her daughter brought the child to a local hospital where he was treated with medication, but Mrs. M wanted our doctors to examine her grandson. We said we could schedule an appointment for him when we returned.

I could tell that Mr. M and my executive director wanted to get down to business so I turned to Mr. M and said, "Well I have made many telephone calls trying to see supporters like you folks and let me tell you, your response that you won the lottery was a first for me." He replied, "Well winning the lottery was a first for me, too." Mr. M worked over 26 years as a plant manager for a national retail sales company. He had eight children to support so times were tough. A group of guys that he worked with always bought a block of lottery tickets as a group, and they wanted him to join. He resisted for a few years, and then he really needed extra money and decided to play the lottery on his own. He purchased lottery tickets each week, a small win every once in a while, and then a year ago, he won the $20 million jackpot.

My executive director wanted to hear about the exact moment when he knew he won—where they were, what they did first, who they told. Mrs. M jumped in the conversation. "He was sitting in the living room writing down the numbers as the television announcer was reading them off one by one. I was in the bedroom. He kept yelling for me to come in and bring the ticket. He always kept his lottery tickets in the dresser drawer near our bed." She went on to tell us that he remembered that he had most of the numbers on the ticket, but he was unsure of the last one. Mrs. M brought him the ticket and sure enough—bingo—they had the $20 million winning ticket.

At the time they claimed their prize, the state would only give the winner "annuity payments," spread over the lifetime of the ticket holder. You could not take the prize as a lump sum. Last month the state legislature changed that rule and now Mr. and Mrs. M had the option to take it as a lump sum. If Mr. and Mrs. M took the lump-sum payment, they would get $13 million before taxes. They wanted the cash now so they took this option, and they anticipated receiving that amount in two months. Their first priority was to use a portion of the money to take care of their children so that they could take care of their grandchildren. Their next two priorities were to give the hospital a gift and to find a way to reduce the taxes on the $13 million. They heard that a charitable trust might be able to give their children money, benefit the hospital, and avoid some taxes.

I sensed that Mr. and Mrs. M had been thinking about this for a long time. I asked if they had an attorney or financial advisor. Mr. M said he had an attorney, and he was the one who told him about this trust. He went to see several financial advisors but thought they all charged outrageous fees. He did find one fellow, a local guy, who he trusted and who would charge him a fraction of what the other planners were charging to manage money. Mr. and Mrs. M had not made any decision to date about how to use their lottery winnings.

Armed with this information, I asked Mr. and Mrs. M if they intended to give our hospital $5 million as Mr. M indicated on the telephone and if this would be an outright gift. They said they were trying to figure all that out when I called. They wanted to know more about this "trust." I told them about how a charitable remainder unitrust works. They would be named the

beneficiaries and receive payments from the trust. With the money from the trust they could make $10,000 gifts each year to each child and grandchild. They could name all eight children as the beneficiaries of the trust, but Mr. and Mrs. M knew that would greatly reduce the income tax deduction they could take for the charitable trust, and they needed the largest deduction they could get to offset the taxes on the $13 million lump-sum lottery payment.

We also discussed wealth replacement. Mr. and Mrs. M could use the payments from the trust to pay life insurance premiums for each other, naming the children as beneficiaries. The policy could be as large as the trust if they were willing to pay the hefty premiums. The income from a $5 million charitable remainder unitrust with a 7 percent payout rate could cover the premiums. I said I would send them some illustrations, and then they could discuss it with their attorney.

My executive director and I had discussed previously what the hospital could do for Mr. and Mrs. M if, in fact, they did make a $5 million gift. He turned to Mr. and Mrs. M and said that he would like to suggest that if this $5 million gift was made to the hospital, that we would like to name the hospital's surgical intensive care unit after them because that was the area where their daughter was cured. They stared as us with blank expressions at first. It had never dawned on them that they would receive something back for their gift. Mrs. M then said softly, "We would love that and so would the kids."

We went back to the office, drew up the illustrations, had our attorney review them, and sent them to Mr. and Mrs. M. We set up an appointment for the grandson to come to the hospital. One week later, Mr. M brought the grandson and daughter to the hospital. Our doctors wanted to see the grandson on a regular basis, so once a month Mr. M brought them to the hospital. With each appointment, I had the chance to spend some time with Mr. M and his daughter. We got to know each other very well, and through them I learned all about the other family members.

During this time period, Mr. M and I had the chance to fully discuss their gift. He and Mrs. M liked the idea of the insurance policy and the charitable trust because the policy would give their children the money while at the same time the trust would benefit the hospital. Mr. M had his financial planner, who had an expertise in life insurance and wealth replacement, contact me.

As one would imagine, you do not get a $5 million life insurance policy overnight. We started this process in February, and it took us to the second week of December before we could finalize the life insurance policy. Mr. and Mrs. M were in their late 70s, and they had some previous heart problems. They had to take a battery of medical tests and examinations that took months. Combine that with the size of the insurance policy they were seeking, and now you know why it took this long to find an insurance company to write this policy. All of us, Mr. and Mrs. M, their attorney, our attorney, and the financial planner, were on the telephone with each other every week. We had this impending deadline of December to make this happen. Mr. and Mrs. M needed the policy written and the trust finalized by the end of the year to offset the tax liability for their lump-sum lottery payment received in that year. We all pulled together and by December 24 the policy was approved and the trust was executed and funded. The hospital had its $5 million gift.

Two months later we had the entire M family at the hospital for lunch in our executive boardroom. All 8 children and 17 grandchildren came. The president of the hospital, executive director, head surgeon, head nurse, and board members were there to join us for lunch and to personally thank the M family. After lunch, we gave the M family a tour of the hospital, leaving the surgical intensive care unit for last. I had the area lined in red ribbon for the ribbon-cutting ceremony.

As we turned the corner to that area, there were several surgeons and nurses flanking the wall to the unit. On the wall in seven-inch gold letters was "The Mr. and Mrs. M Surgical Intensive Care Unit." Mrs. M burst into tears, and I could see Mr. M's eyes were getting filled. Everyone was silent. It was a powerful moment that I shall never forget. Here were two of the most good-natured, kind-hearted people who fell into good fortune and wanted to give something back. When asked why Mr. and Mrs. M made this $5 million gift to the hospital, Mr. M replied, "Our relationship with the hospital stems from our daughter's illness. We wanted these physicians to be able to continue helping others as they helped our daughter." Mrs. M replied, "I know the hospital is a good cause, as a matter of fact, one of the best. After all, we've seen first hand that it is really *a place of miracles.*"

Involve your prospects and donors in the *magic of your organization* and major gifts will happen.

Suggested Bibliography

Here is my "greatest hits" reading list. Some books have been previously referenced, while others will "round out" your total major gifts fundraising perspective.

Andersen, A. 1999. *Tax economics of charitable giving.* 13th ed. Arthur Andersen.

Blanchard, K., and S. Johnson. 1981. *The one minute manager.* New York: William Morrow and Company.

Block, P. 1993. *Stewardship.* San Francisco: Berrett-Koehler Publishers, Inc.

Brinkman, R., and R. Kirschner. 1994. *Dealing with people you can't stand.* New York: McGraw-Hill Companies.

Deep, S., and L. Sussman. 1992. *What to say to get what you want.* Reading, MA: Addison-Wesley Publishing Company.

Kiyosaki, R., and S. Lechter. 1997. *Rich dad, poor dad.* Scottsdale, AZ: TechPress, Inc.

Nichols, J. 1999. *Transforming fundraising.* San Francisco: Jossey-Bass Publishers.

Stanley, T., and W. Danko. 1996. *The millionaire next door.* New York: Pocket Books.

Sharpe, R. 1999. *Planned giving simplified.* New York: John Wiley & Sons.

Williams, J. 1991. *Big gifts.* Rockville, MD: The Taft Group.

Index

About the Author

Laura Fredricks, JD, is Senior Director of Major Gifts at Temple University, Philadelphia, where she identifies, cultivates, and solicits major and planned gifts from alumni, faculty, and friends of the university. In that position she has designed and implemented specific fundraising strategies that have dramatically improved the university's relationship with its donor base. Prior to joining Temple, she served as Major Gifts Manager for Deborah Hospital Foundation, Browns Mills, NJ, where she not only began a comprehensive major gifts program, but also raised more than $6.1 million from several donors in one year.

Ms. Fredricks, a journalism graduate of Rutgers College, New Brunswick, NJ, also holds a law degree from Western New England College School of Law, and a fundraising certificate from the University of Pennsylvania. She is a former Deputy Attorney General for the Commonwealth of Pennsylvania where she practiced over six years in civil litigation, primarily representing health, education, and social service state agencies. Ms. Fredricks entered the fundraising field by serving as the Philadelphia Bar Foundation's Director of Development where she launched a major gifts program that increased individual giving by more than 75 percent.

Prior to her legal career, Ms. Fredricks spent several years as a journalist working for several newspapers as well as for *Newsweek* magazine.

Ms. Fredricks is very active with the National Society of Fund Raising Executives, as an executive board member for the Greater Philadelphia Chapter, and a committee member on the national level. She teaches fundraising and nonprofit management courses at Duke University, the University of Pennsylvania, and the Smithsonian Institution. An active volunteer, Ms. Fredricks for many years has been involved with the Philadelphia YMCA, Big Brothers/Big Sisters of Philadelphia, and her law school advisory board.